T. W. Allies

The Formation Of Christendom Vol. 3

The Christian Faith and Philosophy

T. W. Allies

The Formation Of Christendom Vol. 3
The Christian Faith and Philosophy

ISBN/EAN: 9783742835758

Manufactured in Europe, USA, Canada, Australia, Japa

Cover: Foto ©Lupo / pixelio.de

Manufactured and distributed by brebook publishing software (www.brebook.com)

T. W. Allies

The Formation Of Christendom Vol. 3

THE
FORMATION OF CHRISTENDOM

BY

T. W. ALLIES. K.C.S.G.

VOL. III

THE CHRISTIAN FAITH AND PHILOSOPHY

LONDON: BURNS & OATES, LIMITED
NEW YORK, CINCINNATI, CHICAGO: BENZIGER BROTHERS
1897

My Dear Father Newman,

I DEDICATE to you this work, so far as it has gone, upon the Formation of Christendom, for a double reason. The first is, because it arose out of my nomination to be Reader on the Philosophy of History in the Catholic University of Ireland, which was made when you were its first Rector. The nomination, indeed, led to no more than the delivery of the Inaugural Lecture in your presence as Rector before the University. For though the work which has followed was originally intended to be delivered in like manner, I ascertained, on the completion of the first series, that no need had been felt for Lectures on the Philosophy of History, and my connection with the University practically terminated with your Rectorship. I am therefore offering you the fruit of an appointment peculiarly your own, since it ceased with you. And I may add that your counsels were not wanting to me in the first choice and handling of the subject. My second reason is, that now in mature age I wish to give utterance to the profound gratitude which I have never ceased to feel towards you for the aid which your writings gave me to discern the light of the Catholic Faith, and the force which your example added to follow that light into the knowledge, peace, and liberty of the Catholic Communion. If anything could heighten that gratitude it would be my sense of the value of those subsequent works by which you, who were once the Hector of a doomed Troy, have become in your day and country the Achilles of the City of God; that power which in our own as in every preceding age advances to victory out of defeat, is justified through the calumnies of opponents, and often converts the lance which aims at its life into the sword of a champion.

I am, my dear Father Newman,
Yours affectionately,
T. W. ALLIES.

February 21, 1875.

CONTENTS

THE CHRISTIAN CHURCH AND THE GREEK PHILOSOPHY

LECTURE XV

THE FOUNDATION OF THE ROMAN CHURCH, THE TYPE AND FORM OF EVERY PARTICULAR CHURCH; ITS CONTRAST WITH PHILOSOPHY, AND ITS DEVELOPMENT OF THE JUDAIC EMBRYO.

	PAGE
Moral apathy and unbelief of the generations preceding Claudius	1
This period unexampled in its material prosperity	2
Which is attributed by Philo to the concentration of power in the emperor's hands	3
Unfruitfulness as yet of the long contact between the Hellenic and the Jewish mind	8
Condition of things at the first publication of the Gospel Kingdom	11
Foundation of the Roman Church, A.D. 42	12
Recorded by St. Irenæus, St. Clement of Rome, and St. Dionysius of Corinth	13
Alluded to by Suetonius, A.D. 47	15
Testimony of St. Paul to its growth, A.D. 53	16
Of Tacitus, to its spread among the nobility, A.D. 58	17
And as to the first persecution, A.D. 64	18
Nature of the work thus accomplished	19
Fulfilment of St. Peter's vision seen in the variety of its subjects	20
Its intrinsic contrast with Philosophy in the union of dogma, morality, and worship	23
What Pythagoras attempted	25
The work of Plato	26

CONTENTS

	PAGE
The work of Aristotle	27
The work of Zeno	28
The common effect reached by these four	29
Contrast of St. Peter's work	30
The power of "Follow Me"	32
This work of Peter as represented in the catacombs and monuments of Rome	35
Parallel between Judaism and Christianity	37
Moses, as striking the rock, and as the type of Peter	39
The three powers of dogma, morality, and worship, as continued from Moses in Judaism	41
United and exalted in Christ	42
Transfused from His Person to the Apostles, and especially to Peter	43
The catacombs, the sarcophagi, and St. Leo, bearing witness of these to each other	43
These powers weakened and disjointed in Greek philosophy	44

LECTURE XVI

NEOSTOICISM AND THE CHRISTIAN CHURCH

I. Programme of the subject; gradual leavening of heathen philosophy with Christian sentiments	47
The political and social sphere of the empire in which Philosophy was working	49
The great Latin writers, from Cicero to Tacitus, without any fixed belief in their own religion	51
The Stoic philosophy alone in force in the reigns of Claudius and Nero	54
Summary of its Kosmology, Theology, and Ethics	55
The four chief Stoics formed on these principles	57
Seneca, his life and circumstances	57
His view of the task and function of Philosophy	58
His conception of God, the world, cause and matter, corporeality of good	60
His conception of the human soul	64
Great advance on previous doctrine of his teaching on beneficence, anger, revenge, placability	66
How modified by his view of man's duty to himself	68
His doctrine on slavery	69
Inconsistency between Seneca's life and writings	72

CONTENTS

	PAGE
His superiority to all his predecessors in certain points, a case without parallel	73
His principles purely natural and pagan, his expressions almost Christian	74
What is the solution of this problem?	75
Musonius; general sketch of his teaching	77
Epictetus; what function he assigned to Philosophy	79
What he believes of God and Providence	80
The human mind and its kindred with God	81
No personal subsistence after death. Suicide	82
The bearing of his philosophy towards the gods of polytheism	84
Marcus Aurelius; outline of his philosophy	84
Extinction of the human personality at death	87
Points common to Seneca, Musonius, Epictetus, and Marcus Aurelius	88

II. Points of analogy, contact, or contrast between Neostoicism and the Christian faith . . . 90–110

1. The Stoic doctrine of reason as a portion of the divine spirit enclosed in a human body. 90
2. Virtue, which is reason in action, the only good . 92
3. Subordination of all science to the end of making man virtuous . 93
4. Preference of the philosophical to the public or political life; of the inner to the outward 94
5. The culmination of this in the Stoic cosmopolitanism . 95
6. The evidence of design and final causes in the world's arrangement . 98
7. And the subordination of all things in this design to the good of man . 99
8. The mass of men sinners against the law of reason and so against nature . 100
9. Humanity, philanthropy, beneficence, as a deduction from 1–5 . 102
10. Submission to the will of God, *i.e.*, the course of the world . 106
11. Contrast between the Stoic and the Christian ends of man . 109

Result of Stoicism from the accession of Claudius to the death of Marcus Aurelius. . . . 110

LECTURE XVII

THE FIRST RESURRECTION OF CULTURED HEATHENISM IN THE NEOPYTHAGOREAN SCHOOL

	PAGE
Extinction of the Pythagorean School in the time of Cicero and of Seneca	114
Three positions of Greek philosophy in reference to religion	114
The society in which it started possessed a worship consisting of Prayer, Sacrifice, Oracles, and Mysteries	115
How Philosophy had dealt with these	118
Its result in Stoics, Epicureans, and Sceptics a negation	120
Continuing belief of the mass in the polytheistic worship	122
Rise of a believing movement in Philosophy	123
Philo; his connection with it	123
Date and circumstances of his life	124
He attempts to marry the Greek science with the Hebrew revelation	127
The position which he gives to these two in regard to each other	128
What Philo had in common with Greek philosophy, what he borrowed from it, what he contributed to it	129
The principle of revelation and the principle of holiness	130
His conception of God derived from Scripture and Tradition	131
Metaphysical attributes	132
Attributes relative to man	132
Human holiness a transcript of the divine	133
Philo's doctrine of human weakness and divine grace	134
Subordination of human sciences to theology	135
By which self-knowledge being gained leads us through a sense of our weakness to God	136
The opposition of these principles to the previous course of Greek philosophy down to Seneca	137
Plutarch; time and circumstances of his life	141
First remaining representative of the Neopythagorean school	142
His theodicea; the Supreme God	142
Constructor, not Creator of the world	143
The visible gods and the demons	145
Triple Providence	145

CONTENTS

	PAGE
Plutarch's piety, and the place it takes in his system	146
Two main differences between Plutarch and his predecessors	147
Points wherein Philo deflected from Jewish belief into Greek views, and in which Plutarch agrees with him	150
Points which Plutarch may have derived from Philo:	
1. The doctrine of obtaining knowledge by immediate revelation	152
2. The doctrine of intermediate powers between God and the world	153
Employed by Plutarch to reduce his polytheism to unity	153
Review of the interval between Philo and Plutarch, A.D. 40–90	154
Change from the old Roman world of Cicero	156
Probable cause of this change	157

LECTURE XVIII

STANDING-GROUND OF PHILOSOPHY FROM THE ACCESSION OF NERVA TO THAT OF SEVERUS

Altered position of Philosophy in regard to the vulgar religion from the time of Nerva	160
And in regard to the imperial government	161
Alliance between the empire, philosophy, and the polytheistic worship	161
Change of temper in the educated class generally	162
Religion of Epictetus compared with that of Plutarch	164
What it tended to	166
Contrast in Plutarch	167
Dio Chrysostomus	168
His conception of the universe and the power ruling it	168
Man's intuition of God	169
Its fourfold expression	170
Dio's Supreme God a Demiurge	171
Man's kinship with God, and the humanitarian doctrine as the result	172
Plato's Demiurge, was he the prototype of Dio's?	172
The former distinguished from Zeus, the latter identified with him	173
Contrast between the Greek and Roman mind in contemporaries of this date	175

	PAGE
Tacitus, Pliny the Younger, Suetonius	176
The Stoic philosophy and the old belief united in Juvenal	177
Hatred of Christianity in Tacitus, Pliny, and Trajan	179
The philosophic standing-point from Trajan's time	179
Conception of God and Providence common to Epictetus, Plutarch, and Dio	183
The ideal teacher of Epictetus	184
A messenger sent by God to teach man what is good and what evil	185
His office a bishopric which must be without distraction of domestic ties and duties	186
He must be inaccessible to all fear of men	187
The ideal of Epictetus had only been realized in the Christian Church	188
The sole open reference of Epictetus to Christians a witness to their heroism	189
Epictetus a heathen in his grounds of action	191
But a heathen who has seen Christian teachers	192
Position of philosophers in the Roman empire	194
Function of Philosophy, as described by Plutarch	195
The supervision of the whole life exercised by philosophers—Seneca and Attalus	195
Persius and Cornutus—Taurus and his scholars	197
The house and court philosopher, the public teacher, the strolling Cynic	198
Philosophical standing-point of Maximus Tyrius	201
Apuleius of Madaura	202
Celsus—his conception of the one Supreme God	203
The common standing-ground of the cultured class in the second and third centuries hence deduced	205

LECTURE XIX

THE GOSPEL OF PHILOSOPHIC HEATHENISM

The sense in which a Supreme God was acknowledged by Greek philosophy in the time of Severus	207
Life of Apollonius of Tyana the embodiment of this conception	208
Date and circumstances of its composition	209

CONTENTS

	PAGE
The Life itself a romance devoid of historical truth	210
Apollonius the typical disciple of Pythagoras	211
His birth, youth, and education	212
He assumes the Pythagorean life; its asceticism	213
His arrangement of his day and general conduct	214
He determines to travel in the pursuit of wisdom	216
Visits Babylon and the Indian king	217
The Indian Brahmans	218
Their doctrine of the soul	219
Their account of the constitution of the world	220
How this fits into the life and philosophy of Apollonius	222
After full comparison of his wisdom with the Indian wisdom he returns to Ionia	223
His subsequent life as a public teacher	224
His acts at Ephesus, where he stones the plague in the person of an old beggar	225
He discourses at Athens and casts out a demon	226
Visits Corinth and delivers a young man from a ghoul	227
Braves Nero at Rome and raises a Roman bride to life	228
Visits Spain, Sicily, and Greece; his life in the temples there	229
His intercourse with Vespasian in Egypt	230
Visits the Æthiopian Gymnosophists	230
Whom he finds inferior to the Brahmans	231
Returns and advises the Emperor Titus	232
Summary of his activity as a public teacher	232
Transition to the suffering life of Apollonius	232
He is cited to Rome under the persecution of Domitian	232
His life at Rome	233
His conduct when tried by Domitian	234
Disappears from the Court and appears to Damis and Demetrius at Puteoli	235
His triumphant life in Greece	236
Visits the cave of Trophonius and brings out of it the book of Pythagoras	236
Sees at Ephesus the murder of Domitian at Rome	237
The most reputed account of his death	237
The six periods of the life thus described	238
No reference to Christ or to the Christian religion in the book, while the time and the places are those in which that religion first appeared	240
Apollonius intended to be made an entirely independent figure	243

		PAGE
The character given to him in its chief features	. .	244
1. Miraculous birth		244
2. His life dedicated to the knowledge of the divinity		244
3. He has a knowledge of absent and future things	.	245
4. His power of working miracles		245
5. He is as great in doing as in teaching . .	.	246
6. He is the friend of man		246
7. He encounters suffering without fear . .	.	247
8. His miraculous departure from the world .	.	247
Double imitation here practised by Philostratus	. .	248
Contrast on the other hand with the life of Christ	. .	249
1. Relationship of the human soul with the divinity		249
2. The task of Philosophy to restore the Kosmos in man		250
3. Opposition to tyranny takes the place of opposition to sin		253
4. Suffering is either excluded or unreal . .	.	253
5. The soul escaping from the body as from a prison		255
Attitude of Philostratus towards the Christian religion	.	256
Identical with that of the Emperor Alexander Severus	.	258
Results which we gain from the book of Philostratus	.	258
Seneca, Plutarch, Philostratus, three stages in heathen progress		259
The work, not itself historical as regards its subject, contains important matter for history		261

LECTURE XX

THE NEOPLATONIC PHILOSOPHY AND EPOCH

I. Positive side of the doctrine of Philostratus . . .	263
Its relative side turned to Christianity	264
Identity as to the former with Neoplatonism . .	265
Ammonius Sakkas and Plotinus, their time and place .	265
Plotinus in some respects a real Apollonius . . .	267
His system brought out when Christianity was contesting the world with heathenism	268
Analysis of the universe according to Plotinus . .	268
1. His Primal Being, the Infinite, the One and Good, and the Cause	269

The procession of all things from it necessary	273
And has no separate substantial existence	274
The Second God or divine Mind	274
The Third God, the Soul	275
2. The procession of the visible world from the soul	276
Connection with matter the cause of evil	277
Contradiction in the system hence arising	278
The human soul in its three states—before, during, and after this life	278
Defect of conception of personality in the three states	282
3. Elevation of the mind above the world of sense	283
Happiness, life in accordance with nature	284
Moral good and evil	284
Good, detachment from the body	285
Its highest point the doctrine of Ecstasy	286
Attitude of the system to the polytheistic creed and worship	287
Plotinus, like Philostratus, ignores Christianity	289
Porphyrius arranger and explainer of the Plotinic system	291
Iamblichus	292
The system of the last production and outcome of Hellenism	293
A complete antagonism with Christianity	294
And the heathen analogon of it	294
II. Three great oppositions between the Neoplatonic system and the Christian Creed	295
1. The Primal Being—how reached by Plotinus	296
Original start of Greek philosophy from a conception of physical unity	296
Conception of one mind by Anaxagoras	298
The point reached by Plato and Aristotle	298
Identity of the human Logos with the divine Logos a general doctrine—so stated by Cicero	299
This doctrine not altered in the interval between Cicero and Plotinus	300
Effort to reconcile polytheism with this philosophic unity	301
2. Rejection of the doctrine of Creation by Plotinus	302
The philosophic substitute for it	304

The Church's belief:
1. In one God 305
2. In the Trinity of Personal Relations . . 305
3. In the doctrine of Creation 306
4. In the absolute abyss between the Being of God and the Being of creatures . . . 307

3. The relation between "the Divine," τὸ Θεῖον, and human nature in Neoplatonism . . . 308

Practical scope of human life for the individual and the commonwealth, as set forth in the Pythagoras of Iamblichus 309
The Neoplatonic theory of immortality . . . 311
The culminating point of the system 312
The brotherhood rested on a fiction 313
The opposing Christian truth; results of Personality upon the relation between God and man . . 314
1. Man the creature of God 314
2. The notion of evil and sin . . . 315
3. The freedom of the will 316
4. Redemption and Sanctification . 317
5. Eternal life of the personal being . . . 318
6. The assumption of a human body by the Divine Word 319
7. The unity of the Spirit 320
8. God the Creator as against the Absolute Unity 320

Note to pp. 296, 297.
Connection of ancient with modern Pantheism . 323-5

LECTURE XXI

THE RESPECTIVE POWER OF THE GREEK PHILOSOPHY AND THE CHRISTIAN CHURCH TO CONSTRUCT A SOCIETY

Review of the ground hitherto travelled over . . . 326
Present subject, the power of philosophy in this period to form a society 327
I. Original constitution of human society, in which there was a triple union of belief, action, and worship . . 328
Sacrifice, prayer, and priesthood universally established 328

CONTENTS

	PAGE
The civil authority invariably combined with worship	331
Disturbance of the triple union by the denial of the divine unity	332
Rise of Greek philosophy amid this corruption	334
Traces of original revelation in Greek belief	334
Double aspect presented by the heathen world	336

II. 1. Dissolution of the original union between belief and action on the one hand and worship on the other . . 338
    2. Philosophy accepted by the higher Romans as the guide of life 340
       Want of agreement in the teaching of philosophers . 342
       Split between inward conviction and outward worship 342
       Scandals of the pretenders to philosophy . . 344
       The separation of human conduct from belief and from worship in the best philosophic teachers . 345
    3. Disregard by philosophy of the ignorant, the poor, and the labouring classes 346
    4. Historical result of philosophy as to forming a society, from Claudius to Constantine . . 347

III. The spectacle which met the eyes of Constantine . 349
    The work of Peter at Rome repeated in each city of the empire 350
    The triple teaching, pastoral, and sacerdotal office . 351
    Which runs out in its bearers into three gradations, but is exercised by all simultaneously . . 353
       1. The manifestation to the world of the truth, mainly by word of mouth, under the two divisions of preaching and catechising . 354
       Specimen of its operation by St. Paul in preaching 357
       Force of the catechistic instruction . . 362
       2. Union of the sacramental life with the truth as taught by the Church . . . 362
       3. And with the offering of the Christian Sacrifice to the one God in all lands . 364
       Joint action of these three powers in forming the Christian society 365
       In this joint action consists the definite establishment of the Christian kingdom . 366
       Which is based upon the Person of Christ . 368

LECTURE XXII

THE CHURCH RECONSTRUCTING THE NATURAL ORDER BY THE SUPERNATURAL

	PAGE
Religion and Philosophy the battle of three hundred years	371
St. Jerome's statement of the result	372
Failure of Philosophy to implant a doctrine	373
1. How the Church re-established the belief in one Personal God	375
2. How the Church re-established belief in the continuance of the human personality after death	378
Correction of a grave philosophic error	382
Correction of an intense moral corruption	384
3. How the Church re-established the doctrine of man's creatureship	385
4. How the Church re-established the basis of morality in the relation of man to his fellow-man	390
5. How the Church established the proper relation between the individual and the commonwealth	397
6. How the Church carried in her bosom a law of nations	406
Summary and conclusion	409

THE FORMATION OF CHRISTENDOM

THE CHRISTIAN CHURCH AND THE GREEK PHILOSOPHY

LECTURE XV

THE FOUNDATION OF THE ROMAN CHURCH, THE TYPE AND FORM OF EVERY PARTICULAR CHURCH; ITS CONTRAST WITH PHILOSOPHY, AND ITS DEVELOPMENT OF THE JUDAIC EMBRYO.

THE last word of Greek philosophy had been spoken, and it consisted in imagining the world to be a city of gods and men, ruled by right reason, but of which the denizen man could hope for no future personal life. The work which Pythagoras conceived and attempted, of a religious society bearing in its bosom a divine philosophy, had never in the course of five hundred years been accomplished. Again, the attempt of Plato and of Aristotle to found an universal philosophy had broken down under a race of sceptics and eclectics; and the fusion which had resulted from a selection of tenets based on no principle, had brought with it slackness, apathy, and disbelief of all divine truths in the philosophic mind. Cicero, the spokesman of such a mental state, and the voice of the whole century in which he lived, and well-nigh of that which succeeded him, fluctuated between contending systems whose variety and inconsistency were to him an argument against the existence of any absolute truth. The society of all this period in its intense moral corruption attested the bad effect of this philosophical collapse on the higher thinking minds. The eighty years succeeding Cicero's death form a period which, far either from improving the philosophical standing-point or arresting the dissolution of manners, was conspicuous for its barrenness in the realm of abstract thought, and its descent into the lowest abysses of sensuality.

But it was also a time the greater part of which was conspicuous above all the times which had preceded it for its unexampled prosperity. We have an unimpeachable eye-witness of this in one whose life had been spent exactly in this period; and since he was a man of leisure and wealth, occupying a very high position in the second city of the empire, and was moreover a provincial, and one of the subject races, and at the same time a man of great piety and large capacity, he furnishes the most unsuspicious and telling testimony which we could have on such a point. It was just seventy years after the battle of Actium when Philo described his legation to the Emperor Caius; he reckoned himself at this time an elderly man, and was probably sixty years of age. Thus he would have been born just as that pacification took effect with which Augustus had closed the period of the civil wars. And he speaks of it with a sort of transport as a time like none that had been seen before. His past life fell entirely under the two reigns

FOUNDATION OF THE ROMAN CHURCH

of Augustus and Tiberius. Of the first he says:[1] "This is Cæsar who calmed the storms which had swept down from every side; who healed the common diseases of Greeks and barbarians, bursting out as they did from east and south, from north and west, and filling land and sea with miseries. This is the man who did not merely relax but unbind the fetters with which the world was oppressed; who cleared the sea of pirates while he filled it with merchant vessels. This is he who gave freedom to every city, who reduced disorder to harmony, who civilised and made obedient nations before unsociable and brutal. This is he who multiplied Greece many times over, while he Hellenised the barbarous land in its more important divisions; the guardian of peace; the distributor to every man of his due share; who conferred boundless favours on the general mass; who never once in his whole life concealed or reserved for himself any good or excellent thing." Of Tiberius he speaks as one who enjoyed the supreme power for three-and-twenty years, and never allowed any seed of war to smoulder or raise its head either in Greece or in barbarian territory, but bestowed peace and its blessings to the end of his life with rich and unsparing hand and mind; who was inferior to none in race, to none in accomplishments; for who among those that flourished in his day was better endowed with understanding, or more able to give it utterance? What king or emperor lived to more prosperous old age than he, who for his shrewdness even when young was called an elder?

And it is specifically to the imperial power that Philo attributes this state of things,[2] saying of

[1] Legation to Caius, sec. 21.   [2] Sec. 22.

Augustus that if ever there was a man to whom new and unprecedented honours should be voted, it was he, both as the beginning of the imperial race, and as the first and greatest and universal benefactor, in that instead of the multitude of governors who existed before he entrusted the common vessel of the State to himself as one pilot of admirable skill in the science of government to steer it.[1] For the imperial authority was, it is true, irresponsible, but its concentration in one hand gave it so great a power for good that since its establishment misfortune like a venomous reptile could lurk indeed in corners, but could not attack any large district: that power had discovered and brought to light everything that was good, and banished evils to the extremity of the earth.[2]

On the accession of Caius in A.D. 37,[3] Philo describes him as assuming the supreme power over every land and sea, which were free from all sedition, ruled by admirable laws; east and west, north and south, harmonised together, Greek with barbarian, soldier with citizen, in the enjoyment of one common peace: an extraordinary and unspeakable good fortune, since he had come into a ready-made inheritance of all good things, a vast treasury, well-provided forces by land and sea, a revenue flowing as from an exhaustless fountain, and a territory stretching over three continents, the inhabitants of which admired him as they

---

[1] Thus the view taken by Philo of Roman affairs may be considered the exact contradictory of that on which Tacitus composed his history, whose object, says Merivale (vol. viii. p. 84), was "to show that the supremacy of Rome, the final cause of her existence, depends on the pre-eminence of an oligarchy."

[2] Sec. 5 and 7. The words which Philo puts into the mouth of Macro, as exhorting Caius, may well be supposed to represent his own opinion. See, again, the letter of Agrippa to Caius, sec. 39.

[3] Sec. 2.

had never admired any emperor before, not as those who expected to have the possession and enjoyment of all good things, but as those who felt that they actually had a very superabundance of prosperity. Nothing could be seen from city to city but altars, sacrifices, votaries in white garments and crowned with garlands, festivals, assemblies, musical contests, horse races, revels and feasts, delights for every sense. The rich were not better off than the poor, the masters than the slaves, since the occasion gave equal privileges to all, so that the age of Saturn, sung by poets, no longer seemed a fiction, on account of the universal prosperity and happiness.

This judgment of a provincial and an eye-witness may surely be set against and contrasted with the judgment of Tacitus, as expressed sixty years afterwards from the standing-point of an old Roman aristocrat. No doubt in the time of the latter, not merely the passing madness of Caius, but the long experience of cruelty under Nero and Domitian, had thrown further light upon the nature of the imperial power, and given matter enough for the most gloomy portraiture of irresponsible authority lodged in unworthy hands. But in his own time Philo compared it with what had preceded it, the heathen domination, that very "regnum," in fact, which the Romans themselves so abhorred, that for the mere suspicion of its name they had slain Julius; and with this, whether as seen in such rulers as Herod and Cleopatra, the Seleucidæ and the Ptolemies, their predecessors, or in the proconsuls and proprætors of the later republic, who left Rome as ruined men, to gorge themselves with the spoils of prostrate kingdoms. Now in this comparison, which the practical sense of the moment as well as reflection on the past seemed equally to justify, the emperor appeared to Philo a ruler, not a despot; one whose power was based on law and wielded temperately for the good of the whole mass of nations over whom authority was placed in his single hands in order that every part of so vast and composite an empire might enjoy tranquillity, live in amity, and develop its all but boundless resources. That such was the effect during the reigns of Augustus and Tiberius, Philo declares with a profusion of statement, which, as we have cited him, has been somewhat curtailed; but as one of the subject races, and as one whose moral character and judgment stand far higher than that of Tacitus, how can his testimony to what he saw of the benefits which during all his life he, and his people, and all the other peoples had enjoyed from the imperial power, be rejected? If in estimating the work of Augustus we compare it tacitly in our minds with limited monarchy, as developed in Christian nations under the slow education of principles growing into the fibre of the individual and the community, we are guilty not merely of an anachronism, but of a great injustice. The Græco-Roman world being what it was, could anything better than the rule devised by Augustus have been set up in order to pacify, tame, and educate it?

It may then be said that no previous time had shown anything like the prosperous tranquillity of the two generations following the battle of Actium; nor was it a prosperity merely material, but arising from wise laws, fairly administered.[1] Not only order reigned, but justice; and peace flowed from both. As to self-government indeed, the nations subject to the emperor

[1] εὐνομία in Philo.

did not possess that of which they had shown themselves to be incapable, nor the Romans that which through abuse they had lost; but for good government, both enjoyed such a degree of it as they had rarely attained before:[1] and if the senate trembled at the rumour of conspiracy, Alexandria as well as Jerusalem were profoundly thankful for a consideration which the profligate daughter of the Ptolemies, or the Idumean heir of the Maccabees, had never shown them, while for the rest might it not be as well to live under one Cæsar,[2] as to be liable to a senate such as Cicero describes in his letters, to a Verres, or a Clodius, or a Dolabella, or even a Pompey?[3]

Viewed in connection with its moral corruption and its religious apathy, this singular prosperity of the Græco-Roman world at the time specified by Philo is the more remarkable. Far from there being any longing after divine things, any unsatisfied yearnings after truth and certitude, or any strong conviction as to a future state, no age appears to us more destitute of these than the age of Virgil, Horace, Livy, and Ovid, no period less illumined with high and noble thought than the reign of Tiberius, as pictured for us by Tacitus. And yet at this time the Greek mind had been brought during three centuries into close contact with the Jewish. By the founding of Alexandria, and by the policy of the Ptolemies, when they, the

---

[1] Von Reumont, i. 347. "So war doch unter Augustus und Tiberius die römische Herrschaft in den östlichen Provinzen unendlich milder und gerechter als jemals die der Könige der gestürzten Reiche gewesen war."

[2] "Neque provinciæ illum rerum statum abnuebant, suspecto senatus populique imperio, ob certamina potentium et avaritiam magistratuum; invalido legum auxilio, quæ vi, ambitu, postremo pecunia turbabantur." Tacit. *Ann.* I, 2.

[3] See for this view Merivale, ch. 54, p. 465.

representatives of Hellenic culture, took possession of
the throne of the Pharaohs, a large colony of Jews
was drawn to their new capital, a quarter assigned to
them, ample privileges granted, and almost a Jewish
nationality gradually established in Egypt. Thither
the richly-endowed university drew the most learned
Greeks, and beside them grew up a school of Judaic
philosophy, which, using as its own the language of
Greece, and appropriating its culture, strove to penetrate the heathen wisdom with the divine wisdom of
Moses. The sacred books had long been translated
into that language which was used in cultivated society
throughout the East. Moreover, Jews in no small
number were settled for commercial purposes in all
the great cities of the West; Agrippa speaks to the
Emperor Caius of his city Jerusalem as the metropolis
of innumerable colonies in every region of the habit-
able world, in Europe, in Asia, so far as the Satrapies
beyond the Euphrates, and in Africa.[1] We may be
sure that they were generally among the most prosperous of the population, and that they commonly
united learning and refined taste with their commercial
pursuits. One of such men was Philo; and he possesses for us an unique interest in his still existing
works as a representative of Jewish knowledge, penetrated with Greek culture, who had attained ripe manhood, say fifty years, at the time of our Lord's teaching.
The prosperity which he describes belonged precisely
to that time in which the Three Years' Ministry took
place, and the infant Church arose. His prodigious
superiority in every moral point of view to the con-

---

[1] Legation to Caius, sec. 36. Compare Acts ii. 5, 9-11: the
enumerations in the two cases bear a marked resemblance to each
other.

temporary pagan authors is at once apparent to any one who will read one of his remaining treatises. Considering what he was, and the large dissemination of Jews, such more or less as himself, through the whole Roman empire, considering their wealth, learning, activity, and their comparatively pure life, it is a point very much to be noted how little effect on the Græco-Roman mind up to the time of Claudius this long contact with what has been called the oriental mind had produced. We cannot trace any effective influence exercised by them on heathen society, thought, and manners, in Greek and Latin writers before Philo's time. We might fairly have expected that nobler ideas as to the being and personality of God, as to moral purity, perhaps as to social duties, would have permeated society and laid hold of thinking minds among the heathen from this source. If the loss of self-government by the subject nations, if the sense of their helplessness under Roman power, of national degradation, of human culture in its national form losing its characteristic stamp, of the supports to outward and inward life giving way amid national decline,[1] would of themselves produce a lively feeling of needs craving to be supplied, of our earthly being's wants and failures, of man's moral and spiritual imperfections, of the frailty and worthlessness of all external things, of the endless chasm between the world and God, between nature and spirit, then all these causes were in full operation for generations before the time of the

[1] It is exactly thus that Zeller supposes Christianity and Neoplatonism to have drawn their joint origin from the needs of their time: he first makes Christianity contemporaneous with Neoplatonism, which it preceded by at least two hundred years; and then makes it to arise out of yearnings which itself created. *Philosophie der Griechen*, vol. v. pp. 391, 392.

Emperor Claudius, and yet no indications of such a temper appear in the surviving literature, no traces in the history of that period. All these feelings arose subsequently, but the contact of the Greek with the Jewish mind for two full centuries had not produced them.[1] They were biding their time to become fruitful, when a higher power, which had not yet appeared, should impregnate the nations, satisfying the wants which it had taught the human heart to feel. It is quite another state of mind which Philo portrays to us in his picture of the nations at the accession of Caius, an intense enjoyment of the goods of life, and an exultation in the peace and tranquillity which the strong hand of the Emperor had established over three continents. Men were absorbed in outward things rather than pining for inward sources of strength. The settlement of Jews in the great cities of the world before our Lord's coming must be viewed as a most important disposition of Providence, but to appreciate it fully we must contrast the sterility of the effect produced before with the fruitfulness which ensued after His coming. Up to the time of Claudius, in spite of a large number of Jews settled at Rome, and enjoying Roman citizenship, Isis and Anubis had influenced Roman society quite as much as the religion of Moses. They were the favourite gods which the great Roman ladies worshipped with calamitous results.

If then we would rightly appreciate the external

---

[1] Dubois-Cuchan, vol. i. 382, says, "Le Judäisme resta comme enfoui dans un coin de l'orient, et n'en sortit que par la transformation chrétienne. Jusque là ce ne fut qu'un germe caché, qu'une sorte de chrysalide religieuse, et ce n'est qu'en brisant sa vieille enveloppe que l'esprit qu'il renfermait put planer sur la terre." See also Friedlaender, *Sittengeschichte Roms*, iii. p. 505, who gives good reasons for this.

and internal condition of the times in which the first publication of the Gospel-kingdom took place, we must bear in mind the great temporal prosperity, that "immense majesty of the Roman peace" which a world strained to the utmost by the jealous armaments of rival nations ought at least to admire; and not less that profound corruption of manners which made the domestic lives of even the greatest men, such as Augustus, sinks of pollution, not adequately to be described without contamination, and broke up the union of the married life in nations yet possessing the institution of monogamy, a corruption of manners both represented and authorised by the idolatrous polytheism which was in full possession as well of public as of private life. These two things as to the general mass; moreover, in the realm of thought that lassitude and apathy of the Hellenic mind betokened by the eclectic fusion and faltering accents of its philosophy, and reflected in its Roman scholars. Nor must we forget that cultivated Greeks and Jews had been brought together not only at Alexandria but in all the cities of the empire, without the higher knowledge and purer life of the Jew communicating themselves in any appreciable degree to the Gentile.

The beginning of quite a different state of things is full of interest, and it takes place in the reign of Claudius. Instead now of Jews seated to the number of many thousands at Rome, and invested more or less with the privileges of Roman citizenship, while they remained not indeed without occasional proselytes, but with all their Jewish feelings and convictions isolated amid foreign customs and corrupt worship, we shall trace the foundation of a community absorbing gradually the Gentiles into its bosom, and imparting to them the worship of one God, while it ceased to be Jewish itself. Here, if anywhere in history, we have a definite result springing from a definite cause. From this time forth the publication of a certain great fact conducted by Jewish preachers affected Greeks and Romans as they never were affected before.

Twelve years had passed after the Ascension, during which, according to the precept[1] which they had received from their Lord, the Apostles had preached only to the Jews. These years accomplished, the Chief Apostle had been chosen by Divine Providence to show that the end of this restriction was at hand, and to admit the Gentile Cornelius into the bosom of the Church. By this event a new horizon was opened to the Apostles. At once the great cities of the Roman empire were marked out to them as centres from which the Gospel-kingdom was to spread; but first and most of all the imperial city itself. As soon as it was clear that the gift of "repentance unto life"[2] had been bestowed on the Gentiles, Rome was indicated as the great field for such a work. The very name of Cornelius, "a centurion of the Italian band," pointed Romewards. It was in exact accordance with Peter's position as the bearer of the keys that he should first open the house of God to the Gentiles: and it was no less in accordance with it that he should found the chief and principal Church in the very heart of heathendom. And this was brought about by events seemingly the most unlikely to have such an issue. Towards the conclusion of the thirteenth year, he had been seized by Herod Agrippa, and was on the point of being put to death

---

[1] So stated by Clemens Alex. *Strom.* 6, 5, p. 636, referred to by Sanguineti, p. 197. [2] Acts xi. 18.

when delivered miraculously from prison, upon which it is said he "departed and went into another place."[1] That the kingdom in which Herod ruled would henceforth, so long as Herod was its ruler, be unsafe for him, is plain. But, moreover, that other place, of which, for certain reasons,[2] the Evangelist did not disclose the name, is known by the unanimous testimony of ancient writers[3] to have been the city of Rome, where in the second year of the Emperor Claudius Peter laid the foundation and organised the construction of the Roman Church. The double term used of this event by ancient writers is one of great significance and pregnant meaning. As a house is not a chance collection of stones and mortar, but is constructed on a definite plan for a preconceived use, so when they say that Peter founded and constructed[4] the Roman Church, they mean that he instituted a society with the principle of life in itself, exerting definite action on its members, and possessing a definite government. Nothing can be more distinct than this statement of St. Irenæus, nor more unimpeachable than his authority. But, further, exactly what he had expressed by metaphor had been said in direct words by a contemporary and successor of

[1] Acts xii. 17.
[2] Hagemann, *Die Römische Kirche*, pp. 661-663, suggests the danger of mentioning the beginning of the Roman Church when St. Paul was on his trial before Nero at Rome.
[3] Eusebius, *Hist.* ii. 14; Orosius, vii. 6; St. Leo, Serm. 82, cap. 4, where the two presences of St. Peter at Rome, the first in the reign of Claudius, and the second in that of Nero, are alluded to. "Nec mundi dominam times Romam, qui in Caiaphæ domo expaveras sacerdotis ancillam. Num quid aut judicio Pilati aut sævitia Judæorum minor erat vel in Claudio potestas, vel in Nerone crudelitas." See Sanguineti, p. 194, *De Sede Romana B. Petri*.
[4] St. Irenæus. iii. 3. Θεμελιώσαντες οὖν καὶ οἰκοδομήσαντες οἱ μακάριοι Ἀπόστολοι τὴν ἐκκλησίαν Λίνῳ τὴν τῆς ἐπισκοπῆς λειτουργίαν ἐνεχείρισαν, quoted also by Eusebius, *Hist.* v. 6.

St. Peter in his office, who, writing to the Corinthian Church in the same generation as the martyrdom of the two Apostles Peter and Paul, observes that [1] "a great multitude of the elect were drawn together and associated by them in a holy polity." He adds that "by the endurance of many sufferings and tortures they became among us," that is, at Rome, "a most honourable example." This term, polity, conveys in itself all which has been above indicated, for just as the Principate of the empire was a polity whose subjects were governed by it civilly, so what the Apostles set up was a holy polity for the government of souls. Nor must we omit to remark a point of identity in St. Clement's expression with that of Tacitus. Those whom the third Pope after St. Peter mentions as associated in a divine polity with the two Apostles, and by their admirable endurance of sufferings becoming in Rome a great example, and those whom the heathen historian mentions as victims of Nero's persecution, are "a great multitude." [2] It is only another image of the word polity, when Dionysius,[3] Bishop of Corinth, writing to the Romans about the year 170, calls them "the plantation of Peter and Paul."

It appears then that Peter came to Rome to do exactly that which the Roman law most expressly forbade, since it looked with the utmost jealousy upon any college or fellowship of men bound together by rules of its own, and not recognised by the senate.

[1] St. Clemens, Epist. ad Corint. cap. 6.
[2] πολὺ πλῆθος ἐκλεκτῶν, οἵτινες πολλὰς αἰκίας καὶ βασάνους διὰ ζῆλον παθόντες, ὑπόδειγμα κάλλιστον ἐγένοντο ἐν ἡμῖν. "Quæsitissimis pœnis affecit—primo correpti qui fatebantur, deinde judicio eorum multitudo ingens—convicti sunt."
[3] Quoted by Eusebius, ii. 25. τὴν ἀπὸ Πέτρου καὶ Παύλου φυτείαν γενηθεῖσαν Ῥωμαίων τε καὶ Κορινθίων συνεκεράσετε.

FOUNDATION OF THE ROMAN CHURCH 15

This suggests a sufficient reason [1] why the Evangelist, writing, while Peter was still alive, what would fall into the hands of foes as well as friends, passed over in silence both the sphere of his action and all which he accomplished in it. Again, the narrative of St. Luke ends with the appearance of St. Paul at Rome to justify his conduct before the Emperor Nero, which would supply a further adequate reason for passing over all mention of the founding a Church at Rome. But it is a fact that St. Luke is silent about St. Peter's acts for a period of several years after his delivery from prison, and this period exactly corresponds with the historical statement of the Roman Church's foundation. It is only after St. Peter had been driven out of Rome by the edict of the Emperor Claudius [2] banishing the Jews, who had raised tumults concerning Christ, that St. Luke makes him reappear at the Council of Jerusalem. The mention of this tumult, and of the emperor's decree arising out of it by his heathen biographer, gives us another assurance that at this time the Christian faith had been planted in Rome. His words point evidently to the stir created among the Jewish residents at Rome by that event, which broke them up into antagonistic parties, some accepting, some rejecting the Messiah declared to them. Hence would follow naturally the expulsion of foreign Jews from Rome, who would be represented as the cause of the "tumult." Again, in the year 53, at the end of eleven years from

---

[1] See Aberle's treatise, *Theologische Quartalschrift*, 1868, p. 3, who lays down the important rule, that the writings of the New Testament are the literary productions of a persecuted community, which was forming itself under the pressure of persecution.

[2] Sanguineti, p. 199, makes the expulsion of St. Peter from Rome in virtue of this decree to occur in the year 47. Suet. Claudius, 25. "Judæos impulsore Christo assidue tumultuantes Roma expulit."

the first preaching of St. Peter, we have a very striking testimony to the work which he had done in the capital of the Roman empire, and the chief seat of idol worship. St. Paul, writing to the Roman Christians at that time, renders thanks to God for their "faith being spoken of throughout the whole world," and that "their obedience had reached all men," terms which carry with them the meaning of a completely constituted and very flourishing Church. He calls them besides, "full of goodness and all knowledge, and able to admonish others," and "desires much to see them that he might impart some gratuitous spiritual gift to confirm them, that is, to console himself and them with their mutual faith," language again which implies the complete formation of a Church.[1] But he, moreover, alleges a very remarkable reason why he had not hitherto visited them. He states that it had been his object, while labouring at the publication of the Gospel-kingdom from Jerusalem all round in a circle to Illyricum, and there planting Churches, not to build on another man's foundation.[2] Here he uses exactly the two words applied by ancient writers to Peter's work at Rome, that is, founding and building: and he adds, "For this reason I have been many times prevented coming to you," that is, because you were already founded and built by another. But when St. Paul uses such language, it is evident that this other must be at least of equal rank with himself. Nor did he indeed avoid simple preaching where other Apostles preached, for this he had done in Judæa, but he avoided founding a Church on another's foundation;

---

[1] Rom. i. 8; xvi. 19; xv. 14; i. 11.
[2] Capp. 15, 20. ἵνα μὴ ἐπ'ἀλλοτρίου θεμελίου οἰκοδομῶ. See above. St. Irenæus, Θεμελιώσαντες καὶ οἰκοδομήσαντες.

FOUNDATION OF THE ROMAN CHURCH

and he goes on to say that he will take the opportunity of his going into Spain to visit them, words again implying that they did not need his work as an Apostle to found their Church, because it had already been done by another. And, in fact, five years later his own appeal to Cæsar led him as it were incidentally to Rome, where he was destined to do a great work, to be associated in labour and in martyrdom with Peter, and so, notwithstanding his own words, to have his authority from age to age appealed to, as deposited in the superior Principate of the Roman Church. If, however, we put these several expressions of his letter together,[1] they intimate not only that the Roman Church had been already founded and built, that is, organised, but that it had attained so great a distinction that its faith and obedience were spoken of among Christians all over the world.

The next incident we are told concerning it comes from a pagan source, and assures us that in the year 58, the very year of St. Paul's first visit to Rome, the highest Roman nobility had been brought under the influence of the Faith. In that year Tacitus mentions that Pomponia Græcina, wife of Plautius, the conqueror of Britain, who was charged as an adherent of a "foreign superstition," was committed to the judgment of her husband.[2] It was a charge involving both life and reputation, but the husband acquitted his wife, who continued, says Tacitus, to an advanced age, to indulge her sorrowful mode of existence and sad spirit, words which all commentators had inter-

---
[1] See Sanguineti, pp. 140–143.
[2] "Isque prisco instituto, propinquis coram, de capite famaque conjugis cognovit, et insontem nuntiavit. Longa huic . . . ætas et continua tristitia fuit. . . . Per quadraginta annos non cultu nisi lugubri, non animo nisi mæsto egit."

preted as intimating the Christian profession. But in these days when the catacombs are revealing their secrets to the sagacity and rare learning of one who may be called almost their first true explorer, the name of Pomponius Græcinus, the near relative of the lady named above, has been found in the inscriptions of the cemetery of Callistus, and it is rendered most highly probable that she is the very Lucina known in the times of the Apostles for her devotion to the martyrs, and her burying their relics in her own sepulchre.

Thus when Seneca and Burrus were the confidential ministers of Nero, and when St. Paul was brought a prisoner to Rome by his appeal to Cæsar, and as such was placed in the custody of this very Burrus, as prætorian prefect, one of the noblest Roman ladies was tried on an accusation of having received the hateful foreign superstition. It is of the highest probability both that she was well known to Seneca, and that he was present at the examinations which St. Paul underwent before the emperor. Thus the philosopher and the Faith were at least brought into the closest contact.

Six years later, in the year 64, we have the unimpeachable witness of Tacitus to the greatness of the work accomplished by St. Peter and St. Paul in the twenty-two years which had elapsed since the first coming of the former to Rome. When the persecution of Nero broke out, he records that a "vast multitude" gave the testimony of martyrdom to their belief.[1] We may thus compute what had been the growth of a community, which so few years after its first origin was strong enough to render such a proof of its faith. We may note at the same time how in the centre of heathenism, under the eyes of

[1] *Annal.* 15, 44.

Nero, amid a society eaten out with the most profligate corruption, a work had been accomplished unheard of upon the earth before. It was not merely among Jews, prepared by the knowledge of the one true God, and by the expectation of a Messiah, but out of Gentiles in their worst stage of moral decline, that a spiritual community had been founded, which could pass through such a shock, and far from losing, transmit its life onwards with a yet more vigorous growth. Such a result supposes a vast work of previous charity, the work of converting soul by soul, of instructing, catechising, baptizing, holding assemblies for preaching and for worship within the precincts of private houses, which alone were in a measure safe under the protection of domestic liberty. In this manner the whole sacramental life had to be transfused by the daily operation of its powers into a mass of converts, partly Jewish, partly heathen, and with regard to all these latter it was requisite to implant the new principle of obedience to foreign teachers without public warrant, and to make the new principle of faith in the unseen the spring of every action. We see, then, that the Church, which in its eleventh year was already renowned among all Christians for such a faith and such an obedience, was after another eleven years, and before the episcopate of its founder had terminated, the first to incur persecution from the emperor, in which its witnesses, enduring every extreme of mockery and cruelty, amounted to a vast multitude, as attested by one who denounced their belief as a pernicious superstition, and declared their crimes to merit the severest punishment.[1] Now, be-

---

[1] "Repressa in præsens exitiabilis superstitio . . . sontes et novissima exempla meritos." It is the contemporary and admirer of Trajan,

side the pressure of continued unlawfulness, with all its individual sufferings, history has noted ten distinct attacks of the emperors on the Christian people in the first three centuries. It was fitting that the first of these, the augury and anticipation of the rest, should fall as the token and crown of its eminence upon that Church which possessed the superior principate. But where in human things would it be possible to imagine a greater contrast than between the Rome which lived from Cicero to Claudius, in all pride and sensuality, and breathes to us still in the pages of its great writers, and the Rome which produced its witnesses clad in the skins of beasts and the garments of pitch at the games of Nero, and while his "golden house" occupied three of the seven hills, buried its founders, when their victory was won, in the chamber beside the Ostian Road, and in the sepulchral vault of the Vatican, that first hall of assembly of a more than royal line?[1]

But that we may appreciate the work of Peter, it requires to be more accurately described.

The conversion of the centurion Cornelius, the first-

and the friend of Pliny, who speaks, and his words cast a light upon their conduct in the persecution of Bithynia and the judgment of St. Ignatius.

[1] De Rossi, *Roma Sotter.* ii. 370, notes the sedulous care of the Churches, especially the Apostolical, "dei sepolcri dei lóvo vescovi, come testimoni della successione e della fede derivate dagli apostoli." Thus from St. Peter to Pope Victor in 197, the Popes were buried in Crypta Vaticana: there the successors of St. Peter were ranged in burial round him, as at Alexandria those of St. Mark beside him (tom. i. 31). In the time of Pope Zephyrinus, "Caio publicamente citava in Roma gli eretici a riconoscere nei *trofei* del Vaticano e della via Ostiense i pegni dell' apostolica origine della chiesa Romana, e della sua fede" (ii. 370). ἐγὼ δὲ τὰ τρόπαια τῶν 'Αποστόλων ἔχω δεῖξαι. ἐὰν γὰρ θελήσῃς ἀκελθεῖν ἐπὶ τὸ Βατικανὸν, ἢ ἐπὶ τὴν ὀδὸν τὴν 'Ωστίαν, εὑρήσεις τὰ τρόπαια τῶν ταύτην ἱδρυσαμένων τὴν ἐκκλησίαν. See Euseb. ii. 25, who states that their tombs bore the names of the Apostles.

FOUNDATION OF THE ROMAN CHURCH

fruit of the Gentiles, was accompanied by a visible descent of the Holy Ghost which recalled to mind in its chief circumstances the day of Pentecost itself; for indeed it betokened no less an event than the actual extension of the kingdom of God from Jewish converts to the whole world of the Gentiles. It had been preluded by a vision in which Peter, praying at noonday on the top of the house of Simon at Joppa, had seen "the heaven open, and a vessel like a great sheet descending upon him, bound at its four corners, and let down upon the earth, in which were all four-footed creatures of the earth, wild beasts, reptiles, and birds, and a voice was heard saying, Arise, Peter, kill and eat." Such was the divine intimation of what was presently to be. There followed immediately upon this vision the conversion of Cornelius, his kinsmen and particular friends. But the Apostles at Jerusalem recognised in this act the opening up of the whole Gentile world to their preaching. Peter's imprisonment by Herod, and miraculous delivery by the angel, happened shortly afterwards, upon which he forthwith "departed into another place." And in this other place it was that the vision in all its exactness was accomplished. In Rome, the seat of power, the capital of all the subject provinces, whither congregated all that was rich, ambitious, distinguished, but likewise the central slave-market of the world, the sink of the nations, whither drained all that was vile and suffering—in Rome Peter was to find the four-footed creatures of the earth, its wild beasts, reptiles, and birds, whom he should spiritually kill and eat, that is, amalgamate into one community. What image could more clearly represent the variety of Peter's Gentile converts? here and there a senator, such as Cornelius Pudens, here and there a highborn lady, such as Pomponia Græcina, but many freedmen and slaves from the household of Narcissus, from the imperial palace itself, from hundreds of other houses, whose domestics were like a nation, women of all ranks, the unlearned and the poor. Add to these the foreigners of all nations and all religions, of all climates and of every temperament from the extreme of Eastern superstition to that of Western barbarism, who were to be found at Rome, and from whom the preaching of the Apostle would select the recipients of divine grace. The population of Rome at this time represented all the diversities of human nature, and all the various trials which the vitality of the Gospel-seed was to experience in future times and distant regions were collected here, so that its Church would be an epitome of the Church in the whole world. These were they who had been all in their natural condition "common and unclean," sunk in the impurities of heathenism, though diverse in their qualities, but whom the mouth of Peter was to cleanse by the Word and the power following on that Word, and then to offer up in mystical sacrifice to God; and the Holy Ghost came down visibly to signify and commence a work which had had no parallel since the beginning of the world. The highest effort of philosophy had been to lay hold of choice minds: it never dreamed of admitting the multitude into its lecture-rooms, of associating the slave with the free-born, of setting down the rich and poor to feed at one table, of raising women to the utmost height of its precepts. The hetæra indeed was at times seen at an Epicurean feast, but without putting off the reproach of her life. It is only in the

Gospel that she wiped the Master's feet with her hair, and entering a sinner came forth a saint: only in the Church that Mary Magdalen becomes the first example and the type of a whole class which washes to the whitest purity robes that have been soiled in the deepest pollution. In fine, philosophy never essayed to erect a discipline tender enough to receive the weakest, and strong enough to enable women and children to die, not as an exit from evils, but in witness of truth. The attempt to unite in a moral band men and women of all nations, all ranks, all varieties of mind, education, and outward circumstances, was entirely new in its conception: and this was what Peter did for the first time, in the greatest and most dissolute city of the empire, at its worst period, when a Claudius and a Nero ruled its men, when Agrippina and Poppæa swayed its female society: and the first point in which his work stands in the deepest contrast with any previous philosophy, is the variety of the subjects on which it was exercised.

More remarkable yet is the contrast which in its inmost nature it exhibits.

Peter appeared at Rome as one sent by another. Himself a messenger, an ambassador, he called on men to accept as Redeemer, Prophet, Priest, and King, a Person who a few years before had appeared on earth as man in all these characters. Further, he called on men to discard the thousand gods of heathendom for the one God whose Son this Person claimed to be: and, moreover, to follow a course of life which should be after the pattern of His; and to join in a worship the beginning and end of which centred in Him. The existing pagan religions had inherited a worship from which morality had long been severed: the existing philosophies had cultivated morality, and Stoicism at least had grounded it on dogma, but no one of them had any worship of its own: whereas in this new teaching the dogmas of faith, the rules of morality, and the practices of worship had a common root in the Person whose kingdom was proclaimed, and all these, again, were united in visible symbols, sanctioned by Him, and deriving from Him their power to hold together a visible society. The beginning is laid by the living Word: nothing but the fulness, the persuasiveness, the pliability, the force of such an instrument as human speech would suffice to declare the message, on the acceptance of which all depends, no attraction but that of soul upon soul suffice to render it acceptable. As this double power had been used to the utmost by Him who spoke as never man spake, and from whom virtue went forth, so was it used by all those who spoke in His name. The vocal presence, the living person, is the indispensable basis of the work of conversion to a new faith. But when this has done its first task, when men have listened and believed, the marks of the King are set upon those who receive Him, and they become His by power of another kind. The illumination which the living Word of the vocal presence had prepared was completed in Baptism, by which the name of the triune God was confessed and accepted, and a sacred character impressed on the recipient: and provision was made for daily worship and for daily life in a sacrifice wherein this King and Redeemer communicated Himself to the soul. But in these acts were stored up at once the highest doctrine and the ground of all morality to the Christian. By his baptism he became the consecrated creature of God: by his sharing in the eucharistic sacrifice, the consecration was maintained, deepened, and extended in him. These two rites were to him a revelation of God, and no less did all the acts and all the duties of daily life flow out of them. In precisely the same manner the other five great rites, which make up all that is wanted for the life of a community or of the individuals who belong to it, were derivations of divine power, at once containing doctrine, enforcing morality, and practising worship. Thus the kingdom which took its rise in the fulness and attraction of vocal teaching had its compactness, completeness, and cohesion in the sacramental system, which joined its subjects in one belief, practice, and adoration, being itself the transfusion of Christ into His people, their generation from His Person. This was the nature of the society which Peter set up at Rome, in which nature its contrast with every preceding philosophy was yet more striking than in the variety of its subjects.

To make this clearer, let us take the four most illustrious names of Greek Philosophy and compare the work which they achieved with that of Peter.

And here what was the most remarkable and original idea in that Philosophy appears nearly at its rise. We know but little with certainty of what Pythagoras taught, but every authority concurs in attributing to him the conception of a society of men bound together by a moral discipline and common belief. The name itself, the study of wisdom, he is said to have invented, observing[1] that while some men are the slaves of glory, and others of money, there are a few who, counting all things else as dross,

---
[1] Cicero, *Tus. Dis.* v. 3.

give themselves up to the study of the nature of things. But though himself a man with an extreme thirst for knowledge, and trusting much to his own self-inquiry for the attainment of knowledge, he seems to have attributed the highest importance rather to a practical life grounded upon unity of belief than to mere science,' which he subordinated to a moral end. Simplicity of food, daily self-examination, purity of morals, were required of his disciples. And he trusted his teaching only to the living body of men, for, writing nothing, he actually formed a society which carried on his doctrine. It obtained a considerable success, grew and flourished in Crotona, until the fear which it occasioned as a political union brought on persecution, which finally broke up the society, though all through Grecian history we find individuals, and those the most distinguished of their day, imbued with so-called Pythagorean tenets.

In this conception of Pythagoras there was to some extent a sort of natural anticipation of the Christian Church. And his great personal qualities, combined with a noble religious purpose, produced a result, which, however, was frustrated and dissolved by the first attack of violence. That which he attempted, a political society based upon moral and religious principles, was never repeated with the same definiteness in Greek history again. His successors admired his idea, entertained it in their thoughts, but never ventured to carry it out.

Plato, himself in a measure a Pythagorean, conceived philosophy as a system of teaching to be conveyed orally by the master to his disciples, that is, to the few who can be found fitted for such pursuits by natural gifts, and prepared by moral discipline and by earnestness of purpose. The injunction,[1] "Take care that these things do not ever fall into the hands of unprepared and uninstructed men," may be called his keynote. In a school so selected, so laboriously trained, and in which the gifts of nature should be ripened by the finest art, the most careful study, he looked, if anywhere, for that immortal line of living men which was to continue on his own work. But at this point he stopped. He composed indeed an ideal republic, and he modified in another treatise his ideal views for the actual needs of what, if not the best in itself, should be the best that was practicable: but to the formation of an actual society, such as Pythagoras both conceived and attempted, he did not aspire. The fate of Socrates as well as the result of Pythagoras were before his eyes, and he only founded a school, which went through five modifications. We know him now entirely by those writings which he would not himself allow to represent his whole mind, inasmuch as he thought it impossible for any fixed type to convey the full system of any art, much less the secrets of philosophy.

Aristotle, in his conception of philosophy, stood very much on the same standing-ground as his master Plato. With prodigious industry, curiosity, and learning, with a most subtle, penetrating, and accurate intellect, he set himself to obtain truth by the force of the human reason in logic, ethics, and physics. No one man, perhaps, by the power of his own reason ever effected so much. He may be termed the father of literature, being the first to collect books, and the

---

[1] Epist. 2, p. 314. I follow the original Alexandrine editors and Mr. Grote in believing the authenticity of this epistle against the suspicions of some Germans.

great Alexandrine library, the formation of which we might call the beginning of literature, owed its first origin to that zeal for knowledge which the great master communicated to his royal pupil, and which that pupil's successors carried out in their famous foundation. He, with Plato, and still more than Plato, is the representative through all time of human culture. Like Plato he limited himself to the formation of a school, and with all his love for books subordinated the written to the spoken word. His writings have been considered the note-books of his lectures. Aristotle created two sciences, logic and ethics, but he made no society of men. He conceived and described all polities, but he too shrunk from the attempt to create that noblest one which should rest on the precepts and practices of philosophy.

In Zeno we find a considerable modification of the mental standing-ground occupied by Plato and Aristotle. No longer aspiring to universal knowledge in and for itself, it was pre-eminently a practical system, to found which he limited his efforts. In him the study of logic, ethics, and physics, the whole force of his reason was directed to afford an inner support to man amid the troubles of life. Those studies were pursued indeed, but not as a part simply of human culture, which had its end in itself. They were subordinated to a moral purpose. Philosophy became the instructress of humanity, and of a humanity felt to be sick in almost all its members. Man, as a spark of the universal reason which ruled the world, was to direct his life in conformity with that reason, represented in the laws of nature, and to live according to those laws was the conception of virtue. Philosophy thus took up at least in part the standing-ground proper to religion, and Zeno, passing at a bound the limits of states and nations, conceived the race of man as a flock in one pasture feeding on a common law, the law of reason. If we go on from the conception to its realisation, we find that Zeno too established a school: and as the many were foolish, and the few only in progress towards wisdom, his school was to be composed of such proficients. Now, although the Stoic was sometimes driven to confess that a wise man had never yet been found, as a matter of fact the strongest and most earnest natures among the Greeks and Romans during the three centuries which followed his teaching down to the time of Claudius were attracted by that elaborate system of duty—the subordination of the individual to the universal reason—drawn out in Stoic morality.

What then is the common effect of philosophy as seen in these four examples of Pythagoras, Plato, Aristotle, and Zeno, and their several systems? Certainly the powers of the human mind cannot be expected to rise higher than in the three former instances, nor the steadfastness of human purpose to exceed the fourth. What had been the result upon human society? So much as this. A few minds here and there out of the mass had been affected. Such minds accepted and professed certain tenets: it can hardly be said that they conformed their lives and actions to the tenets. Pythagoras, indeed, attempted to form a body of men so acting, but his society was dissolved. The Stoics afterwards approached nearest in their system to the attainment of a practical end, but, not to say that the profession was severed from the practice, the professors of Stoicism remained single and isolated. No such thing as a Platonic Peripatetic, or Stoic city, town, village, or even family existed. Cato of Utica was a Stoic, but he ruled his household as a Roman slaveholder, and when, in accordance with Stoic rule, he put an end to his own life, his hand was still swelling from the effects of a blow given to a slave. Where were the men, women, and children, the fathers, mothers, husbands and wives, brothers and sisters, living a Pythagorean, Platonic, Peripatetic, or Stoic life together? Philosophy, then, constructed no social building: its professors remained single stones. This was one defect betokening its impotence. And another was that it carefully abstained from attacking in practice that system of worship which its teaching tended to deny. It had, indeed, from the time of Zeno taken up, so far as concerned the formation of the interior life, the standing-ground of religion, and claimed to be the instructress of human nature and the guide of human actions: it had professed, as in Zeno's sect, the belief in one power ruling all things with an inexorable chain of cause and effect, but the whole world around was left in full possession of polytheism: the altars in countless temples smoked as before with sacrifices to Jupiter, and a crowd of conflicting deities, while the Stoic philosopher was seen, like the rest, taking part in his country's worship. He had no tangible sacrifice to offer to the universal reason, which he professed to believe, but hecatombs to gods and goddesses whom in his heart he despised.

Now measure what Peter did at Rome during the principates of Claudius and Nero with what these great men and their followers had all failed to do. During about the same number of years as those in which Pythagoras is said to have formed at Croton a society of the most distinguished inhabitants, Peter had formed at Rome a society including the highest and lowest, the young and the old, in one bond. In the former case the brilliant circle of educated men formed by Pythagoras was scattered by a persecution, and never was restored again. In like manner the arm of Nero came down upon Peter's society, which he had drawn out of the four-footed creatures of the earth, the wild beasts and reptiles, and birds of the prophetic vision, and a "great multitude" died. But the society lived; it lived to meet many such another storm in successive generations; to yield up again and again a great multitude to the same sufferings. It lived on in the self-same city: after eighteen hundred years it lives still, and in the self-same chair in which Peter taught, his two hundred and fifty-eighth successor teaches still.

But the disciplines of Plato, of Aristotle, and of Zeno afford us absolutely nothing to compare as a society with that of Peter. They produce individual and diverging specimens of certain schools of thought, but a community ruled by such thought they have not to show. It is not that they did not wish to create such a community; they had the wish, but were far from having the power. It is expressed exactly in Zeno's conception of the human polity, which Plutarch speaks of as so much admired; expressed, but never realised. This impotence of philosophy running through eight centuries from the time of Pythagoras, was shown two hundred years after Peter, in the case of the most fervent, most consistent, most elaborate, and the last of Grecian systems. Plotinus besought the Emperor Gallienus to grant the philosophers a city wherein a system of life could be carried out after Plato's model. It was to be called Platonopolis, and be situated in Campania. But the emperor did not assent, and Neoplatonism, like its predecessors, went without its city. Before that time, in the two centuries preceding the lectures of Plotinus at Rome, a divine city had been built up in the teeth of imperial persecution, there and in every centre of human intercourse and thought throughout the empire. St. Laurence could have shown Plotinus the treasures of that city in a multitude of the poor and destitute such as philosophy had never fed; and St. Laurence's own life and death might have imparted to him the secret how he who was carried from the Mamertine prison to execution founded under Nero's eyes, and in his despite, a permanent Christian polity, whilst imperial favour was solicited in vain to grant a single city for the trial of a philosophic experiment.

Such is the nature of Peter's work as contrasted with the work of philosophy.

But in calling it Peter's work, we must not forget that it was the work of Another, administered by Peter. As the impotence of philosophy lay precisely in this that it had no one to follow, so the power of the new faith lay in those two words, "Follow Me." The contrast here with the ancient philosophers is most striking. Pythagoras, Socrates, Plato, Aristotle, Zeno, Cleanthes, Plotinus also, Porphyrius, and the rest would have liked to form a society after their own principles, but it never entered into their thoughts to say, "Follow me." The ancient wisdom had indeed said, "Follow God."[1] It remained for Him alone when He appeared on earth to say, "Follow Me." The words in the mouth of a mere man are

[1] See Cicero, *De Fin.* iii. 21.

absurd. They had disciples, but no one of them ventured to set up himself as the germ of a polity, though they did conceive a polity, as the medium of teaching a doctrine. Not one of them thought of associating truth with his own person, or imagined that union of the truth with the life of a single man transfused into a body of men, which is the idea of the Church. The only faint resemblance of this is the fact, if it be one, that the Stoics framed their doctrine of the Wise Man after the living character of Socrates. It is true, indeed, that several generations after Christ had come, the Neopythagoreans idealised their conception of the philosophic life first in the person of Pythagoras, and then in that of Apollonius; that is, with the picture of Christ in the four Gospels before them, and the sight of the Church growing out of that model under their eyes, they bethought themselves to construct a heathen Christ, and to attribute whatever was great, noble, and attractive in human nature as they conceived it to two dead men. One of these had lived seven hundred years before, leaving behind him a great name, but scarcely any authentic documents as to the details of his life and teaching: the other had been contemporaneous with the Author of Christianity, but his life had passed almost unnoticed by any one of his own time, and without any effect on the world. Thus, after the lapse of a hundred years, the legend of Apollonius, like that of Pythagoras, lent itself to every embellishment of fiction. Far otherwise in the case of Him whom they feebly attempted to copy. "Follow Me" was as creative as "Let there be light." Uttered by the side of the Lake of Galilee, those words aggregated Apostles to Him who spoke them: uttered by those Apostles afterwards, they built up the Church.

On Peter's mind especially they had been impressed as those words which conveyed the greatness of his office, and his resemblance therein to his Lord, his supreme pastoral power, and his crucifixion.[1] But they contained likewise the whole structure of the Church, as the great "Following of Christ," the society which carried His truth in them, and with His truth His power. As then the philosophers were the theologians of heathenism, so the propagation of philosophy which they contemplated was by means of the society which the teacher instituted. In this the Academy, the Lyceum, the Portico, and the Garden were at one: and, indeed, no other propagation was at that time possible. There was philosophy long before there were libraries, and libraries again for ages before even the notion could arise of substituting a book for a society, which, indeed, before the invention of printing was inconceivable. The school was a collection of living men, and the idea of philosophy was bound up with this. But the Christian Church actually carried out what each philosopher attempted with so little success, and that because it was the school of Christ. Our Lord taught not as the Scribes and Pharisees, that is, commenting on a law, but as one having authority, that is, as being Himself the fulfilment of the law, that to which it pointed, and for whose coming it was instituted. He is the Lawgiver come in person, who delivers the law to His disciples, perpetuating His presence among them by His Spirit, by means of whom they carry on and propagate His law. Thus as with regard to the Jew, the synagogue was the embryo, which remained in the womb of the

---

[1] See John i. 44, where these words stand at the very beginning of our Lord's ministry, and xxi. 19, where they occur at the end of it.

Jewish nation until the Person of Christ should put life into it, and bring it to the birth, so with regard to the Gentile, philosophy with human power attempted to form an order of teaching, which changed and so to say evaporated with every teacher, recommencing an ever unachieved work. But the Teacher, who alone could say, "Follow Me," established not a school but a kingdom, whose law was the truth, Himself, whose power was grace, Himself, which by personal agency communicated both from Himself, and in His "Following" consisted the perfection of individual character and the fulness of corporate strength. "Follow Me" was said alike to Apostles and to others at their first call, as the foundation and watchword of Christian life: it was repeated emphatically to all the disciples, as being that in which their whole profession consisted: it was said also in a special manner to the Universal Primate, as the token of his divine vicariate.[1] Thus it formed the entire system between these two extremities. The point of union for dogma, morality, and worship lay in this "Follow Me," by which worship was no longer severed from dogma and without truth; nor morality without faith, and without authority to rest on: but the temple had found its God, man his Lawgiver, truth its Author: and the school had passed beyond the limits of a nation into a kingdom, worldwide and eternal.

This work of Peter in the midst of the heathen world, and especially at Rome, its centre and capital,

[1] (1) To Apostles and others of their calling, *e.g.* to Peter and Andrew, Matt. iv. 19; to Philip, John i. 44; to Matthew, Matt. ix. 9, Mark ii. 14, Luke v. 29; to another disciple, Matt. viii. 8, Luke ix. 59; to the rich young man, Matt. xix. 21, Mark x. 21, Luke xviii. 22. (2) To all, Matt. xvi. 24, Mark viii. 34, Luke ix. 23, John xii. 26. (3) To St. Peter, with regard to his Primacy and Crucifixion, John xxi. 22.

was represented to Christian eyes in the ancient paintings of the catacombs and in the sculptures of sarcophagi under a symbol which cannot be mistaken. There often recurs the image of Moses striking the rock with the rod of power, from which the streams of salvation issue. The rock, according to the Apostle's interpretation, signifies Christ; the stream that one fountain of grace on which the Christian life depends, and which accordingly the sheep are represented as drinking. The allusion to the Old Testament narrative is plain, but usually no name is given to the man striking the rock: in two instances, however, of the ancient glasses the name of Peter is written above this image, to signify that in the new Israel of God he occupies the place which Moses occupied in the old. But, moreover, this scene of Moses striking the rock is found constantly in juxtaposition with another scene of Peter taken captive by the satellites of Herod, and the features of the captive Peter and the man striking the rock are frequently made with a studied similarity to each other. For the repetition of these scenes close to each other no reason can be assigned but that Peter's imprisonment and miraculous deliverance immediately preceded that "going forth into another place" in which he founded the Roman Church, the most signal instance wherein he appeared as the Moses of the new covenant, causing the stream of grace to flow from the rock of Christ in the very centre and high place of pagan idolatry. The exhibition of such paintings on the walls of Roman catacombs and of such sculptures on Roman sarcophagi, conveyed a whole history to the beholder's mind. There was the local tradition of the Roman Church, and the universal tradition of the whole Church embodied in colour or in stone as to the part which Peter had taken in founding the great See wherein he would deposit his jurisdiction: but that jurisdiction itself is indicated in the rod,[1] the symbol of divine power, given in these paintings and sculptures to three persons alone, the Incarnate God Himself, Moses who prefigured Him, and Peter who followed Him. And the work accomplished is conveyed under the image of Moses striking the rock with a fulness and pregnancy of meaning such as reminds us of our Lord's own parables, for it would require a great space adequately to develop the thoughts suggested by the representation of Peter discharging to the new people of God functions which corresponded to those discharged by Moses when he led the typical nation through the desert.

But we may fitly exhibit some of the truth conveyed by this speaking symbol, and so elucidate the idea which the Christian artists of the third, fourth, and fifth centuries intended to portray: and that especially because in their delineation of Scriptural scenes "they did not treat them either accurately as facts of history, or freely as subjects of the imagination, but strictly with a view to their spiritual meaning."[2] The transit of the Jewish people from their slavery in Egypt through the wilderness to their promised possession is the type of the Christian people delivered from their darker slavery, and led through

---

[1] See *Roma Sotterranea* (Northcote and Brownlow), pp. 286-289, and also pp. 302, 303, for a description of the remarkable sarcophagus in the Lateran Museum, wherein to three groups above representing our Lord with the rod of power changing the water into wine, multiplying the loaves, and raising Lazarus from the dead, there appear three answering groups below, of Peter bearing the rod, apprehended by Herod's soldiers, and striking the rock. The same authors remark that the parallel event in the life of St. Paul, his imprisonment and deliverance at Philippi, is nowhere represented in early Christian art (p. 288). [2] Northcote and Brownlow, p. 240.

the desert of the world to their divine inheritance. But in that transit Moses was the leader and lawgiver of his people. As their mediator with God he received from God and gave to them a revelation of doctrine and a code of morals. Into his people as a receptacle he poured the knowledge of one personal God, the Creator and rewarder of men, and as a deduction from that truth he gave them a code of duties in which the first table contained all their relations to God, and the second all their relations to each other. Thus in the person of Moses were combined the two great powers of the Prophet or Teacher, and of the Lawgiver or King, but both as the deputy of Another, with whom he communed on the mount. And in the same character, as the deputy of that Other, who was not only the Revealer of truth and the Source of authority, but the Object likewise of worship, he instituted the third great power, the priesthood, not however in his own person, but in his brother Aaron and Aaron's sons. It is in this triple mediation, as the instrument through whom a revelation was conveyed and a law promulgated, and a priesthood together with its worship instituted, that the pre-eminence of Moses consisted. He thus made a complete society, feeding his people with truth, governing them with law, and sanctifying them with sacrifice and prayer. In the union of the three he educated them for their promised possession, and constituted them a nation. For their nationality was to consist in the continued joint possession of these three things, by maintaining which they were to be distinguished from all other nations down to the coming of the great Chief whom they expected. Thus it is to be observed that in the work of Moses, doctrine, morals, and worship all depended upon a close personal relation between the people and their God. "Hear, O Israel, the Lord thy God is one God." "Be ye holy, for I am holy." This was to be the sanction of doctrine and of morality: and the perpetual sacrifices were to deliver the chosen people from the guilt of disobeying One who expressed His absolute sovereignty by the often-repeated word, "I am the Lord." The whole life of the Jew, then, and of the Jewish people, as conceived and set forth by Moses, consisted in the maintenance and discharge of a personal relation in belief, in conduct, and in worship to One whose own personality was conveyed in that most significant expression, "I am the jealous God," of whom "Israel was the first-born[1] son."

But the three powers which were thus united in the mediation of Moses, while they were continued in the nation which he moulded, were not deposited in the same hands. We need not enter here into the various manners in which during the course of fifteen hundred years they were exercised. It is enough for the present purpose to note that in the nation as ultimately constituted we find the synagogue, the temple, and the throne of David,[2] that is, the teaching office which communicates doctrine, the priesthood which celebrates worship, the royalty which is the guardian and the transmitter of the kingdom promised to David. As Moses left these three powers in the Jewish community, so after all the changes through which it had passed they were found at the time of Christ still existing. The great Council of Jerusalem sat in the seat of Moses,[3] guard-

---

[1] Exod. iv. 22. [2] Döllinger, *Christenthum und Kirche*, p. 228.
[3] Matt. xxiii. 2.

ing and applying the double code of revelation and of morals which was contained in the law and the prophets.; the high-priest occupied the place of Aaron, and Herod filled the throne of David. The Prophet, the Priest, and the King, three rays of the divine sovereignty, made up "the polity of Israel,"[1] but they were separate and distinct in their holders until He came unto whom each of them pointed. The priesthood, with all the elaborate arrangement of sacrifices connected with it, was instituted only to mark out the office and prepare the way for the great High-priest. The prophet who had established the law both as the disclosure of divine truth and the rule of life, gave it as the image of that prophet like unto him who was to be raised up among his brethren. The throne had only been consecrated in David's person as the typical seat of the Eternal King. The whole polity which contained these three powers had been prepared during so many ages to be taken up and transfigured by Him who should unite all these offices in his own Person.

But these offices, upon their being received by Him, acquired an augmentation of dignity proportionate to His Person. The bearer of them being divine, the things borne rose to His height. The Incarnate God willed that the law should prefigure His truth, the priesthood His atonement, the seat of David His royal power: that thus there should be continuity between the Jewish type and Christian antitype, but continuity attended by an immeasurable exaltation. First He joined together in Himself these powers which make the perfect kingdom; then He imparted them so joined to the Apostolate which He

[1] Ephes. ii. 12.

created, and especially to Peter, whom alone He made the Rock, the Foundation, and the Door-keeper, the Confirmer of his brethren, the Shepherd and the Ruler of the Fold. He extended that which had been confined within the limits of a nation to the whole race of man : He detached the carnal covering which veiled the promises, and disclosed them in their full spiritual light. For the priesthood which offered the sacrifices of bulls and sheep, He instituted the priesthood which offered at His own table the sacrifice offered by Himself, and He made it a royal priesthood, ordering that its possessors should sit upon twelve thrones judging the twelve tribes of Israel, and so be perpetual guardians and maintainers of the law of truth and charity which He left in that new Israel. Thus He disposed to them the kingdom which had been disposed to Him.[1] In this manner the covenant, the legislation, the worship, the adoption, the glory, and the promises, which made according to St. Paul the distinction of the Jewish Church, passed over to the Christian, which became in a higher sense than the former, in the words of St. Peter, " a chosen race, a royal priesthood, a holy nation, a purchased people." Moses, Aaron, and David having been gathered up into the one Christ, the race of Abraham became the race of the God-Man.

Now, what Moses did in the type, Peter did in the antitype. As Moses drew out the life of the Jewish people as a personal relation to God in what they believed, in what they worshipped, and in what they did, which made up the adoption of sons, so the

---

[1] Luke xxii. 29, 30, in which passage, as Döllinger notes, while creating the royal priesthood in the Apostolate, He marks that there should be one that is greater among them.

Christian life which Peter set up at Rome was the
establishment of the same relation to Christ in doctrine, worship, and morals. Obedience to him in
these three things formed his kingdom. The whole
domain of truth was guaranteed to the Christian as
the illumination given by the one Prophet. His
worship was the perpetual recognition of the Redeemer in the very act of His sacrifice; while his
morality was summed up in charity, the filial spirit,
which raised the cardinal virtues to the level of
divine gifts, and was thus "the fulfilment of the
law" as perfected by Christ. The painter in the
catacombs of the second and third centuries, the
sculptor on the monuments of the fourth and fifth,
conveyed all this when they represented Peter on
the very scene of his spiritual triumph, the centre
of the world's power, and the seat of idolatry, striking
with the rod of divine power which he alone received
from the hands of his Lord, that Rock which is
Christ, and so drawing forth the one stream of salvation, the grace which works in the great Christian
priesthood, which conveys to the sheep the faith and
the sacraments, the whole supernatural life. In
their eyes as but one Moses was the mediator of the
old covenant, so but one Peter was the master-builder
of the Church, the deriver of the stream to the sheep.
They anticipated in colour and on stone what St. Leo,
at the same spot, has set forth so powerfully and distinctly in language. The living mind of the Church
in their day, as seen in their works and in his words,
is the same, which he declares to his brethren, the
Bishops of Italy: "Whatever we do rightly and
discern clearly is of his own working and his merit,
whose power lives and whose authority is pre-eminent

in his own See—for throughout the whole Church Peter is daily saying, 'Thou art Christ, the Son of the living God,' and every tongue confessing the Lord is imbued with the teaching of that Word of His." For, "out of the whole world Peter alone is chosen to preside over the calling of all the nations, over the whole number of the Apostles, and all the Fathers of the Church: so that though there be in the people of God many priests and many shepherds, yet Peter rules all with ordinary whom Christ rules with sovereign power."[1]

Now, from the time of Zeno onwards the Greek philosophy had, in a certain sense and degree, taken up the standing-ground of religion. It essayed to satisfy the human mind in its aspirations after truth, to afford man a security for a happy life, independent of outward circumstances, to supply him with a compensation for the loss of political freedom by its intrinsic principles, to teach him, if not how to die, at least how to live. Such is the part assigned to it in the name of all who went before them by Cicero and by Seneca. Such was notoriously the Stoic boast. We are, then, entitled to ask how it stood as to these three powers, doctrine, morals, and worship, in the intimate connection of which the perfection of society consists.

As to the first, to attain truth with respect to the universe and man its occupant was its primary object, and if we abstract that portion of its teaching which was the continuation of the original tradition descending to the Greeks as to all other men from the patriarchal religion, it could only by the force of the human reason acting in conjunction with the natural

[1] St. Leo, Serm. iii. 3, iv. 2.

conscience reach truth. It did not claim to possess
any such gift as the Jew recognised in Moses and
the prophets, and the Christian found in the Apostolic
teaching. And so in it we find its physical science
and its theology made identical.

Again, as to its morality, that likewise was the
produce of human reason. No doubt, indeed, in this
case as in that of doctrine, the most self-reliant philosopher was still influenced, and much more, perhaps,
than he was conscious of, by precepts which had come
down from the ancient religion, and which coalesced
in his mind with the judgments of the natural conscience. But so far forth as each philosophic system
had a distinctive morality, it was formed by a process
of reason working upon that supposed truth which
the intellect had attained. Thus the three virtues of
Plato, prudence, fortitude, and temperance, were deduced from his triple division of the human being's
constituents, and represented the three parts which he
derived severally from the divine mind, the world-soul,
and matter. In a more remarkable instance there
can be no doubt that Stoicism, which claims our notice
above all the rest as a moral system, worked out its
morality as a strict deduction from its conception concerning God or Nature on the one hand and man on
the other, which involved the subjection of the particular to the universal reason: but likewise an identity
with it. And so the ground of its morality was the
intrinsic dignity of man as a rational being, not the
acknowledgment that he was a creature. It seems
then that the grand modern invention of independent
morality was entirely anticipated by the Greek philosopher, not, however, as a thing desirable in itself,
but as that to which he was reduced by the necessity

of his position. This will be more apparent when we consider the third great constituent of society, worship. Now of this Philosophy was entirely destitute. It had none of its own, and it fell throughout its course and in all its sects into the fatal weakness of consenting to take at least an external part in an ancestral worship to which its inmost belief was opposed. Thus in the most important act of human life the philosopher was a hypocrite. He joined in rites the efficiency of which he disbelieved, and which were offered to powers whose existence he denied. This is true of Plato and of Aristotle as well as of Zeno and Epicurus, of Cicero and of Cato, of Seneca too and of Marcus Antoninus. The result was that in philosophy the two forces of doctrine and morals were entirely detached from that other great force which raises man above himself, and exalts him in proportion to the idea which he has conceived of the Being who rules him. In fact, the personal relation, which ran all through Jewish life, and bound together worship, doctrine, and morals, which was exalted to its highest expression by the mystery of the Incarnation, and from it formed and impregnated the whole Christian life—which is but to be a child "of the great Father, Christ"—this was wanting to Philosophy,[1] and far more wanting to the philosopher than to the ordinary heathen, in whom the natural conscience still left a feeling or imperfect conviction that he was a creature under dependence and rule.

In the disruption of these three forces we see the permanent and universal cause of that weakness and powerlessness to persuade, which marks the Greek philosophy in all its sects, and of that inability to form

[1] See Kleutgen, *Phil. der Vorzeit*, ii. 830.

a society after its tenets which runs through all its history. And this will be found no less true of Philosophy, with the example of the Christian Church before it, than of its previous efforts to find the truth and improve human life.

LECTURE XVI

NEOSTOICISM AND THE CHRISTIAN CHURCH

I.

We have hitherto considered what Philosophy, working in the most intellectual of human races, had done up to the time of our Lord's teaching. Then, in order to illustrate the grounds of its insufficiency we traced the foundation of the greatest and most celebrated Church, the special work of the chief Apostle, to whom the keys of the kingdom of heaven were given, in the principates of Claudius and Nero. It remains to consider in the same manner what Philosophy was able to do during the period in which the teaching of our Lord was being embodied before its eyes in a visible institution by His disciples. The first study gave us the measure of what human reason was able to do, mainly by its own power, in solving the mysteries of human life, while the nations were covered with darkness. The second will unfold to us a scene not less interesting. We shall see the same human reason pursuing in the main its old course and resting on the same fundamental principles, but gradually awakening to the sense of a great rival power arising in the world of thought which it had claimed for its own. And it is acted upon, more and more, whether consciously or unconsciously, by this power. It remains unconverted by it, but not unaffected. Its great thinkers are heathen still, but of a very different stamp from the heathen of the republic. Already Seneca, the

tutor and minister of Nero, whether he conferred with
St. Paul, as he might most easily and naturally have
done, or not, spoke as no Greek or Roman ever spoke
before him, of mercy, brotherly kindness, humanity to
slaves, and compassion with the weak and suffering.
He has a moral standard not only immeasurably above
his own practice, but equally above the moral standard
of such men as Aristotle and Plato, far exceeding him
in genius. If we go on another fifty years, Epictetus and Plutarch seem to belong to quite a different
world from that in which Cicero lived and moved, and
Marcus Aurelius is no less distant from Julius Cæsar
or Augustus. As we advance the contrast deepens.
Philostratus and Plotinus are far from being productions of the Christian Faith which they opposed, but
their works are a powerful testimony to what that
Faith was doing in the world. The ideal character
which the one tries to exhibit, and the philosophy
which the other attempts to restore, show the divine
example which had flashed on the mind of the one
without converting him, and the conception of divine
things which the other had witnessed, admired, and
endeavoured to convert to the behoof of heathen
wisdom. Before the end of the third century, every
thoughtful heathen mind had undergone a revolution.
Porphyrius teems with Christian sentiments which
stud his invectives against Christianity. Thus the
period which ends with the conversion of Constantine
has, besides its other wonderful attractions, a special
interest as the battlefield between the heathen philosophy and the Christian Church. It is true that the
battle continued afterwards, and an emperor even
became its champion out of the very family of the
imperial convert, but the contest was practically de-

cided, and the Church both as a doctrine and an institution had gained the victory, when the edict of toleration was published.

We have already seen how poor and meagre a part Philosophy played between the death of Julius Cæsar and the accession of Claudius. The political and social sphere in which it moved may be thus epitomised. Augustus reduced to peace the warring elements of Roman political life. From the battlefield of Actium, A.U.C. 723, which placed in his single hands the destiny of the Roman world, to his death in 767, a period of forty-four years, he watched over and maintained the equilibrium which he had created. Tiberius received from him the republic at the mature age of 55, and governed it in tranquillity for nearly twenty-three years. The short madness of Caius succeeded, and when he was swept away in the year 794, Claudius inherited the supreme power over the vast confederacy of nations subject to Rome, which now for seventy years had been welded into an imperial republic enjoying the benefits of a common civilisation. If, outside the walls of Rome, and beyond the interests of the Roman nobility, we compare the state and condition of all these nations as to the enjoyment of such benefits, during these seventy years, with their state and condition during the century preceding the battle of Actium, it will be impossible to deny that they had greatly gained by the establishment of the imperial government. In spite of individual abuses of power, the provinces as a rule were no longer used up as the private spoils of profligate nobles. They possessed instead laws administered with equity, could develop their commerce, and be secure of their wealth. If Augustus could only have ensured successors like himself, wielding with the modesty of a senator, who was but the princeps of his order, that vast central power which so great a mass required to hold it in cohesion, the gain would have been as permanent as it was great. That was the empire which Virgil and Horace saw and celebrated with a heartiness and a sincerity which their own previous sufferings, and that of all men under the republic, might justify. If those in whom an exclusive Roman patriotism was strong might feel thus, was not the whole world of the subject provinces ready to cry out with them,

" O Melibœe, Deus nobis hæc otia fecit" ?

That, no less, was the empire which, fifty years later, Philo praised in glowing colours as the reign of law, and described as the voluptuous enjoyment of civilisation without a rival and without an enemy. But the dark side of the picture remained to be filled in, and when another seventy years had passed after the death of Tiberius, Tacitus drew this portrait with a master's hand. Mental apathy, disregard of high thought, and intense corruption of morals make up the Rome which he describes. And certainly the whole surviving literature of that time bears out his censure. Writers for whom the undying grace of outward form and elegance of language have secured the admiration of all posterity, if judged according to a moral standard by any feeling or longing after divine things which they show, would betray a state of society which seemed to value nothing else but the material goods of civilisation, peace, plenty, bread, and games. Philosophy gives scarcely a sign of life during this period. From Cicero to Seneca it is almost silent: during this most important century when the world-empire was forming, it can show only the honourable but uninfluential school of the Sextii. That city of gods and men ruled by reason as the common inheritance of all, the standard of their progress and the bond of their union, which Cicero had so grandly imaged out, clothing his Stoic teachers in the stately toga of the Roman tongue, found little favour in the eyes of those to whom the dominion of the world was only precious for the abundance of peace and the refinements of scientific vice. Such was the temper which rose to its utmost height in the twenty-seven years during which Claudius and Nero ruled, when the utter corruption of human society filled the few who thought with blank despair.[1] Yet precisely this people and their rulers were chosen by the Divine Providence to be the scene of that work of Peter within the walls of Rome, which has shown itself to us as alike without a parallel in the ages before it, and without, as it seemed, any aptitude for accepting it in the population where it was carried on.

For the work of Peter was pre-eminently a work of faith in the unseen, a disregard of the temporal for the sake of the eternal. But if we take the line of writers from Cicero to Tacitus, which includes all the great names of Latin literature, this is precisely that which is wanting to them. From the first to the last they speak as men without faith in the popular religion which they had inherited; and likewise without any firm mental grasp of a power superior to man ruling the world with wisdom and justice; and equally without any clear assurance of a personal subsistence of the individual man after death. Their uncertainty about God and Providence draws with it an equal uncertainty

[1] Döllinger, *Heid. und Jud.* p. 576.

about their own destiny. They were citizens of an empire holding the fairest regions of the earth, formed of the finest races of men, enjoying the accumulated fruits of learning and thought which many past ages had laid up for them, and moreover during the latter part of this period, they dwelt in the midst of the most majestic material peace which the world has seen. This was the condition of outward things during the reigns of Augustus, Tiberius, Caius, and Claudius. But when we look on the inward life of the soul, when we try to realise what such men as Julius Cæsar, Cicero, Catullus, Virgil, Horace, Livy, Ovid, thought concerning those problems which most engage our own minds, we find an utter uncertainty and a hopelessness which moves us to the deepest commiseration. What expectation had the imperial spirit of Julius formed concerning his own future when he entered the senate on those ides of March, to fall before the statue of Pompey? What did the great orator, who in his unwilling moments of forced leisure ransacked the treasures of Greek philosophy, anticipate for himself when he stretched out his neck from his litter and fixed his eyes on his assassin? What did the poet who has embodied in majestic verse the house of Æneas, and the Capitol's immovable rock and the empire of the Roman Father, think of his own individual destiny when he laid down his life at Parthenope? What did the haunter of the Sabine hills, the skilled painter of Roman society, look forward to, when eleven lustres of his life were over, when the time of flowers and fugitive loves was past, and Mæcenas left him with but half of his soul remaining? What consolation, when banished from that scene of brilliant corruption which his verses paint with so fatal a skill, could Ovid find on his Scythian shore in any hope of his own spirit having power to replace the goods of outward life which he had lost? Cæsar and Cato agreed in the senate that death ended all things, and that there was neither joy nor sorrow beyond it, and the tragedian bearing Seneca's name cries: "After death is nothing, and death itself is nothing: then thou wilt be where the unborn are." There is profoundest pathos in the last words of the man whose great genius made him the second and real founder of this prodigious empire. Augustus, enthroned in uncontested power, had complacently reviewed, on tablets of brass, as in presence of the human race, his acts during more than forty years, recounting the pacific victories of a long prosperity. And his dying comment on all these things was, as he turned to those who should presently close his eyes, "Have I played my part well? *Vos valete et plaudite.* All the world's a stage. Clap me as I make my exit."

In the midst of a people, emperor, senators, knights, freedmen, and slaves, who thought and acted just as these leaders of thought and action had done, that "great multitude" of whom the Roman historian speaks, died under the persecution of Nero for their faith in an unseen world, and in a never-ending life of soul and body to be reunited together. Unless we have this present to our minds we shall utterly fail to recognise the power which characterised that work of Peter. At a later period we shall find a yearning after union with God awakened even in pagan minds, but when the Gospel was first preached we have all the evidence which a surviving literature can give that it was wanting there, at least in the intelligence of cultured men.

After the Christian Church had acted for a certain time on the Gentile world we shall find who and what God is become the first and most pressing of questions, and the way by which the human soul may approach that God the question which is become next in urgency to it. But nothing can be further from the spirit of the Latin world, as all its extant writings show, than these questions in the time of Claudius, when Peter first appeared at Rome.

The only form of Philosophy which existed in any force at this time was the Stoic. Now this was a system penetrated with unbelief. The never-ending and never-broken series of cause and effect, the icy chain of physical and material necessity applied unrelentingly to mind also, this being indeed the only God —a God of its own creation—which the Stoic philosophy admitted, had dethroned the Platonic God, a pure spiritual essence. It treated the popular gods of the current mythology as mere manifestations of this supreme power, and viewed as such it found no contradiction in their number, and no embarrassment in their various functions. They had ceased to be persons and become mere agencies. As we are about to consider particular tenets of the four chief Stoics after Christianity was preached, of Seneca, Musonius, Epictetus, and Marcus Aurelius, let us endeavour to obtain a clear and succinct view of the general system of thought, to which Cato and many others of the noble Romans had addicted themselves, which reappeared in the senate of Nero, inspiring Thrasea, as afterwards Helvidius and Rusticus, and was alone, it may be said, standing on its feet when St. Peter began to preach at Rome. It may be viewed, in fact, as the outcome of the Greek wisdom respecting God, Providence, and man, his present and his future, when the Epistle to the Romans was written.

That our picture may be perfectly unbiassed I take it from an accurate modern compendium of philosophy.

The term Physics embraces with the Stoics not only Kosmology but also Theology.[1] Everything actual with them is held to be corporeal. Matter and Force are the two superior principles. Matter is in itself without motion or form, but capable of taking every motion and form. Force is the active, moving, and forming principle. It is inseparably bound up with matter. The working force in the whole mass of the world is the Deity. The world is limited and spherical. It has a permeating unity together with the greatest multiplicity of particular shapes. The beauty and design of the world can only spring from a thinking mind, and therefore demonstrate the being of the Deity. As further the world has conscious parts, the universe which must be more perfect than each individual part cannot be without consciousness. But the consciousness in the Universe is the Deity. This permeates the world as an all-pervading Breath, as an artistically-shaping Fire, as Soul and Reason of the Whole. It contains in itself the particular germs and seeds of reason.[2] The divine original Fire changes itself in constructing the world into air and water: the water becomes in part earth, in part remains water, in part evaporates in air, whence again fire is enkindled. The two grosser elements, earth and water, are chiefly passive; the two finer, air and fire, chiefly active. After the lapse of a

---

[1] Ueberweg, pp. 195, 198.
[2] λόγοι σπερματικοί.

certain world-period the Deity takes back all things into itself, since all passes by the burning up of the world into fire; out of this divine fire the world then again and again comes forth anew. In the arising and passing away of the world there rules an absolute necessity, which is identical with the regularity of nature and with the divine reason. This necessity is Fate, and likewise [1] Providence, which rules everything. The human soul is a portion or effluence of the Deity, and stands in reciprocal action with it. It is the breath of heat in us. It overlasts the body, but yet is transient, and endures at the utmost only to the burning of the world. Its parts are the five senses, the faculty of speech, the power of reproduction, and the ruling power,[2] which has its seat in the heart, and to which notions,[2] desires, and understanding belong.

The supreme end of life or the highest good is virtue, that is, life in accordance with nature, the harmony of human conduct with the all-ruling law of nature, or of the human will with the divine will. Man's highest task lies not in contemplation, but in action. But action refers to human society. All else is come into existence for the sake of gods and men, but man for the sake of society. Virtue is sufficient for happiness. It alone is good in the full sense of the word: all which is not virtue or vice is likewise neither good nor evil, but something between; but in this between there is something that is to be preferred, something that is to be avoided, something too that is entirely indifferent. Pleasure is something superadded to activity, and it should not be the end of our endeavours. The cardinal virtues are prudence,

---

[1] εἱμαρμένη, πρόνοια.   [2] τὸ ἡγεμονικόν, φαντασίαι.

fortitude, temperance, and justice. He only who unites all virtues in himself can truly possess them singly. The perfect fulfilling of duty [1] is the doing right with a right intention, such as the wise man possesses. Right conduct, as such, abstracting from the intention, is the suitable.[2] Only the wise man performs the perfect fulfilling of duty. The wise man is without passion, though not without feeling: he exercises to himself and others not indulgence but justice. He alone is free. He is king and lord, and is inferior in inward worth to no other reasonable being, not even to Jupiter. He is likewise master of his own life, and may end it according to his own free determination. The later Stoics admitted that no one perfectly answered the ideal of the wise man, but that in fact there only existed the distinction between fools and those in progress towards wisdom.

There are four illustrious productions of this philosophy, who happen singularly enough to represent the four chief constituent parts of the Roman commonwealth. Seneca gives us an instance of the Stoic senator; Musonius of the Stoic knight; Epictetus of the Stoic slave; Marcus Aurelius of the Stoic emperor. All are formed, whatever may be the differences of individual character, out of the common tissue of these principles, and to understand their language aright we must interpret it by this general charter of Stoic thought.

Seneca, from the time and circumstances of his life and the large amount of writings which he has left, is full of interest and instruction as a specimen of the wealthy, cultured, and philosophic Roman of that day. We may count his years with those of the

[1] τὸ κατόρθωμα.   [2] τὸ καθῆκον.

Christian era. Born at Corduba,¹ of knightly parentage, he was early brought to Rome. The years of his youth, he says, were passed under the principate of Tiberius. Though of delicate constitution, he gave himself up with zeal to study, especially to philosophy, in which Sotion of Alexandria, the pupil of Sextius, and Attalus the Stoic, instructed him. He subsequently became a lawyer, married, and was rich and fortunate in his condition. After being threatened by Caligula, he was banished to Corsica, under Claudius, at the instigation of Messalina. Here he remained about eight years, and only upon her fall was recalled by the influence of Agrippina in the year 49. He was then made prætor, and for five years conducted the education of Nero. On Nero's accession he became with Burrhus the chief minister of that emperor, and to these two men the famous quinquennium of Nero is probably due. But with the death of Burrhus Seneca's influence came to an end. After a period during which he was treated with jealousy and suspicion the conspiracy of Piso in the year 65 gave Nero an opportunity to get rid of one whom he feared probably as well as hated, and the philosopher with courage and equanimity put himself to death at the command of Nero.

Now as it would require a large space to draw out the doctrine of Seneca, let us dip into the strata of his mind on three principal points. The first shall be the office which he assigns to philosophy; the second, his conception of God; the third, his conception of man.

As to the function of philosophy he says, "The mind is made perfect by one only thing, a fixed

---
[1] Zeller, iv. 616.

unchanging knowledge of goods and evils, and this belongs to philosophy alone. . . . One study only is there truly liberal, which makes man free, the study of wisdom, source of sublimity, fortitude, and magnanimity. . . . Wisdom is the perfect good of the human mind, and philosophy is the loving and the laying hold of wisdom. . . . It is the art of life, and its law. . . . Philosophy teaches to do, not to say, and requires every one to live according to its law, that the life may not disagree with the language. . . . It is the chiefest duty at once and sign of wisdom that words and actions should agree, and the man be everywhere like himself. . . . Why does no one confess his own vices? Because they still master him. The man awake tells his dream, and the confession of one's vices shows one's convalescence. Awake we then, that we may have power to refute our own errors. But philosophy will be our sole awakener; alone will she shake off our deep sleep. Dedicate thyself entirely to her. Thou art worthy of her and she of thee; embrace each other. Deny thyself firmly, avowedly, to every other: thou canst not philosophise by fits and starts. . . . Philosophy has her kingdom; she gives her own times, does not accept yours, is not a thing of leisure moments; she claims the whole, is mistress, is beside you, and commands. A certain city offered Alexander half its territory and its property. He replied, ' When I came into Asia, it was not that I should accept what you offered, but that you should keep what I left you.' So says philosophy to all : ' I shall not accept your superfluous time, but you shall have what I assign to you.' Give your whole mind to her, sit by her, reverence her. There will be a huge interval between you and other men. You will surpass all men in your life; not much will the gods surpass you. What will be the difference between you and them? They will last longer. But in very truth it shows a great master of craft to enclose a whole in a small space. As wide is his own age to the wise man as all age is to God. There is a point in which the wise man surpasses God. God by nature's gift is incapable of fear, but the wise man by his own. That indeed is a great thing, to have in the weakness of man the security of God."[1]

Let us proceed to Seneca's conception of God.

He himself puts the question, "What is God?" He replies, "The mind of the universe." He repeats: "What is God? The whole which thou seest and the whole which thou seest not. His due magnitude, than which thought can reach to nothing greater, will at last be accorded to him, if he alone is all things, if he grasps his own work both from within and from without. What then is the distinction between God's nature and ours? The better part of ours is the mind: in him there is no part outside the mind. He is all reason, while our minds are possessed by such error that men deem that which is fairest in form, most ordered in arrangement, most constant in purpose, to be fortuitous, tossed about by chance, and therefore driven hither and thither amid lightnings, clouds, and storms, and such-like, which strike the earth and the regions adjoining it. . . . Jupiter is the ruler and guardian of the universe, the mind and spirit of the world, this work's lord and artificer, whom every name suits. Will you call him Fate?

[1] Epistles lxxxviii. 28; lxxxviii. 2; lxxxix. 4; cxvii. 12; xciv. 39; xx. 2; liii. 8.

You are not wrong: he it is from whom all things are suspended, the cause of causes. Will you name him Providence? You are right: for he it is by whose counsel this world is provided for, so that it proceeds without tripping, and unfolds its acts. Will you entitle him Nature? You will not err. He it is of whom all things are sprung, by whose spirit we live. Will you call him World? You are not deceived, for he is this whole which you see, infused into the parts of himself, and supporting himself and his."

But further. "Our Stoics say that there are two things in universal nature out of which all comes, Cause and Matter. Matter lies inert, prepared for every change, idle if no one moves it. But Cause, that is Reason, forms Matter, and turns it whithersoever it will, produces out of it various works. Thus there must be that out of which something comes, and then that by which it comes. This is Cause, that is Matter. . . . We are now inquiring after the prime and general Cause. This must be simple. For Matter too is simple. We are inquiring what is Cause, that is, Reason as agent, that is, God. . . . In fact, all things consist of Matter and of God. God tempers them and they being circumfused follow their ruler and leader. But that which acts, which is God, is more powerful and more precious than the Matter, which is passive of God. The place in this world which God holds, the mind holds in man. What there is Matter, in us is body. Let the inferior, therefore, serve the superior."

But this God is corporal. "We are agreed that what is good, is a body, because what is good is an agent: whatever is an agent, is a body. What is good, profits, but it must be an agent of something in

order to profit: if it is an agent, it is a body. . . .
This, therefore, which you call being wise, is it an
agent or a patient of wisdom? Whether it be an
agent or a patient, in both ways it is a body. For
both that on which the action takes effect and that
which is an agent, is a body.[1] If it is a body, it is
good." . . . For " we are of opinion that there is no
good which consists of separated things. For the one
good must be contained and ruled by one spirit: the
principle of this one good must be one. . . . And
why should you not think that something divine
exists in him who is part of God? This whole, in
which we are contained, is both one and God. We
are both his fellows and his members. Such is our
mind's capacity."[2]

To make the above expressions clear, we must have
present to us the absolute Stoic conception of God.
It is this.[3] The opposition between God and Matter
is only secondary. If we take in the conception of
the Godhead in its full meaning, it must be described
as the Primal Matter as well as the Primal Force. The
collective mass of the Actual is nothing else but the
Divine Breath which moves forth out of itself and back
into itself. The Godhead itself is the Primal Fire
which bears within itself in germ God and Matter,
is the world in its primal state of spirit, the Universal Substance, which changes itself into particular
concretions, and restores itself back from them again:
which, therefore, considered in its pure form, or as
God, embraces at one time the All, at another time
only a portion of the Actual. Thus Origen speaks of
the Stoics as introducing a corruptible God, as term-

[1] "Nam et quod fit et quod facit corpus est."
[2] *Nat. Quæst.* Prol. 13; *Ibid.* ii. 45; Epist. lxv. 2, 12, 23; cxvii. 2, 10; cii. 7; xcii. 30.   [3] Zeller, iv. 133.

ing his substance a body, subject to change, conversion, and transformation, as at some particular period destroying all things, and reducing God to solitariness. And again he says, that the Stoic God, being a body, sometimes possesses his whole substance in a condition of ruling, at the time, that is, of the burning of the world; sometimes is embodied in a portion of it, when the world is arranged in its order. These statements of Origen are justified by Seneca, when he asks, "What will be the life of the wise man, if he be cast into prison, and left without friends, or be destitute amid some foreign nation, or kept on a long voyage, or tossed out upon a desert coast?" And replies, "It will be such as the life of Jupiter, when, after the fusing up of the world, and the pouring back of the gods into one, and the cessation of nature, he rests in himself, delivered over to his own thoughts."[1]

It is by the above statements that we must interpret the beautiful passages of Seneca preserved for us by Lactantius. "Dost thou not understand the authority and the majesty of the judge, the ruler of the earth, and the God of heaven and of all gods, from whom those deities whom we severally adore and worship are suspended? ... He it is, who, when he cast the first foundations of this most beautiful structure, and traced the web of that which in grandeur and in goodness nature cannot surpass, in order that every part might have its proper commander, although he had stretched himself throughout his whole body, yet begot gods to be the ministers of his kingdom."[2]

---

[1] Origen, *Contra Celsum*, iii. 75, iv. 14, quoted by Zeller; Seneca, Epist. ix. 16.

[2] "Quamvis ipse per totum se corpus intenderat," an expression of exact Stoicism, the τόνος which they so often repeat. Lactantius, *Divin. Instit.* l. 5.

Let us complete Seneca's conception of God by passing on to his conception of the human intelligence.

"Good is an agent, for it profits. That which is an agent is a body. Good moves, and in a sense forms and contains the mind, which are properties of a body. The goods of the body are bodies; therefore those of the mind also, for it too is a body. The good of man must be a body, he being himself bodily. . . . As a flame cannot be grasped, for it evades pressure; as air is not hurt by a stroke, nor even divided, but pours again round that to which it yields; so the mind, consisting of that which is thinnest, cannot be laid hold of, nor pressed within the body, but by help of its own subtilty escapes through what would bind it. As lightning, however widely it may have struck and shone, can come back through the finest aperture, so the mind, which is thinner even than fire, can escape through every body. . . . Heat draws out curved beams, and their natural growth is shaped to what our need requires. How much more easily does the mind, being flexible and more pliant than any liquid, accept a shape. For what else is the mind but a breath under certain condition? But you see that breath is more shapable than any other material, as it is thinner."

And the human mind or soul, so conceived, is a part of God. "You do what is very good and saving to you, if, as you write, you persevere in going to a good mind, which it is foolish to wish for, when you can get it of yourself. There is no need to raise hands to heaven, nor to beseech the sacristan to let us in to whisper at the ear of the statue, as if we could be better heard. God is near thee, with thee, within thee. So it is, Lucilius. A sacred spirit is seated within us, the observer and the watch over our good and our bad. As he is treated by us, so he treats us himself. But no one is a good man without God. Can any one rise above the strokes of fortune except by His assistance? He gives great and lofty counsels. In every one of good men a god there dwells, though it be uncertain what god. . . . Praise in the man that which can neither be taken away nor given: that which belongs to the man himself. Ask you what it is? The mind, and perfect reason in the mind. For man is a rational animal. And so his good is consummate if it fulfil that for which it is born. But what does this reason require of him? A most easy thing, to live according to his own nature. . . . What then is reason? The imitation of nature. What is man's supreme good? To bear himself according to nature's will."

Again: "He had a perfect mind, as being raised to his own highest, above which there is nothing but the mind of God, from whom a part has flowed down into this mortal breast. And this is never more divine than when it thinks of its own mortality, and knows that man was born for this, to pass through life: that this body is not a home but a hospice, and a short one too, which has to be left when you find yourself troublesome to the hospitaller. My dear Lucilius, it is the greatest proof of a mind coming from a higher dwelling, if it deems its present occupations low and narrow, if it fears not to go forth. For he who remembers whence he is come knows whither he is going." And "the gods are not fastidious nor envious; they receive those who come up and lend them a hand. Do you wonder that a man should go to the gods?

God comes to men; nay, rather, which is nearer, comes into men. There is no good mind without God. Divine seeds are scattered in human bodies: if a good gardener cultivates them, they come up like their origin, and equal what they spring from: if a bad, it is just as when a barren and marshy soil kills them, and then makes refuse instead of a harvest."[1]

The divine assistance thus spoken of must be understood in the sense of the system: it is nothing supernatural, but identical with the use of our reason, and its natural powers. God's stretching out the hand means that an effluence of the Deity, which is man's intellectual nature, connects itself, as the seminal intelligence, with a human body.[2]

So far as this Seneca stands on the old Stoic foundation. From Zeno's time philosophy was made to assume the exact function of religion as the moral teacher and physician of man. And in this material view of God and the soul, and in the kinship with God which he assigns to the soul, as part of the one divine seminal intelligence, a kinship belonging equally to the whole race of man, he is likewise true to his sect. But now in the conclusion which he draws from this view of the divine and the human, and which runs through and colours all his writings, and more especially the writings of the last period of his life during his disgrace and retirement from Court, the letters to Lucilius, he goes far beyond all who preceded him. From this dignity of human nature, as part of the Godhead, he proceeds directly to the equality of men as such among each other, and the duty of mutual

[1] See Epistles cvi. 4; lvii. 8; l. 6; xli. 1, 8; lxvi. 39; cxx. 14; lxxiii. 15.
[2] This is Zeller's inference, iv. 649.

kindness. Now[1] the Stoic school had indeed summed up its whole moral teaching as concerning the relations of men to each other, in the two duties of Justice and Humanity, so that there was a side of severity and a side of mildness in their teaching, but then the side of severity had greatly predominated. Justice had been so urged that it assumed an aspect of inhuman hardness. Humanity and kindness had quite receded into the background. In Seneca, on the contrary, all the virtues which belong to kindliness are set forth with a warmth, a detail, an inspiring sympathy which before him had no example. In this respect he far surpasses all classical antiquity, including therein Socrates and Plato as well as Cicero.

It would require a treatise of considerable length to bring out with adequate force how far his doctrine on certain subjects not merely goes beyond, but is opposed to that of the greatest intellects and the best hearts of the heathen world preceding him. Thus his language on the duty of beneficence to all men, on the unseemliness of anger, in censure of revenge, and in praise of placability, is without precedent, if we take it in its fulness, and as part of a system of thought. For instance, through the whole line of Greek and Latin writers down to his time the principle prevails that hatred of enemies and revenge are not only upright, but an indispensable duty for a man of worth. Even among the Greeks, with all their kindliness of disposition, no doctrine was so often expressed, and in ways so various, as that a proper revenge was something good and honourable. A kindlier Grecian

---

[1] See a paper on "The Humanitarian Doctrines of Heathen Philosophy about the time of Christ," by Dr. Ott, in the *Tübinger Quartalschrift* for 1870, pp. 355-402, of which I have availed myself in various places, in what follows.

gentleman than Xenophon is not to be found, and he
puts in the mouth of Astyages the hope respecting
his grandson, the elder Cyrus, that he may grow up
to be a man able to help his friends and punish his
enemies: and of his favourite the younger Cyrus he
has not forgotten to praise the wish that he might
live long enough to surpass those who did him good
and who did him evil, in the one respect and in the
other. In spite of slight indications on the other
side, such as the saying ascribed to Pittacus, that
pardon is better than revenge, or an expression in the
Georgias of Plato, that if the choice be offered between giving or suffering offence, it were better to
choose the latter, there was a general and over-
whelming prejudice the other way. Now in Seneca,
on the contrary, the idea of reconciliation grounded
upon a distinct view concerning mankind is maintained as a part of a whole system of humane principles. But it is remarkable that the love of enemies
has no part in this system. Seneca stops short of
what without a thorough reception of the Christian
spirit would be impossible.[1]

But also against this fair view of man's duties
towards others must be set a much less attractive view
of man's duties towards himself. If we were to take
by themselves and put together all the passages of
Seneca which speak of beneficence, kindliness to others,
forbearance, avoiding anger and revenge, they would
express to us a very different character from what is
revealed when man is considered with regard to his
duty towards himself. Thus the ground upon which
Seneca denounces revenge is based in fact upon a
subtle egotism, which runs up from this forced exal-

[1] See Ott, pp. 361-368.

tation of human nature into three degrees. Firstly, the wise man holds himself free from anger and revenge in order to maintain the even calm of his own mind. Insult must make no impression on him. Should it succeed in doing that he would not be without care: but freedom from care is his proper good. Secondly, the wise man exercises no revenge because he has overcome all impulse to revenge by the sense of his own moral dignity, of which he ceases not to be conscious. Thirdly, the wise man revenges no offences because he despises them as not touching his real being. The most contemptuous manner of revenge is when one is not thought worthy of it. The extreme feeling of his own moral dignity will likewise prevent his descending to pardon. And in the same manner he is not compassionate, because compassion involves passion. But he will take no notice of injuries, as if he pardoned, and he will show all the acts of compassion, such as harbouring the destitute, and giving to the needy, as if he were compassionate.[1] Thus so far is Seneca as a moralist from being able to grapple with the egotism which is at the bottom of human nature in its actual condition, that in his view of the wise man the acts of seeming virtue proceed from it while they disguise it.

It is most of all upon the question of slavery[2] and the treatment of slaves that the doctrine of Seneca goes beyond the greatest thinkers of antiquity who preceded him. From the joint possession of reason by all men and the kindred thence subsisting between the divine and the human, he deduces not only the dignity of man in general but his universal brotherhood, whether Roman or barbarian, rich or poor, bond or free: and the

[1] See Ott, pp. 375-379.   [2] Ibid. pp. 368-375.

duty therefore of the fraternal treatment of slaves. For such being the origin and the nature of man, the only difference which he allows between men is that of moral qualities, which each man gives to himself, virtue is shut out to none, admits all, invites all, gently born, freedmen, slaves, kings, exiles. It chooses not the house or the rent-roll, but is contented with the bare man. The world is the single parent of all: to this the first origin of every one is carried, whether through a splendid or sordid lineage. What is a Roman knight, freedman, or slave? Names which are sprung out of ambition or injustice. From the meanest corner you may rise to heaven; only spring up, and make yourself worthy of God.[1] It is thus that from a purely natural standpoint Seneca by scientific reasoning makes out for the slave a position worthy of human nature. And he does this at a moment when the internal economy of the country in which he wrote was based upon slavery, and a slavery of such a character that its victims were abused, not as if they were men, but as if they were beasts. In describing vividly as an eye-witness these very abuses, he exclaims, "They are slaves, nay, men; I say, they are slaves, nay, comrades; they are slaves, nay, humble friends: they are slaves, nay, fellow-slaves, if you consider that fortune has as much power over you as over them." And he writes thus in a city where shortly before he had seen four hundred slaves of a single household[2] led to execution because their master had been slain by one of them. "The sum of my rule," he adds,

---

[1] Epist. xlvii. 15; *De Benef.* iii. 18: Epist. xxxi. 11.
[2] The death of Pedanius Secundus and the execution of his whole household took place in the year 62. Seneca died in 65. The letters to Lucilius are supposed to have been written in his last years when he was in disgrace at Court, and retired from it. He just survived to see the Christian persecution in the year 64.

"is this: To live with your inferior as you would wish your superior to live with you. As often as you think of your power over your slave, think of your lord's having as great power over you. 'But,' you object, 'I have no lord.' You are young and may have one, as Hecuba, and Crœsus, and Plato, and Diogenes. Live with your slave forbearingly, nay, kindly; talk with him, advise with him, sit at table with him."[1]

Now, to estimate the advance which Seneca had here made, consider what the greatest men had said on the subject before him. Slavery is to Aristotle an institution inseparably bound up with social order. It is necessary, because a true family cannot subsist without slaves. It is lawful, because it rests upon a direction of nature; since by nature one portion of mankind is formed to rule, and the other to serve and obey. These are those who are in a state of intellectual pupilage, the barbarians, who have only so much reason as to know that it exists, not enough to possess it for their own independence. These are the born slaves, of use only to understand and execute commands, bound to their master as the tool to the artist and the body to the soul. And yet more instructive, perhaps, is the language of Cicero, who lived but a hundred years before Seneca. He stands on the ground of Aristotle, whose reasons in justification of this institution he exactly reproduces. Seneca, it is true, does not attack slavery as a legal institution, but he endeavours so to soften the actual condition of the slave as to make it something quite different from what it had hitherto been in theory and practice. And, moreover, in his moral conscience it is so shaken as an institution that he can scarcely suppress a confession of its unlawfulness.

[1] Epist. xlvii.

It was natural that, in the case of a man who more than any other in the heathen world assumes the tone of a preacher, his life should be compared with his doctrine. And here the inconsistency is striking. Seneca sets forth the equal dignity of all men by nature, in virtue of the divine quality of reason, and in spite of all variety in wealth, birth, rank, and outward fortune, proclaiming aloud that the only standard whereby men should be measured is the use which they make of this divine quality within them, and that as it affects their actions. He recognises therefore the standard of moral worth as his only criterion. And he preaches this as tutor, minister, and favourite of Nero, as the possessor of numerous palaces, sumptuously furnished, in the fairest spots of the earth. Again, all countries are the same to the wise man, whose origin is from heaven, and whose home is the world, declares the man, who, when banished to Corsica, though without the loss of his wealth, found no tone of complaint abject enough to express his misery. He enjoins firmness and consistency in our moral judgments, having exceeded all men in fawning flattery of the living prince as the model of justice and wise government, and in contemptuous abuse of the same prince when dead as a worthless and besotted despot. The man who holds human life as sacred in the meanest slave, is minister by Nero's side when Britannicus, the young and innocent brother, is swept out of his way, and when Agrippina, the dangerous and guilty woman, but the mother still, perishes by her son's command. If we grant upon the testimony of Tacitus that Seneca was esteemed as one of the best Romans of his day, and that his own life in the midst of boundless wealth was simple, and his example as a

husband especially without reproach, still these are
heavy drawbacks in the character of a moralist so
severe in his judgment of others, and who measures
all men and all things by the standard of reason.

That a man's doctrine should be far above his
practice is nothing rare in human life. But what is
so rare as to be perhaps without a single other example
of it, is that such a man's moral standard of judgment
should rise in a whole system of teaching on certain
points of great importance far above the standard of
all who had preceded him, however great their genius,
and however consistent their life was with their precepts. Yet Seneca in proceeding from the joint possession of reason by all men to the conclusion that
there is an universal brotherhood of all men, who,
whatever their nation and their outward condition,
have a right to be treated with kindliness, sympathy,
and forbearance, was far outstripping his predecessors.
Again, when, with the severest exercise of slavery
before his eyes, and when slavery formed the indispensable condition of the empire's existence, he termed
the meanest slave fellow-man, friend, and even fellow-
slave, and denounced cruelty inflicted on such an one
as a wrong to humanity, he was using a language
hitherto unknown. In all this he was doing what
had never been done by Socrates, or Plato, or Aristotle,
or Cicero, or any other Greek or Roman writer before
him: what neither the Plinies nor Tacitus reached
after him. If it be said that this is but a deduction
from Zeno's fundamental view about men, it is a deduction which the Stoics for more than three hundred
years had not made. He presents with the maturity
of a consistent system doctrine of which a scattered
seed may be found here and there in preceding writers.

In fact his whole temper of mind and his whole body
of teaching on the above entire range of subjects have
a softness, a tenderness even about them, equally
alien from what had hitherto been the temper of
Stoic philosophy and from the Roman character at
all times.

In the principles nevertheless which lie at the
basis of his teaching he is undeniably Stoic. Such
are his conception of God, of the human mind or
soul, of reason. The participation of the divine
by the human, on which the whole of the prevailing doctrine is grounded, is entirely natural
and pagan, Stoic in an eminent degree. If we
add that he is a praiser of suicide, and a disbeliever
of personal existence after death, we must admit that
Seneca is far enough from holding Christian principles
on the most important problems of human life and
duty. And yet, this being so, his expressions are often
surprisingly Christian. Fifty passages at least in his
writings have been quoted so remarkably similar to
passages of Scripture, especially in the New Testament,
as to suggest that he had seen what we are so familiar
with. Now let us add to the above an unquestionable
fact. During the last twenty-three years of Seneca's
life, a Christian community had been formed in Rome,
and to that community one person, at least, of the
highest nobility, Pomponia Græcina, the wife of
Plautius, is known to have belonged. Many more
Roman nobles are, with good reason, believed to have
been converted. Seneca lived long enough to witness the immolation of that vast multitude by Nero's
cruelty, which furnished to Roman eyes the first instance of men dying for a faith. We have preserved
for us, in his own words, a description of the good

man which would at least vividly express the sufferings undergone by the Christians in the gardens of Nero.[1] This, says he, "is the man of worth, who, when he sees death near, is not disturbed, as at the sight of a new thing, but whether he has to undergo tortures in every part of his body, or draw in the flame with his mouth, or stretch out his hands on the gibbet, asks himself not what he has to suffer, but how well." The letters to Lucilius, written in the last years of Seneca's life, when he had withdrawn in great part from the Court of Nero, and was in disfavour, contain the most remarkable passages of his humanitarian doctrine. Now the easiest solution of the problem presented to us by this doctrine is that the philosopher, who all his life long had foraged everywhere for information, and borrowed from every store, and is the largest retailer of the views and opinions of others, had become acquainted with some of the teachers of the sect which had planted itself at Rome under his eyes. If, as Christian antiquity believed, he met and conversed with St. Paul, he would find in the author of the Epistle to the Ephesians, and to Philemon, one with whose doctrine he could in many points sympathise. St. Paul, indeed, taught that men were to be treated with fraternal kindness, even if they were slaves, not only because God had made all nations of one blood, as he declared to the philosophers themselves in the main seat of their doctrine, but because He had redeemed all by the blood of the Son of God. This folly of the Cross may have been too great for "an illustrious senator of the Roman people"[2] to accept,

---

[1] Passages relating to sufferings strangely akin to those inflicted on the Christian martyrs are Epist. xiv. p. 29, lxxviii. p. 199, lxxxv. p. 231.   [2] St. Aug. *De Civ. Dei*, vi. 10.

while he was touched with the beauty of the teaching which derived its inspiration from the Cross. May not Seneca have been one of the first to do what so many have done after him; may he not have admired the morality of the Gospel without accepting its conditions; have remained a Stoic in his principles and practice, while he appropriated what pleased him, and so far as it would agree with these principles, out of the Apostle's love of man? However this may be, it is certain that the doctrine of human brotherhood in its practical application to all men, even to the slave, was not set forth at Rome and by Roman writers until He who had become man's brother had stretched out His hands to embrace all nations on the gibbet of Calvary. And it is no less certain that all which is most attractive in Seneca's writings as to kindliness, forbearance, and brotherly affection, while it appears in his teaching as a mere work of fancy, a mere decoration of rhetoric, had been practised in the city where he wrote, and under his eyes, as part of a coherent doctrine, by a number of men at the cost of their life. For the difference of the guise in which the doctrine appeared on the one side and the other must be noted as a material part of the fact. One of the richest of the Romans, in the midst of a sumptuous retirement, out of a palace sparkling with luxury, writes letters to a friend upon the equality of men, the right of slaves to compassion, the duty of brotherly kindness. Already while he wrote, all that he suggested and much more had been done. A spiritual bond had connected together some of the noblest Romans and the meanest of slaves in the common hope of an eternal life, was leading them to run counter to the general tendencies of the age in which they lived, to face danger and distress and death in the direst form. How far removed was the talk of the Stoic, which incurred no danger and cost no sacrifice, from the life of the Christian, which might end in the Mamertine prison, or the fiery torment of the Vatican gardens!

No less the influence which the Stoic teaching and the Christian respectively exercised upon the world was in proportion to this difference between the teachers. The noble whose millions were lent on usury while he preached forbearance, and extolled the mind of the sage immovable amid poverty and suffering, was read by the rich and leisurely, but did not convert them; the Christians who acted and suffered propagated their doctrine and formed an universal people upon its precepts through the course of eighteen centuries.

Stoicism in its further course pursued the like direction with that given to it by Seneca: the features only in which he differed from his school's original character became still more marked. We have a most distinguished representative of it in Musonius Rufus,[1] a Roman knight, younger by about twenty-five years than Seneca, the friend of Thrasea, Rubellius Plautus, Soranus. He has the great advantage over Seneca that his life was in harmony throughout with his teaching. More decidedly yet than Seneca he restricts philosophy to its moral purpose. Men in the moral point of view are to be dealt with as patients who need for their cure a constant medicinal treatment. Philosophy alone can supply this. It is the only road to virtue, and therefore every one, the female sex included, must have to do with it. On the other hand

---

[1] I have drawn the following notice of Musonius from the account of Zeller, iv. 651-660, which is carefully put together from the fragments preserved of him.

virtue is the sole object and matter of philosophy, which is nothing else but the consistent study of a life in accordance with duty. Philosopher and upright man are equivalent terms. Virtue is much more matter of practice than of learning, since vicious habits can only be overcome by habits which are opposite. The disposition to virtue, the germ of it, is planted in all men by nature. Musonius directed his instruction entirely to this practical end. The teacher of philosophy is to produce not assent but improvement. He must give his hearers the moral medicine which they need, and if he do so rightly, they will not have time to wonder at his discourse, but will be entirely employed with themselves and their conscience, and filled with emotions of shame and repentance, and so will be improved. His scope being so entirely practical, it is not new thoughts, or the accurate carrying out of a system, which can be expected from him. He generally applies the well-known Stoic principles. His leading thought is man's inward freedom, which is attached to two conditions, the right handling of that which is in our own power, and the giving ourselves up to what is not in our power. In our power is the use we make of the notions which our mind forms of things, and on it rest all virtue and happiness. All the rest is not in our power. That we must leave to the course of the world; throw in our vote with God's, and give up contentedly children, or country, or body, or anything else. For instance, we must court banishment as no evil, but feel at home in all the world; must not seek death, nor yet shrink from it. It is the great praise of this man that, when banished by Nero at the time that Seneca was put to death, he carried out in practice exactly what he had taught. He is supposed to have lived down to the end of Domitian's reign, and seems fairly a specimen of what a good heathen might be in the worst times.

The most illustrious of the Neostoics, the man whose writings have had most weight with those who came after him, is Epictetus. A slave of Epaphroditus, a freedman of Nero, weak in body and lame, he became while still a slave a disciple of Musonius. He must, later in life, have obtained his freedom. Under Domitian he had to quit Rome with the other philosophers. He was probably born about 50, and lived to about 120. His view of philosophy is that it consists pretty much in what is to be desired and what is to be avoided. Its foundation is the consciousness of one's own weakness and helplessness. "Hast thou the wish to be good? believe that thou art bad." "The philosopher's school is a physician's house. You ought to leave it not in pleasure, but in pain. For you come as patients, one with his shoulder put out, another with his head aching, a third with an ulcer, and so on. And am I to take my seat and address you with fine sentences and striking thoughts for you to break out into praise of me, and then for you to go away each of you with his shoulder or his head or his ulcer just as he brought them? Is it for this that young men take long journeys, leave parents, friends, relations, and their property too, that they may cry 'Bravo!' at my witticisms? Did Socrates, or Zeno, or Cleanthes, so?" The really important thing is to speak to their consciences, to bring them to the feeling of their misery and ignorance, to call forth in them the earnest resolution to improve, to make them philosophers, not in their opinion but in their conduct. "Show me," says Epictetus, "a Stoic, if not one formed, yet one in process of forming. Show me, one of you, the spirit of a man purposing to be of one mind with God, never hereafter to blame God or man, to be disappointed in nothing, to be hurt by nothing, not to be angry, envious, or jealous, in a word, desirous from man to become God, and in this narrow body of mortality to have communion with Jupiter. Show me one. There is none such. And now, I am your teacher and you my disciples, and it is my purpose to deliver you from hindrance, compulsion, impediment, to make you free, prosperous, happy, looking to God in everything great and small."[1]

For Epictetus[2] is filled with the thought of the Godhead, which knows our words and our thoughts, from which all good originates; in whose service the philosopher stands; without whose commission he cannot set about his work; which he must have ever before his eyes. Epictetus proves the government of Providence from the unity, the order, and the connection of the universe. He praises God's fatherly provision for men, and the moral perfection which makes Him our model. He recognises in the world the work of the Godhead, which directs everything for the best, has formed the whole faultless and perfect, all its parts corresponding to the need of the whole, which intends all men for happiness and has provided them with its conditions. In the spirit of his school he celebrates the design which is apparent in the regulation of the world, which meets us so momentarily at every step, that our whole life should be a perpetual song of praise to the Godhead; nor

---

[1] Frag. 3; Diss. iii. 23, ii. 19.
[2] I take this short summary from Zeller, iv. 665.

does He disdain to show this design in the smallest and most outward things. Nor is he disturbed in his belief by the apparent evils and injustices in the world, since he has learnt from the Porch to unite these also with the perfection of God and His works. This belief in Providence is, according to the genuine Stoic sense, always referred by Epictetus to the universe as a whole, and to the individual only so far as it is determined by its connection with the whole. If he exhorts to devotion to the will of God, that in his meaning falls in with the requirement that man should suit himself to the order of nature.

Now to estimate all this language at its right value, we must ever remember what sort of a God it is to whom the Stoic shall so look up. And as to this, for Epictetus as for all his school, God and the world are one and the same thing.[1] Thus he says: "All things obey and serve the universe; earth and sea and sun and stars and plants and animals; our body also, in its sickness and its health, in its youth and in its age, and in its transition through all other changes. It is reasonable then not to set that which is in our power, the judgment, to struggle alone against the universe. For this is strong, and superior, and better minded towards us, ruling us together with the whole." "For such the nature of the world both was and is and shall be, and it is not possible for what takes place to be otherwise than as it is. And in this change and succession not men only share, but all other living things upon earth, nay, and divine things too."[2] In God and in Providence thus understood, Epictetus is a firm believer. How should he not feel the highest interest in that of which he is

[1] Zeller, iv. 666, 4. [2] Frag. 136, 134.

a portion and an effluence. Man must be conscious of his own higher nature: from this thought he draws the sense of his dignity and moral obligation, and independence of all outward things. He resigns himself absolutely to that of which he is a part. "See you not how small a portion you are in comparison of the whole? That is in body: for as to the reason you are neither worse nor smaller than the gods. For the greatness of reason is judged not by length or by height, but by its decrees. Being then in something equal to the gods, are you not willing to place your good in that something?" And he says elsewhere, "A man who has realised the greatness, the glory, the extent of this universe, the system of men and God, from which the seeds have fallen not on his father or his grandfather only, but upon all things generated and produced on earth, and eminently on the things possessing reason, for these alone by this connection of reason have a natural communion with God, why does not such an one call himself not by the name of any particular country, as an Athenian, or a Corinthian, but a world-denizen? Why not son of God? Relationship with the emperor or any magnate at Rome gives security of life, but to have God for maker, father, and carer of us, shall it not deliver us from all pains and fears?" He imagines his disciples coming to him and saying, "Epictetus, we can no longer endure to go on in the bondage of this wretched body, giving it food and drink, resting it and cleaning it; we are kinsmen of God; thence we came, thither let us go; free us from these chains which hang on us and bear us down." To which he will reply: "O men, wait for God; when he gives the signal and releases you from this service, then depart to him." But that we may not be misled by this language, he says elsewhere: "When God no longer gives you what is needful, he sounds the recall, he opens the door, and bids you come! Whither? To nothing dreadful. To that from which thou camest, to the friendly, and the cognate, to the elements. What was in thee of fire departs to fire; what was in thee of earth, to earth; what of breath, to breath; what of water, to water.[1] There is no Hades, or Acheron, no river of wail, or fire. But all things are full of gods and genii." And again, "As the harvest is reaped and the stalk of wheat perishes, but not the world; as the leaves drop, as nature is full of these minor changes, so death is a greater change, not from that which is now existing into the non-existent, but into the non-existent as it is now. Shall I then no longer be?

---

[1] This philosophy is in fact the Anaxagorean view of immortality, which is found distinctly formulated in Euripides. Thus in *Helen*, v. 1013, he says—

"Mind in the dead lives not indeed, but yet
Plunged in the deathless ether has a knowledge
Undying."

And in a fragment from *Chrysippus*—

"The earth in all her greatness, and the ether
Of Jove; ether the sire of gods and men;
Earth in her bosom fecund rains receiving,
Bears mortals, and their food, and kinds of beasts:
Whence is she justly called, Mother of all.
What springs from earth goes back to earth again;
What from ethereal germ has flowered, returns
To that same bourne of heaven whence it came:
What has been ceases not to be, but each
From each distinct bears then its own impress."

Nägelsbach, who in his *Nachhomerische Theologie*, p. 461, quotes these, comments on them thus: "The mind of the individual, after loss of the personality which was linked to the life, merges in the universal mind, and has part in its immortal consciousness, without any more animating a single being; and death is the sundering of the production into its elements, by which each of them assumes again its proper form."

Thou shalt be, but as something else, of which the world has now no need."[1] That is, by this change of death, greater only than the changes which pass under our eyes in nature, but not different in kind from them, thou passest from embodied to disembodied mind, and rejoinest that from which thou camest. But the individual man, who has joyed and sorrowed, hoped and feared, done well and done ill, will exist no longer. Such is the end of the self-sufficient son of God; the extinction of personal subsistence.

And thus it is also that the Stoic Pantheism takes up the popular Polytheism into itself. The derived gods are to be distinguished from the primal divine being. Heré, Athené, Apollo, and the rest do not outlast the burning of the world, but are resolved into the original primal force.[2] And this reason of man, thus extolled and prized, is so resolved, when the body of death, which he bears about with him, is broken up. Thus the belief in God and Providence, in the dignity of man by virtue of his reason, and his kinsmanship with God, are united with the doctrine of the "open door," that is, suicide, with the restriction of man's personal subsistence to this life, and with the admission of a countless multitude of gods, whose number and variety do not matter, since they are emanations of the one primal force, into which they fall back again, like the human soul, but somewhat later.

Epictetus the slave, like Musonius the knight, was faithful to his principles throughout his life. Let us proceed to another great Stoic, who in the highest of all ranks showed a similar fidelity to his philosophy, the Emperor Marcus Aurelius Antoninus.

[1] Diss. i. 12; i. 9; iii. 43; iii. 24.
[2] Zeller, iv. 666.

This disciple of Epictetus, born just as his master was leaving the world, reproduces exactly the views of that master as to the function which he assigns to philosophy, as to the nature of the power ruling the world, and as to the human soul's relationship to it.[1] The centre of his philosophy lies in the moral life of man, and this also makes his greatest resemblance to Epictetus. The main points on which he dwells are the drawing back of man into himself, devotion to the will of God, and the unvarying duty of humanity to others. He calls out to man, Why trouble thyself with what is external? draw back into thyself. Thou canst find rest and well-being only within. Busy thyself with thyself; cherish the divine genius within thee; sever thy true self from all which hangs about thee. Bethink thyself that nothing outside can touch thy soul: that it is but thine own notions of things which weigh on thee; that nothing hurts thee unless thou think that it hurts thee. Consider that all is changeable and worthless; that only within thee an unfailing source of happiness springs; that passionless reason is the only fortress in which man must take refuge, if he would be unconquerable. His action as a reasonable being is the only thing in which a being possessed of reason has to seek his happiness and his good. All the rest, which has no connection with man's moral constitution, is neither good nor evil. He who limits himself to his inward being, and has cut himself free from all without, has extinguished every wish and every desire. At each moment he is contented with the present; he suits himself with unreserved assent to the world's course, he believes

---

[1] This summary is drawn by Zeller, iv. 682-684, from a great number of passages of M. Aurelius.

that nothing happens but the will of the Godhead, that what is good for the whole, and lies in its nature, is likewise the best for himself; that nothing can happen to man which he may not make material for his action as a reasonable being. Besides, he recognises for himself no higher task than that of following the law of the whole, of honouring by strict morality the God within his breast, of fulfilling his place each moment as man and as Roman, of advancing towards the end of his life, whether it come sooner or later, with the tranquil serenity which contents itself simply with the thought of what is in accordance with nature. But how can a man feel himself to be a portion of the world, and subordinate himself to the law of the world, without at the same time treating himself as a member of humanity, without finding his worthiest task in working for humanity? And how can he do this without giving to his country, in the more restricted sense, all the attention which his position requires of him. Nor does Antoninus exclude from his affection even the unworthy members of human society. He reminds us that it befits man to love even those who stumble, to help the thankless and the unkindly. He bids us remember that all men are our relations; that the self-same divine spirit lives in all; that a man may not expect to find no wickedness in the world; that the erring only fail against their will, and only because they do not recognise their real good; that he who does wrong only harms himself, whilst our own being can suffer no harm through the action of another. He therefore requires that we do not suffer anything to lead us astray in doing good, that we either instruct men or endure them, and instead of being angry or astonished at their faults only compassionate and pardon them.

From a number of passages we gather the belief of M. Aurelius that the human personality ceases at death. It is true that no part of man perishes, neither the portion of matter, nor the portion of mind, which make up the human conglomerate. The matter passes into an endless round of change; the mind rejoins the seminal intelligence. But the man himself is nowhere again. He calls to mind men of old, and especially the Cæsars preceding him, and then asks, "Where then are those men? Nowhere, or nobody knows where. For thus continuously thou wilt look at human beings as smoke, and nothing at all, especially if thou reflectest at the same time that what has once changed will never exist again in the infinite duration of time." "I am composed of what is causal, and of what is material: neither of these will perish into non-existence, as neither come to subsistence out of non-existence." As buried bodies last a time, and then corrupt, "so the souls which are removed into the air, after subsisting for some time, are transmuted and diffused, and enkindled by being received into the seminal intelligence of the universe, and in this way make room for the fresh souls who come to dwell there." And if a charge be brought against the Divine Justice "that some men, and very good men, and men who, as we may say, have had most communion with the Divinity, and through pious acts and religious observances have been most intimate with it, when they once have died should never exist again, but should be completely extinguished," he answers, not that it is not so, but "if this is so, be assured, that if it ought to have been otherwise, the gods would have done it." And "consider that before long thou wilt be nobody and nowhere, nor will any of the things exist which thou now seest, nor any of those that are now living. For all things are formed by nature to change and to be turned and to perish, in order that other things in continuous succession may exist."[1]

Looking at these four together, Seneca, Musonius, Epictetus, and M. Aurelius, we find them coincide in the following points. Philosophy as the rule of life takes the place of religion, and its office is to restore a sick humanity. It has the means to accomplish this purpose by enjoining and practising a life according to nature, or reason. For the dignity of man consists in possessing reason, which is an effluence, or a portion, of "the divine." And, therefore, the earth is a city common to gods and men, who are all of them, and they alone, in possession of reason. And in consequence of this, men possess equal rights, and differ from each other in moral worth and real value only according to the degree in which they live in correspondence with reason. And the universe, being this great city of gods and men, which is ruled by an inflexible reason, the absolute submission of the part to the whole, of the individual man to the course of the world, is the first duty, encompassing human life with a never-ceasing pressure. But also from this joint possession of reason by men the duty of beneficence and humanity in its widest extent is deduced: and it is chiefly in the enforcing this duty, in the kindliness and even tenderness of tone which they assume herein, that these writers differ so widely both from

---

[1] M. Aurelius, Medit. x. 31; v. 13; iv. 21; xii. 5; xii. 21. Other passages referring to man's state after death are, ii. 17; v. 33; viii. 18; ix. 32; x. 7; xi. 3; xii. 1, 31, 32.

their own school before them, and all preceding philosophers. While, however, the expansion of their view in this respect is remarkable, for it is indeed the culminating point of Greek intelligence as to the social character of man, and applies to the whole race the noblest and most touching thought of the dramatist,

"Homo sum, humani nihil a me alienum puto,"

the contraction, or rather, an unnatural severance of their view on another side is equally remarkable. It is as though they had gathered the countless myriads of individual human destinies into one great channel of waters only to conduct it to a precipice whence it shall fall into an abyss, and be dissipated for ever. For the existence of man after death, if continued so far as his intelligence is concerned, about which their language is confused and uncertain, is not the existence of a personal agent rewarded or punished for what he has done. His intelligence, reunited to the divine intelligence of which it was originally a part, is become universal, but the man who did well or ill, is extinct. Out of the city of gods and men, the citizen has perished. A system of future reward and punishment forms no part of Stoic morality; enters neither into their fears nor their hopes. They are not to fear or to hope about it. It accords with this, that suicide, the open door, is for adequate causes justified and commended, these causes being when providence, that is, the course of the world, indicates to man by withdrawing from him the means of living according to nature that it has no further need of him here. And finally this system assumes an attitude of neutrality, or even of support, towards the established religion of Polytheism by considering its gods, how numerous soever, as names for agencies of the one divine force which rules the world, as evolved from it, and to be reduced back to it at each burning of the world. And so M. Aurelius, a rigid believer of the Stoic divine unity, can be a zealous defender of the ten thousand gods of Rome.

II.

Let us now consider the system of those writers from a somewhat different point of view, that, namely, which presents certain points of analogy, contact, or contrast between it and the Christian Faith.

1. The generative principle of Stoicism, and the key, therefore, to its whole doctrine, is the relationship of the human intelligence to the divine. "As light," says Posidonius,[1] "is perceived by the vision which is akin to light, and sound by the hearing which is akin to air, so the universal nature must be perceived by its kindred reason." Thus Seneca: "God is near thee, with thee, within thee. A sacred spirit is within us—in every one of good men a god dwells, uncertain though it be who that god is." "Reason is nothing else but a part of the divine spirit plunged in a human body." And Epictetus: "Our souls are bound into God, are in contact with him, as being portions and fragments of him." "Thou art a fragment of God; thou hast in thyself a portion of him: how knowest thou not thine own nobility? Why dost thou not recognise whence thou art come? Carriest thou God about with thee, and knowest it not?" And Marcus Aurelius: "Every man's intelligence is God, and an efflux of the Deity." "The

[1] Quoted by Zeller, iv. 70, 3.

understanding and reason of every one is the divine spirit whom Zeus has given to him for guardian and guide, a portion of himself." And as all souls are portions of the divine intelligence, so all together may be considered as one soul or reason. "There is one light of the sun, though it is distributed over walls, mountains, and other things infinite. There is one common substance, though it is distributed among countless bodies, which have their several qualities. There is one soul, though it is distributed among infinite natures and individuals: one intelligent soul, though it seems to be divided."[1] And to complete this view it must be remembered that the human soul is not merely, like all other living forces, a portion and effluence of the universal living force, but by its rationality stands in a peculiar relationship to it.[2]

Thus the basis of Stoicism was the physical identity of the human soul with what they called "the divine":[3] and as they had not the conception of immateriality, it was an identity as well in quantity as in quality. To use their own expression, the soul was a part torn off from "the divine."[4] It is this natural identity which would stand in opposition to the supernatural relationship of son bestowed on man, according to the Christian faith, by the Incarnation. A kinship founded in nature, belonging to the whole race, and so incapable of being lost, formed a strong contrast with that filiation which is a pure gift,

---

[1] Seneca, Epist. xli. 66; Epictetus, Diss. i. 14, ii. 8; M. Aurelius, xii. 26; v. 27; xii. 30.
[2] Zeller, iv. 184.
[3] τὸ θεῖον. No translation conveys the force of this neuter and abstract term in the original. It is of very constant recurrence in Greek philosophical writers, and strongly suggestive of Pantheism.
[4] ἀπόσπασμα.

merited for the whole race by the Divine Redeemer, but finally bestowed only on the elect, and as the reward of a battle won. When this contrast is stated, a sufficient ground is given for the deep-seated antagonism which the Stoics showed to the Christian Faith.

2. It is impossible to overrate the importance of this doctrine in the Stoic system. Let us consider some deductions from it. First of all is the conception of virtue. Now it follows from the soul being a portion of the divine reason that the rational activity of the soul is virtue, which is the only good. And this conception of virtue rules the whole domain of Stoic morality. Seneca thus exhibits it: "Human virtues are included in one only rule, for right and simple reason is one only. In the divine and celestial there are no degrees of comparison. Mortal things are subject to diminution, extinction, deterioration and growth, exhaustion and increase. Therefore, in so uncertain a lot they suffer inequality. But there is one only nature of divine things. Now reason is nothing but a part of the divine spirit plunged in a human body. If reason is divine, and no good without reason, all good is divine. Moreover, there is no difference between divine things; therefore not between goods. Tranquillity, simplicity, liberality, fortitude, equanimity, endurance, are equal to each other, for one single virtue underlies all these, which preserves the mind upright and unswerving."[1]

Thus the Stoic doctrine is a most absolute form of naturalism. And as there is a physical identity between the particular and universal soul, so the virtue of the particular soul is to act according to its nature,

[1] Epist. lxvi.

and its nature consists in being rational. Reason then being divine invests with its own divinity all the actions of its subject. Thus reason in the Stoic system is a sort of natural anticipation of grace in the Christian system. Now charity in theology is the representative of grace. And so Seneca's expression, "One single virtue underlies all other virtues," is in very exact analogy with St. Paul's, " Let all your works be done in charity ;" and, " If I have all knowledge, and all faith, and bestow my goods on the poor, and give my body to be burned, and have not charity, it profiteth me nothing."

3. But inasmuch as the rational activity of the mind is virtue, which is the only good, it follows that the pursuit of knowledge, and the attainment of it, which is science, are subordinate to virtue. It is to be pursued, not for its own sake, but for the sake of virtue. All knowledge of the laws of the world is valuable, because it will serve to establish the sole supremacy of virtue. "Not knowledge as such, but the obedient following of the divine order of nature, is our supreme duty."[1] Thus a moral purpose runs through the logic, the physics, and the metaphysics of the Stoic, and binds them together. As it is the purpose of the Stoic to live according to the laws of nature, it is of great importance to him to know them. Hence his study of them, which has a moral origin and a moral determination. He has no other means of knowing them but by studying them. He can therefore give himself up to earnest study both in the field of matter, of abstract thought, and of mental science, but throughout he will have a moral purpose. It was Zeno's guiding thought to attempt to found the

[1] Ueberweg, p. 200.

supremacy of virtue on the scientific knowledge of the world's laws.[1] And in the last age of Stoicism this purpose comes out most strongly. Seneca, Musonius, Epictetus, and Marcus Aurelius disregard any logical, physical, or metaphysical studies which are not conducted for this end. In this point of view it is that Stoicism is rather a religion than a philosophy. Its historical importance consists in this position. In this subordination of all science to the end of making man virtuous, which springs, as we have seen, out of its very conception of virtue, the Stoic doctrine presents again an analogy with the Christian. As the obedient following of the divine order of nature in the one case, so in the other the knowing and loving God, and the imitation of Him by loving Him, is the end which gives its value to all knowledge.

4. Hence follows what is no less a marked feature of the whole Stoic line, a preference of the philosophical life, as thus conceived, to the public or political life. For the cultivation of that virtue, which alone the Stoic recognised, to which he subordinated all study, and for which he exercised all action, belonged to the interior life, the life of the mind. To procure tranquillity within the domain of the mind, to be independent of the fluctuations which assault the outer life, which attend all forms of government, and run into all human occupations, was the very effort which gave rise to the philosophy. And it remained on the whole faithful to this principle throughout its course. If the Stoic became soldier, lawyer, or statesman, this according to his sect's doctrine, though a necessary, was an inferior sphere of action. Epictetus[2] expresses this: "You inquire whether a man is to

[1] Zeller, iv. 326.   [2] Diss. iii. 22.

embrace political life? Do you then ask for a greater polity than that which he administers? He has to converse with all men, whether it be at Athens, at Corinth, or Rome, not about ways and means, nor about peace and war, but about happiness or misery, good or evil fortune, servitude or freedom. And when a man lives in such a polity, do you ask me if he is to embrace political life? Do you ask me if he is to take office? Foolish man, I retort, what office is greater than that in which he bears rule?" The Stoic herein took precisely the ground of all true religion. He was repeating after his fashion and on his natural basis, "The kingdom of God is within you." This is, within the limits of the law of nature, the very counterpart of that spirit which Tertullian gives as the characteristic of Christians in his time; which before his time caused Christians to be denounced as men "of the most contemptible inertness," because they drew back from the Roman magistracy and the cares of public life; which a profound observer of our own times [1] has so deeply regretted as forming a note of Catholics in his own day.

5. But this culminated in what may be called the glory of Stoic doctrine, the sense, that is, that men as men had a common life, interest, and cause, and belonged to each other, and in each other to the Divine Being. "When," says Seneca, "we have given to the wise man a commonwealth worthy of himself, that is, the world, he is not outside of this commonwealth, though he withdraw into retirement; nay, rather, if he leave a corner of it, he advances into larger and ampler regions." And again, "Our thoughts embrace two commonwealths, the one vast and truly public,

[1] Tocqueville.

which contains both gods and men, in which we regard not this or that corner, but measure by the sun the limits of our state; the other that to which the condition of our birth has attached us. This may be Athens, or Carthage, or any other city, belonging not to all, but to certain men. Some men at the same time labour for both these commonwealths, the greater and the smaller, some for the smaller only, some for the greater only. But we can be servants to this greater commonwealth in retirement, and perhaps better there, as in the inquiry, what is virtue, one or many? What does a man engaged in these contemplations do for God? He prevents works so great being without a witness."[1] Marcus Aurelius especially has set forth this view in striking language. "My nature is rational and social, and my city and country, so far as I am Antoninus, is Rome, but so far as I am a man, it is the world. The things then which are useful to these cities are alone useful to me." And again, "If our intellectual part is common, the reason also, in respect of which we are rational beings, is common: if this is so, common also is the reason which commands us what to do and what not to do: if this is so, there is a common law also: if this is so, we are fellow-citizens: if this is so, we are members of some political community: if this is so, the world is in a manner a State. For of what other political community will any one say that the whole human race are members?" And so he calls man a citizen of the highest city, of which all other cities are like families, and such a world is a body, of which each man is not a portion only, but a member.[2]

---
[1] Seneca, Epist. lxviii. 3; *De Otio*, 4.
[2] M. Aurelius, vi. 44; iv. 4; iii. 11. Portion, μέρος; member, μέλος.

In like manner, then, as for the individual the inner life is the Stoic's kingdom, so further he exalts the whole race of man, as possessing reason in common with the one divine power which goes through all things, into an ideal city or republic. The outer kingdom is a transcript of the inner, the single wise man leads on to a community of the wise. And as in the former so in the latter case the analogy with the Christian Faith is striking. And it is well to observe how far the heathen philosophy could go, and to acknowledge its remarkable merit in going so far. For this conception as to a community of human nature, consisting in the joint possession of reason, was reached by the force of that reason alone. The key to it, that is, the descent of all men from Adam, had been lost: and notwithstanding this the Stoic, overleaping all differences of race, all varieties of condition, as between conqueror and conquered, civilised and barbarous, freeman and slave, white and black, pronounced boldly and absolutely that all men by birth were equal; that all had a divine quality within them, and as partaking it were members of an universal city, conterminous with the earth, associated with "the divine." Man and all men belonged to this; man and man only, for every class of beast was alien to it. Rationality was its token, pledge, and possession. Marcus Aurelius and Tertullian use parallel expressions about the great republic of men. That of the former is rooted in this community of rational human nature: that of the latter gathers up this same human nature, derived of old from one head, fallen in him, and propagated from him, in a new head, the incarnate God, from whom proceeds a new unity of mankind. The joint possession of grace,

restoring and exalting the rational nature, is the token
and pledge of this unity, as rationality was of the
former. Thus, as the one virtue of the Stoic, ruling
the whole inner man, his living in accordance with
nature or reason, was analogous to the Christian doing
all his works in charity, so the one rational nature of
mankind, uniting the whole race in one with itself,
and with "the divine," was analogous to the Christian
City of God, in which the Second Head of the race
unites as companions with himself and brethren all
who preserve the divine gift of grace, which He has
merited for them and bestowed on them.

6. It was part of the Stoic conception of the universal reason governing the world to lay the greatest
stress upon the evidences of design which every part
of nature supplies. They studied physics with a
view to final causes. A chain of cause and effect
never broken in any single instance through all
the multitudinous processes of mind and matter they
called Providence. That this Providence acted ever
with perfect intelligence was part of their conception.
The proofs of design and purpose which they saw all
around them in the visible course of nature, in the
changes of the seasons, in the orderly arrangement of
the heavenly bodies, in the structure of animals, in
fact, in everything without and within them, they
considered an irrefragable assurance of this Providence.
The Stoic argument on this head may be seen exhibited with a skill and a detail which a Christian
moralist might admire in Cicero's treatise of the
nature of the gods. This doctrine was part of the
Socratic legacy, and came to them besides through
Plato and Aristotle. But as set forth by them it
bore their own special impress upon it. The evolu-

tion of cause and effect, revealing to them the boundless intellect of the universe, was also a necessary process. It admitted of no single break; it could be no otherwise than it was. It is made up of power and wisdom, but there is no indication of Will. It is not a blind power in nature certainly, for no men ever drew more peremptorily than the Stoics the conclusion, "He that made the eye, shall He not see?" except that they expressed it in the neuter, and said, "*That* which made the eye, shall *it* not see?" In this they departed from their master, Socrates, who expressed, with almost Evangelical tenderness, his belief in a personal Providence. But still their recognition of final causes is so specific and continual, that it seems to stimulate even Christian language. And their conception of the world as a whole ruled by infinite wisdom and intelligence stood out in the strongest contrast with the Epicurean doctrine of chance, and furnishes a point of contact with Christian doctrine.

7. Still more is this the case when that wisdom and intelligence are viewed as ruling all things for the good of man. This too was part of the Socratic view, and inherited by the Stoics. But to this also they gave their own impress. For as man alone shared reason with "the divine," all the effects produced by "the divine" were for the sake of itself, of which man was the representative among living animals. Thus man is the centre from which they regard nature. The order and arrangement which they saw everywhere in the processes of nature were for the good of man. The supreme reason acknowledges and works for its kindred, which is in man. Not only then the Stoic conception of Providence, but in that Providence the subordination of all things to man, the ruling, for

instance, the seasons of the year, the growth of plants, the production of animals, the whole economy of visible nature, for his advantage, coincided so far with the Christian Faith. It wanted but one element, the conception of Will in the ruling power, to make it Christian. But as the motive supplied by the Stoic doctrine for this special care of man was his possession of rationality, which belonged to him in virtue of a physical, which was also a necessary union with the divine power in the universe, so the motive supplied by the Christian Faith was the special love of God for man, as shown forth in the work of his redemption. And here in that element of Will, in which the Stoic conception of "the divine" was so deficient, the Christian on the contrary superabounded. For only in a choice of the Divine Being, the fountain-head of which is concealed from man in the abysses of the divine nature, could the cause of such an act as the Redemption be sought. And so the Christian God is pre-eminently one who chooses, one who wills. And as He willed to create, so He willed to redeem.

8. From their fundamental principle, that virtue is the only good, and consists in living according to reason, the divine part of man, or according to nature, which is as it were the sum of the mass of the operations in which the divine reason works, the Stoics could not but divide men into two classes—the wise, or those who followed reason; the foolish, or those who disregarded it. Their morality mainly consisted in maintaining that this difference was the only real and essential one among men: all other differences, arising from the portion of external goods which might fall to the lot of each, were superficial. But once judging men by this test, neither could they fail to see and to

affirm that the vast majority of men were unwise. And this statement, characteristic of them from the beginning, was made with still greater emphasis by Seneca and those who followed him. His words may serve to speak for all. "We shall always have to say the same thing of ourselves: bad we are, bad we have been, I am sorry to add, bad we shall be. ... Of this our forefathers complained, of this ourselves complain now, and our descendants will hereafter: the overthrow of morals, the reign of wickedness, the perpetual deterioration of human things. ... We all are evil: whatever a man blames in another, he will find in his own heart. Why mark how pale one man is, how lean another? It is a common infection. We may each be quiet: we live among people as bad as ourselves: one thing only can tranquillise us, an agreement to be mutually indulgent. But such an one has done me an injury; I have done him none. But you have injured or will injure some one else. Do not count this or that hour of the day, but examine the whole habit of your mind. Even if you have done no evil, you are capable of doing it." We have all sinned, the one more lightly, the other more heavily, and we shall sin to the end of our being. One pushes the other to evil, and the mass of the bad does not endure individuals becoming better. Whoever would be angry over the crimes of men, instead of lamenting their errors, would find in the mass of miseries no end. And once more: "We do not say that all vices are in all men in such wise as certain vices are conspicuous in some, but that the bad and the foolish are without no vice. The bad man has the seeds of all wickedness in him."[1]

[1] Seneca, *De Beneficiis*, i. 10; *De Ira*, iii. 26; Epist. xli. 9; *De Beneficiis*, iv. 27, and other places, referred to by Zeller, iv. 233, 234.

In this picture of men, the striking similarity of Seneca's language with the language of one who is his exact contemporary, the Apostle St. Paul, has often been remarked. But their differing standing-points being on the one hand bare reason, and on the other reason penetrated with grace, the analogy between the natural and the supernatural standard is to be expected. In all this view, which the later Stoics, Seneca, M. Aurelius, Epictetus, present with such detail, reiteration, and pathos, the law of nature, according to which they spoke, would carry them up to the very threshold of the Christian Faith. St. Paul, in expressing the struggle of the regenerate man against sin, falls almost upon the words of the heathen poet: but as his standard is far higher, and his scale more minute, and his vision of sin more clear and terrible, so his language exceeds in intensity. "I see and approve the better and follow the worse," says the one; "O wretched man that I am," says the other, "who shall deliver me from the body of this death?"

The Stoic then made the mass of men as much sinners against the law of nature, as the Christian makes them against the law of God.

9. The points hitherto noted belong to Stoicism from its beginning, though the last one, the general corruption of mankind, is enforced by Seneca with an intensity unexampled before, and the great human republic, in its full and practical development, appears only in him and his successors.[1] But we now pro-

---

[1] Friedlaender, *Sittengeschichte Roms*, iii. 610, observes, "In fact an unprejudiced consideration must reach the conclusion that Stoicism and Cynicism raised themselves at this time by their own strength to a height and purity in the moral conception of human rights and human duties which had not been reached in an earlier antiquity.

ceed to a deduction from Stoic principles, which was certainly legitimate, and which as a pure process of reasoning ought to have been worked out by its founders and first professors; which, however, as a fact scarcely appeared before Seneca, and is strikingly characteristic both of him and of those who followed him, Musonius, Epictetus, and Marcus Aurelius. From the Stoic conception of virtue, as grounded on reason, which is the common possession of all men, uniting them in one mass with the gods and with each other, would follow undoubtedly, if men simply drew conclusions,[1] "All virtues of the widest and most unreserved humanity, beneficence, mildness and gentleness, an unbounded good-will, readiness to pardon in others whatever admits of pardon." But in fact up to the time of Seneca Stoicism had shown to the world quite another side of its character, which likewise, as is admitted, had been contained in its principles. Their wise man was called upon to exhibit a severity of justice which knew no compassion or indulgence. If he was forbidden to envy the rich, so was he likewise to succour the poor. The poet's

It was the Stoics of this time who first carried out in its whole range and to its last consequences the Stoic principle of all men belonging to each other, who, according to the expression of Epictetus, have all God for their Father, and so are brethren." The admission that the Stoics of this time were the first to do this I take to be much more certain than the assertion that they did it by the mere strength of Stoic principles. It remains to show why this conclusion was not drawn by Stoics before the preaching of the Christian Faith. How far it was drawn we see in Cicero, that is, the intellectual conception of the universe, as the city of gods and men, of which reason was the joint possession and the common law. The difference between Cicero, and Seneca, Epictetus, Plutarch, and those who follow, is to be accounted for. All the causes, relied upon by Zeller and others, arising out of the condition of the Greek and other races, had been in operation for several generations, without producing any such fruit. The only new thing was the Christian Church.

[1] Zeller, iv. 267.

ideal was embodied in this icy product of one-sided reason—

"Neque ille
Aut doluit miserans inopem aut invidit habenti."

It is thus Cicero[1] set forth the Stoic doctrine: "Compassion and envy belong to the same subject, for he who grieves over another's adversity, likewise grieves over another's prosperity. But just as compassion is a sickness arising from another's adversity, so envy is a sickness arising from his prosperity. Thus he who is liable to compassion is liable to envy. The wise man is not liable to the latter; therefore not to the former." And Zeller sums it up, saying:[2] "He can feel no compassion, and exercise no indulgence, since what he would esteem in his own case as no evil, he cannot compassionate others for: he can as little for their sake as for his own give himself up to an unhealthy emotion, and if justice demand punishment, his feeling will not mislead him into forgiving." If Cicero, following Panætius, mentions justice and benignity as the two component parts of that virtue by which human society is held together, he stops in depicting the latter very far short indeed of the part which Seneca gives to it. And Cicero, as an exponent of Stoic doctrine, probably gave as large a share to this virtue as was to be found in their teaching up to his time. A hundred years later another spirit, whencesoever it came, had breathed upon Seneca. Remaining entirely on the Stoic standing-ground, he drew from the cardinal doctrines of the sect conclusions which for three hundred years none had drawn before him. In this respect the

[1] *Tusc. Disp.* iii. 10. [2] iv. 216.

following portrait exactly describes him.[1] "The proper crown of his moral teaching lies in the universal love for man, the purely human sympathy, which shows itself to all without distinction, even the most insignificant and despised, which even in the slave forgets not the man; in that mildness of sentiment to which nothing is more opposed than anger and hatred, violence and cruelty, and nothing appears more in accordance with nature, and worthier of man, than indulgent kindness, than unselfish benevolence, bestowing happiness in secret, imitating the divine goodness towards good and evil; which bearing in mind human weakness, rather spares than punishes, does not exclude even enemies from its good-will, and refuses to return injury for injury."

All this, which was truly a revelation in Greek and Roman heathendom, appears suddenly in Seneca, and in it he is followed in different degrees by Musonius, Epictetus, and M. Aurelius. These sentiments often simulate Christian charity with a nearness of expression which is surprising, which suggests contact. They are based, however, purely on a natural ground, on the fact that man, of whatever clime, or race, or condition, has within him the same reason, that "particle of divine breath" which makes all the world akin. It may be well to compare and contrast the philosophic and the Christian treatment in the radical case of the slave. Epictetus,[2] urging on the master forbearance to his servant, says: "O slave, will you not bear with your own brother, who has Jove for his ancestor, who is a son from the same seed, of the same descent from on high." How definite and absolute is the Apostle's exhortation. For master and for servant alike he

[1] Zeller, iv. 647. [2] Diss. i. 13.

touches the unhallowed relationship of slavery with the doctrine of the Incarnation, and tranfigures it by the touch. On the one hand he puts the Christian's Lord in the person of the master, bidding the slave obey him with fear and trembling, not with eye-service as a man-pleaser, but from the heart with good-will, as doing the will of God in that very service, and knowing that whatever good he does he shall receive it back from the Lord. On the other hand he turns the same great doctrine's light and heat upon the master, and with equal force bids him to act in the same spirit to his slave, using no threat, and knowing that he too has a Lord in heaven with whom is no respect of persons. Thus the Christian dogma severs from the heathen the pantheistic alloy, and exalts the rational creature to an infinitely higher participation of the divine nature by grace than the Stoic imagined by reason. The brotherhood with Jove was vague and distant: that with Christ touched every fibre of the Christian's heart. Still the Stoic doctrine herein maintains, as in the former instances, a striking natural analogy with the Christian.

10. But in no point is the resemblance and at the same time the contrast between the Stoic and the Christian conception more remarkable than in the doctrine of the submission of man to the order of the world. "The Stoic[1] picture of the wise man is completed by his resignation to his lot. With this come repose and happiness of mind, mildness and philanthropy, the fulfilling of all duties, that harmony of life in which virtue according to the Stoic definition consists. As morality begins with recognition of the general law, so it concludes in

[1] Zeller, iv. 283.

unconditional submission to its arrangements." Thus Seneca says: "Good men labour, they spend and are spent, and that willingly; they are not dragged by fortune. ... How does the good man act? he gives himself up to fate. ... Follow God, but what madness is it rather to be dragged by him than to follow him. ... Whatever has by the constitution of the universe to be suffered, receive with a great mind. To this oath we are enrolled, to bear the conditions of dying things. ... We are born in a kingdom: to obey God is freedom. ... I do not obey but assent to God. I follow him cordially, not because it is necessary." And Epictetus: "Dare to look up to God and say, 'Use me for the future for what thou wilt. I am of the same mind with thee. I am thine. I repine at none of thy decrees. Lead where thou wilt.'" "This is the way which leads to liberty: this alone is escape from servitude." And Marcus Aurelius: "To the reasonable living being alone is given to follow voluntarily events: to follow them simply is a necessity for all."[1]

In all this, nowhere does the expression come nearer the Christian, and nowhere is the sentiment really at greater distance. What is this god, or fate, or nature, or providence, or eternal law, or common reason? Zeller will reply for us. "Man is considered merely as an instrument of the universal law. The Stoic morality leaves him as little freedom of action, in face of duty, as the Stoic physical system leaves him freedom of will over against the course of the world. It recognises only the general moral obligation; the right of the particular man to act in accordance with

[1] Seneca, *Provid.* v. 4; *Vita beata*, xv. 5; Epist. xcvii. 2; Epictetus Diss. ii. 16, iv. 1; M. Aurelius, x. 28, quoted by Zeller.

his peculiar state, and to develop himself is for it as good as non-existent." And in this he says that it followed the intrinsic necessity of the system. "For if every particular thing in the world is only a sequel of the universal enchainment of causes and effects, only the completion of the universal law, what remains for us in relation to this absolute necessity but unconditional submission?"[1] All here depends on the nature of the God to whom submission is required. Submission to the unfree, impersonal, unbroken, everlasting sequence of cause and effect, is as terrible a doom as submission to a free, loving, remunerating Creator is "to reign." But the pantheistic conception of God rules every part of Stoic doctrine, and interpenetrates the whole mass with a rigorous naturalism. "The real ground of Stoic fatalism is expressed in the statement that nothing can happen without sufficient cause, or under given circumstances can fall out otherwise than it actually falls out. For this, as the Stoics believe, is as impossible as that anything should come out of nothing, and if it were possible it would destroy the unity of the universe, which consists exactly in this fast-closed chain of all causes, in the unbroken necessity of all things and all their changes. This is the immediate consequence of its Pantheism. The divine force which rules the world could not be the one absolute cause of all things if there were anything which in any relation were independent of it; if an unchangeable connection of causes did not embrace everything."[2]

The fiction has been imagined of a prisoner confined in an iron room, the walls of which he at length perceived to be daily contracting upon him, until at

[1] Zeller, iv. 339; iv. 282.   [2] *Ibid.* iv. 149.

no great length of time they would join and crush him. Such is the treatment which man, as a personal being, having affections and conscience, as well as reason, experiences at the hands of the Stoical god. The common reason, which runs through all things, pervading the minutest point of matter and the whole universe, crushes every sentient and intellectual nature in its grasp, eternally destroying and reproducing them. Is it any wonder that a spirit such as M. Aurelius, in presence of such a conception, should be shrouded as it were in the blackness of despair, stifled with the "bitter smoke" of its own imaginings?

Thus the Stoic and the Christian both proclaim, and almost in identical terms, that the sum of life is to follow God and to do His will: but the Stoic god is the absolute contradiction of the Christian, to whom the soul cries, "Thou God seest me," and is pacified, comforted, and exalted.

11. And this last thought leads directly to the contrast which the Stoic and the Christian ends of man present.

Stoicism is mainly a system of morality which is founded upon the intrinsic dignity of each individual man as possessing in his intelligence that which is akin to the one divine intelligence. To live in accordance with this, or with nature, is the whole Stoic rule, under which all individual duties are ranged. And this deification of man, whose duties depend on his sense of his own dignity, and are a realising of the god within him, comes to an end at his death. This "Son of Jove" terminates in non-existence, as a personal being. And so a relationship with "the divine" which is founded in boundless pride finishes in absolute nothingness.

The Christian rule of life on the other hand springs[1] from an act of infinite humiliation by which the Son of God becomes man, and as man a sufferer above all His fellow-men. Thus humiliation and suffering come before man as personal acts of God, and likewise as the price of the sonship bestowed on him. Christian morality, having a divine model for its rule, is itself an imitation of these acts: Christian life is based upon them. The sonship itself is the working of God in the human will, and the human action, and the two comprehend the reason deified by the Stoic. But death, which ends all to the Stoic, puts the Christian in possession of the infinite good, which consists in the personal enjoyment of a personal god.

Reviewing Stoicism in its course from the commencement of the reign of Claudius to the end of that of Marcus Aurelius, we may note that at the first period it is that system of philosophic thought which has most possession of cultured Latin society. In the course of these one hundred and forty years it loses this ascendency. Another movement of the Greek mind, which we shall next have to trace, and which starts from about the beginning of this time, is preferred to it.

If we try to measure its results in this period, they will seem to be that it produced three such men as Musonius, Epictetus, and Marcus Aurelius; and few and far between such senators as Thrasea and Rusticus. Lucan was its poet. Whatever of dignity and opposition to tyranny existed in the Senate of Nero, whatever in Persius and Juvenal we find concerning a moral end of life, the value of man, and his dearness to the gods, with the emptiness of human things, is

[1] See Philip. ii. 5, 13.

drawn from this source. The elder and younger Pliny, and Tacitus, belong more or less to this school. But we can only trace its effect on individuals. The most notable intellectual work which Neostoicism can show are the sayings of Epictetus, collected and handed down to posterity by his disciple Arrian. Beside their intrinsic value they had whatever weight the consistent life of their author could give to them. From youth to age he appears to have practised the tenets which are here preserved to us under his name. He had the reputation of an honest man and a real philosopher. But he does not seem to have created any living school of philosophy. What effect had either his life or his writings upon his age? It is in this respect that we ought to note the contrast between the action of the Christian Church and the impotence of that philosophy which, when it began to teach in Rome, it found in vogue, with the credit of having been in that and the preceding age professed by many noble Romans. During these five generations of men the Church formed in every city of the Roman empire a society swayed by its principles, a society strong enough to produce in the capital during the reigns of Claudius and Nero, a vast multitude of martyrs: strong enough to produce after another generation a like sort of harvest in the reign of Domitian, and to exhibit under Trajan and Hadrian, and still more under Marcus Aurelius, fruits of the same kind. During the same five generations Neostoicism gradually decreases in influence. One indeed of the school mounts the throne, but he is the last considerable person who belongs to it. Now, Stoicism in its original growth, and without that colouring of humanitarian sentiment given to it by its latest professors, when the Christian Church was already in the world, showed more than any other system the force of the purely heathen thinking mind. It had nearly dethroned all other competitors: its god was not a restoration of the original father of gods and men, but a force created by its own thought, and its morality was the result of this creation. It claimed to make man independent in this life and without any life to come. Such it was when it lifted its head once more amid the deep corruption of Nero's reign. But while it has worked itself out by the time that its imperial votary dies, with such results as we have seen, the Christian Church was performing in an ever-increasing degree the wonderful work of gathering to itself out of the bosom of a corrupt society men who should act on new principles of life, and confirm their belief, if need were, with their blood. In this interval the proudest and most self-reliant of philosophic schools produces here and there an able writer, and more rarely a disciple whose life was in accordance with its doctrines, but in the work of putting together a society which shall enforce its principles fails so absolutely that we can discern no trace of any such attempt. Yet it is not from want of will to oppose the Christian Church that it fails to imitate it in this its highest work. So bitter is the antagonism between the Stoic and the Christian mind, that the imperial philosopher whose rule in all other respects is a model of moderation, clemency, kindness, and generosity, departs in the case of Christians, and of these alone, from all these attributes. Marcus Aurelius, as he spoke of Christians scornfully, so he persecuted them bitterly. The patient endurance of death, which would have called forth his highest admiration in one of his own sect, moved him but to sarcasm in them, a sarcasm the more savage because some of their noblest martyrs obtained their crown in consequence of orders directly transmitted from himself. But while those whom he thus treated were spreading more and more through every city and town of his empire, his own book of thoughts, the most interesting study of a pagan mind which we possess, exhibits a deep discouragement, a hopelessness about himself and human affairs, which indicate how little his philosophy satisfied either his mind or his heart. Removed by about two centuries from Cicero on the one side and St. Augustine on the other, his meditations hold a sort of middle ground between the outwardness of the one and the intense introspection of the other. They bear witness to the new thoughts about life and death, man's work and destiny, stirred up by the teaching of the Christian Church. There is in them a yearning unfulfilled, a blackness of despair quite unknown to the earlier time. Perhaps it may be said that the greatest result of the Stoic school was one which Stoics never intended or foresaw. Their argument, deriving the unity of the human race from its joint possession of reason, which was akin to the one divine intelligence, carried with it a most rigid doctrine of the divine unity. But that unity, as conceived by them, being without personality, which the human heart bears witness to and yearns after, raised a longing which it could not satisfy, and so prepared the way for the reception of a personal God, when He should come before men with the attraction of the Christian revelation, as the God who not only creates but redeems.

LECTURE XVII

THE FIRST RESURRECTION OF CULTURED HEATHENISM IN THE NEOPYTHAGOREAN SCHOOL

CICERO, in a philosophic treatise written towards the end of his life, about fifty years before the Christian era, remarks that the Pythagorean philosophy might be said in his day to be extinct. Seneca, writing as it would seem in the year 64, the last before his death, and that in which the great fire at Rome occurred, followed by the first persecution of the Christians, expresses himself thus: "Who regards philosophy or any liberal study except when the games are interrupted, or a rainy day makes amusement necessary? Thus it is that so many philosophic families fail for want of an heir. The old and the young Academies have left no representative. Who is there to communicate Pyrrho's tenets? The Pythagorean school, disdainful of the multitude, finds no teacher. The new line of the Sextii, full of Roman vigour, after beginning with great force, was presently extinguished."[1]

Whatever allowance we make for the usual exaggeration of Seneca's language, heightened, as it might be conceived in this case, by the excessive claim on behalf of philosophy which one who reckons its dignity so high might put forward, there is nothing remaining

[1] Cicero, *Timæus*, i.; Seneca, *Nat. Quæst.* vii. 32.

to show that this was not an accurate estimate of the condition of philosophy, and of the little power which it had exercised in the world during the century preceding the time at which he wrote. This is a point on which I have dwelt in preceding chapters, and therefore need not pursue here, but I would note the three periods which have been assigned to Greek philosophy, and the three corresponding attitudes in which it stood to the national religion. It was originally identical with theology, but this position lasted but a short time. As soon [1] as Thales, and from him downwards, men philosophised no longer on the basis of the popular belief. From his time philosophy, dividing itself therefrom, sought for an independent solution of the highest problems of life, and worked itself out in opposition to popular belief, which it tended to break up. This period lasted for several hundred years, and its end coincides with the first preaching of the Christian religion. Its third period and its third attitude was when, in proportion to the advance of that religion to the conquest of the Græco-Roman world, it took up the defence of the ancient worship of the gods, with all its rites and customs.

Before proceeding to the third period of the Greek philosophy, let us note the course which it had taken during the long second period. After reaching its culminating point in Plato and Aristotle, it had followed three main directions, the Stoic, the Epicurean, and the Sceptic. The proper movement of Greek and Latin heathenism had completed itself in these three. But what sort of a thing was the heathen society in the midst of which philosophy started on its course?

[1] See Lasaulx, *Ueber den Entwicklungsgang des griechischen und römischen Lebens*, p. 55.

The people among whom Thales and Pythagoras, Xenophanes and Heracleitus, Anaxagoras and Democritus, Socrates and the schools which sprung from his disciples, arose, had been from time immemorial possessed of a certain belief and worship. This may be said to have comprehended in its completeness four great parts, which are prayer, sacrifice, oracles, and mysteries. Let us look at these in the idea which lay at the bottom of each. Prayer is founded upon the belief of man's continual dependence on a higher and invisible power, supporting human life, a power which has sympathy with man, and will answer his supplication with protection. Sacrifice, viewed as an institution, is the expression of man's belief that he needs an expiation in the sight of this higher invisible power. It was the general belief of the ancient world that the freely-offered life of the innocent had power to save the forfeited life of the guilty.[1] The bloody sacrifice of animals, with all its accompanying rites, so wonderfully significant of the victim's supposed free-will as to his own offering, and of the transference of guilt to him, accomplished in the shedding of his blood, wherein lay his life, rested on the basis of this belief. And these acts of sacrifice, accompanied with prayer, encompassed the whole daily domestic as well as political life of the people. Thirdly, the recurrence to the knowledge of this superior invisible power in the frequenting of oracles testified in respect to the darkened knowledge of man the same sense of dependence and need of aid which sacrifice testified in respect to moral guilt.[2] If men fell into trouble, public or private, if they were perplexed as to how they should

[1] See Lasaulx, *Die Sühnopfer der Griechen und Römer*, p. 277.
[2] Stiefelhagen, *Theologie des Heidenthums*, p. 134.

act, they came to ask the higher power, and their coming to do so was a perpetual testimony to the need which they felt of enlightenment, and to their assurance that it would be given. Fourthly, in the mysteries of the heathen lay the notion of pacification and communion with this higher invisible power. These, it is true, were connected with prayer and with sacrifice so far as man's preparation went, but so far as the act of the higher power was concerned, the communication of these came in the mysteries. As knowledge was conveyed to man by the oracle, so his will was cured by the rites of initiation. And the sense of the need of this curing of the will is manifested in the universal existence of such rites of initiation and purification in the mysteries of the heathen world.[1] The corruption of such rites and their passing over into superstitious usages and customs, such as magic, enchantment, and all the dark arts which belong to them, testify in their very deepest debasement to the need from which they spring.

If we view this fourfold worship in its mass, however it had been overladen with corruption, to whatever extent prayer had been misdirected in the persons to whom it was addressed, and the requests which it made to them, however much the meaning of sacrifice had been obscured, whatever trickery and falsehood had been mixed up with oracles, and whatever the debasement of mysteries, still the whole covered a belief in the divine providence ruling the world in justice, rewarding man and punishing him, and, though more obscurely, guiding him in a way of probation. As we look back upon it, it is not difficult to trace the original revelation from which it sprung. And the

[1] Stiefelhagen, *Theologie des Heidenthums*, pp. 147, 162.

existence of its parts in many various nations of antiquity points back to this original revelation with a certitude like that which the comparative grammar of the various Aryan nations creates in the mind as to the original Indo-Germanic language. If the identity of the verb To Be, of the numerals, and of the words betokening the primary relations of life, in Sanscrit, Greek, Latin, Teutonic, and the other members of the family, proves that in a far back antiquity the hearth existed at which they all sat as brethren, so the existence of this fourfold system in the time preceding the Christian faith in Greece and Rome and other heathen nations, proves the voice which communicated it to man, and the hand which impressed it on him. That voice indeed spoke, and that hand was impressed with such force in the institution of the bloody sacrifices of animals, that man carried on from age to age an arrangement of peculiar and intricate rites based upon one notion so specific that many various nations could not have hit upon it separately, and so singular that reason could not have devised it for itself.

When the pursuit of wisdom arose among a people whose life had been moulded by institutions such as these, what should we expect its proper work to be? Was it not to disengage the truth from its corruption, to purify and strengthen the positive belief which formed the ore, to detach and reject the scoria which had adhered to it. And indications of such a course in the early Greek philosophy are visible. Thus at its very rise in the sixth century before Christ, Xenophanes leaped at once by the conclusions of his own reasoning to a conception of the deity which formed the strongest contrast with the popular Polytheism. Looking upon the heaven, he exclaimed, "God is unity. If there be what is supreme in power, he must be one; for, were there two or more, he could not be mightiest and best. One God there is, the greatest among gods and men, like to mortals neither in shape nor understanding. Without toil by his mind he rules the universe. He is all eye, all mind, all ear. Homer and Hesiod have attributed to the gods whatever is vile and blameful among men, theft, and adultery, and mutual deceit. Mortals conceive as if the gods were born and had clothes as we, and our voice and shape. So if oxen, lions, and horses had hands to construct works of art like men, they would make their gods such as themselves: just as the Æthiopians make them black and flat-nosed, the Thracians ruddy and blue-eyed, and each people after its own likeness. But it is an equal impiety to say that gods are born or that they die, for in both cases they once were not." And when his country people asked him if they should sacrifice to Leucothea, and if they should mourn for her, he replied, "If she be a goddess, do not mourn for her: if she be human, do not sacrifice to her." Thus clearly spoke reason as to the unity and spirituality of the Godhead at the very rise of Greek philosophy, and as clearly condemned the worship of false gods with which it was surrounded. So in the next century Anaxagoras, the teacher of Pericles and Euripides, recognised no other God than the mind which orders the universe. So Plato believed that the causes of apparent things are the eternal Ideas, which may be referred back to three, the Idea of the Good, of the Beautiful, and of the True, but the highest cause and the unity of these three is God. And when reason had reached after and found such a God, to whose presence conscience would bear witness in the secret heart of every man, both would unite to enjoin that prayer be made and sacrifice offered to such an one alone: that from him alone sitting in the midst of the earth as a fatherly councillor in his oracles instruction and advice should be sought; from him alone purification and healing of the will be asked for in mysteries. For he, in Plato's words, "according to the ancient tradition holding the beginning, the end, and the middle of all things by his own nature while he encompasses them, directs them aright, and upon him follows justice, the avenger of those who desert the divine law."[1]

Here then is ample proof that reason and conscience, not to speak of that ancient tradition to which Plato appeals, were strong enough both to see the truth as to the one God, and condemn the error which had divided His worship and corrupted it in the division. But now what we have to note is that such had not been the prevailing course of philosophy up to the first preaching of the Christian faith. It had been hostile indeed in the main to the established religion, and had discredited its rites, to which yet every philosopher in his time had accommodated himself, for one and all, like their master Socrates, sacrifice a cock to Esculapius; but these noble conclusions of Xenophanes, Anaxagoras, and Plato had not purified that religion, and brought out the basis on which it rested, a belief in the divine providence, which is the witness of prayer, in man's need of expiation, which is the witness of sacrifice, in the ignorance of his mind looking for continual instruction from above, in the perversion of his will,

---

[1] Plato, *Laws*, iv. 354.

demanding union with God, though these two latter needs lay hidden in the frequentation of oracles and mysteries. On the contrary the outcome of the three centuries and a half which intervene between the death of Aristotle and the publication of the Christian Faith was that philosophic thought had thrown itself into three channels, each of which terminated in negation of these primary truths to which even the polytheistic worship scorned by the philosopher bore witness. For the Stoicism, which we have seen described in the pages of Seneca, admitted indeed one only power which ruled the universe, but it was a force impervious to prayer and sacrifice, an interminable series of cause and effect, in which the laws of necessity which belong to matter were applied to mind, nay, the very distinction of mind and matter was done away with; in which providence was the course of the world, and God was nature, and man a particle of nature. If the nobler and firmer minds among the Romans were attracted to this philosophy by its theory of duty, and of man's dignity as possessing reason, a much larger number, it is believed, were contented with the Epicurean view of things, that is, with the conclusion that there were no gods who concerned themselves with the course of human actions, no providence in short, no judge, rewarder or punisher of man. They were famous, it is said, for the cultivation of friendship with each other. They were made up chiefly of the wealthy class, and the kernel of their philosophy consisted in making the most of the goods of life, and the least of its evils. In fact we should probably do them no wrong if we said that the only thing they worshipped was the civilisation of the day. The other tendency which

existed in the thinking world at this time was that
of the Sceptics. If they had no teacher to set forth
their principles in Seneca's day, as we have heard
him assert, there is every reason to believe that there
were many whose only conclusion about the most
important problems of human life was that there is
no such thing as certitude. Perhaps these cut at the
root of worship and all that belongs to it at least as
deeply as either Stoics or Epicureans.

From the point of view in which we are now
regarding them these three philosophies are but
branches growing on one stem. The denying spirit
pervades them all. Far from developing, they had
not discerned the good which still existed in that
complex system of rites and the belief embedded in
them, out of which the ritual sprung. Far from
purifying religion of its corruptions, they had extinguished its essence, the sacred fire of piety in the
human heart, the human person's recognition of the
Creator and Father of all. They had not merely
degenerated from Socrates in his tender acknowledgment of an all-wise overruling providence: they were
far behind Homer, who proclaimed a father of gods
and men, the judge and rewarder of human actions.

But at the same time that the cultured classes had
assumed this attitude of coldness, unbelief, or even
direct hostility to the established worship, which the
name of Stoics, Epicureans, and Sceptics conveys, and
which the still existing literature reflects, it must not
be forgotten that this worship was in full possession
of the mass of society.[1] The poor and the rich, the
cultured and the uncultured, formed then as now,
and much more than now, two worlds. If a portion

[1] This is shown by Friedlaender, *Sittengeschichte Roms*, vol. iii. ch. 4.

of the rich and cultured then exhibited only an outward compliance with rites and ceremonies which they inwardly disbelieved, yet a vastly larger number ruled by habit, custom, and ancestral belief, frequented them still with undiminished faith. It would seem that the evidence of remaining inscriptions and votive tablets bears as decisive a testimony to this temper of mind in the mass, as the spirit of the literature bears to a prevailing unbelief in that far smaller class to which it is addressed.

It was not until after the time of Seneca, and only when the Christian Church had been spreading itself during forty or fifty years in the Roman empire, that what may be called a believing movement in cultured heathenism can be traced. This constitutes the third period of Greek philosophy, when, over against the extending influence of Christianity, it took upon itself the explanation and defence of the worship of the gods. Its characteristics are on the one hand a religious feeling of piety, on the other an endeavour to give a logical and doctrinal foundation to heathenism, and so to reconcile together popular belief with philosophic thought.[1]

All existing evidence points to Alexandria as the place at which this school arose, and those who studied there, whether Greeks or Jews, as taking part in the movement, among whom the learned Helleniser, Philo, was conspicuous. It is difficult to trace the exact time at which it appeared; in Philo, at any rate, it first reached importance. If before him a number of writers under the assumed names of old Pythagoreans had composed works which pretended to be the

---

[1] See this state of mind set forth by Möhler, *Geschichte*, i. 208, 262; Döllinger, *Heidenthum*, p. 598. Lasaulx, *Studien des klassischen Alterthums*, recognises the motive I have given to it.

authentic utterances of the Samian philosophy,[1] yet so far as can be inferred from the fragments of them which remain, a good judge pronounces that the ethical and political remarks were but a colourless and weak repetition of well-known propositions from the Academic and Peripatetic and, in a smaller degree, from the Stoic system of morals.[2] In all of them there was nothing peculiar to distinguish them from opinions generally prevailing in that day. But we find strongly marked in the Alexandrine Judaism of that time certain peculiarities of the Pythagorean and Platonic revival of which we are about to speak. And in the Jewish speculation of Philo, the common direction taken by the Jewish and Grecian schools, both of which had their root in Alexandria about the same time, is developed more rapidly and powerfully than in the whole Hellenic science down to Plotinus.[3] It does not seem an unfair inference from such a fact that his writings may have been the means of disseminating this tone of thought in the Gentile world.

Philo is every way worthy of our attention, both from the time at which he lived, from the position which he occupied, and from the effect which we are justified in attributing to his writings. He belonged to a rich and distinguished Jewish family at Alexandria, of which great capital his people mainly occupied two quarters out of five, while they formed a million out of the seven or eight at which the then population of Egypt is computed. His brother's son was the Alabareh or chief-magistrate of the Jews. He was born about twenty-five years before our era; he lived, it is supposed, far into the reign of Claudius.

---

[1] See a list of these enumerated by Zeller, v. 85, n. 2.
[2] *Ibid.* v. 123.   [3] This is asserted by Zeller, v. 62.

This date makes him, considering that he is a writer who has left large remains, an object of the highest interest with respect at once to the Roman empire, the Jewish people, and the Christian Church. About five years before his birth Egypt had passed from Cleopatra, the last of the Ptolemies, under the dominion of Rome. His manhood up to the age of fifty years witnessed the consolidation of the monarchy under Augustus and Tiberius. When he reached that age the preaching of our Lord began. We cannot indeed tell whether he himself went up to Jerusalem during any of the four passovers over which that preaching extended; but we cannot think that a person so well informed of all matters which concerned his people remained in ignorance of the stir which the events of our Lord's life created. Thus his writings were composed at the very last period of the Jewish people before the appearance of the Christian Church. There could not be a matter of greater interest than to know how a Jew at once zealous for the religion of his own people and learned in the literature and philosophy of the Greeks would speak at such a moment. For many generations there had been a large colony of his people in Alexandria. During all that time the great city continued to be the central point of meeting for the Greek and the Oriental mind, and the world's mart for intellectual speculation no less than for commercial exchange. When it fell under Roman dominion, it took rank at once as the second city of the empire, being however far superior in the beauty of its buildings and in the regularity and stateliness of its structure as a city to what Rome was up to the end of the reign of Augustus, or rather to the fire of Nero. At the same time it was perhaps even more cosmopolitan,

at least in the cultured part of its population, than
Rome itself, for there was no institution at Rome like
the University of the Ptolemies which would collect
together by honourable salaries and the attraction of
erudite society, the learned of many races and religions.
From this time forth it became the point at which
the Western as well as the Greek and the Eastern
minds were brought into contact and collision. Thus
the Greek writings of an Alexandrian at the time of
Philo would either directly or indirectly affect the
whole cultured society of the Roman empire, of which
Greek was more the language than Latin; and especially all those who were interested in philosophy
would become acquainted with any view or doctrine
of importance set forth in any school of Alexandria.
When Philo thus in his learned leisure looked out
upon the world, he would find it ruled by Roman
power and Greek mind. As a practical man he could
not but appreciate what was pre-eminently the Roman
art, the art of government. As a thinker, he could
not but be drawn towards the people who for five
hundred years had been engaged in solving with the
instrument of an almost matchless language, and in
the main by efforts of reason, the most important
problems which concerned man whether singly or in
society. Thirdly, as a Jew he believed with all his
heart that his own nation was in possession of truths
yearned after but imperfectly reached by the thinkers
whom he most admired. Quite different in the circumstances of his life from a Jew of Palestine, he
would be exposed to the full force of the Greek civilisation in the midst of which he was placed, and he
would be inclined to look with favour on that Roman
power which secured for his people a second country

wherein they throve and were honoured. And yet, while he speaks of the government of Augustus and of Tiberius almost with veneration, and while he calls Plato not only great but holy, he believes that the sole rule of life was delivered by Moses to his people, that he was the legislator and divinely-taught sage from whom truth not only shone in full lustre to the Jews, but streamed over to the Gentiles.

It was under such circumstances no wonder that a man of high intellectual gifts, who was profoundly penetrated with the truth and goodness of the Hebrew revelation, yet by education and learning was a Greek, should wish to join together in a sort of marriage the two parts of his own being. He would in fact espouse the fair Grecian captive, whose beauty had delighted his senses, with the Hebrew husband whose dignity and authority were paramount over his soul. And to this end, according to the precepts of his law, he would prepare her for the ennoblement she was to meet. The myths which disfigured her worship were to be explained and purified by a moral interpretation, just as on the other side revelation itself in condescension to human weakness had veiled high spiritual truths under a homely literal expression. But here we must note that while on the Hebrew side the allegory simply draws the truth out of its image, on the Greek side the interpretation employed removes from the myth the falsehood which had debased it. Thus, however, in the view of Philo, the human gifts which formed the dowry of the bride, that is to say, the circle of sciences, which the philosophic subtlety of the Greek mind had produced, were to be carried to the home of the husband, who had for his divine portion the knowledge of God and the goodness of virtue.

In the mind of Philo, philosophy, as such, was the handmaid of theology: in the mixed religious and philosophical system which he was attempting to construct, he was exalting her to the rank of a wife, but she was still to be subordinate to the husband. The form of Greek thought [1] was to be fused with the substance of Jewish belief. This was his intent and purpose, which he supposed himself to have carried out, and to which he was never consciously untrue.

In this attempted union of Jewish revelation with Greek science, the position of Philo is, that the Holy Scriptures of his own people contained the sum of all knowledge; that they were given by a divine inspiration which excluded all error and imperfection. He recognises no other source of wisdom. The exposition of the sacred books is to him the proper philosophy of his people: Moses the greatest of all prophets and of all men. On the other hand a practical limit is set to his belief in authority, by his recognition of a true wisdom outside of his own nation and religion. Thus he speaks of the holy community of Pythagoras, and of the godlike men, Parmenides, Empedocles, Zeno, and Cleanthes, and admits that Greece is distinguished as the cradle of science and a truly human civilisation above all other lands in the world. Further, his veneration for Greek philosophy is shown more strongly than any particular expressions can exhibit, by the wide use which he has made of Pythagorean, Platonic, Peripatetic, and Stoic doctrines, and by the influence which he has allowed these to have upon his own view of things. The central point of all wisdom to him is theology, in which, as is natural, he follows his Jewish doctrinal system. But philosophy and

[1] Döllinger, *Heidenthum*, p. 837; Zeller, v. 295.

RESURRECTION OF CULTURED HEATHENISM 129

even the encyclical sciences are in his opinion an indispensable help to this theology. Now these sciences could be found only among the Greeks. The legislator of his people is exalted far above Greek philosophers, but the relation which he conceives of the Greek philosophy to the Jewish religion is yet the essential similarity of their contents. The Jewish law contains the purest and most perfect wisdom, but philosophy contains the same wisdom less purely and less perfectly. The difficulty which a Jew would feel in allowing this was softened to him by the belief that the Greek wisdom itself was derived from the Jewish revelation.[1]

But the chief interest of Philo to us in the present inquiry lies in three particulars, which are, first, the tendencies which he had in common with the Greek philosophy of his day; secondly, what he borrowed from it; thirdly, what he contributed to it. On the first and second points we will say but a word, dwelling more largely on the last.

Now as to the eclectic connection of diverse doctrines which gave the name to his school, that was a tendency which had been a considerable time at work : so likewise the neglect of logical and physical studies, and the devotion to religious and ethical questions, and again the representation of philosophy as a religion. These things had been seen in Antiochus, Cicero, and those who followed, and are marked enough in the Stoicism of Seneca. So far Philo's Alexandrine speculation presupposes what had been up to his day the course taken by Greek philosophy. Again, which was our second point, from it he borrows scientific form and method, and a number of particular concep-

[1] See Zeller, v. 295–297, 300.

tions and propositions derived from Plato, Aristotle, the Stoics, and others.¹

But now we proceed to a much more important point, to consider, that is, what Philo's own contribution to Greek philosophy may have been. As to this we note that the distinguishing peculiarity of the Neopythagorean school lay in the attempt to attain, by means of a divine revelation, to a knowledge and to a happiness which no effort of mind by a process of reason and science could acquire. Secondly, in order that the individual might obtain this revelation, it was considered necessary that he should stand in a similar relation to the Godhead with that in which those stood to whom such a revelation was originally made.² These two things may be termed in a word the principle of revelation and the principle of holiness. Now both of them had been strange to Greek philosophy down to Philo's time. Any assumption of supernatural revelation, any requirement of contact with the Divine other than what might be produced by the effect of thought itself, was either entirely unknown to Plato, Aristotle, and their descendants, down to the rise of the Neopythagorean school, or remained without any real significance to them.³ The Greek principle always had been scientific thought, and this, twenty years after Philo's time, continued to be the principle of Seneca, as it had been of Cicero, and all their predecessors. The introduction into philosophy of two such principles as the need of revelation in order to acquire true knowledge of God and of the great problems which concern human life, and the need of holiness in man in order practically to avail himself

---

[1] Zeller, v. 63.   [2] See Zeller, v. 56.
[3] See this avowal made by Zeller, v. 58.

of such knowledge, amounted in fact to a revolution. This has been virtually admitted by those who date from this time a third, which forms the last period of Greek philosophy.

But now the whole mind of Philo was filled with the thought that a complete revelation had been given to his people, and that this was the only well-spring of true knowledge; and not less earnestly did he hold that the participation in such knowledge depended on the religious and moral state of the man.

Let us turn to that which rules the whole religious and philosophical system of Philo, his conception of God.

And first it is derived to him from the theology of the Old Testament; it comes to him as a gift from above, not as an elaboration of his own mind. Almost all his treatises are comments on the sacred writings, and it is in so commenting that he draws out his conception of God. The effect is remarkable. If Plato[1] had declared that the Maker and Father of this universe was hard to find, and when found impossible to utter to all, Philo's mind on the contrary ran over with the thought of God, and disclosed His attributes without stint, from the ground of that tradition which he inherited as a Jew; and, moreover, the sense of God was wrought into his inmost being by the special relation in which God stood to his own people. The contrast between this strong conception of Philo and the abstract relationless impersonal neuter which the Greek philosophy up to his time called "The Divine," is most striking. It is expressed most vividly by Philo's own often-repeated name, "the living God," for truly, in comparison with it, that philosophical abstraction is a dead thing.

[1] *Timæus*, sec. 9.

The God thus conceived by Philo is one, simple, eternal, unoriginated; He is self-existent, and absolutely distinct from the world, which is His work. Whoever holds the world itself for the Lord God, is fallen into error and wickedness. God is in His own being incomprehensible; we can only know that He is, not what He is. We can only predicate of Him that He is "He who is." He is most pure and absolute mind, better than virtue and better than knowledge, better than the idea of goodness and the idea of beauty. "He is His own place, and full of Himself, and sufficient for Himself, filling up and embracing all that is deficient, or empty, but Himself embraced by nothing, as being Himself one person, and yet everything."[1]

But as He is the Maker and Father of the world, so is He likewise its preserver, governor, rewarder, and punisher. "Those who would make the world to be unoriginated cut away, without being aware of it, the most useful and necessary of all the constituents of piety, that is, the belief in Providence. For reason proves that what has an origin is cared for by its father and maker. For a father is anxious for the life of his children, and a workman aims at the duration of his works, and employs every device imaginable to ward off everything that is pernicious or injurious, and is desirous by every means in his power to provide everything which is useful or profitable for them. But with regard to what has had no origin, there is no feeling of interest, as if it were his own, in the breast of him who has not made it. It is a worthless and pernicious doctrine to establish in the world what would be anarchy in a city, to have no

[1] ἅτε εἷς καὶ τὸ πᾶν αὐτὸς ὤν. *Legis Allegor.* I, xiv. p. 52.

superintendent, regulator, or judge, by whom everything must be distributed and governed."[1]

To God accordingly, as Maker, Philo ascribes the absolute knowledge of everything which He has made, and especially as the moral governor of man, the knowledge of His most secret thoughts. "To God, as dwelling in pure light, all things are visible, for He penetrating into the very recesses of the soul, is able to see transparently what is invisible to others, and by means of prescience and providence, His own peculiar excellencies, allows nothing to abuse its liberty or exceed the range of His comprehension. For indeed there is with Him no uncertainty even in the future; for there is nothing uncertain and nothing future to God. It is plain then that the producer must have knowledge of all that he has produced, the artificer of all that he has constructed, the governor of all that he governs. Now Father, Artificer, and Governor He is in truth of all things in heaven and the world. And whereas future things are overshadowed by the succession of time, longer or shorter, God is the maker of time also. . . . For the world by its motion has made time, but He made the world, and so with God there is nothing future, who has the very foundations of time subject to Him. For their life is not time, but the archetype and model of time, eternity, and in eternity nothing is past, and nothing is future, but there is the present only."[2]

But His goodness is as perfect as His power and His wisdom. His holiness is the pattern of all holiness. "It is God who sows and plants all virtue upon earth in the mortal race, being an imitation and image

---

[1] *De Mundi Opificio*, sec. 2.
[2] "Quod Deus sit immutabilis." Sec. 6, p. 72.

of the heavenly."¹ Thus commenting on the four rivers of Paradise, he says, "The greatest river from which the four branches flow off is generic virtue, that is, goodness, and the four branches are so many virtues, prudence, temperance, fortitude, and justice. Now generic virtue derives its source from Eden, which is the wisdom of God, and it rejoices and exalts and triumphs, having its glory and its beauty only in its Father, God; and the four particular virtues are branches from the generic, which like a river waters all which each does well² in an abundant stream of good actions."

But not only is God the archetype of all holiness, and not only is the origin of all human virtue in God, but man in the weakness of his sensual nature, and in the sinfulness which springs from it, can only look to God for help. Man³ is bound to free himself from the influence of sensuousness, but as a sensuous being he cannot do this. What remains for him but to betake himself to a higher power, and receive from it as a loan that strength for good which fails in himself? Hence Philo teaches that all virtue springs from the divine wisdom. To God alone it belongs to plant virtues in the soul, and it would only be a self-seeking delusion if we were to ascribe them to ourselves. The powerful drawing of God alone makes it possible for us to rise above the senses, and grace often so entirely prevents our own desire that it

---

¹ *Legis Alleg.* i. 14, p. 52, and 19, p. 56.
² τὰ κατορθώματα ἑκάστης. This is a fair instance of Philo's union of philosophic morality with Scriptural revelation. The four cardinal virtues are Stoic, and κατόρθωμα is the special Stoic word for the good intention carried into a good act.
³ I take the following account of man's weakness and his need of grace, as set forth by Philo, from Zeller, v. pp. 354, 355, 357–60. He supports it by many references to Philo's works.

chooses out its instruments before every good deed, nay, before birth itself. So perseverance in good-will only succeed to one who is under the defence of the Divine Word. From this point of view the task of man naturally would be not merely to exhibit human reason in life and action, but the most necessary thing for him is to put himself in relation to God, and take the motives of his conduct from this relation. True morality is imitation of God. Whoever follows only his own conviction of good and duty, however right and pure this conviction may be, does not yet possess right virtue, which belongs to him who does everything only out of regard to God. If then Philo agrees with the Greek philosophers in founding virtue upon wisdom or knowledge, still this wisdom is of another kind from theirs. True science has in his meaning one only object, the Godhead. The unfailing ground of wisdom, nay, true wisdom itself, is only faith. Thus the negative description of virtue, according to which it would consist in deliverance from sensuality, receives its positive completion, which lies however not in human nature and action as such, but only in their relation to the Godhead.

But knowledge itself has only value so far as it bears on the moral and religious state of man. Not only the encyclical sciences, mathematics, grammar, and the rest, but many philosophical inquiries have only a subordinate importance for Philo. They are only a preparation for wisdom, not wisdom itself: only milk-food for children, Chaldean arts, attendants upon true science. Perfect virtue is Sara, encyclical knowledge Hagar. If a man must first be versed in this, and if even the friend of wisdom must embrace Hagar before he can have children by Sara, and as

Abram pursue Chaldaic astronomy before as Abraham he reaches on to theology, yet so soon as the maid attempts to put herself in the place of the mistress she is thrust out: and when the sciences, which serve as an introduction, seek to be the highest and final object, they become perverted and ruinous. But it is no better with philosophy itself, if it does not seek its end in the knowledge of God and in moral self-knowledge. It is true, Philosophy is the highest gift of the Godhead. In it knowledge is matured and perfected. Other sciences are occupied with particular parts of the world: Philosophy searches out the essence of things itself. Everything actual is its subject. Nevertheless its proper aim lies only in man and his salvation. The philosopher is a physician who is called in to heal the sicknesses of human life, to make the inward man sound. The self-knowledge, which is its chief task, goes beyond itself. The deeper we penetrate into ourselves, the more shall we mistrust ourselves, the plainer recognise our nothingness. We shall see that God alone is wise, but the human mind far too weak to comprehend the nature of things. We shall remember how often our senses deceive us: how feelings and judgments change with persons and circumstances: how relative are our notions; how uneven and dependent on their convictions even the moral conceptions of men are; how little we know even the essence of our soul; how even philosophers are at issue with each other on the weightiest questions; and we shall renounce all claims to knowledge of our own. Thus only can we hope to attain to truth. He who will know God must give up himself; must turn away his sense from everything perishable. He who gives up himself, knows Him who is.¹ No created being can of itself know anything of Him; if we would see Him, He must reveal Himself to us.

The attitude of Philo's mind to God may be summed up in his own words. "Do thou therefore, O my soul, hasten to become the house of God, His holy temple, to become strong from having been most weak, powerful from having been powerless, wise from having been foolish, and very reasonable from having been doting and childless." Man's taste is to imitate God: to follow God: "His supreme happiness to stand firm and unswerving in God alone."²

Union with God, as satisfying the mind of man, which nothing on earth, neither intellect nor sense, can satisfy, is the ultimate point of Philo's system. This union, like everything perfect in human nature, is an immediate gift of God. On the one hand vividly conscious of human weakness, of our moral and intellectual helplessness, Philo yearns after communion with the infinite God:³ on the other hand he is convinced that the needs which neither our own strength nor the finite world will satisfy, will meet their full satisfaction in a power beyond the world, beyond man's heart and intellect. But the inseparable condition of attaining such a state is holiness on the part of man produced by grace on the part of God.

Now all that we have been hitherto considering in Philo's state of thought, this conception of God, drawn from revelation, of God who is one and infinite, yet personal, who is absolutely distinct from the world, yet its constructor, who is the maker, father, governor

¹ ὁ γὰρ λίαν καταλαβὼν ἑαυτὸν λίαν ἀπέγνωκε τὴν ἐν πᾶσι τοῦ γενητοῦ σαφῶς προλαβὼν οὐδένειαν· ὁ δ'ἀπογνοὺς ἑαυτόν, γινώσκει τὸν ὄντα. *De Somniis*, i. 10, p. 629.
² *Ibid., De Somniis*, i. 23.   ³ Zeller, v. 365.

of man, the very archetype of holiness himself, and the giver of it to man by grace, union with whom is the end of man's life; a God who is to be reached not by the effort of a scientific knowledge on the part of man, but by His own gift, dependent on a moral and spiritual state in man, which likewise springs from God, all this is completely unlike the course of Greek philosophy up to Philo's time. We cannot assure ourselves better of this fact than by comparing him in these respects with Seneca. Philo was older than Seneca by about twenty years. When he visited Rome in the commencement of the reign of Claudius, he was already a grey-haired man. He is supposed to have died a few years later, but twenty-five years after this visit of his, Seneca was the representative of such philosophy as then existed at Rome. Now in certain points these writers show a similarity of tendencies. If Seneca exalted philosophy into a sort of religion, assigning to it the solution of the most important problems of human life, and requiring submission to it as the guide and teacher of man, Philo, on the other hand, sought to penetrate his theology with philosophic thought, and scrupled not to select Platonic, Peripatetic, and Stoic doctrines, which he attempted to reconcile with the doctrine of Moses. In this process he was unconscious of being in any point untrue to the supremacy which he accorded without doubting to that doctrine. Nevertheless in picking and choosing from the Greek schools he was an eclectic like Seneca. Again, in their ascetic doctrine of subduing the flesh to the reason, in their view of the antagonism between mind and matter, there was much in common. Philo also agrees with the Stoic in declaring that the wise man knows himself to be as a citizen of the world not confined to any particular country, but feels himself to be a member of the whole race of man, and a portion of the world. And in his treatment of slavery he requires it to be considered as an external lot which does not derogate from the regard due to the common human nature in the slave.[1] This, it will be remembered, was one of the points in which Seneca is so far superior to his predecessors, and in this he had been preceded by Philo; and if we could suppose him to have been familiar with Philo's works it would solve a portion of the difficult problem respecting the source from which he derived a moral tone so little borne out by his own life. But while there is in the above-mentioned points an agreement in the two thinkers, there is in the mental attitude and spirit of the men a total dissimilarity. Philo's view of everything in man's life is dependent on his conception of God. He has an intense regard and affection for Him as his own God, a person for a person. He annihilates himself before God's holiness, and admits that he is nothing without God's grace, and yearns for His communion. These sentiments are absolutely strange to Seneca, and to the whole course of Greek philosophy[2] down to his time. And this is the more remarkable in Seneca, because, as he tells us himself,[3] he had imbibed a love for Pythagoras and a regard for some portions of Pythagorean doctrine, such as the abstaining from animal food and the transmigration of souls, from his teacher Sotion, an Alexandrian,

---

[1] Zeller, v. 353.
[2] As Zeller admits, v. 360. "Durch diese Sätze, welche mit seiner ganzen Denkart so eng verwachsen sind, trennt sich Philo's religiöse Philosophie ganz entschieden von der reinen, in sich befriedigten Wissenschaft des hellenischen Alterthums."
[3] Epist. cviii. sec. 17-22.

who must have been just of the same age as Philo. But there is no trace of any such doctrine respecting God or man's relation to God having been received by him. On the contrary, there is not a particle of piety in all the writings of Seneca. How should there be, since his God is a primal force dwelling in the whole body of the universe, and how should man worship force, or pray to an unbroken series of cause and effects? Then, as to the relation between God and man, Seneca would reach knowledge and virtue by the exercise of his own reason, which is the principle of scientific thought, and had been the animating principle of Greek philosophy down to his time. Philo would reach them by the gift of God, bestowed through his grace, to which man must correspond, though the first movement comes from God. And Philo dwells on all those moral relations of God, as maker, provider, governor, judge, which had well-nigh disappeared from philosophic thought and from literature in Seneca's time, though not from the popular conscience nor the reason of mankind. And what has just been said of Seneca would appear to be true of all writers of so-called Pythagorean tendencies, outside of the Jewish circle of thought, in Philo's time. The most anxious search [1] cannot produce in them any resemblance to Philo in the particulars we have just now cited, but these form the whole basis of his thought and his distinctive character.

Thus down to the end of Nero's reign there is no spirit in Greek philosophy or in its Latin affiliations bearing resemblance to the spirit of Philo, requiring, that is, a special divine aid, distinct from a man's own reason, in order that he may attain knowledge, and

[1] Such, for instance, as that made by Zeller, v. 81-141.

a special moral character in the recipient, formed by this aid, to make him capable of it. It is almost the same thing to say there is no clear conception of moral character in God or of man's personal relation to Him.

But thirty years after Seneca's time there appeared in Greek literature an author of great name and wide influence, who may almost be termed a heathen counterpart of Philo. For Plutarch and Philo in their view of the relation of philosophy to religion, in the general identity of their philosophical tenets, and in the attitude of their minds to religion, hold, the one being a Greek and the other a Jew, an analogous position to each other. The time and outward circumstances of Plutarch's life were these. He was born at Chæronea in Bœotia about the year 50. At the time of Nero's visit to Greece he is found studying philosophy at Athens under Ammonius of Alexandria. He is known to have visited Egypt. He was more than once at Rome, and seems to have given lectures there in the time of Domitian, which were largely frequented by persons of consideration. He formed friendships with noble Romans, and dedicated works to them. In later years he is said to have been held in high esteem by the Emperors Trajan and Hadrian, and he is supposed to have died in the reign of the latter, about the year 125. During this long life he was devoted to philosophy and literature, and still more to the religion of his country. On these subjects he was probably acquainted with every movement of thought in the cultured world of the Roman empire. Thus from the beginning of Domitian's reign to the middle of Hadrian's, his works may be taken as an index of the philosophic mind then prevailing. He speaks as a priest of Apollo in his ancestral religion, as the friend of Trajan and Hadrian in the Roman government, while in literature he is the exact contemporary of Tacitus and the younger Pliny, as well as of Epictetus. He was a young man when St. Peter died, and the sphere of his mental activity extended over the Pontificates of six successors to the Primacy, St. Linus, St. Anacletus, St. Clement, St. Evaristus, St. Alexander, and St. Sistus. About the time when he was lecturing at Rome Domitian was persecuting the Church, and he outlived by many years the martyrdom of St. Ignatius.

He is the first representative we have remaining of the Neopythagorean or Platonising tone of thought. He fully and exactly reflects it, and his whole view of the world is framed upon it. It is this. At the head of the universe as its author and orderer is the mind and will of the Supreme God. Under him the rulers and administrators of human affairs in general are the heavenly and visible gods, as the sun, moon, stars, planets, with which are identified the gods of the Greek mythology. Subordinate to these are the "demons," as "watchers and inspectors" of things in particular, and lower yet, but superior to men, the souls of heroes.

Let us specify these somewhat more exactly.

First, as to the Supreme God, Plutarch expresses himself thus:[1] "What is that which really is? That which is everlasting, unproduced, and incorrupt, to which time brings no change. For time is something subject to motion, and forming itself into the appearances of matter in motion, always in a flux and never holding in its contents, like a vessel of corruption and

[1] Περὶ τοῦ Εἰ ἐν Δελφοῖς. 19, 20.

production; in which the very terms 'before' and 'after,' 'shall be' and 'has been,' confess that there is no real being.... But of God we must say, He is, and is in no time, but in a motionless, timeless, uninclined eternity, in whom there is neither before nor after, neither future nor past, neither older nor younger, but being One he fills eternity with one now.[1] And that alone is which in such wise truly is, neither past, nor future, nor beginning, nor ending. So ought worshippers to salute and address it, or indeed as some of the ancients, saying, "Thou art one." For the deity is not many things, as each of us, a heterogeneous mixed collection, made up of countless differences which spring from being subject to passion. But that which is must be One, as that which is One, must be."

To the God so conceived every moral perfection is attributed. "Being[2] perfectly good, he wants no virtue, least of all justice and friendship;" and "the blessedness of the eternal life which God possesses consists in his knowledge never failing by the succession of things, for if knowledge and wisdom were taken away, immortality would not be life, but mere time."

But this God, though the orderer and arranger and in this sense the maker of things, is not their creator. Outside of him and independent of him he found matter, and something moreover within matter which he could not entirely tame and reduce to his will. This principle is called by the most different names, by the Persians Ahrimanes, by the Egyptians Typho, by the Greek mythology Hades and Ares, by Empedocles Conflict, by the Pythagoreans the Second, by Aristotle

---

[1] ἀλλ' εἷς ὢν ἑνὶ τῷ νῦν τὸ ἀεὶ πεπλήρωκε.
[2] *On the failure of Oracles*, 24; *On Isis*, 1.

Privation, by Plato the Other, and, which is best of all, the evil World-soul. Thus in fact Plutarch admits of three principles: the first, the Godhead or good; the second, the unordered World-soul, which is the origin of everything that is evil; and the third, Matter, the substratum, itself without quality, but which therefore being receptive of opposites is moved and determined by the powers which act upon it.[1]

Thus, then, the universe came into being by the action of God upon Matter, in which He reduced to order the irregular soul, and so made the Soul of the World. The ordered movement of the world is time, before which there was no time nor any world. Thus the world had a distinct beginning, and its constructor only found in existence its original parts, Matter without quality, and Soul without reason. The rest is all His work. He is to the world not merely as the artificer is to his work, for the builder, when he has built his house, has done his work, but its father, inasmuch as the power of the generator is infused into the child, and holds nature together as being a portion of Himself. The Soul of the world is not merely a work but a portion of God, and is not only made by Him but of Him and from Him. But in it the inferior element exists by the side of the superior. It is composed of the divine reason which has poured itself out upon matter, and of that disorderly power which we termed the evil soul, of the principle of unity and its opposite; therefore in all parts of the world there is evil beside good, disorder beside order, change beside permanence.[2] "The generation and constitution of this world is mixed out of opposite but not equivalent forces; the better has the superiority, but it is impos-

[1] Zeller, v. 152.   [2] *Ibid.* v. 154, 155.

sible for the bad to be exterminated, since with great abundance is it seated in the body and in the soul of the whole, and ever fights a battle with the better."[1]

The Supreme God communicates himself to the world, and first of all to the heavenly gods,[2] the sun, and the stars, and planets, with whom the gods of the Greek mythology are identified. The sun is the chief of these, and is the visible image of the Supreme God. But far below these are ranged the "demons," intermediate beings, greatly surpassing men in knowledge and power, but in the construction of their soul and body subject to sensuousness. They are capable of pleasure and pain, they are of a changeable, and in a certain sense even mortal nature, for though very long-lived, they are not absolutely free from death or a change corresponding to death. Further, they are exceedingly diverse in moral qualities. Bad gods are never spoken of, but there are bad demons. It is possible for a demon to turn himself to evil by his free-will; and as not only men can become heroes, and even demons, but demons also can become gods, so on the other side the case may occur that demons are drawn down into human bodies through sensual inclination. The gods are too far from the human world to interfere themselves in its course, but they take part in this through their servants the demons, to whom is entrusted the providence over particular things.

In accordance with this hierarchy of intelligences superior to man, Plutarch recognises a triple providence. This in its primary ground and origin is nothing else but the thought and will of the Supreme God. This will is fulfilled in a triple manner. The disposition of the universe and its general laws proceed

[1] *On Isis*, sec. 49.   [2] See Zeller, v. 157.

immediately from the maker of the world. The origin and maintenance of mortal beings are effected by the visible gods, the sun, planets, and stars, in the manner prescribed by those laws. The actions and the fortunes of particular men stand under the protection and guidance of the demons.

In connection with his belief in providence is his belief in the continuance of the human intelligence after death. He declares that these two beliefs stand or fall together. This continuance applies only to the divine part in man, which springs from the divine reason, not to the body or to the sensuous soul. And it seems to rest on three things in his mind, the kinship of the human spirit with the divine, the necessity of a future retribution and recompense for the evils of life, and the consolation which the thought of a future existence and recognition bestows.

This doctrine of providence is of great importance in Plutarch's conception of the world, and in defending it he vehemently attacks two sorts of opponents. First, the Epicureans, who were willing to admit that "all things were full of gods," but gods who did not trouble themselves with human affairs; so that those of this sect denied entirely the doctrine of providence; and secondly, the Stoics, whose fatalism destroyed, as he averred, the conception of possibility, and the freedom of the will, and made error and wickedness into something necessary, and the godhead the cause of evil.[2]

Plutarch's view of all moral obligation runs up into religion. Piety is the attitude of his mind. In legislation the first and the greatest thing is the opinion entertained of the gods. It is the bond

[1] Zeller, v. 164.   [2] *Ibid.*, v. 159.

which holds together all communion and making of laws. A city could subsist without its foundations as easily as without belief in the gods, without oaths, vows, divinations, sacrifices. No time is spent more joyously than in the temples. No sights, no actions convey more delight than what we see and do for the gods, by presence at their rights and sacrifices: and the ground of this joy is the good hope and belief that God is present propitiously, and receives graciously what is done. All things belong to the gods, and the possessions of friends are in common, and the good are friends of the gods: and that a friend of God should not be happy, or the temperate and just man not be a friend of God, is impossible. What is done by the gods we should expect to be good; but that these things are done by the gods is a source of great delight and boundless confidence.[1]

Now in this view of the world and man wherein does Plutarch differ from his Greek and Latin predecessors?

At the head of the universe he placed one God. Now the conception of which doubtless he felt the need, which he yearned after, like other Platonics of the later school, was that of a God who should be living, superior to nature, external to the world, a God who has intelligence and who has will.[2] In fact, Plutarch's God is the author of the universe, but at an immeasurable distance above and beyond it. Somewhere in that distance, but far below him, are placed the visible heavenly gods, the gods to whom Plutarch's people offered worship, but who in this system are reduced to be ministering powers under the Supreme

---

[1] These various passages from Plutarch's works are referred to by Zeller, v. 170.   [2] Döllinger, *Heidenthum*, p. 578.

God, yet not creatures, inasmuch as the spirit which is in them is a portion of the one divine spirit. These gods rule the destinies of men, yet not immediately, but by the demons under them, and in obedience to the will of the Supreme God over them. And lastly, there are the souls of heroes and the souls of men. And as the heavenly gods participate in the divine nature as spirits, so in an inferior degree do demons, heroes, and men, in their several order. And all these intelligences are not mere forces, but personal beings. Herein lies the great contrast of this system with that of Stoicism. For the Stoics also had reduced the universe to unity, and to a unity which was not without intelligence, for it was rigidly ruled by the "common reason"; but it was without will, the solid adamant of an eternal machine. Now Plutarch's conception of personality is not complete, just as his conception of God falls short of reaching that which he yearned after, a being entirely superior to nature and outside of the world: but his God is sufficiently personal to be very different from that of the Stoics, and to give quite another spirit to the system of which he stands at the head.

Secondly, this philosophic system appears as the friend and supporter of the polytheistic worship, which at the same time it strives to purify and reduce to perfect order. Now Stoics and Epicureans both tolerated that worship, and both adapted themselves to it: but the spirit which ruled them was adverse to all worship. Epicureans, who denied a divine providence, certainly could not really favour prayer and sacrifice. But the rigid fatalism of the Stoics also struck at the root of these. Necessity knows not prayer or sacrifice. Stoicism had likewise attempted by its physical interpretation of myths to get rid of all the incoherencies, all the unseemly and immoral elements, all the corrupting tales, which attached to the vulgar worship: but in reducing all these to the abstract operations of one force, termed indifferently God, nature, fate, or providence, it had banished personality from the universe. Now all worship is between persons, and therefore whatever aspect of conformity to this vulgar worship Stoicism could assume, it was in its essence profoundly impious. In Plutarch, on the contrary, was a system which strove to give a logical foundation to the existing worship; which conceived both a personal God, and a hierarchy of personal intelligences under him, which took delight in acts of worship, which preserved the names and the rites of the existing gods, and strove to make acts of homage paid to them, as servants and ministers of the Supreme God, to be part of a worship due to him; and which, finally, fathered upon demons, who had given way to sensuous attractions, all stories unworthy of the heavenly gods. Thus in Plutarch for the first time in Greek and Roman heathenism the bewildering world of Polytheism seems in process of reduction to order under an ever-mastering sense of the divine unity, in which, however, all the beings who take part and subserve it have personal relations. Here was an attempt to make a true and inward reconciliation between philosophy and the popular religion; for the gods of the popular religion, however debased in certain moral aspects the conception of them might be, were always personal beings; an attempt to give a reasonable basis to that religion, which would lead naturally to a pious observance of its rites. From his standing-point Plutarch could really believe that he who denied worship to his god Apollo was impious; and could himself venerate all the rites of his country's worship as parts of a worship at the head of which stood the Supreme God. Philosophy in his hands did at least in some degree endeavour to bring back the component parts of that worship, prayer and sacrifice, oracles and mysteries, to the positive meaning which lay beneath them, to detach the corruption and draw out the truth.

In so doing Plutarch's spirit of piety is in striking contrast not merely with Seneca, not merely with the frivolous love of infidel negation, which breathes through the poets and historians of Augustan literature, but with Cicero, with Aristotle, and even with Plato, from whom he assumes to derive his notion of God. There is in him an intimacy of relation between man and God as his author, ruler, and provider, such as had been strange for ages at least to those minds which can be said to have been formed or influenced by Greek philosophy, and have come down to posterity in their works.

But here I would recur to Philo in order to note certain very important points in which his love of Greek philosophy had led him, as it seems unconsciously, to desert the divine tradition of Moses and the orthodox Jewish belief. Thus God to Philo is not, strictly speaking, the world's Creator, but only its constructor or builder, for Philo asserts the independent existence of matter, which God found in a chaotic state at the beginning, and moulded by His divine power the universe out of it. In like manner he admitted the Stoic doctrine of the human soul being a fragment or derivation of the divine spirit; and after thus conceiving the origin both of matter and spirit, he places the origin of evil in the conflict of these two. From [1] God only what is good and perfect can derive only life and order; the imperfection of the finite, the strife and opposition between things, the necessity of nature, the lifelessness of material things, the evil in the world, can be traced back only to a source distinct from the divine operation. Accordingly the body is an absolute contradiction to the mind, and as such the source of all evils; the earthly shell is a prison out of which the spirit longs to be set free, a carcase which the soul drags about with it. Thus it is the conflict between the flesh and spirit, rather than the abuse of free-will, which is made the source of evil. Philo is further notorious for his extravagant use of allegory, both in the interpretation of Scripture on the one side, and in giving a moral sense to the Greek myths on the other.

Now in all these four points, the conception of the Supreme God as the builder of the world but not as its Creator, of matter as existing originally and before the divine operation, of the human soul as an effluence of the divine, and of the conflict between matter and spirit viewed as the cause of evil, the doctrine of Plutarch is the same as that of Philo, while he vies, to say the least, with Philo in the extravagance with which he uses allegory in order to draw a meaning in accordance with his system out of the Greek mythology. But in all this it is Philo who Grecises, not Plutarch who Judaises. In another doctrine, however, which in Philo forms the crowning point of union between God and man, Plutarch

---

[1] Zeller, v. 336, who observes that this train of thought in Philo is clearly seen not only in particular passages, but from all his statements respecting Matter. See also p. 349.

approaches him nearly, and this is the more remarkable because it is a doctrine quite foreign to the natural genius and previous course of Greek philosophy. This is, the attainment of knowledge by an immediate gift of the Godhead rather than by the natural exercise of human faculties. Whence,[1] he argues, could knowledge of the Godhead come to us unless the Godhead itself communicated to us this its most proper possession, as it does all good. But if it rests upon a communication of the Godhead, the less we mix in it of our own the more perfect it will be. The higher revelation is a passivity of the soul, wherein it has become an instrument of the Godhead. It is a state of divine possession. And if the soul will never succeed, so long as it is encompassed with the body, in surrendering itself pure and undisturbed to the higher operation, and if therefore every revelation is to be considered as the result of two movements, one natural and one divine, and in every one the divine operation is to be distinguished from the human ingredients, it still remains our task to repress, as much as possible, all activity on our own part, and to bring to meet the divine spirit an apprehension as far as possible undisturbed and virginal.

Once more. Philo, out of a mixture of Platonic and Stoic notions with his Jewish belief, constructed the following theory as to the intermediate beings between God and the world. When[2] God would make the world, He knew that every work presupposes an intellectual archetype, and for this purpose He framed first the supersensuous world of ideas. But the ideas

---

[1] From Zeller, v. 173, who refers to *De Pyth. Orac.* sec. 21–23; *Amator*, sec. 16; *Defect. Orac.* sec. 48 and 40.
[2] Zeller, v. 314, 315.

are not simply patterns, but at the same time efficient causes, powers, which reduce to order the as yet unarranged elements, and impress on everything their qualities. Thus it can also be said that the archetypal world consists of the invisible powers which as a train surround the Godhead. It is through these invisible powers that God is active in the world, and works in it what on account of His exalted majesty He cannot produce immediately. They are the servants and deputies of the Supreme God, the messengers through whom He communicates His will to men, the agents mediating between God and finite things, portions of the universal reason, which forming and ordering bear sway in the world, the indissoluble bands wherewith God has encompassed the universe, the pillars which He has set under it. Hence they can be also described as the ministering spirits and instruments of the divine will; they are those pure souls which are called by the Greeks demons, by Moses angels, and thus they come to be invoked by man.

If a Greek philosopher, who desired above all things to restore the doctrine of the divine unity, yet to maintain the rites and worship of his ancestral gods, and to reconcile the one with the other, met with such a theory set forth in his own language, what could be more likely than that he would avail himself of it to present to his countrymen such a view of the world as that above drawn from the works of Plutarch? He would strip off from it everything which had a special relation to the Jewish people, and he would be silent as to the source from which it was derived. The angelic messengers enjoying a celestial life and presiding over nations and individuals in Philo might well suggest a place for the national gods and heroes of Greece, nor of Greece only, but of all other nations, and the view would come out as we actually find it in Plutarch, who thus attempts to reduce all religions to one. "God is not a lifeless thing subject to men (as those who confounded the gifts with the giver, wine with Bacchus and wheat with Ceres, were prone to imagine), but we deem them to be gods because they bestow their gifts upon us in an abundant and never-failing stream. Nor are they different according to place, nor barbarous and Grecian, nor of the north or the south, but as the sun and the moon and the heaven and the earth are common to all though they have different names, so there is one reason which arranges and one providence which controls the world, and ministering powers which are set over every part, to whom divers honours and appellations are assigned by the laws in different places, and symbols are used, sometimes obscure and sometimes clear, guiding the thoughts to divine things not without peril."[1]

Now let us look back for a moment to the space we have traversed since Philo bore part in a legation to Rome in the last year of Caligula. The Christian Church had not then begun to preach to the Gentiles. It is probable that most of Philo's works had then been composed, but we have no means of judging whether they were as yet known in the West. Philo himself is supposed to have been by no means the first of his school, that is, the first who attempted at Alexandria to unite Jewish belief with an eclectic Greek philosophy, and who used as an instrument for that purpose the allegorical interpretation of the Old Testament Scriptures on the one hand, and the moral or physical interpretation of Grecian myths on the other. For

[1] *De Iside,* 67.

three centuries at least Greeks and Orientals had been thrown together under one government and in one place of study. And Jews had been settled in all the cities of the Roman empire, and far beyond it in the East, and probably in every place some male, and still more some female proselytes were attracted either to a complete or to a partial observance of their religion. Of Rome in particular we know that since Pompey's conquest of Jerusalem Jews were in large numbers there, and reference to their peculiar rites is not infrequent in Roman authors. Moreover, whatever reasons existed in the condition of the provinces subject to Rome for the rise of such a state of mind as is shown in the philosophy which is called a revival of the Pythagorean or Platonic mode of thinking, had existed equally for several generations of men, and this still more notably since the pacification brought about by the battle of Actium, and the establishment of one empire embracing so many races and religions. But though certain philosophic tendencies of Philo—doctrines which he imbibed from Platonic, Peripatetic, or Stoic sources—were in the air around him, and may be considered as the result of the education which he received in the midst of Hellenic life, yet up to the time of Philo's visit to Rome nothing like his religious system could be found in the heathen life of Greeks or Romans. The Jews were bodily in every place, but their nation and their religion kept them apart in spirit. They were looked upon with antipathy and contempt, and their bearing towards Polytheism was that of strong abhorrence and exclusion, but not of aggression. Their position was one of defence, not of conquest, and so they were allowed the open exercise of their worship throughout the empire. Whatever and supplementing them with a host of demons who fill up the gap between them and men.

What can be more unlike the old Roman world of Cicero, and his bearing towards the immortal gods whom he parades, and the smile which he attributes to the augurs when they meet each other? What can be more unlike the stage religion or thinly-veiled unbelief of Julius, Augustus, Tiberius, Strabo, Diodorus, Horace, Virgil, and Ovid? But the contrast is brought home to us because the successors of these men are still to be found in some of Plutarch's exact contemporaries, in Tacitus and his friend Pliny. These stand very much upon the ground of Cicero still. Tacitus thinks the facts which he records as historian to be the severest comment upon the notion of a divine providence extending over the fortunes of men. He maintains the ancestral worship as a thing of custom and as connected with the dominion of Rome. But it is an outward, hesitating, sceptical maintenance, more of the politician than the man. Both he and Pliny are utter strangers to Plutarch's heartiness of belief and spirit of piety.

But had anything happened between the accession of Claudius and that of Trajan which would throw light upon this change? Certainly something had happened quite unknown to the history of philosophy since it arose with Thales six hundred years before. Men had gone throughout the whole empire preaching the divine unity, spirituality, holiness, providence, and personality. Jews, and going forth from Judea, they had first approached the synagogues of their own countrymen which were to be found in every city, and strove within them to form a nucleus of believers in the new doctrine: next they proceeded to associate therein the inhabitants of the empire, to whatever race, sect, or religion they might belong. These things were not done in a corner, but spoken in the market-place, discussed in the Areopagus. Whatever philosophy had in the course of these six centuries divined about the unity of the Godhead had been imparted in dark and doubtful intimations to congenial breasts: but a ringleader of this new sect said openly to Stoics and Epicureans in the place of their power concerning that unknown God, "whom you worship without knowing Him, the same declare I unto you." Philosophy, up to the time these words were spoken, had acted as a dissolvent of the popular belief, but had never announced a positive doctrine which could take visible form and produce effects in the practical world. This was one novelty, but there was another as important involved in it. In the declaration of this one God an attack was made upon the whole polytheistic worship. For He was an exclusive God, a God so entirely jealous of giving His glory to another, that the proclaiming of Him must be the overthrow of the rest. This was an attack totally dissimilar to the previous hostility of philosophy, as shown in the three chief sects, Stoics, Epicureans, and Sceptics. The worship which their doctrine attacked from within and secretly ruined had no enemy from without which it feared, or which was feared by philosophy itself. The rise of the various Socratic sects in the bosom of heathenism may be likened to the internal contests within a state for a redistribution of civil power. The combatants are bone of its bone and flesh of its flesh; they do not mean to destroy their country, but strive to get possession of it for themselves. But this preaching of the One God, who would not give His glory to another, was like an assault from a foreign power, which aims at overthrowing and thoroughly subjecting what it attacks. If the attack is strong enough, it is wont to unite against itself those rival parties for civil pre-eminence which betoken a state of internal security. Foreign invasion brings about domestic union. Was not something like this apparent in that complete change of front which in the time of Trajan philosophy had made? At all events, the change corresponds exactly to the two points of attack by the foreign invader. Plutarch has a doctrine of the divine unity, and at the same time he is the warmest friend of the polytheistic worship. And the civil power has no objection at all to such a statement of monotheism as that of Plutarch. It is compatible with the full maintenance of the established religion; indeed, it is made by a priest of Apollo, who is most assiduous in the due performance of his rites. Accordingly Trajan promotes to a post of honour Plutarch, who believes, as we have seen, in one God, and states his belief, while as soon as St. Ignatius avowed that he carried the one God in his bosom, Trajan ordered him to be thrown to the wild beasts.

LECTURE XVIII

THE STANDING-GROUND OF PHILOSOPHY FROM THE ACCESSION OF NERVA TO THAT OF SEVERUS

THE Greek philosophy, whether as seen in the pre-Socratic schools, in the Sophists, or in the Platonic, the Peripatetic, the Epicurean and the Stoic sects, or again in the Eclectics, who made a mixture of them all, having acted without a break from the time of Thales to the preaching of the Gospel in the reign of Nero as a dissolving agent of polytheism, takes up in the later years of Domitian, and from the time of Nerva onwards, another position. It puts under its protection the assaulted fabric of pagan belief and worship; it strives to introduce reason and order into the Olympian heaven of deities; to restore the shaken supremacy of Jupiter, and to put it on a larger and firmer basis. It aims to defend scientifically that whole system of worship, the objects of which it had so often exposed to ridicule, with bitter censure of its scandals and exposure of its endless incongruities. We have seen that it had not taken up this new position even in the last writings of Seneca, which reach to the year 64; for the Stoicism of Seneca, however eclectic and mixed, however tinged with peculiarities not before seen, certainly did not point to a restoration of the ancient religion, but to a substitution for it of the god within us, that is, human reason; and set up a system of

THE STANDING-GROUND OF PHILOSOPHY 161

duty disjoined from worship altogether, which derived all its sanction from the possession of this reason, and so, at the bottom, from man himself.

Another thing also is to be remarked, that the philosophy then in vogue was connected with opposition to the government or imperial rule. For this it was persecuted by Nero and even by Vespasian, as afterwards by Domitian. Seneca and Lucan, Thrasea, Helvidius, and Rusticus were put to death, and many more were banished, at three distinct intervals, by these emperors, for their political, which were connected with their philosophical, opinions. But from the accession of Nerva another state of things commences. Philosophy accepts frankly the imperial government, and as frankly the polytheistic worship. It swears by the genius of the emperor, and offers its cordial vows to the Capitoline Jupiter. Note also that this double alliance is not broken down to the time of Constantine. We must view the second and third centuries of the Christian era under this aspect; and it is full of instruction. It points unquestionably to the working of influences which Roman historians dissembled as long as they could and Grecian philosophers carefully ignored, which we shall find Tacitus, Plutarch, and Epictetus pass in silence, but which we are not therefore to conclude that they knew nothing about. Ignoring is often the most convenient mode of dealing with a peculiarly obnoxious adversary.

From the accession of Nerva the empire answered the altered temper of philosophy with a different mode of treatment. From that time forth it favoured its studies and promoted its teachers. The younger Pliny in his panegyric praises Trajan for encouraging those studies which the vices of a former ruler had viewed with fear, and the studies specified are rhetoric and philosophy. Dio of Prusa, self-banished under Domitian, returned joyously under Trajan, and was distinguished by him. Hadrian sought intercourse with philosophers as well as with learned men in general, and is supposed to have been the first who appointed public teachers of philosophy in Rome. Antoninus Pius established them in all the provinces. The salaries of the learned who were drawn to the University of Alexandria continued on, and public professors of the four chief schools were named at Athens with ample appointments by Marcus Aurelius. Janius Rusticus, probably the grandson of the Rusticus whom Domitian had put to death, was the bosom friend of the last-named emperor, and as governor of Rome gave the crown of martyrdom to Justin Martyr, who had tried the various sects of philosophy, and finding satisfaction in none had taken refuge in the Christian faith. It was a crime worthy of the most ignominious death in the eyes of a descendant of a Stoic who had perished for his political and philosophical opinions.

The second century, then, and the third, are the age of a triple alliance between the empire, philosophy, and polytheism as seen in belief and worship. The enemy of imperial rule in Nero's time had become a friend in that of Trajan, just as the prayers and sacrifices which Seneca slighted had been encouraged by Plutarch's warmest devotion. The inward and outward revolution is complete, whatever may have been the causes leading to it. That which ensued from this time was not a mere natural sequence or unfolding of the previous civilisation, but a change of front betokening the approach of a new enemy. Plutarch and Epictetus are not wholly legitimate successors of Cicero, but a light has arisen in the East, the reflection of which is seen on their faces, though their hearts refused to receive the warmth of its beams.

But this altered front of those who professed and taught philosophy is itself a phase of the change which had taken place in the feelings of the whole cultured class. During the civil wars, which began with Cæsar's passage of the Rubicon, and ended with the establishment of monarchy by the victory of Actium, indifference to religion had been the prevailing temper of the times. So it had continued during the reigns of Augustus and Tiberius. The culmination of this temper and its turning-point lie in the reign of Nero. Already in that great break-up which followed his death, and which wrapped in flames the Capitol while it threatened with destruction the whole fabric of the empire, another widely different temper is found to prevail. Men's faces are set towards the East. Eastern rites and religions are in vogue. Instead of indifference to religion there is a longing for satisfaction in it. By the end of the first century after Christ this current has set in with force, and it continues to the time of Constantine. Religiousness in a thousand different shapes, with a strong leaning to Egyptian and Syrian deities, running in its excess into magical rites and theurgy, takes the place of that apathy which is so marked a feature of the classic times of Roman literature. Horace, that "spare and infrequent worshipper of the gods," who too often verifies his own confession that he was "a porker of the sty of

Epicurus," is the type of the former frame of mind: Plutarch, who finds the hours spent in their service a delight, of the latter. Here however we are met by two contrasts: the Stoic and the Platonic character on the one hand, the Greek and the Latin mind on the other.

There are two men of this period, exact contemporaries, both Greeks, one a writer who has had great influence, the other a man whose sayings as collected by a disciple are among the most noteworthy utterances of heathenism. Both are remarkably religious, if compared with Cicero or any man of the Augustan or Tiberian time. But the character of their religion is quite different. Epictetus is a rigid monotheist in so far as this that the only God whom he worships is the reason which is in every man, and is part of the one divine being. Upon this single ground he estimates every action, and divides his day into its several duties as a Christian might. All external goods, rank, wealth, beauty, talent, health, are viewed by him with regard to this one standard. A man is fulfilling his duty as man, not in proportion as he possesses these, but as possessing more or less of them, since he has it not in his power at all to determine the degree in which he has them, he uses what he has of them according to the dictates of reason. And all other men, since they possess this divine attribute, as he does himself, are by nature brethren, common children, he even calls them, of one God: but in reality they are rather parts of one God, and go back to him, or more properly to it, with no conscious existence after death. If piety be possible to such a frame of mind, Epictetus is pious. But it is plain that he does not aim at a restoration of heathen polytheism. His whole system is a most complete dethronement of "the immortal gods," and a substitution for Jupiter and all his Olympian assessors of pantheistic Deism, that tremendous form of necessity, out of which heaven and earth, gods and heroes, men and animals are formed in endless evolution, and return back again into its exhaustless bosom. Epictetus has been admired and copied in every age by those who, born and nurtured in Christianity, have been unable to sustain the weight of the Cross and the glory of a conscious eternity, or have loved and fostered the pride of an independent human nature rather than embrace the shame of a suffering God. He is the parent of modern Deism.

The old rugged temper of Stoicism is wonderfully softened in Epictetus. Humanity and kindliness breathe in his precepts. You feel the slave who has gone through all the trials to which man's life is subject, and learnt by his own sufferings to sympathise with the sufferings of others. He is supposed to have been born in A.D. 45 ; he would thus be twenty years of age in the year 65, and was a young man at Rome at the time of Nero's persecution of the Christians. It is an impossibility that the slave of Epaphroditus, Nero's freedman, could have been ignorant of the torments inflicted on them. It is a very great improbability that he was not aware of many circumstances respecting the Christian life in those who professed it. When he asks, "Why should not the wise man call himself not by the name of any particular country, but son of God," was he ignorant of that Son of God who had already come into the world, who had been crucified for assuming that very title, so many of whose disciples had perished before his eyes for their fidelity in following His precepts, in imitating His life, and in actually practising that brotherly love which Epictetus warmly commends? We cannot answer this question with certainty; but since Epictetus lived to the end of Trajan's reign, and by that time there was a Christian congregation in every great city, since this subject of religion was that upon which the mind of Epictetus was specially curious, and specially informed, since he would naturally examine every form of belief in his own day existing in the empire, we can by no means conclude from his general silence about Christians that they were unknown or unobserved by him. Moreover, if there are resemblances in him to Christian tones of thought which no Greek heathen showed before him, the inference is, to say the least, fair that we see in these resemblances a working of that leaven which touched numberless bosoms among the heathen, in whom desertion of the heathen standing-ground did not follow.

The system of Epictetus would have transformed the existing heathen worship, but could never have restored it. It would have allowed the mythological gods to continue their existence as parts of a physical whole. It is convenient to Epictetus to vest his conceptions in the usual phraseology. Thus he continually entitles his own supreme God, Zeus. In this sense his system might be called a reconciliation between philosophy and religion; but neither the supreme God nor the subordinate gods were personal beings at all in the mind of Epictetus. Such a teaching could not obtain any hold upon the mass of mankind; but if it could have rooted itself in men's minds, the worship and its deities must have dropped away, silently absorbed in the all-embracing and all-consuming whole of which they had been partial and temporary manifestations. But the character of Plutarch's piety was essentially different, for he attempted to range all souls of men, heroes, demons, stellar or heavenly gods under the headship of one supreme God, and all these were to him real beings, as the last and highest was real. His conception of personality is no doubt imperfect, like that of his master Plato; and on his mind, as on that of Plato, the eternity and independence of matter impinged as a hostile power which he could not subdue: but nevertheless souls from the highest to the lowest have in his conception not only intelligence but will. Thus worship to him was a reality, and his attitude to his country's gods was that of a religious mind. He would undo the work of mythology, disengage from the fables of the poets the truths which lay beneath them, and so restore the divine monarchy. The reconciliation here between philosophy and religion was genuine. The philosophy, if it prevailed, did not tend to transform the character of the religion, but to purify and renovate it. However much the Neostoic and Neoplatonic school, under the influences surrounding them, inclined to agree together in certain humanitarian doctrines, which are very marked both in Epictetus and in Plutarch, such as the recognition of man's dignity in the slave, the enforcement of men's universal brotherhood, the injunction of kindness to all and sympathy with all, there is this essential divergence between them. The Stoic is simply a pantheist; the Platonist acknowledges a God independent of matter, though unable fully to subdue it, whose will corresponds to his intelligence.

Epictetus and Plutarch were the most distinguished

of their own time, the former as a teacher, the latter as a writer: as well as those who have had by far the greatest influence on the generations which have succeeded them. They represent the Stoic and Platonic mind in the phase which it assumed at the beginning of the second century. Let us add to them another Greek who is likewise of the same epoch, Dio of Prusa, surnamed for his eloquence the golden tongue, the most successful Rhetor, or as we should now call him Lecturer, of the day. Dio's occupation was to go from city to city of the great empire, and deliver addresses to the cultured class of society. Eclectic in his creed, that is, serving up such a mixture of Stoic and Platonic views as would please the palate of his hearers, and only partially a philosopher, he yet professed to be a physician of souls. He was born about A.D. 50, and he lived at least to the end of Trajan's reign, say to 120. When Domitian made his raid upon the philosophers he was expelled from Rome, and wandered for some time among the barbarians on the banks of the Danube. But with Nerva's accession a new time opened for him, which was one of unbroken prosperity until his death. His lectures procured him fame, while they increased his already large patrimonial wealth, and he enjoyed the special favour of the Emperor Trajan. Thus he was acceptable both to the class which he addressed, and to the ruling sovereign, and we can be sure that what he put forth fairly exhibited the prevailing spirit of the time. Now two of his extant orations, the twelfth and thirty-sixth, give us in considerable detail his conception of the universe and of the power ruling it. Thus he considers the only [1] strong and indissoluble principle of communion

---

[1] Orat. xxxvi. p. 46. Edit. Morel.

and justice to be the conjunction of the human race with the divine in the common possession of reason. According to this the universe may be well called a city not under the dominion of indifferent or petty rulers or tyrants, or democracies, or oligarchies, not severed into seditions and parties through all time by such-like diseases, but arranged as the best and wisest of kingdoms, whose law is a law of harmony and friendship. For a supreme legislator, who is the absolute lord of all being, enjoins the same thing upon mortals and immortals, and gives as a sample his own government. Divine poets learned from the muses to call him Father of gods and men. For[1] this whole universe, when it came forth completed by the wisest art, fresh from its Maker's hands, brilliant and lucid in all its parts, knew no infancy or weakness, after the fashion of human and mortal nature, but was from the beginning in its prime, and its maker and father beholding it, took not pleasure, for this is a mean and low expression, but rejoiced and exulted to see the gods present before him. . . . For[2] he is the common king and ruler and judge and father of men and gods, the dispenser also of peace and war, if only we be able to chant his nature and his power in few words falling far beneath his worth.

Now[3] the opinion and conception concerning the nature of the gods in general, and especially respecting the ruler of them all, is first of all common to the whole race of man, Greek and barbarian alike, being necessary and innate in every one who has reason without mortal teacher and initiator; and thus it is infallible, both because of the kinship existing, and the many evidences of the truth which do not admit of

[1] Orat. xxxvi. p. 454.   [2] Orat. xii. p. 199.   [3] *Ibid.* p. 201.

dulness or neglect. For the divine wonders of heaven and the stars, of the sun and moon, of day and night, the many-voiced sounds of winds and forests and rivers and sea, of tame and wild beasts, and the human voice itself so full of sweetness and of beauty, which has power to give a name to every object of the intellect, these are the things in the midst of which men live, not far off nor outside "the Divine," so that they could not remain without understanding. How then could they be ignorant or have no conception of their own Sower and Planter, Preserver and Nourisher, filled as they were with the divine nature by seeing and hearing and every sense, living on the earth, but having light from heaven and food in abundance by the gift and provision of their first father, God?

This innate conception of God finds further a fourfold expression, in the poet, in the legislator, in the artist, and last of all perhaps the truest and most perfect in the philosopher. And [1] here we must excuse the necessity under which the artist lies of expressing by the human shape that intelligence and wisdom which neither painter nor sculptor can render as they are in themselves. Thus the human body is put upon "the Divine" as a shape to express that reason which has no embodiment to the sight and no form in the conception. It is a symbol better than those forms of animals used, as is said, by some barbarians to express "the Divine." It is better to have such a symbol than to be without any visible representation, because of that strong love which is in all men to honour and worship, to touch "the Divine": just as little children, torn away from father and mother, have an inexpressible yearning in their dreams to stretch forth their

[1] Orat. xii. pp. 207-211.

hands to them. Thus it is that men justly loving the gods for their benefactions and their relationship are eager in every way to be with them and to converse with them.

Now [1] this first and immortal parent, this giver of life and all good things, this common Father and Saviour and Guardian of men, is none other than all who are of Greek lineage term their ancestral Zeus, and he is represented by Phidias as watching over serene and peaceful Greece, so far as it was possible for mortal conception to imitate the divine and unattainable nature.

This Father of gods and men is the architect and arranger of the whole universe, which he administers for the general good of all. He has impressed perfect order and harmony on it from the beginning, so that it had no infancy, no weakness. He maintains that order and harmony in it. The relation between him and the other gods is not defined further than that he is called generally their father and leader. Are they parts of him, or ministers? This question is left unsolved. It seems as if it were unasked. He is the sovereign reason, and they are immortal, and share that reason, as men who are mortal share it, but in a lesser degree, so that the whole race of gods and men form together "that which has reason." [2] But while this supreme God is the architect of the universe, and is so exhibited with all the pomp of language which Dio can command, the notion of creation is absent. His wisdom is impressed upon matter, and the result is that infinite variety of form combined with purpose which the world presents, but the question how matter came there to be operated

[1] Orat. xii. pp. 205, 215.   [2] τὸ λογικόν.

upon is avoided. "For¹ this first and most perfect architect took for that in which his art should work the universal matter of the whole." All power, wisdom, and goodness, which can be assigned to a God who is not a Creator, are assigned to him by Dio.

Again, the kinship between God and man—the sharing, that is, of the divine reason, which distinguishes the divine and the human race, and it alone—is strongly dwelt upon, and that on its two sides; on the side of the deity as a reason for the unfailing divine solicitude about all men, on the side of man as a reason for reciprocal philanthropy between all men without regard to national distinctions. For the contracted view of nationalism is entirely overleapt by Dio. The divine² polity is a communion of gods and men sharing law and citizenship between all who possess reason and prudence, and Zeus presides over hospitality by his name Xenios, because we must esteem no man strange to us, and he draws together all men and wills them to be friends to each other, and no one an enemy. In short, the whole humanitarian doctrine is as completely the possession of Dio as of Epictetus and Plutarch. It is a point in which the Stoic, the Platonist, and the Eclectic are altogether of one mind, and which forms a basis of their teaching.

But whence did Dio derive the conception of this supreme architect of the universe who put the world together by His moulding art out of universal matter, and who rules it with equity and unfailing care? He alleges that all men by an intuitive judgment accept

---

¹ οὗτος γὰρ δὴ πρῶτος καὶ τελειότατος δημιουργὸς χορηγὸν λαβὼν τῆς ἑαυτοῦ τέχνης . . . τὴν πᾶσαν τοῦ παντὸς ὕλην. Orat. xii. p. 217.
² Orat. xxxvi. p. 448; xii. p. 216.

THE STANDING-GROUND OF PHILOSOPHY 173

such a God; that the legislator, the poet, the artist, and last of all the philosopher, do but exert their several powers to give expression, as each best may, to this intuitive judgment. But was he in this likewise a Platonist? Had Plato preceded him by nearly five hundred years in setting forth such a God? In the *Timæus* we certainly find delineated an agent conceived as preceding the world, a divine constructor or artist who puts together the universe, which is a mixed generation of mind and necessity: who, so far as mind, or intelligent force, can persuade matter, which it finds pre-existing, and in which resides an "erratic,[1] irregular, random causality," to yield to its sway, produces what is best under the circumstances. The Kosmos, the orderly arrangement which extends through all nature, is the result of his skill. "This Kosmos, having received its complement of animals, mortal and immortal, has become greatest, best, most beautiful and most perfect, a visible animal comprehending all things visible, a perceivable God, the image of the cogitable God: this Uranus, one and only-begotten."

So far as this Dio's Demiurge is the reproduction of Plato's. But now we come to an important variation between them. The Demiurge of Plato is entirely distinct from the generated gods. First he makes the Kosmos, which has both a soul to itself implanted by him, and a body of the primordial matter, and so is itself a god, but with many separate gods resident within it, or attached to it. Such are the sun, the moon, the planets, the stars, which are generated or constructed by the Demiurge as portions or members

---

[1] Grote, who (*Plato*, iii. 293) translates, as follows, the last words of the *Timæus*.

of the Kosmos, their bodies out of fire and other elements, their souls of the Forms called Identity and Diversity. Here, then, Plato supposes the physical construction of a complete world by his Demiurge. But after such a construction, what is he to do with the mythological gods believed in by the people among whom he lived? The account which he had given of the formation of the world, or, as he terms it,[1] "what we have said of the nature of the visible and generated gods," was plainly quite incompatible with the existence of these others. He dismisses them in the following words: "To speak of the other deities and to know their generation is beyond our faculties, but we must trust to what those of old have said, for they were, as they said, descendants of the gods, and surely knew their own ancestors. It is impossible, then, to disbelieve the children of gods, although what they say is destitute both of probable and necessary proof; but as they assert that they are recounting family matters, we must obey the laws and credit them. Now according to them the generation of these gods was thus:— Oceanus and Tethys were children of Earth and Heaven, and Phorcys, Kronos, and Rhea and the rest were children of these; but children of Kronos and Rhea were Zeus and Hera, and all that we know are called their brethren, and others still who were their progeny."[2] Thus all the traditional gods of Greece, including Zeus, are practically got rid of by Plato, while his Demiurge stands at an immeasurable height above the gods whom he has generated. For Plato next supposes the Demiurge to call together both all those who revolve around us visibly, being

---

[1] *Timæus*, sec. 15.   [2] *Timæus*, sec. 16.

the physical gods first described, and those who show themselves when they please, being the traditional gods whom he had just shunted aside, and to address them thus: "Ye gods of gods, of whom I am the constructor and father, all things formed by me are in virtue of my will indissoluble. Whatever, indeed, has been composed is dissoluble, but to desire to dissolve what is beautifully harmonised and well disposed would be a mark of evil. Now inasmuch as you are generated, you are not immortal, nor absolutely indissoluble, yet you shall never be dissolved, nor be subject to the lot of death, in virtue of my will, which is a greater and more powerful bond than what at your generation bound you together."

Thus the Demiurge of Plato has no resemblance to the Zeus of Grecian tradition, whereas, on the other hand, Dio's supreme God is simply the ancestral Zeus exalted by all the attributes of power, wisdom, and goodness which can be given to a constructing intelligence until he becomes the Demiurge of Plato; that is, Dio has united himself with that mythology which Plato put aside. He has invested the form of the son of Kronos with a certain divine unity, so that the gods and goddesses who were of equal lineage and like power with himself recede into something like his ministers. They would be simply his ministers, if the notion of creation had entered into Dio's mind. A species of monotheism tries to arrange itself with the manifold forms of the Greek polytheism. It is the alliance of philosophy with the established worship under the empire, whose lord is the god upon earth, the bearer of the whole civil power, but likewise the visible image of the Capitoline Jupiter.

Now these three men, Epictetus, Plutarch, and Dio

Chrysostomus represent very sufficiently all the phases of the Greek mind of their time. In one we have the Stoic, in another the Platonist, in the third the popular semi-philosopher and lecturer, who combined the Stoic doctrine of reason with the Platonic view of the divine unity. All profess a strong belief in the divine providence, and are never weary of extolling the wisdom of its rule. Again, all three are thoroughly penetrated with the doctrine of the universal brotherhood of men, and draw as a conclusion from it the reciprocal duties of kindness and friendship. They are not so much citizens of Rome as preachers of a human race.

But now, turning from these varieties of the Greek mind, let us compare them with four distinguished writers and an emperor, who were all Latins and just of the same time. How do they stand in reference to Tacitus, the younger Pliny, Suetonius, Juvenal, and Trajan? Tacitus is neither a Stoic nor a Platonic monotheist: he seems to accept the gods of his country, to acknowledge their power and their interference in the affairs of men, yet he is full of painful doubts as to the fact of a divine providence. The lot of men is dark to him altogether. He would fain hope that at least the more deserving have some existence after death. He may be said to acknowledge and defend the Olympian assembly as part of the Roman constitution. He is indefinitely nearer to Cicero's world than his Greek contemporaries. For philosophy altogether he had somewhat of the old Roman scorn. Thus he quotes his friend and father-in-law Agricola as saying of himself that in early youth he would have pursued the study of philosophy more keenly than a Roman and a senator should, but for his mother's prudent tempering of that burning love of knowledge. So he makes Helvidius Priscus an exception to the majority, inasmuch as he did not prosecute Stoic philosophy as a cover for a life of lazy inactivity, but to find in it a dauntless spirit for the dangers of a statesman's duties.[1] The world of Tacitus, in short, is not a world for Greek thinkers, but for Roman workers. Trajan fulfils his ideal of an emperor, and the great soldier whose days are given up to the ceaseless labours of government, who rules by and with his senate, is as a light which shines before Tacitus "at the beginning of that most blessed age." The principate, borne by him, almost redeemed, by maintaining liberty while it saved society, the "headlong servitude" of Rome under Tiberius, the madness of Caius, the stupidity of Claudius, the fiddling, the debauchery, and the cruelty of Nero, the suspicious tyranny of Domitian. The same is the attitude of his friend the younger Pliny, who built temples as well as inaugurated schools for his poorer neighbours. Suetonius is a more decided believer than either in the gods according to the popular belief. The same tone and temper may be observed in Juvenal, but then it should be added that in him some of the noblest precepts and principles of Stoicism are found together with belief in the old gods. Thus in his own town of Aquinum he dedicated an offering to Ceres in fulfilment of a vow. It is of the gods collectively that he expresses his belief in a providence answering man's prayers better than the suppliant himself would know how to answer them. It has been said that all the records of classical Greek literature do not produce a sentiment so favourable to the heathen gods as that contained in

[1] Tacitus, *Agricola*, 4; *Hist.* iv. 5; *Agricola*, 3.

his famous verse, "More dear to them than to himself is man;" and this sedulous worshipper of the old gods has likewise blent together the best parts of Platonic and Stoic theory in a passage which represents the divine unity, the gift of reason proceeding from the common nature of man, and the reciprocal duties of men to each other derived from this common origin.

> "This marks our birth,
> The great distinction from the beasts of earth.
> And therefore gifted with superior powers
> And capable of things divine, 'tis ours
> To learn and practise every useful art,
> And from high heaven deduce that better part,
> That moral sense, denied to creatures prone
> And downward bent, and found with man alone.
> For he who gave this vast machine to roll
> Breathed life in them, in us a reasoning soul,
> That kindred feelings might our state improve,
> And mutual wants conduct to mutual love."[1]

Here Juvenal in one of his happier moments breathes a sense of the dignity of man's destiny which is far above the moral tone of his three contemporaries, for they may be said to be heathen of the old block. The currents which have reached the Greek mind have but slightly touched them. Not that even Trajan, the unliterary soldier, and much less the philosophic historian and the well-read man of letters, were ignorant of the theories which we find in Epictetus and Plutarch and Dio. They knew of them doubtless: they listened to them: they would themselves be auditors of many philosophic lectures at Rome, or Athens, or Alexandria: but they reckoned philosophy a Greek science, just as before and after them even Romans who philosophised wrote in Greek. Such were Cor-

[1] *Sat.* xv. 142-150. Gifford's translation.

nutus, Musonius Rufus, Favorinus, Marcus Aurelius,
while the vast majority of philosophical teachers
throughout the empire, in the western as well as
the eastern parts, were Greeks. But the life of
these five, who may be said to represent very fairly
the senate, the bar, and the literature of Rome in
their day, was on the old Roman standing-ground of
Augustus, though they would have claimed to be
Roman gentlemen of a more advanced civilisation,
which began already to concern itself with the education of the poor, and even with orphanages. Further,
in considering this latter tendency it should not be
forgotten that Tacitus in his language and Pliny and
Trajan in their acts showed a very complete hatred of
Christianity. Trajan in his rescripts to Pliny appeals
to his age as having a standard of humanity superior
to the preceding time; and it was he who established
on a firm basis the condemnation of Christianity as an
illicit religion. Again, the learned and elegant lawyer
who appears in his letters with all the refined tastes
and pursuits of an English gentleman in the nineteenth century, dismisses to summary execution men
and women against whom nothing could be alleged
but meeting together to address worship to Christ as
God. Thus the heavy sentence which concludes the
acts of martyrdom of St. Ignatius receives the fullest
verisimilitude from the official proceedings of Pliny, as
described by his own pen to his master Trajan, who
replies to him with affectionate commendation. The
emperor who sentences the martyr corresponds exactly
to the emperor who instructs the prefect.

Taking these seven men, Epictetus, Plutarch, and
Dio on the one hand, Juvenal, Tacitus, Pliny, and
Suetonius on the other, they offer no inadequate

specimen of that compound society which the great
Emperor Trajan ruled. The contrast in them between
the Greek and Latin mind is striking. Certainly
Tacitus is the ablest and most original of the seven:
but his religious and philosophic standing-ground is
perhaps the most obscure. Indeed, religion and philosophy for him belong to the policy of the empire.
They have no deep place in his heart. It is not the
destiny of man but the destiny of Rome which moves
him. And if he does ever make a remark upon providence or human life in general, doubt and gloom seem
to invade his clear practical intellect, and despondency
to quench his feeling as a patriot. Pliny is the careful administrator, the polished man of letters, who is
ready for any philosophic discussion with his friends,
and worships his country's gods without hesitation.
These are the Latin friends and servants of the emperor, while in Trajan himself we see the embodiment
of the valour, the statesmanship, the practical governing qualities which sustained the Roman world, and
which met with entire homage from such men as
Tacitus and Pliny. But it is to the Greeks that we
must look for any theory as to the deeper problems
which surround human life. It was the provincials
who thought for the humanity which Rome governed.
Now Epictetus, Dio, and Plutarch were likewise valued
and honoured by Trajan: they represent the learning
and intellectual activity of the Greek portion of his
empire: and in them we find a very definite standing-
ground taken up as to the relation between philosophy
and the existing belief and worship. From their time
we may say that philosophy, as disseminated by Greek
teachers to the cultured classes, contained two main
elements, of which the first is the entertainment of

THE STANDING-GROUND OF PHILOSOPHY 181

an exoteric mind much after Plutarch's pattern with regard to a supreme God, of whom all the mythological or elemental gods are parts or ministers; and the second is the maintenance in practical life of all the worship sanctioned by the laws. This means that the Greek thinkers were attempting to give a scientific basis to the belief in the heathen gods which was expressed in their worship, and on this basis to reconcile philosophy with religion. Such a reconciliation had never been thought of up to the times of Augustus and Tiberius, for its need had not been felt. Philosophy under various forms had been persistent in one thing, its enmity to the existing religious worship. By it the thinking and cultured classes were alienated from that worship, and the alienation was equally complete whether the Stoic, the Epicurean, or the Sceptic form of thought was preferred. But then the worship from which the bias of cultured thought led men away had during all this time encountered no external enemy of its own kind. I pass over the attraction of individual minds in the time of the empire to Syrian or Egyptian gods as not counting on a large scale. Viewed as a whole, no other worship had competed with it. It was in no danger of falling by those various forms of philosophy, which, as a whole, consisted mainly in negation. Prayer and sacrifice supply an universal need in man which cannot be satisfied by denying that it exists. So in the times we have mentioned philosophic unbelief went on to a certain extent in the few minds which form the cultured classes, while the great mass still found support in frequenting the established rites: and, further also, the philosopher in practice did not sever himself from that worship as a custom and habit of life. But this new reconciliation between philosophy and religion, by which it was attempted to restore a certain monotheism, and to reduce to order and harmony the vast multiplication of heathen deities, indicated that some new power had arisen, which it was attempting to meet. Why did Epictetus speak of man as being the son of God, possessing in his own nature a dignity universal and indefeasible, which is superior to all gradations of fictitious rank, and places the beggar who realises that dignity above the emperor who is only proud of the rank? Why did Plutarch and Dio bring forth again Plato's Demiurge, but no longer half concealed in the intricate recesses of philosophic thought, "hard to find out and impossible to describe to all"? Why did they not only invest him with all except creative power, wisdom, and goodness, but further identify him with the Zeus of Greek mythology? In the system of the Stoics, it is true, as we find it delineated in Cicero, the universe had become a city, a kingdom ordered with supreme wisdom and friendship towards man by the best of legislators and fathers, when so it pleased them to represent, as in the hymn of Cleanthes, that creation of their abstract reasoning, the terrible form of necessity. But now the crowd of Olympian deities, the peers of Jove who in the popular belief held over them but an undefined primacy, appeared his obedient satellites in the fervent exaltation of his throne which Plutarch and Dio celebrated. Something more powerful than philosophy had set the heathen worship on its defence, when philosophy, deserting its old ground, applied itself to build up the temple and to justify the rite, and to defend the gods to whom the temple was built and the rite

offered. Yet this is what we see from the beginning
of Trajan's reign, and that standing-ground thus taken
up is never again relinquished. It continues to be
the basis of operation on which the heathen defenders
of Olympus stand, until the termination of the conflict
with the Christian Church.

Whatever appears in common in three such teachers
as Epictetus, Plutarch, and Dio Chrysostomus may be
securely predicated of the whole Greek mind which
they represent. Now such is the notion of God and
Providence which is of perpetual recurrence in them.
The universe is most wisely governed according to
them by one maker, that is composer and arranger,
and for the good of man, who is distinguished from
all other animals by the possession of reason, which
he has in common with this God. When speaking of
God and Providence in this general relation they are
rigid monotheists, but then, whenever it suits their
turn, they are as completely polytheists, using the
gods, like men, as parts of the divine intelligence.
By this sort of legerdemain two results are accomplished: on the one hand, for the philosophic mind
they approve the unity, wisdom, and power of the
universe; on the other hand, for the popular mind
they defend and justify all the existing worship of all
the established deities. Moreover, the God whom
they so exalt as the maker and maintainer of the
universe is called by the name of the national god of
the Roman empire, Zeus or Jupiter; and as they thus
exalt him, every other power seems to sink into insignificance before him, so that passages may be taken
from them which seem to convey almost a Christian
conception of God; but then immediately other passages may be cited in which the deities are mentioned

collectively, or any particular deity is specified, and piety to them is inculcated on the common ground of piety to him, and the worship paid to them is exactly identical with the worship paid to him—as for instance in the great and most significant rite of sacrifice —nor is their relation to him anywhere distinctly stated. So far, indeed, as the passing from the singular to the plural appellation, and the reverse, so that the monotheistic and polytheistic expression is interchanged, as if equivalent, this is found in the classical age of Greek literature, in Thucydides, Xenophon, Pindar, Æschylus, and the poets generally.[1] If this were all, Epictetus and Plutarch would in this only be instances of a common and ancient interchange, or as it were unconscious indifference in the use of *one* or *many* when speaking of "the Divine." What distinguishes them is the force and explicitness with which they bring out the conception of a divine monarchy, leaving as it seems no place for any other ruling power than that one which they have so exalted.

But if what we have now noted in these three conspicuous specimens of Greek thought supplies ground for the conclusion that a moral force was acting on the thinking part of the heathen world so strong as to alter the bearing of philosophy towards religion, let us examine more closely one of these teachers and see whether he does not supply specific imitations of the power which had thus arisen, and which he studiously keeps out of sight. Epictetus gives us, under the name of the Cynic, his ideal character of the teacher who is to propagate the philosophy which is likewise

[1] See Nägelsbach, *Nachhomerische Theologie*, ch. ii. sec. 22, pp. 139, 140, for some remarkable instances of this.

THE STANDING-GROUND OF PHILOSOPHY 185

his religion. It is well worthy of being considered. The occasion[1] is this. One of his disciples, who had an inclination to be a Cynic, asked him to give his conception of that work. "Well," said he, "let us consider it at leisure. So much I may say at once, that whoever sets his hand to such a work without God is heaven-struck, and will only disgrace himself publicly. For no one enters into a well-ordered house and says, 'I am to be steward.' Or else its lord turning upon him and seeing him ruling with insolence takes him and cuts him in two. So, too, it happens in this great city, for here also there is a master[2] of the house, who arranges everything in due order. Thou art a sun: thou canst make the year and the seasons by thy revolutions, increase and nourish the fruits, raise and lay the winds, and warm sufficiently the bodies of men. Go: make thy revolution, and move things from the highest to the lowest. . . . Thou art a calf: when the lion shows himself, get out of his way, or thou wilt fare ill. . . . Thou art a bull: go and fight, for this is thy part and thou canst do it. Thou canst lead the army against Troy: be thou Agamemnon. . . . Thou canst fight a duel with Hector: be thou Achilles. . . . But if Thersites had come up and claimed the command, either he would not have got it, or he would have made an ignominious failure before many witnesses. So therefore thou: take good counsel: know thyself: examine thy con-

---

[1] Epictetus, iii. 22, pp. 443-472. Upton's Edit.
[2] δικοδεσπότης, the word which occurs so often in the parables. It is curious to compare this passage with Luke xii. 39-48. In both there is the δικοδεσπότης and the οἰκονόμος. In the one the master seeing the steward behaving himself in an unseemly manner, ἐλκύσας ἔτεμεν. In the other, διχοτομήσει αὐτόν. But the similarity of *tone* is even more striking than that of the words or the thought. I suspect that Arrian had St. Luke's narrative before him.

science: attempt it not without God. But first of
all make that which rules thee pure and clear. Conscience alone can give thee this power. But you
must know that the teacher is a messenger sent from
Jupiter to men concerning what is good and evil, to
show them that they are in error, and seek the essence
of good and evil where it is not, but lay not to heart
where it is. . . . Tell us then, sir messenger and
watchman, where good is. 'O men,' he says, ' whither
go ye? What do ye? You seek happiness and that
which should rule you where it is not, and believe
not when another shows it you. Why do you seek
it *without?* Is it in the body or in wealth? See
those who are now rich, of what sorrow their life is
full. Is it in holding office? Not so, or those who
have been twice or thrice consul would be happy, but
they are not. It is where you think not, and where
you will not seek it. For had you willed, you would
have found it in yourselves.' . . . And remember, the
teacher must be entirely in the service of God without
distraction, able to visit men, not bound to his private
business, nor embarrassed with relations, which if he
disregard he will lose his character for integrity, while
if he maintain them he will destroy the messenger,
the watchman and the herald of the gods. For think,
if he has got to provide for a father-in-law or the
other relations of a wife, or a wife herself, or children
and their needs. Where, I pray you, would be that
king who provides for the common good, to whom
peoples are committed and who has so many cares,
who has to be [1] bishop over others, over the married,
over those who have children, to see who treats his

[1] ὃν δεῖ τοὺς ἄλλους ἐπισκοπεῖν, p. 462, and οἱ ἐπισκοποῦντες πάντας κατὰ δύναμιν ἀνθρώπους, p. 463.

wife well, and who ill, who quarrels, what house is well and what ill managed; who must make his rounds like a physician, and feel pulses. To one patient he says, 'You have a fever;' to another, 'You have headache;' to another, 'You have the gout, You, sir, must take exercise; You, sir, must eat; You must avoid the bath; You must have an operation; You must be cauterised.' How can one who is bound by domestic duties find leisure for this? Must he not find clothes for his children, send them to school with satchel? . . . Considering, then, the present distress,[1] we think not marriage good for the teacher. But then, say you, how will he maintain society? Good heavens, is it a greater benefit to men to bring two or three ill-conditioned children among them, than to be a bishop over them, to see what they do, how they live, what they take care of and what they neglect? Which did greater good to the Thebans, they who left them children, or Epaminondas, who died childless? Who contributed most to society? Priam, Danaus, Æolus, with their wretched broods of fifty, or Homer? Shall military or civil command debar from marriage and family life, and the teacher's royalty not be deemed an equivalent? Do not we fail to see his greatness? For, my friend, he has made all men his children; the men he counts for sons, the women for daughters. Thus he approaches all; thus he cares for all. Do you suppose that it is as a busybody that he censures? Nay, it is as father, as brother, as servant of the common father, Zeus. . . . Kings and tyrants have guards with arms

[1] τοιαύτης οὔσης καταστάσεως, οἵα νῦν ἐστιν, ὡς ἐν παρατάξει, p. 461. οὕτω] ζητοῦντες οὐχ 'εὑρίσκομεν ταύτῃ τῇ καταστάσει προηγούμενον τῷ Κυνικῷ τὸ πρᾶγμα, p. 463.

in their hands, and so they can punish, but it is conscience only which gives the teacher a power which makes up to him for the want of armed force. When it is seen that he has kept vigil and laboured for men; has gone pure to bed and risen purer still; when all his thoughts are those of a friend to the gods, of their minister, of one who shares the government of Jupiter; why should he not speak freely to his own brethren, to his own children, his own kinsmen? Therefore he is no busybody or meddler, when he acts the bishop over human things, for they are his own. Or else call the general a busybody, when he inspects and reviews and punishes his soldiers. . . . What to him is emperor, or proconsul, or any one, save he who sent him, and whom he serves, Jupiter: and whatever he suffers from them he knows that he is tried and examined by Jupiter. And how is it possible for one who possesses nothing, who is naked, houseless, hearthless, squalid, a servant, citiless, to lead a tranquil life? Behold, God has sent one to us to show by facts that it is possible. Behold me, that I am citiless, houseless, without possession or servant. I sleep on the ground. I have no wife, no children, no reception-room, only the earth and sky and one mat. And what is wanting to me? Am I not without pain? Am I not without fear? Am I not free?"

Let us realise by whom these words are said to be spoken. They were collected some time after his death, not earlier certainly than the year 130, by the disciple of a heathen philosopher, who was a man of middle age at the death of the last surviving Apostle, St. John. What is remarkable about them is that no such conception of the teacher as they give had ever been carried out by any one in the heathen world of whom word has come down to us before the time when Epictetus is supposed to have spoken them. A single Stoic in the lifetime of Epictetus, by name Demetrius, had indeed won universal respect by the independence and freedom of his life, but neither he, nor Diogenes, to whom Epictetus refers, represents the other features of this character, which are stamped with a divine messenger's solicitude for his fellow-men, a sacred charge committed to him from above which he must execute, an abnegation of self, and a sacrifice for others of the dearest family relations. But on the other hand the Roman world for sixty years before these words are said to be uttered, for ninety years before they are published, had been sown by such teachers, who carried their lives in their hands, fearing neither emperor nor consul; who proclaimed themselves to be messengers, to be stewards, to be heralds of God; who claimed to inspect the lives and thoughts of those whom they taught, to treat the men as brethren, the women as daughters, who abstained from marriage, because "no man being a soldier to God entangleth himself with secular business." Two of such men Epictetus in his youth, when a slave in the house of Epaphroditus, had known to have disregarded all the terrors of a tyrant, had known them to have been the one crucified, the other beheaded, at Rome for their teaching, and to have encountered this death simply for carrying out to the very life the portrait of a teacher which he has here drawn. Now it is singular that the only passage in which Epictetus refers by name to Christians informs us that he was acquainted with this their heroism. "What,"[1] he says, "makes

---

[1] Epictetus, iv. 7.

the tyrant terrible? His guards and their swords. If a child then feels no fear in approaching these guards, is it because he has no perception of these things? Suppose then a man to perceive these guards and their swords, but to approach the tyrant for the very purpose of seeking death, will he fear the guards? He seeks the very thing for which they are terrible. Suppose, then, one caring neither to die, nor to live, but as it may turn out, to approach him, may he not do so fearlessly? But as this man is minded in regard to his body, let another be minded in regard to possessing property, or children, and wife, and in a word through some madness or want of sense be so disposed as to care nothing for having or not having these things; or as children play with oyster-shells, caring nothing about the shells but much about the game, so let this supposed man care nothing about the subject-matter, but everything about the game and his conduct therein, what tyrant, what guards or their swords will cause him fear? Well then, can a man be so disposed towards these things by madness, and *the Galileans, because it is their wont*, and can no one by force of reason and proof learn that God has made all things in the world, and the whole world itself effecting its purpose and being its end in itself, and its parts for the use of the whole?" Epictetus then was well aware that the Galileans, "because it was their wont," had resolution to confront death and suffer the loss of all things. He knew that there was something in their life which enabled them to reach the utmost height of heroism which he imagines for his ideal teacher. He portrays that teacher in colours which irresistibly remind one of St. Peter and St. Paul, and all that race of Apostolic missionaries of which they were the leaders. His own heathenism supplies him with no original for a portrait, which at least had been exhibited during his lifetime in a great number of instances by these Galileans: one point of which, the most striking and the rarest, he himself in another place of his sayings attributes to them as specially characteristic of them. Taking into account the time and the places at which Epictetus lived, and the studies on which his mind was engrossed, is there any sufficient reason to think that he was so ignorant about Christians in general, their doctrine and their mode of life, as his silence with respect to them has led some to conclude? If he who drew the character of the teacher above cited was not acquainted with Christians, how came he to put together a very original and marked portraiture such as in its entirety had never been seen among Greeks or Romans, but had been presented again and again in his own time by the first teachers of the Church? Where was the Stoic ever seen who had treated all men of whatever nation or race or quality of rank as his brethren, all women as his daughters, who had watched over them with solicitude, and with utter disregard of self, who had resigned all domestic affections, not out of apathy, but in order to bestow himself, his life, and its labours upon others? Myriads of Christian teachers have done this. No philosopher has ever done it. But whence did Epictetus draw the conception of doing it? If Stoicism from its origin contained within itself the germ of such a flower, why did it never produce a specimen until the Roman world had been filled with the fragrance of the Christian fruit?

Not but what Epictetus is entirely heathen in the ground which he assigns for his teacher's fearlessness.

To him the body and the soul do not make the one personality of man. "This[1] poor body is nothing to me: its parts are nothing to me. Death, let it come when it will, in whole or in part. ... For if death be any evil it is equally an evil, whether in company with others or alone. But will it be anything else but the separation of this poor body and the soul? Nothing." And he proceeds to mention that there is always in case of need the option of suicide. "Is the door shut? May you not die? You may."

The fair conclusion is that Epictetus having had the sufferings of Christians brought vividly before him in his youth, and acknowledging their heroism, was more or less acquainted with their doctrine, and that he was not unaffected by the two things, but nevertheless preferred his old heathen standing-ground: as so many since in the full blaze of Christian light and the full knowledge of Christian practice during hundreds of years before them, have done like him in their day. But it results that the heathenism of Epictetus, as that of Plutarch and Dio Chrysostomus, is not that of Cicero or Augustus. A new light has shone upon their moral world, a new order of ideas has passed before their minds. A very learned writer[2] observes that "their doctrines concerning the relation of the individual to humanity in general breathe as strongly a Christian spirit as they bear witness to the most decided break with what had been, specifically, the ancient views of the world." "Stoicism and Cynicism raised themselves in this time to a height and a purity in their moral grasp of human rights and human duties which had not been reached in

---

[1] Epictetus, iii. 22, p. 447.
[2] Friedlaender, *Sittengeschichte Roms*, iii. 609, 610.

earlier antiquity." "The Stoic principle that all men belong to each other, who, as Epictetus expresses it, all have God for their father, and therefore are brethren, was first followed out by the Stoics of this age to its full range, and to its last consequence." This very important and pregnant fact is not only stated by this writer, but admitted by the most able historians of Greek philosophy. Some who admit it maintain that this consequence lay in the conception of Stoicism from its beginning, and was produced by its own power. They have to show why a philosophy which existed for three hundred years before our Lord came, never produced these fruits until after these doctrines had been preached by His disciples on the ground of His example, and at the cost of their lives, through the length and breadth of the empire. They have to show why Cicero, with all the stores of Grecian thought before him, and regarding philosophy as the guide of life, never produced such a view of the teacher as we have just quoted from Epictetus. They should further show why his view of slavery is the hard cold view of Plato and Aristotle, without a glimpse of the tenderness for the rights of human nature, which appears in Seneca and Epictetus, and the subsequent school. It is a fact that in the interval the great sacrifice on Calvary had taken place, and the Creator of man had died upon the cross the death of a Roman slave. Before the slave Epictetus obtained honour as a philosopher, the slave Onesimus had become a bishop in the Church. Before the character of the teacher had been sketched by the Stoic, all its fine and exalted points had been exhibited during two generations in the settled order of the Church's missionaries. The reasoned unbelief of modern infidels—who lay special claim to science—is strangely regardless of chronology.

We must now mention the position occupied by philosophers in the Roman empire from the accession of Nerva at the end of the first century until far into the third. Scanty as are the notices which we possess of the intellectual condition of those times, there is enough to warrant the belief that during this period there was in the higher classes of Roman society a lively and a wide-spread interest in philosophy. Philosophical lectures formed a regular part of Roman life, not only in the capital, but in the other great intellectual centres, such as Athens, Alexandria, Marseilles, Tarsus, Rhodes. The great majority of the teachers, whether in the West or East, were Greeks. Whatever opposition there had been to philosophy in the natural character of the Romans, whatever suspicion entertained against it as an unpractical study, leading men away from the duties of active life, whatever dislike of it from the number of its professors who only sought in it the means of enriching themselves, and whose own life was a scandal to the precepts which they enjoined on others, yet undoubtedly much the larger portion of the cultured class even in Rome and the western parts of the empire was fully convinced that philosophy was the best guide to the highest morality.[1] As such it laid claim to the education of youth, and for the greater part the years of philosophical study began after the conclusion of the grammatical and rhetorical course. The ordinary rule was that with the assumption of the toga young men entered upon that discipline which was to introduce and guide them into an upright and well-regulated manhood. Philo-

[1] Friedlaender, iii. 572, 580.

sophy properly comprehended three divisions, Logic, Physics, and Ethics, but the former two of these retreated so far into the background that Ethics appeared to be the essential if not the only subject treated. But it was [1] especially the education of youth in moral virtue which was expected of philosophy. "As gymnastics and medical science provide for the health and strength of the body," says Plutarch in his treatise on education, "so philosophy alone heals the weakness and sickness of the soul. By it and with it we learn what is noble and what base, what right and what wrong, what to strive after and what to avoid: how we have to behave towards the gods, our parents, old age, the laws, strangers, our rulers, our friends, women, children, and men; that we should fear the gods, honour parents, reverence age, obey laws, comply with rulers, love friends, be modest with women, treat children with tenderness, and slaves without insolence: but especially that we be neither thrown off our balance in prosperity nor cast down by adversity, that we neither allow ourselves to be overcome by pleasure, nor become passionate and brutal in our anger. This I hold for the chiefest of all the goods which we gain through philosophy." In another place he says: "Foolish parents who have neglected to give a good education to their children generally begin to pay for this neglect when their sons approach manhood, and instead of leading an orderly and reasonable life plunge themselves into extravagances and low pleasures, draw around them parasites and other ruiners of youth, fall into loose living, gluttony, gambling, commit adulteries and other excesses, by which they risk their lives for pleasure. Had they enjoyed the instruction of a philo-

[1] I take the following from Friedlaender, iii. 586.

sopher, they would not have given themselves up to such courses. As the gardener plucks the weed from the field, so the philosopher plucks the bad impulses of envy, avarice, concupiscence out of the youthful soul, though it must be done sometimes with deep cuts which leave wounds behind. In other cases he works cautiously, as the pruner trims the vine, in order not to cut out the noble together with the base."[1]

From these expressions of Plutarch and from Epictetus it is apparent that in their time philosophy had completely assumed that function of forming the inward life which we assign to religion. Cicero indeed recognised it as the guide of life. Seneca is never weary of extolling it as such. Further also, the philosopher[2] being esteemed not merely as a giver of lessons but as an educator, as one really charged with a cure of souls, necessarily considered it his duty to advance by every means in his power the moral growth of his scholar outside the ordinary time of instruction. By consequence he assumed a right of supervision over the whole conduct which was exercised by giving counsel and exhortation, warning and reproof. We have some remarkable instances of this preserved to us. Thus Seneca described himself in his youth, in the reign of Tiberius, as the first to attend the school of Attalus, and the last to leave it. But not only so: he followed Attalus with questions in his walks, where he found him not only ready, but anxious for learners. And he quotes him as saying that the teacher and the taught should have the same purpose before them, the one to impart, the other to receive, good. He adds that one who frequents a

[1] Plutarch, *De Educ. Puer.* cap. x. 7; *De Vitioso Pudore*, cap. ii.
[2] Friedlaender, lii. 587.

philosopher should every day carry off something good with him, for philosophy exercises a good influence, not merely in the process of study, but by living intercourse, as the sun's light tints one who comes within it, though he came not for that purpose.[1] Thus thirty years later, in the reign of Nero, Persius reminds Cornutus, "the dear friend who was so great a part of his own soul," how when, trembling in the liberty of opening manhood, he was free to cast his eyes on the seductions of Rome, he had fled for refuge to his guidance:

> "Nor did you, gentle sage, the charge decline;
> Then, dext'rous to beguile, your steady line
> Reclaimed, I know not by what winning force,
> My morals, warped from virtue's straighter course;
> While reason pressed incumbent on my soul,
> That struggled to receive the strong control,
> And took, like wax tempered by plastic skill,
> The form your hand imposed: and bears it still."[2]

A hundred years later, in the reign of Antoninus Pius, about the middle of the second century, we have a picture of the relations which the Platonic philosopher Taurus maintained with his scholars. He allowed them not only to ask him questions after the day's instruction, but constantly invited those who wished to be more intimate with him to a frugal supper, in which a dish of Egyptian lentils and a salad made the chief repast. Here they were expected to propose questions and problems which the philosopher resolved. Again, when they were sick he was wont to visit them. Whatever displeased him in their manner of life he could freely censure. "So," says Gellius,

---

[1] Seneca, Epist. cviii.
[2] Persius, v. 30-40. Gifford's translation.

"Taurus used every sort of exhortation to lead his scholars to what was right and good."

It appears that there was no concern of life too important to be beyond the reach of the philosopher's inspection, none too minute to be beneath it. Thus Epictetus gives particular directions as to the dress and the personal habits of those who frequent him, such as the wearing a beard, the arrangement of the hair. In all scruples of conscience, in all difficult positions of life, the philosophers were consulted. When Gellius, who had been appointed a judge at the age of twenty-five, found himself unable to determine a suit, he suspended the sitting and betook himself immediately to the philosopher Favorinus, of whom he begged a decision for this particular case, as well as instruction generally in the office of judge. It would seem that philosophers had to complain rather that they were consulted too much than too little. Epictetus says men came to him as to a greengrocer or a shoemaker, to get articles ready made, and say they had conversed with him, as if he were a statue, without giving themselves the trouble to learn the moral principles on which particular decisions should be founded.[1]

The function of philosophy and the supervision exercised by philosophers over the life of their adherents being in general such as have been described, there were three sorts of relation in which it was exercised. First, there was the house-philosopher. In many great Roman families it had become the usage to have such an appendage. Such a man would serve not only as the educator of the children, but as the counsellor and guide of the elders. Especi-

[1] Epictetus, iii. 9. I take the above examples from Friedlaender.

ally they were considered to prepare people for death, and so in the Cæsarean history the victim not unfrequently spends his last moments in a conversation "with his own philosopher." "Thus[1] Julius Kanus, condemned by Caligula, did not cease to search for the truth in his very end. 'Why are you so sorry?' he said to his friends. 'You ask whether souls are immortal: that I shall presently know.' His philosopher was following him, and now they were nearing that hill on which daily offerings were made to our god, Cæsar. 'What are you thinking of now, Kanus?' said he. 'I intend,' replied Kanus, 'to observe whether at that most rapid moment the soul has a sense of its own going forth.'" In like manner Rubellius Plautus was encouraged by Musonius to prefer death to an uncertain life; and the messenger of death found Thrasea in conversation with the Cynic, Demetrius. "It might be judged," says Tacitus,[2] "by the earnestness of his face and some words more loudly spoken than the rest, that he was inquiring as to the nature of the soul and the separation of body and spirit."

Another species of the house-philosopher was the court-philosopher. Such are mentioned at the courts of Augustus, Nero, Trajan, Hadrian, the Empress Julia Domna. Plutarch defends such a position on the ground that philosophers who give themselves up to form the moral life of private persons deliver only individuals from weaknesses and passions: but he who ennobles the character of a ruler advances and improves thereby the whole State. For such advan-

---

[1] Seneca, *De Tranquill.* 14. "Prosequebatur illum philosophus suus."
[2] Tacitus, *Ann.* 16, 34.

tages he must bear the imputation of courtiership and servility.[1]

But, secondly, a greater and more honourable position for the philosopher was that of holding one of the public chairs in a great city. At central points, like Rome or Athens, the influence of a teacher might extend over the flower of the youth drawn from all the provinces of the empire. A large salary was likewise attached to such a place. This undoubtedly was the greatest field for the dissemination of its doctrine which was open to philosophy.

But, thirdly, while even these public schools were limited in their influence to those who attended them, it is said that a class of philosophers, who gave themselves out as general teachers of morality to the whole human race, were to be found passing from place to place through the empire. These were Cynics, and, though most of them bore a very evil name, now and then men were to be found among them who renounced for the sake of this office the goods and conveniences of life, and gained thereby, like Demonax who lived chiefly at Athens, general consideration and honour. But the character of Demonax, whom Lucian has so greatly extolled, though full of independence and rugged honesty, was totally wanting in that tender regard for the good of others with which Epictetus has invested his teacher. Demonax, who, feeling the weakness of age approaching, put himself to death by fasting when nearly a hundred years old, is supposed to have[2] lived between 50 and 150, or perhaps ten years later.

Plutarch's mode of thought is continued on by his

---

[1] Plutarch, on philosophising with princes, ch. ii., quoted by Friedlaender, iii. 595.   [2] Zeller, iv. 691.

successors in the Platonic school. Three of these may be mentioned whose lives extend from about the time of Plutarch's death to the end of the second century. They are Maximus of Tyre, Apuleius of Madaura, and Celsus. These survive in part to tell us what was probably the teaching of the philosophers whose position in the empire we have been sketching at least as concerns the important points which most interest us. Maximus of Tyre lived under the Antonines: he was half philosopher, half lecturer, that is a Rhetor. Forty-one of the compositions thus delivered remain to us. This then is what a fashionable Platonist would say to his audience at Rome in the time of Marcus Aurelius: "God,[1] as the highest spirit and the highest good, is one only, exalted above time and nature, invisible, ineffable, to be known only by pure reason. He is the architect and ruler of the world, whose never-resting providence embraces and maintains everything, from whom good only comes, without whom no one can be virtuous. Matter serves him as stuff for the forming of the world, and out of this in the last resort all evils spring, the physical immediately, the moral mediately, inasmuch as free-will fails to control the sensual appetites. Between the supreme godhead and the world there are besides innumerable visible gods, demons as middle beings, inferior gods of immortal but passible nature, who dwell on the borders of the heavenly and earthly world, servants of the gods and inspectors of men, various in perfection, temper, and occupation, assigned to the good as personal guardian spirits." Maximus considers these middle beings as the connecting link between the

[1] This analysis is drawn by Zeller, v. 186-188, from a number of passages in the dissertations of Maximus.

sensuous and supersensuous world. He is so strongly convinced of their existence that he not only credits the simplest stories of demon apparitions, but can himself tell of such apparitions, which he has had in a waking state. The human soul likewise is of divine essence, but is imprisoned in the body during its earthly life, and experiences a sort of dream-state, out of which it only incompletely wakes to the remembrance of its true being. It is only in the future life that it may hope for a purer knowledge of the truth, and an immediate intuition of "the divine." Maximus sees in the many kinds of divination a proof of the divine care for man, uniting it as he does with the freedom of the will by the assumption that only what is necessary is foretold unconditionally. Sensuous representations of the godhead by images and myths are defended as helps which most men need, and poets are praised on this ground as being the most ancient philosophers. The particular form of the image is in itself indifferent, but Maximus finds his people's artistic preference of the human form the worthiest.

Syria was the mother of Maximus, and Africa produced in Apuleius of Madaura one very similar to him in philosophical character. He[1] names as the first grounds of being the Godhead, Matter, and Ideas. The Godhead, the perfect Spirit, is ineffable and immense, exalted not only above all passion, but also above all activity. Ideas are simple and eternal forms, the incorporeal patterns of things. Next to God and the Ideas, he calls Reason, or Mind, and the Soul, a being of higher nature, though we are not to seek in him for a definite gradation of divine forces. Like Maximus he places gods and demons between the

[1] This analysis is from Zeller, v. 190.

highest God and the world. He reckons among these gods not only the visible deities, or stars, but likewise invisible beings as the twelve Olympian gods, who as scions of the highest God are described as everlasting pure spirits, raised above all contact with the corporeal world. But as the gods enter into no immediate intercourse with men, demons are required to form a link between them, and Apuleius enters with great detail into their nature, occupations, and classes. He maintains guardian spirits, supposing that Socrates not only heard but saw his demon. Apuleius also like others refers to demons the sacrifices, consecrations and religious usages, the images and temples of the gods. He derives from them divination and the other disclosures of the future which he readily credits. The human soul is also reckoned to belong to the race of demons, as well during its earthly life as especially after its delivery from the body. But it is only demons of a lower order which enter into a body.

Celsus possesses for us a higher interest than either of the foregoing, for he is, so far as we know, the first heathen who set himself to oppose the advancing Christian faith with the arms of the intellect. Nothing more definite is known of his age than that he is believed to have flourished in the later half of the second century. He may be supposed to have written in the reign of Marcus Aurelius. When Origen had reached the fulness of age and maturity of mind, he was besought by his friend Ambrosius to write an answer to a work entitled "The Word of Truth," which had great credit among the heathen. His refutation of that work supplies us with many fragments of it; and from these we can gather what was the philosophical standing-point of its author.

Thus he[1] declares there to be one supreme God, the absolute Being, who is. He distinguishes between this highest original Being and the Universe, as the second god and son of the most high God, declaring itself by its generation. The stars are divine beings, animated by superior intelligences, visible gods, as distinguished from the invisible deities, who do not show themselves. There are subordinate deities who preside over particular parts of the earth, national gods, to whom different portions of the earth are subject, and to whom therefore fitting veneration must be paid. He recognises the divine origin of the human spirit, the power of matter, which as resisting the divine and formative principle is the cause of all evil. From this are derived the forces, or evil spirits, which resist "the divine," that is, God, who is the Reason of all things that are. He can give a high conception of God. Thus he says,[2] "That which is, is the subject of the intellect; that which becomes, of the senses. To the one belongs truth; to the other, error. Science is about truth; opinion, about error. Intelligence belongs to the intelligible, as sight to the visible; mind knows the intelligible as the eye the visible. What then the sun is to visible things, being neither eye nor sight, but the cause to the eye of seeing, and to sight that it takes place, and to visible things that they are seen, and to all objects of sense that they are generated, and to himself, that he is beheld, such in things intelligible is he who is neither mind, nor the action of mind, nor science, but the cause to the mind of its action, and to this action that it exists by

[1] See Werner, *Geschichte der christlichen Theologie*, i. 172.
[2] Origen, *Contra Cels.* vii. 45.

him, and to science that it knows by him, and to all things intelligible, to Very Truth and to Very Being, that they are. Being beyond all he is by some ineffable power the object of the intellect." This on the one side, while on the other the whole heathen world of divine things, demigods, heroes, sacrifices, oracles, finds in his system convenient space and room enough. Then as for the idol worship, "if [1] any pay them not honour, because the stone or wood or brass or gold which any particular artist has wrought cannot be a god, that is a pitiful wisdom. For who that is not a mere simpleton thinks these things to be gods, and not rather things offered to them and representing them?"

The work of Celsus is generally aggressive, but I am not now concerned with his attacks on the Christian Faith; I speak here of his own positive standing-ground. It will be seen to coincide exactly with that of Plutarch at the beginning of the century. And I think we may fairly conclude that it was the ground which every man of cultivated mind among the heathen attempted to take, and that from the last years of St. John, during the whole second and third centuries, when any Christian argued against the multiplicity of gods, the idolatrous worship paid to them, and the impure and monstrous tales of the heathen mythology, the instructed class would meet him with this counter-belief in one supreme God, shared, as we have seen, and most distinctly expressed by Epictetus, Plutarch, Dio of Prusa, Maximus, Apuleius, Celsus, under whom the mythological gods would be ranged as parts or members of the "race possessing reason," while the offensive myths, imputing crimes

---

[1] Origen, *Contra Cels.* vii. 62.

to the deities, would partly be repudiated as the invention of poets, partly interpreted in a physical or moral sense, partly again attributed to an inferior and intermediate class of deities, demons as they were called. The unlettered crowd in the meantime, that is, the vast majority of mankind, held to their ancestral belief in its crudity, worshipped Jupiter and Venus in the temples and by imitating their conduct, and were ready to tear to pieces "the atheists," who denied them. Meanwhile Trajan and Hadrian, Antoninus Pius and Marcus Aurelius patronised and rewarded such men as Epictetus and Plutarch, and Dio and Maximus, attended their lectures, and admired their conception of "the divine," each being Pontifex Maximus of the State religion, zealously practising and defending its rights; in accordance with which they put to death on due occasion such teachers of the Unity of God as St. Ignatius of Antioch, St. Symphorosa and her sons, the ex-philosopher Justin, and the martyr bishops, against whom in the theatres of Lyons or Smyrna the crowd cried out, "Away with the impious!"

LECTURE XIX

THE GOSPEL OF PHILOSOPHIC HEATHENISM

IN[1] the last two lectures we have been tracing a reformation of heathenism in the Neopythagorean and Platonistic school of thought, of which Plutarch has remained to posterity as the chief representative. This school, dead as we have seen in Cicero's time, and dead in Seneca's time, by the time of Domitian had revived, prevailed more and more, and in less than a hundred years became the foremost if not the sole champion of Grecian thought. In the reign of Septimius Severus the whole philosophy of the Greeks had come to the acknowledgment of one supreme God, and that a God not distinct from but embracing the deities of the popular mythology. When the Christians attacked the polytheism of the established religion, it replied, "We grant what you teach. We also know that there is one Lord over all; but we maintain that the gods likewise whom we honour are gods. As there is one Cæsar who has many servants, Consuls, Prefects, Tribunes, Centurions, Decurions, so there is one God under whom are ranged the other gods, who rule the affairs of men."[2] We now come to a very

---

[1] In this chapter I have followed the original life by Philostratus throughout. I have likewise had specially before me the work of Baur, *Apollonius und Christus*, and Kellner's chapter, *Flavius Philostratus, der Neopythagoräer*, as well as Zeller, v. pp. 131-144; but while availing myself of all these writers, I have endeavoured to form my own opinion.
[2] Tzschirner, *Fall des Heidenthums*, p. 556.

remarkable work, which sets forth this idea in the detail of what pretends to be the veracious biography of a Neopythagorean philosopher. In this we shall find that what Plutarch, Dio, Maximus, Celsus also, and many others had taught in bits, is exhibited full length and clothed in flesh and blood as the birth, education, discipline, travels, labours, sufferings, triumph, and death of an actual man. The reformation of the heathen religion which we have hitherto followed in fragmentary disclosures is embodied in an example and illustrated by a hero.

Such was the thought of that great patroness of literature and philosophers, the Empress Julia Domna, the wife of Septimius Severus, at the beginning of the third century. She commissioned Philostratus, one of the ornaments of her learned Court, to carry it out, and the life of Apollonius of Tyana which we now possess is the result. The occasion of writing this work is told us by its author. "There was," he says, "a certain man named Damis, who was well read in philosophy, a citizen of the ancient Ninus, who became one of the disciples of Apollonius, and wrote the account of his travels, wherein he set down his opinions, discourses, and predictions. A person nearly allied to Damis introduced the Empress Julia to a knowledge of his memoirs, which till then were not known, and as I was a part of her circle, for she encouraged all literary works, she commanded me to transcribe these commentaries, and pay particular attention to the style and language, for the narrative of the Ninevite was plain but not eloquent. To assist me in the work I was fortunate in procuring the book of Maximus, the Ægean, which contained all the actions of Apollonius at Ægæ, and a transcript of

THE GOSPEL OF PHILOSOPHIC HEATHENISM 209

his will, from which it appeared how much his philosophy was under the influence of a sacred enthusiasm. For credit should not be given to Mæragenes, who has written four books about Apollonius, but was ignorant of many things concerning him. I have now explained the manner of my collecting my materials, and the care taken in their compilation. I trust the work may do honour to the man who is the subject of it, and be of use to the lovers of literature, inasmuch as it will introduce them to the knowledge of things with which they were before unacquainted."[1]

Now as the work thus undertaken at the bidding of the Empress Julia came out not dedicated to her, it is believed to have appeared only after her death, which took place by her own hand in the year 217, in the troubles which ensued upon the death of her son, Caracalla. As Elagabalus succeeded the next year after the short usurpation of Macriuus, we may conclude that it was published in his reign, which coincided with the pontificate of Pope Callistus. At this time the Christian religion was enjoying the longest period of tranquillity which occurs in the first three centuries, and which extends from the cessation of the persecution of Septimius Severus at the beginning of the century, interrupted only by the short interval of the reign of Maximianus, to the outbreak of the persecution under Decius in the year 250. Origen and Tertullian were in the midst of their career, and Christianity a well-known religion, and a force which was stirring society to its depths. First we must note that the Apollonius, of whom Damis is here said to have written memoirs, had been already dead about

---

[1] *Life of Apollonius.* By Philostratus. Berwick's translation corrected, lib. i. ch. 3.

one hundred and twenty years. The work of Damis, which Philostratus states not to have been known when it was thus presented to the Empress Julia, is only known to us now by the reference to it throughout this work of Philostratus. The work of Mæragenes has perished, but we learn from Origen that he held Apollonius to be a magician, and stated that certain philosophers were deceived by him through this art of his. What we know of Apollonius from other sources than Philostratus is that he lived in the first century and died in old age in Nerva's reign. Origen calls him both magician and philosopher. Lucian classes him with Alexander of Abonoteichos, his model of an unprincipled impostor. Dio Cassius terms him a skilful wizard and magician. With reference to the remaining circumstances of his life there is silence. Thus learned men, considering that there is no guarantee whatever for the incidents assigned by Philostratus to Apollonius, are unanimously agreed that this pretended life is a romance, which, taking up the person of a man who had really lived in the first century with the reputation of a Pythagorean philosopher and a magician, puts together, four generations after his death, an ideal picture of one who should carry out what the writer meant to be taken for the ancient philosophy of Pythagoras, and what was really the Neopythagorean philosophy as it had been constructed by a certain school in his own time. Thus of the real Apollonius hardly anything is known; little notice was taken of him in his day. The representation of him by Philostratus has no claim whatever to historic truth. If real facts are mentioned in it, no one can distinguish them from the fictions with which they are surrounded, so that in nothing can it be trusted. The whole interest lies in the picture thus given us of the Neopythagorean doctrine and discipline, which at the beginning of the third century was devised by the Greek mind as the only efficient means for the moral and religious elevation of man, the restoration of his intercourse with the gods, nay, even a deification of human life.[1] Accordingly, for what concerns the person and adventures of Apollonius, this biography is worthless; but it is of great importance for what concerns the thoughts of learned Greeks bent upon the defence of heathenism some twenty years after Tertullian had cried out of the Christians, "We are of yesterday, and yet we have filled every place belonging to you, cities, islands, castles, towns, assemblies, your very camp, your tribes, companies, palaces, forum." It conveys to us a measure of the effect which the Christian Church had produced on the Greek and Roman world six generations after it had been first introduced at Rome.

The biographer begins with a commendation of Pythagoras, for throughout his work Apollonius is represented as embodying in his life the precepts of that sage, who had conversed with the gods and had learnt from them what conduct in men pleased and what, again, grieved them. Now whatever was taught by Pythagoras was observed as a law by his disciples, who reverenced him as a man come from Jove, and silence respecting "the divinity"[2] was enjoined upon them, for many divine and unspeakable things they heard which they could not retain and comprehend without having first learnt that "silence is understanding." Apollonius then devoted himself to the pursuit of wisdom with even a diviner impulse than Pythagoras: he vanquished tyrannies, and he lived in

[1] Zeller, v. 135.   [2] ὑπὲρ τοῦ θείου, i. 1.

times neither remote nor modern, and yet he is not recognised by men for that true wisdom which he cultivated. Some have admired this or that action of his, but others, knowing that he conversed with the Magi of Babylon, the Indian Brahmans, and the Egyptian Gymnosophists, impute to him the practice of magic, yet they did not so in the case of Empedocles, or Pythagoras, or Democritus, nor again in the case of Plato, much as he borrowed from Egyptian priests, arraying it in his own artistic colours: nor did men impute magic to Socrates or Anaxagoras on account of their foreknowledge. "I am then determined," says Philostratus, "to give accurately the history of the man, and the sort of wisdom in virtue of which he reached to being considered not only as one led by a good genius but as divine.

"He was born in Tyana of Cappadocia, of an ancient family, aboriginally Greek, with considerable fortune. Of the manner of his birth no one should be ignorant. As his mother was near the time of his delivery, she was warned in a dream to go and gather flowers in a meadow. When she came there, while her maidens were dispersed up and down amusing themselves with the flowers, she fell asleep on the grass. Then a flock of swans, which was feeding in the meadow, formed a chorus round her, and clapping their wings, as their custom is, sung in unison, while all the time the air was filled with a gentle zephyr. The singing of the birds caused her to start out of sleep, and at that moment she was delivered of a son. The natives of the place affirm that at the instant of her delivery a thunderbolt which seemed ready to fall on the ground rose aloft and suddenly disappeared. By this the gods prefigured, I think, the splendour of the child, his superiority over earthly beings, his nearness to themselves, and the deeds which he was to do.

"When he grew up and was capable of instruction he showed great strength of memory and persevering application. He used the Attic dialect, and never suffered his speech to be corrupted by the place of his birth. The eyes of all were attracted by his beauty. At fourteen years of age his father carried him to Tarsus, and committed him to the care of Euthydemus the Phœnician, a celebrated rhetorician. But though he liked his master he disapproved of the manners of the city, and obtained his father's permission to retire with his master to Ægæ, a neighbouring town, where he found a tranquillity more adapted to science, and studies more suitable to his years, as well as a temple of Æsculapius, who sometimes showed himself to his votaries. Here he studied philosophy with the disciples of Plato, Chrysippus, and Aristotle. He heard also and did not reject the tenets of Epicurus, but those of Pythagoras he embraced with ineffable zeal: and at sixteen, impelled by some superior power, he gave himself up to the Pythagorean life. For his sister he obtained from his father a house with a garden and fountains belonging to it. 'Here,' said he, 'live you in what manner you please, but I shall live after the manner of Pythagoras.' In accordance with this he declined to eat anything which had life, as being impure, and making dull the understanding. He lived on fruit and vegetables, esteeming the productions of the earth alone to be pure. Wine, as a beverage produced from a tree good for men, he allowed to be pure, but thought it adverse to a settled state of mind, as disturbing the ethereal nature of the soul. Having thus purified the appetite, he went barefoot and clothed himself in linen, and rejected the use of all garments made from living creatures. He let his hair grow, and lived in the temple, all the officers of which were astonished at his conduct, and Æsculapius himself once said to the priest how he had pleasure in performing cures of the sick before such a witness as Apollonius. Thus his fame spread far and wide.

"In his twentieth year he lost his father, and hastened to Tyana to bury him beside his mother with his own hands. He divided a splendid inheritance with his brother, and being still under age went back to Ægæ, where he made the temple a shrine of the Platonic and Peripatetic philosophy. When he came of full age he returned to Tyana, and ceded the half of his patrimonial portion to his brother, in the hope of reforming him, in which he succeeded. Most of the rest of his property he gave to other relations who needed it, reserving but little for himself. The famous saying of Pythagoras, that a man should be strictly faithful to his wife, was intended, he observed, for others; for himself, he would never marry, nor indulge in the delights of love. And he practised the precept of silence for five whole years, though it was a great labour to him, having things to say which he refrained from saying, often provoked to anger, which he might not indulge, often wishing to censure, which he forbore.

"After he had fulfilled the law of silence he visited Antioch the Great and the temple of Apollo at Daphnæ there. And his mode of life in general is thus described: At sunrise he performed apart from all certain rites which he communicated only to such as had been prepared by a four years' silence. After this, if it was a Greek city, and its worship known to him, he would call together the priests, and philosophise about the gods, and correct them if in anything they departed from the lawful rites. If the worship was foreign and peculiar, he would inquire who had established it, and for what purpose; and having learnt how it was observed, and suggested anything which might appear to him an improvement, he would go to his followers, and bid them ask him any questions which they wished to put. For it was his saying that they who practised wisdom as he did should at dawn converse with the gods, as day advanced converse about them, and spend the following time in things that regarded men. When he had answered all the questions proposed by his friends, and satisfied his intercourse with them, he would address the general multitude, but not before noon. Then he would be anointed and rubbed, and take a cold bath, for he denounced hot baths as the old age of men. His language was neither swollen nor affectedly refined. He did not use elaborate divisions of discourse; he was never ironical or magniloquent: but he spoke as with absolute truth, in short and serried sentences, in proper terms, and his words had a sound as if they came from a sceptre of royalty. Once a subtle disputant asked him why he did not take a side in a question. 'So I did,' he replied, 'when I was a youth: but now, I do not investigate, rather I teach the result of my investigation.' And when the other rejoined, 'How will the wise man converse?'[1] 'As a legislator,' he replied; 'for the legislator will enjoin the multitude to do what he is convinced ought to be done.' And thus at Antioch

---

[1] Compare "He spoke as one having authority, and not as the Scribes and Pharisees."

he converted to him people who were strangers to all knowledge."[1]

Such in brief is the birth, education, and manner of life which Philostratus assigns to Apollonius, whom he has thus conducted to the age of full manhood. He is in all this represented as the pure offspring of the Greek mind, having shown qualities such as Empedocles, Democritus, Plato, and Anaxagoras had shown in ages long past, but especially he is as it were a resurrection of Pythagoras. In short, he is one whose culture and wisdom, like his language, are eminently and indigenously Hellenic, while he has the advautage of living exactly at the opening of the Christian era; for it is curious that his birth coincides as nearly as possible in time with that of Christ. "At this point of his life," says Philostratus, "Apollonius determined that a young man should travel, and go beyond the boundaries of his own land. The object which he set before himself was to visit the Indian wise men called Brahmans, and on his way to see likewise the Magians who inhabited Babylon and Susa. This he proposed to his seven companions, but when they attempted to divert him from his purpose, he told them, 'I have consulted the gods and declared to you their will, to make trial of your courage, whether you have strength for what I undertake; but since you have not the resolution to go, I bid you farewell and desire you to study philosophy. I must go where wisdom and my good genius lead me.' And so saying he set out from Antioch with two servants of his family, one remarkable for the speed, the other for the beauty, of his writing. In passing through the Syrian city of Ninus he met with

---

[1] I have drawn the preceding account from the "Life of Philostratus," Book i. 1-16.

Damis, who offered to accompany him, and mentioned as a recommendation that he knew the Armenian, Persian, Median, and Cadousian languages. 'My friend,' said Apollonius, 'I know them all, though I have learnt none;' and when Damis stood in amaze, he continued: 'Do not wonder if I know all the languages of men, for I know also their secret thoughts.'[1] Upon this Damis adored him, considering him a deity, and henceforth followed him, remembering and storing up his wisdom." It does not however appear that in his travels Apollonius used this assumed gift of foreign tongues, for he is nearly always described as conversing either with foreigners who understood Greek, or by means of an interpreter.

We have in the course of this journey a description of Babylon, as if it subsisted still in the grandeur which Herodotus saw; and of its king, who appears as a great monarch, and honours the philosopher. But of the Magi we only hear that Apollonius saw and conversed with them, upon which he gives this judgment: "They are wise, but not in all things." After staying eight months with the king of Babylon, Bardanes, he is sent forward with great honour to the Indian king, Phraotes, and passing the Indus arrives at Taxila. He finds this sovereign a philosopher, living with the utmost simplicity, and prizing his friends more than his treasures. Like Apollonius, he ate only vegetables. He had also the advantage of speaking Greek perfectly, and loving Grecian literature. After an interval of three days spent in philosophic conversations, Phraotes sends him forward with costly gifts of precious stones, and a letter to the

---

[1] Compare John ii. 25—"He needed not that any should bear witness about man, for He knew what was in man."

Indian wise men, in which he said, "Apollonius, the wisest of men, deems you wiser than himself, and is come to learn what you can tell him. Send him forth, therefore, instructed in all your knowledge, for nothing of it will perish, since he speaks better than all other men, and remembers what he knows." I pass over all the strange stories inserted in this journey from Antioch to the land beyond the Ganges, in order to bring Apollonius at once to the object of his travels, the seat of the wise men of India. As after many days' journey, in a land teeming with wonders, he approaches within a furlong of the hill where they dwelt, a very dark Indian youth appeared, bearing in his hand a golden anchor, the symbol of the herald's sacred office, and addressing Apollonius in Greek, while he passed the others by, "Leave these," he said, "here, but come thou as thou art, for it is *They* who command." In this Apollonius recognised the Pythagorean *Ipse dixit*, and followed rejoicing.

The Indian sages are described as having a sort of enchanted dwelling upon a hill rising out of a plain to the height of the Acropolis of Athens, defended on all sides by rocks. Here they cover themselves with clouds, or disclose themselves at pleasure, open or shut the vessels of the winds and rains, which they dispense to India. Apollonius approaching sees statues not only of the Indian and Egyptian gods, but likewise of Minerva, Apollo, and Bacchus, and these too worshipped with Hellenic rites. "I saw," he says, "the Brahmans living upon the earth, and yet not on it, fortified without walls, possessing nothing and yet possessing all things." Iarchas, the chief of the wise men, with his seventeen companions, receives Apollonius with great honour, saluting him in the Greek tongue, and giving him forthwith an instance of his knowledge by stating that the letter of recommendation which Apollonius had not yet shown was deficient in a delta. While Apollonius is in amazement at this knowledge, Iarchas asks him, " What is your opinion of us? " " That," he replies, "is plain from my coming to see you, which no one of my countrymen hitherto has done. I esteem your knowledge greater and more divine than my own, and if I should learn nothing from you, I should have the satisfaction of knowing that you have nothing to teach me." Upon this Iarchas in clear distinct order gives him the history of his family, of his past life, and his journey thither. And when Apollonius, in spite of his knowledge of men's thoughts, is astonished at this, Iarchas says, " You too are a sharer of this wisdom, but not yet in its completeness." " Teach me then," he replies, "all wisdom." " That I will," replies Iarchas, "without stint, for it is wiser to communicate than invidiously to conceal what ought to be known." In further conversation Iarchas says, " Propose what question you please, for you are come to men who know all things." "What," asks Apollonius, "is your opinion of the soul ? " " The same," replied Iarchas, " which Pythagoras delivered to you, and we to the Egyptians." And he proceeds to enforce and illustrate by his own pre-existence in the King Ganges, the doctrine of the transmigration of souls. Thus it is plain that Philostratus represents his hero in the character of a Pythagorean as recurring to the Brahmans of India because he esteems them the fountain-head of that wisdom which Pythagoras received immediately indeed from Egypt, but ultimately from them through an Ethiopian colony. And the purpose of his visit is to compare his own doctrine as a disciple of Pythagoras with theirs, and if necessary to enlarge it, or at any rate to confirm it by conference with those who held it at its original source. Now he is said to remain four months with the wise men, and to hold innumerable conversations with them, and to be initiated in all the secrets of their science. The most important matter which we learn from the thirty-five chapters in which Philostratus describes this intercourse, is the account of the constitution of the world. Apollonius, being bidden to ask any question, inquires how the world was composed. They reply, "Of five elements, the fifth being ether, whence the gods have their generation, for whatever things breathe air are mortal, but whatever breathe ether are immortal and divine." "Which element then existed first?" "All together," replies Iarchas, "for that which lives is not produced by parts." "Is then the world a living thing?" "Yes, for it produces all things alive." "Is it then feminine, or both male and female?" "It is both, for by an act of self-coalescence it performs the functions both of father and mother in the generation of that which lives, and is more ardently fond of itself than other things having life of each other. This love it is which harmonises and unites it. And as in a living thing its movement and the mind which is in it, the source of its impulses, perform the work of hands and feet, so we consider the parts of the world through its mind to be capable of providing what is needed for all its productions. And even the calamities arising from drought happen according to this mind, as punishments for human depravity. And this living thing is ruled not by one hand but by hands which none can count or express, and in spite of its size is obedient and docile. It may further be likened to a great Egyptian merchant ship, with many compartments, many pilots, under the command of one, the oldest and wisest, many skilful sailors and armed combatants. We may consider the world in the likeness of this ship. The chief and most conspicuous place is to be assigned to God, the progenitor of this living thing, and next under Him to the deities who direct its parts. And here we assent to the poets when they tell us that there are many gods in heaven and in the sea and in the springs and rivers, and likewise about the earth, and some too under the earth. But that place under the earth, if such a place exists, which they describe as full of horror and the abode of corruption, let us separate from our conception of the ordered world."[1]

Now we have been told that Apollonius in his diet avoided wine, as disturbing the ether of the soul. Thus he viewed the human soul as sharing that fifth element which the Indians said that the gods breathed. Again, Apollonius especially loves to converse with Iarchas on the subject of foreknowledge. Iarchas highly praises him for this, and says, " They who take pleasure in the art of divination become by it divine, and work for men's salvation. For I consider that man most happy and equal in power to the Delphic god who possesses in himself the power of foreknowing and foretelling to others ignorant of it what we learn by approaching the oracles. And since the art of divination enjoins all who consult the oracle to go thither with pure hearts, or orders them to depart, it seems to me that he who wishes to know the secrets of futurity should keep himself pure, should have no stain upon his soul, no scars of sins upon his mind.

[1] Book iii. 34, 35.

Thus he foresees the future through understanding himself and the tribunal of his own breast. And so his oracles will be more true and pure. Hence it is not surprising that you should possess this kind of knowledge, who have so great a portion of ether in your soul," the ether, that is, which is the substance of the gods. It is in full accordance with this tenet as to the nature of the soul that when Apollonius asked the Indians whom they esteemed themselves to be, Iarchas replied, "Gods." "But for what reason?" "Because we are good men:" an answer which Apollonius thought so full of wisdom that he cited it afterwards to Domitian. "Why," said the accuser then to him, "do men call thee god?" "Because," he replied, "every man that is deemed good is honoured with the name of god." And when the Indians take leave of him they assure him that he would be considered a god not only after his death but during his life.[1]

In fact the passages we have thus cited concerning the constitution of the world, the gods, and the human soul, and its capacity of knowing the truth and future things, contain the kernel of the whole Neopythagorean philosophy, in which the pre-existence and transmigration of souls, the immortality of the soul's substance and its identity with the substance both of the supreme God and the particular gods, and the right therefore of the good man who lives according to this nature of the soul to be called god, cohere together. "If[2] the essential nature of the divinity is immortal and imperishable being, it is especially in the immortal essence of the human soul that the relationship of the human nature with the divine is mani-

---
[1] See Book i. 8; iii. 42; iii. 18; viii. 5; iii. 50.
[2] Baur, *Apollonius und Christus*.

fested. Hence every human life has a certain share in the divine being: but as only the purest nature of light and an all-embracing knowledge in union with the highest clearness of consciousness can be attributed to the deity itself, it follows in this philosophy that whoever is conscious to himself in a high degree of the immortal nature of the soul and of his own being before the present life, will likewise in the same high degree participate in the divine being."

This is the key to the whole life and character of Apollonius in the description of Philostratus, and the motive-power of that reform in heathendom which he is supposed to work. This too explains, if it does not justify, his syncretistic worship of all deities in all temples, "the[1] various forms of the gods in the polytheistic religion being so many various symbols of the one divine being."

But the Indian sages unite power with knowledge, and Apollonius, before he leaves, witnesses their miracles. Thus a mother comes to intercede for her son, who is possessed by a lying wicked demon, upon which one of the sages takes a letter from his bosom, which he gives to the mother, and tells her that it will command the spirit to relinquish his hold. Again, a lame man recovers by touch the use of his limb, and a blind man his sight.

Finally, Apollonius having had communicated to him all their public and their most secret knowledge, takes leave of Iarchas and the other sages, and sends back to them the camels which they had lent him, thanking them for the wisdom which they had bestowed on him in showing him the path to heaven, and promising to impart this to the Greeks, as if they

[1] Baur.

were present with him. And so by the Indus, Babylon, Ninus, and Antioch, after a visit to the Isle of Cyprus, where he instructs the priests in the temple of Venus, and explains the meaning of its symbolical statue, he sets sail for Ionia, amid the applause and salutation of all who esteemed and valued wisdom.

Here is completed the first stage of the public life of Apollonius, in which one, who is described as more devoted to wisdom than even Pythagoras was, having formed his youth upon the model of his master, visits the fountain-head of that knowledge whence the master drew. He treats the Indian wise men with a certain reverence, but he finds and they recognise his wisdom to be identical with their own. He does not then receive anything new from them, but is as it were confirmed in the knowledge of possessing the same wisdom with them. He is honoured by the kings of Babylon and India as the true representative of the highest civilisation, which belongs to Greece. And so he comes back to his native land to dispense wisdom to his countrymen as a public teacher, and with it everywhere to strengthen, correct, and encourage the public worship, as it is celebrated in the rites of the various gods, in all which he is a perfect master.

To this public life of Apollonius as a teacher three books are given by Philostratus, in which he is made to traverse the whole Roman empire. The effects of his wisdom are seen in promoting piety and worship everywhere in public life, in correcting and improving the private life of all whom he meets, in braving tyranny in the bad emperors, Nero and Domitian, in advising and preparing for sovereignty good emperors, such as Vespasian, Titus, and Nerva, in a continual foreknowledge of future events, whether concerning

THE GOSPEL OF PHILOSOPHIC HEATHENISM 225

the Roman State or his own life, and in working miracles, especially such as consist in detecting and expelling evil spirits. He is accompanied not only by Damis, who never leaves him, but by a number of disciples.

He begins by residing at Ephesus for some time, where ambassadors from the surrounding cities wait upon him, esteeming him "the guide of life," and the adviser in the erection of altars and statues. The chief act which he performs at Ephesus is that when the plague has made its way there, he, being at Smyrna, transports himself in a moment thither. As soon as he arrived,[1] he collected all the people together and said to them, "Be not afraid, for I will this day put a stop to the disease." Saying this he carried the people of all ages to the theatre where now stands the statue of the Averter. Here they beheld an old man begging alms, who had a strange way of winking with his eyes. He had a wallet in his hand in which he carried crusts of bread. He was clad in rags and had a most squalid appearance. Apollonius bade the Ephesians surround him and pelt him with stones. They were shocked at the thought of killing a stranger in so wretched a plight, for at this time the poor man appeared in the act of supplication, and doing all he could to excite their compassion. But Apollonius, unmoved by this, insisted that what he commanded should be executed, and bade them not let him escape. When some of the bystanders began to throw stones, he who lately appeared only capable of winking with his eyes, darted them flaming with fire and fury. Hence the Ephesians saw that he was a demon, and continued pelting him with stones till they piled a

[1] Book iv. 10.

heap over his head. Whereupon, a pause ensuing, Apollonius ordered the stones to be removed, that all might see the wild beast they had destroyed. But, lo, what they thought was destroyed had made its escape, and a dog like one of the Molossian breed, but as big as the largest lion, appeared when the stones were taken away, vomiting foam as madmen do. Now the statue of the Averter, Hercules, was erected on the very spot where the spectre was stoned.

Apollonius now travels into Greece, visiting on his way the tomb of Achilles, whose ghost appears to him as a shape of ineffable beauty, and tells him among other charges to warn people against discontinuing religious ceremonies. At Athens the philosophers welcome him with delight, and ten young men declare that they were just on the point of sailing to Ionia to meet him. Finding the Athenians much given to religious worship, he made sacrifices the subject of his discourse, wherein he specified the kind of offering best suited to each god, and the precise hour of day or night when they should sacrifice, offer libations, or pray.[1] Here among his auditors was a youth whom he saw to be possessed by a demon, though the youth knew it not. And when Apollonius fixed his eyes upon him, the spectre broke out into cries of fear and anger like those who are racked, and swore that he would depart out of the youth, and never again enter into another. Apollonius rebuked him as a master does a cunning, saucy, insolent slave, and commanded him to come out, and give a visible sign of his departure. Upon this the demon said, " I will overthrow a certain statue," to which he pointed.

[1] Book iv. 19.

The statue first shook and then fell, upon which the people shouted with joy. The young man, having rubbed his eyes as if he recovered from a dream, turned to his right mind, and followed henceforth the rule and manner of life which Apollonius led.

Apollonius visited all the temples of Greece, attended by his disciples, and the priests whom he instructed, and his biographer says, "His words were collected as in goblets, out of which all who would quenched their thirst." When at Olympia he stood upon the steps of the temple discoursing upon wisdom and fortitude and temperance and all virtues, striking all men with wonder not at his thoughts only, but at the forms of their expression.[1] At Corinth he meets with the famous Cynic philosopher, Demetrius, who felt for him the reverence which Antisthenes felt for Socrates, and he delivered Menippus, a friend of Demetrius, from a ghoul, who appeared to be a beautiful woman. The youth was on the point of marrying her, but Apollonius presenting himself at the marriage-feast, the gold and silver vessels, the cup-bearers and cooks vanished at his bidding into air, whereupon the phantom appeared as in tears, and besought him not to torment her, nor force her to confess who she was. But Apollonius was peremptory, and compelled her to confess that she was a ghoul feeding on human bodies, and Menippus, being delivered from her, became his disciple, and followed in his train.[2]

From Sparta and Crete, which he visited, warned

---

[1] Compare "Never man spoke as this Man;" and John vii. 57, "If any man thirst, let him come unto Me and drink."
[2] Book iv. p. 25. τὸ φάσμα ἐδεῖτο μὴ βασανίζειν αὐτό. Compare Mark v. 7—ὁρκίζω σε τὸν Θεόν, μη με βασανίσῃς.

by a dream, Apollonius proceeded to Rome, and this he did at the moment when Nero was banishing the philosophers. The peril was so great that at Aricia Apollonius was met by a fugitive philosopher, who warned him not to go on. And here out of his thirty-four companions all but eight deserted him. With the rest he entered Rome. And he remained there a considerable time, publicly practising and teaching philosophy in spite of Nero, and visiting the temples, which the Consul Telesinus, attracted and subdued by his conversation, authorised him to do. In vain did Tigellinus attempt to daunt him; the evil minister of Nero was quelled in spite of himself by the divine knowledge of the philosopher, and not wishing to contend with God, "Go," he said, "where thou wilt, for thou art too great to be subject to me." That he had reason to say this appears from what follows. A girl died on the eve of her marriage, and the intended bridegroom followed the bier weeping, and all Rome wept with him, for she was of a consular family. Now Apollonius happening to meet the funeral procession, "Set down," said he, "the bier, for I will dry up the tears which you are shedding for the maid." Upon which he asked her name. Now the spectators thought he was going to pronounce a funeral oration over her. But all he did was to touch her, and uttering something in a low tone of voice wakened the maid from that seeming death. She immediately began to speak, and returned to her father's house, as Alcestis of old when recalled to life by Hercules. When the relations offered Apollonius 150,000 drachmæ, he added this to her dowry. "Now whether he found in her a spark of life, which those who attended her did not see, or whether, when the soul had departed, he kindled it afresh and brought it back, neither I nor the bystanders can tell."[1]

All this purports to have taken place just at the time when Nero was persecuting the Christians, before his visit to Greece. But when he published an edict forbidding the philosophers to remain in Rome, Apollonius left it, and went, accompanied by his disciples, into Spain. From Spain he went to Africa, Tuscany, and Sicily. And here at Catana he asked his disciples, "Is mythology any real thing?" And answering his own question he preferred to it the fables of Æsop as being more adapted to convey wisdom. For heroic fables, which make the matter of poetry, corrupt the hearers by introducing absurd amours, incestuous marriages, blasphemies against the gods, devouring children, unbecoming stratagems and disputes. These being represented as realities, invite the lover, the jealous man, the miser and the ambitious, to carry them out in life.[2] From Sicily he passed over to Greece, and on the way having sailed prosperously in a certain vessel, he said, "Let us leave the ship, for it is not good to sail in her to Achaia." Only those who knew him took note of his words, and followed him into another ship. The one he left presently afterwards foundered. He passed the winter in the various temples of Greece, visiting the several cities, and dispensing praise and blame as he saw them to be required. He pursued his journey into Egypt in the spring, where, says his biographer, as he disembarked from the ship at Alexandria, the people looked upon him as a god, and made way for him in the narrow streets, as is done for those who carry

[1] Book iv. 45. All have been struck with the imitation here of the raising the widow of Naim's son. [2] Book v. 14.

sacred things. Here he fell in with Vespasian, and
being consulted by him, strongly advised him to
assume the empire. Vespasian accepted his advice,
treated him with great reverence, and wished to be
accompanied by him; but he excused himself as
having a great desire to compare the Egyptian wisdom
with the Indian, and for this purpose to visit the
Gymnosophists, and to drink of the source of the Nile.
Leaving then twenty of his disciples at Alexandria,
he took the other ten, after warning them that life is
a contest for victory, as is shown in the Olympic,
Delphic, and Corinthian games, and ascended the river
with them. No city, or temple, or sacred spot in
Egypt was passed by unobserved, but in continual conversations on sacred subjects an interchange of knowledge took place, and the boat in which Apollonius
sailed resembled a sacred galley carrying pilgrims to
a shrine.

The interview of Apollonius with the Ethiopian
Gymnosophists is described at great length. They
lived on a small rising ground not far from the banks
of the Nile, but were further surpassed in wisdom
by the Indians than they themselves surpassed the
Egyptians. And the assurance of this, obtained by
actual intercourse, seems to be the fruit which we are
intended to suppose that Apollonius sought after in
his long journey to them. Thus their chief, Thespesion, in a lengthy discourse recommended to him
the independence and freedom from care which their
philosophy secured, and tried thereby to incline him
to their simplicity and rude mode of life. Apollonius
in reply told them that being older than them all,
except Thespesion, he had not come thither to take
them as counsellors of his life, having already chosen

his mode of life according to the doctrine of Pythagoras, who in his unspeakable wisdom knew not only what he was, but what he had been. They had formerly instructed Pythagoras in his philosophy, having themselves derived it from the Indians; but he had seen it in its source, and had gone to the Indians rather than to them, "as men of sublimer genius, living in a purer atmosphere, and next, as holding truer opinions respecting nature and the gods, by reason of being nearer heaven, and the fountain of an ethereal and vivifying substance." Such men best knew the nature of the soul, "of whose generation that which is immortal and immutable is the source."[1] "The Indians," he farther told them, "having instructed me in all those points of their wisdom which I thought of service to me, I do not forget my instructors, and I go about teaching what I have heard from them, and I may be of service to you, if you send me forth acquainted with all you know, for I should never cease imparting it myself to the Greeks and writing it to the Indians." He then reproached them that while the Greeks represented their gods only in a noble and beautiful shape, they made them ridiculous and unseemly by figuring them as beasts. Thespesion replied that the Egyptians dared not venture to give any forms to the gods, but represented them only in symbols and allegories, that they might be more venerable. Apollonius retorted by asking what there could be symbolical or venerable in a dog, an ibis, or a goat.

Apollonius thus quitted the Egyptian Gymnosophists in full assurance that the wisdom of Egypt possessed nothing which he as a Pythagorean had to

---

[1] Book vi. 11. ἧς τὸ ἀθάνατόν τε καὶ ἀγέννητον πηγαὶ γενέσεως.

learn. This was in the year 70, and on his return he had a correspondence with Titus, who had just taken Jerusalem, and by his invitation visited him at Tarsus. He gave Titus much the same advice as to his government, and with the same assumption of superiority, as he had given to his father, Vespasian.

"These," says the biographer, "were the countries which Apollonius visited in his ardour to give and receive instruction. He made no further journeys to nations unvisited before, but he continued to visit Phœnicians, Ionians, and Italians, ever remaining consistent with himself: and hard as it is to know oneself I esteem it harder for the wise man to remain always like himself. For that man will make no improvement on the corrupt minds of others who has not first so ordered himself by discipline as not to change." Then, after giving certain anecdotes respecting his life at different times, he concluded this whole period with saying, "Such were the deeds of the man in behalf of temples and cities and peoples, the dead, or the sick; such his intercourse with the wise and the foolish, and with emperors who made him their counsellor in virtue."[1]

The seventh book of Philostratus opens a new period in the life of Apollonius. He had visited the Indian wise men in early manhood, and the Ethiopian wise men in the full maturity of age, only to find his doctrine identical with that of the former and superior to that of the latter. The meaning of this obviously is, that the Greek wisdom and culture which he carried in his person found nothing outside of Greece to surpass or compete with it. And he as representing it has traversed the Roman empire from end to end,

[1] Book vi. 43.

blending philosophy with religion, and by his encouragement of every rite and worship proclaiming and enforcing the practical identity of the one divine power which they expressed. He has everywhere been received with honour, as the mouthpiece of wisdom and the restorer of religion. The priests crowd to hear his instructions; the young attend upon his steps; he rescues victims from evil spirits; he foresees dangers and avoids them. He braves Nero in his persecuting mood, but departs unscathed. He selects, as it were, and places Vespasian and Titus upon the throne. One thing only remains. All things have hitherto prospered with him. He has not yet suffered. But his biographer recognises that, in order to be perfect, suffering is necessary. He considers that the conduct of philosophers under despotic governments is the truest touchstone of their character.[1] And the tyranny of Domitian is to furnish Apollonius with the opportunity of bearing witness for his principles.

Apollonius, then, having fallen under the suspicion of Domitian, when in the last years of his life he persecuted the philosophers, is cited to Rome. But he goes at once, and his old friend the Cynic, Demetrius, whom he meets on the way at Puteoli, in vain attempts to frighten him from appearing before the emperor to answer the charge of conspiring against him. Apollonius pursues his way, attended only by Damis, reaches Rome, and is put into prison, where, with unbroken equanimity, he consoles the various fellow-prisoners. In due time he is brought before Domitian, at first privately; he answers fearlessly, but is treated with great contumely, has his beard and hair shaven, and is sent back to prison among the lowest malefactors.

[1] Book vii. 1.

While thus in fetters, to show Damis that he can at any moment deliver himself, he withdraws his leg from the chain, saying, "You see the liberty which I enjoy." Then, said Damis, he first understood that the nature of Apollonius was divine and superior to man; for without offering sacrifice—how could he in a prison?—without praying, without uttering a word, he mocked at his fetters, and replacing the leg therein resumed the demeanour of a prisoner. At length, his public trial being appointed, Apollonius dismisses Damis, bidding him travel to Puteoli by land, salute Demetrius, and there, he said, you will see me. "What! alive," said Damis, "or how?" Apollonius laughed and answered, "Alive in my opinion, but in yours raised from the dead." Damis says that after this he set out much against his will, doubtful between hope and fear, and not knowing whether Apollonius would be saved or perish. Arriving at Puteoli on the third day he heard of a violent storm at sea, which had sunk and dispersed vessels, and then he understood why Apollonius had told him to go by land.

In the meantime Apollonius meets the public trial without the least fear. The court is fitted up with the greatest solemnity, and the chief men of the State are present, on an occasion on which the emperor is bent upon convicting the prisoner. But the prisoner refuses even to cast a glance at the omnipotent judge; and when the accuser charges him to look upon one whom he terms "the god of all men," Apollonius raises his eyes to the ceiling, showing by his gesture that they were turned to Jupiter, and that he considered one who admitted flattery so gross to be viler than the flatterer himself. He defends himself with great moderation, and the emperor pronounces his acquittal, but orders him to stay until he has had some private conversation with him. Then Apollonius, bursting out, replies, "I thank you, O emperor, for this, but on account of the wicked informers by whom you are surrounded, your cities are ruined, your islands filled with exiles, the continent with groans, the army with fears, the senate with suspicions. Listen, if you please, to me; if not, send to take my body, for my soul you cannot take, or rather, even my body you cannot reach. Slay me thou wilt not, for I am not mortal." And, as he spoke, he vanished from the tribunal. This was before mid-day. In the evening he appeared to Demetrius and Damis at Puteoli. They were at this moment sitting down by a cistern of white marble, and Damis cried out, " O ye gods, shall we never see again our good and virtuous friend ? " Apollonius was already standing by, and replied, " You shall see him, or rather you see him now." " What, alive?" said Demetrius, "for if dead we shall never have done lamenting you." Hereupon Apollonius stretching out his hand, said he, " Feel me, and if I escape you, hold me as a shade just come from Proserpine, such as the terrestrial gods present to the afflicted; but if I abide your touch, persuade Damis also that I am alive and have not lost my body." Doubting no longer the truth of what he said, they rose and ran to him and embraced him. They asked him about his defence, and how he had come to them in so short a time. "Ascribe it not," said Apollonius, "to the ram of Phrixus, or the wings of Dedalus, but to God." Then he described his defence, and how he had disappeared at the words, " Thou shalt not kill me." Demetrius upon this is full of fears respecting the persecution which Domitian will institute, but Apollonius is quite tranquil, says

that he only requires sleep, and after a prayer to Apollo
and the sun, casts himself on a couch, and addressing
sleep in the words of Homer, rests without anxiety.
The next day he determines to sail to Greece, accompanied by Damis, and the remainder of the biography
contains what we may call his triumphant life, after
he has defied the utmost power and malice of Domitian, and escaped by a sort of resurrection.

In Greece he appears at Olympia, where he takes
up his abode in the temple of Jupiter. Rumour had
gone abroad that he had been burnt, or hung upon
hooks, or cast into a pit, but when it was ascertained
that he was there alive, all Greece flocked to see him
with more eagerness than it had ever gone to the
Olympian games. They almost worshipped him when
they heard with what modesty he described so wonderful an escape. His life at this period may be thus
summed up. He conversed on matters of great importance for forty days at Olympia. Then he said:
" I will for the time to come converse with you, O
Greeks, from city to city in your public meetings,
your processions, your mysteries, your sacrifices, your
libations:[1] but now I go to see Trophonius." In the
cave of Trophonius he remains seven days, putting to
him the question, "Which is the most perfect and
the purest philosophy?" and he issues forth in a strange
manner bearing a book which contains as an answer
to his question the precepts of Pythagoras. And now
we are told all his followers, "whom Hellas calls the
Apollonians," come forth to meet him, forming an
admirable company from their numbers and their zeal.
People went in crowds to hear his philosophy, and as
the ancient kings, Gyges and Crœsus, opened the doors

[1] Book viii. 19.

of their treasury to those who wanted money, so did Apollonius impart his wisdom to those who were filled with the love of it, permitting them to ask him any questions they pleased.

Having thus passed two years in Greece, he sailed to Ionia with all his company, dwelling chiefly in Smyrna and Ephesus, but likewise visiting the other cities, and everywhere welcomed with delight. It is at Ephesus that he has a vision of the murder of Domitian as it is happening at Rome. He was conversing in one of the groves, when he paused in his discourse, lowered his voice, hesitated, looked on the ground, advanced three or four steps and cried out, "Strike the tyrant, strike!" as if the whole scene was passing before him. Thirty days afterwards a message from the new emperor, Nerva, reaches him, which said that he was reigning by the counsels of the gods and Apollonius, and would be more secure if he had his presence and advice. Therefore Apollonius answered enigmatically, " We shall live together a very long time, in which we shall not command others, nor shall others command us." And presently he parts with Damis under pretext of charging him with a letter for the emperor, but in reality to carry out the word which had been always in his mouth, "Conceal your life, but, if you cannot do that, conceal your death." Wishing then to separate from Damis, that he might have no witnesses of his departure, he invented this letter with which to send him to Rome. Now Damis said, that though he knew not what was coming, he was affected at leaving him; but Apollonius, who knew it well, said nothing to him, as if he should not see him any more, but had so full a conviction of living for ever as to charge him,

"Damis, when you are alone and philosophise, keep me before your eyes."

"Now here," says Philostratus, "the account of Damis ends, but I can find no certain account how Apollonius died, if indeed he did die. Some say he lived to be eighty, some ninety, some more than a hundred years old, sound in all his body, and more agreeable than in his youth." The story which Philostratus seems to prefer is that he lived in Crete more honoured than ever, and used to frequent the temple of Diana, which was guarded by savage dogs, who however did not bark at him, but fawned upon him even when he approached at untimely hours. The priests who had the care of the temple seeing this seized him and bound him, as if he were not only a magician but a robber, saying that he had given the dogs a sop to tame them. But he about midnight freed himself from his chains, and called those who had bound him, to show that he did nothing in secret. Then he ran to the gates of the temple, which opened before him and closed after him, but the voice of virgins singing was heard, and their song was, "Leave the earth— Come to heaven—Come:" as if they told him to ascend on high.[1]

Looking back on the life which has been thus epitomised, we find it divides itself into six periods. The first embraces the birth of Apollonius, his education, and manner of life as a Pythagorean, or rather as a new Pythagoras, more than equal to the original. The second contains his visit to the Indian Brahmans, to test and confirm, as it were, his doctrine, the doctrine, that is, which embodies the Greek wisdom, and all the civilisation and glory which it has produced.

[1] Book viii. 30.

The third takes in his life as a public teacher, in which, coming back as accredited by the Indian sages, yet as an equal, not as an inferior, he meets with universal acceptance throughout the whole realm which is the dominion of the Greek mind; teaches and instructs all orders from city to city, enlightens priests as to their duties, encourages and revives worship according to the several rites of the various divinities, admonishes emperors, and finds by personal converse with the sages of Egypt—the rival of Hellas —that its wisdom is inferior to his own. In the fourth period we pass to his suffering life, in which in the fulness of years he goes of his own accord in defiance of warnings to Rome in order to encounter the tyranny of Domitian, when philosophers cower before him, and when also, it may be added, Christians are put to death by him, the result being that Apollonius is treated by him with contumely, but escapes by miracle in the open court, and laughs his power to scorn. The fifth period carries us to the triumphant life of the sage, following upon this sort of resurrection, wherein Greece in the very central point of its varied life, Olympia, is stirred at his presence, hangs upon his lips, follows his footsteps with a crowd of disciples, the flower of the land, who are called after his name Apollonians, while in all this he is but reproducing the wisdom of Pythagoras, as he shows by emerging from the oracle of Trophonius with a book containing the precepts of the Samian sage. Thus in all his life he is but inheriting the heirloom of the Greek mind, is but the manifestation of the Greek spirit, what any one may be who knows "both what he is and what he has been," that is, is conscious of the imperishable soul which has lived before and will live after him through a series of transmigrations. Thus Apollonius, fairer in age than in youth, unimpaired in senses, in mind only matured and enriched, approaches a hundred years, the utmost bound of human existence. Sixthly, and lastly, this long life is crowned with a death—if so it can be called—in keeping with it, for his tomb can nowhere be found though Philostratus searches for it; rather as swans hymned his entrance into life on the flowery meadow, so the temple's gates open before him and close behind him, and he is seen no more, while the voice of virgins is heard welcoming the ascent to heaven of the man who is the representative of Greek wisdom, a god in fact because a good man, because he unfolds the deity within him; the veritable man-god, the highest conception of the heathen mind.

Now through the whole of this biography, which makes in the original a volume of 343 pages, rather larger than the four Gospels, there is not a single mention of the Christian religion, or that there had been any such person as Christ, or any people called after His name. But nevertheless as to the time at which Apollonius is said to have lived, and the places in which his activity was chiefly exercised, there are some curious points to be noted which seem to indicate a hidden reference to all these. First, as to time, Philostratus makes him die at a very great age, after the accession and before the death of the Emperor Nerva. If he be given, as some accounts according to Philostratus gave him, full a hundred years, this would bring his birth exactly to the date of the birth of our Lord. But at any rate his exit from the earthly scene coincides exactly in time with the death of the Evangelist St. John. Thus his life comprehends the whole period of our Lord and His Apostles. Moreover, he is described to be traversing the Roman empire from end to end as a public teacher precisely at the time that the Author of Christianity and His immediate disciples began to propagate the Christian religion. Then, as to place, his sojourn is dwelt upon at Ephesus, Athens, Corinth, and Rome, at each of which cities he is said to work a notable miracle. But there is something much more remarkable in the way in which he is said to visit Rome. There were two emperors who persecuted the Christians at Rome during the supposed duration of his life, and he visits Rome twice precisely at the time of these two persecutions, and expressly to measure himself, as it were, with the tyranny of Nero and Domitian. Apollonius first goes to Rome just before Nero visits Greece, and boldly preaches his philosophy there at the moment other philosophers are flying from Nero, also at the time when the great Apostles Peter and Paul lay down their lives. But Apollonius after preaching without fear departs without molestation. The very Tigellinus, who is the instrument of Nero's cruelty to the Christians, acknowledges and venerates his power. Thus Apollonius departs unscathed out of the furnace which consumed the chief Christian teachers, proceeding on his course to Spain with the tranquil superiority of a higher nature. Again, some twenty-five years later he returns to Rome, and this time it is exactly at the moment that Domitian is putting to death his relation Flavius Clemens and other Christians. Domitian tries his hand likewise upon Apollonius, and brings him to a public trial on a charge of conspiracy and other accusations, among which is one of being a god: but is constrained to acquit him, when the philosopher, as if disdaining so to escape, and to accept a tyrant's pardon, exercises his divine power, makes himself invisible, and appears suddenly afterwards to his friends at Puteoli. Thus, as the Apostle St. John was delivered out of the hands of Domitian just about this time, after encountering the risk of martyrdom before the Latin gate, so the Greek teacher triumphs over all the power and malice of the tyrant in his worst time, but in a manner which would seem to the writer of his life much more distinguished. And it may be noted that in the last period of his life he appears in Ionia, crowned as it were with glory, and attended by his whole company, "philosophising, it is said, most part of his time whilst there at Smyrna and Ephesus, without overlooking the other towns, of which there was not one wherein he was not well received." [1] But these were just those seven Churches of Asia to which the Apostle directed his letters in the Apocalypse, and where he taught in the last years of his life. On the other hand, there are two places to which Apollonius shows a marked dislike. One is Tarsus, to which he is sent by his father at the age of fourteen, but which he quits because he finds "the manners of the city absurd and not suited to philosophical pursuits, and the people insolent scoffers, addicted to pleasure, and more passionately fond of fine clothes than the Athenians of wisdom." [2] This is that Tarsus, "no mean city," of which the Apostle Paul declares himself to have been a citizen, and it should be noted that he would have been living there just at this time, as he was contemporary with the supposed Apollonius. The

[1] Book viii. 24.   [2] Book i. 7.

other city is Antioch, where Apollonius found the temple at Daphnæ "beautifully situated, but no zeal in the worship there, the people semi-barbarous and without education."[1] And Antioch, it must be remembered, was the place where the disciples were first called Christians, and the seat, when Philostratus wrote, of one of the largest and most distinguished Christian communities.

The result of all this will be that Philostratus, drawing as an artist the portraiture of his ideal teacher, makes him a positive and independent figure. He is by no means to appear in the world as a teacher of the highest Greek wisdom, and the supporter of Greek worship, because another wisdom and another worship had arisen to compete with these. On the contrary, he is a new Pythagoras, more than equal to the old. His wisdom is the same as that of Pythagoras, and this is attested by the book containing his precepts with which in the last period of his life, as if to set the seal on all his teaching, he returns from the cave of Trophonius. It is then no new thing, as might be objected by a Greek to the mission of Christ, but on the other hand he is near enough to the time of Philostratus to show that Greece possessed its original vigour in undiminished force by producing such a man, and he tacitly appears when and where the Christian religion appears, but outbidding as it were its original Author and its first teachers, who are ignored while they are surpassed.

Let us examine the chief features of the character which Philostratus thus presents to us in independent majesty as the pure and genuine offspring of the Greek wisdom.

[1] Book i. 16.

There is a certain unity of conception running throughout his book. From beginning to end it is knit together by one thought, which is that of a great religious and moral reformer and restorer. Apollonius is described as animated by such a zeal. All his actions are to illustrate and effect the purification and revival of the old religion. He is the bearer and establisher of this movement, which in his person as a Greek by blood, and down to the very niceties of his Attic diction, springs as it were out of the heart of the old belief, and appeals to all its customs. As parts of this one conception we may enumerate the following points.

1. His birth was miraculous. His mother when expecting his birth has an apparition of the Egyptian god Proteus, who in reply to her question whom she would bear, tells her, "Thou shalt bring forth me." And this god is described as taking all shapes, as knowing and foreknowing all things. In this perhaps he is an image of that unity in multiplicity of worship which the conduct of Apollonius was to show, and of the wisdom which is ascribed to him, one and yet multiform, grasping all sacred rites, yet caught in none of them, because consisting of the doctrine which is the essence of them all. Proteus is the immutable substance under the ever-changing shape, which is the one thing which Apollonius worships.

2. Accordingly the knowledge of the divinity is from his youth forward the one knowledge to which the mind of Apollonius is given up. Having tried all the schools of Greek wisdom—in which it is to be observed that he discovers no incompatibility with each other—he finds the complete truth in that of Pythagoras. He devotes himself for five years to the law

THE GOSPEL OF PHILOSOPHIC HEATHENISM 245

of silence, and then visits the Indian sages, to verify and compare his wisdom with theirs. Returning back, he commences an active life, of which he says, "I go about and teach." In fact, Philostratus would have us believe that during a period of sixty years he traverses all the parts of the Roman empire, extending his action over all countries and all men, and with the purpose of making the wisdom which he possesses the common good of all whom he meets. While he is eminently Greek in mind himself, yet he deems all men as possessors in various degrees of the same divine substance in their souls to be of one family, capable of improvement and correction. In his eyes all the rites of the various deities, however differing in circumstances, not all of which he approves, are yet but as it were Protean shapes and symbols of the one divinity. In accordance with this view, though he has his own special religion, he frequents the various temples and confers with the priests.

3. In this function of public teacher a knowledge not only of absent but of future things is ascribed to him. He possesses all the languages of men without having learnt them, nay, the things which they keep secret he knows. He quits a ship which is presently to founder; he anticipates future events by turning the conversation upon them. He has a vision at Ephesus of the tyrant's murder at Rome. He knows when persecuted what will happen and what will not happen to himself.

4. His power corresponds to his wisdom. Thus he works miracles, and we are carefully told that this power does not arise from magic, but is a power inherent and working in him, as when without uttering a prayer he withdraws his foot from the fetters.

In particular the whole world of spirits is subject to him. He stones the plague at Ephesus in the shape of an old man; casts a devil out of a young man at Athens; forces at Corinth a ghoul to reveal herself, and give up her prey; and finally at Rome raises a Roman maiden to life, the description of which reads like a copy of the raising the widow of Naim's son. He passes instantaneously from Smyrna to Ephesus, and again from the judgment-court of Domitian to Damis and Demetrius at Puteoli, where his appearance seems once more like a copy of our Lord's appearance to His Apostles after His resurrection.

5. But he is to be as great in practice as in doctrine, and if his wisdom as prophet and teacher collects all the scattered beams of light which proceed from the ethereal substance wherein consists the nature of the divinity, so his conduct is to correspond. He practises an ascetic life in food and drink, goes barefoot, wears linen vesture, since he must not outrage the principle of life by wearing the skins of animals any more than by feeding on their flesh; he maintains absolute continence, surpassing herein the fidelity of Pythagoras to one wife, and throughout his life is superior to every blandishment of female love. Moreover, possessing himself the most astonishing beauty of person, he resists every attempt on his own virtue from that perverted sin of his age and country to which this beauty exposed him. All virtues of self-control and temperance, all mastering of sensual tendencies and passions, all disregard of outward goods are ascribed to him.

6. In all his relations with his fellow-men he is pre-eminently the[1] friend of man, filled with the

[1] As Baur remarks, whose words I here take.

purest affection to the race. In his service to the divinity, whose visible image the perfect wise man should be, he consecrates himself wholly to the spiritual and bodily good of humanity. Thus the extraordinary gifts and powers which he possesses above all other men are only used by him for the noble purpose of lessening the sufferer's need, improving the condition of social life, and by the confidence which he thus wins extending more widely his influence as a religious and moral teacher.

7. But the last and crowning trial of virtue is to encounter the fear and danger of death without quailing, and Apollonius, we are told, is betrayed by a former friend and follower from motives of jealousy and avarice, and is denounced to the emperor as plotting against him. Hereupon he might escape, but of his own choice proceeds to Rome, disregarding the entreaties of his disciples. There with imperturbable serenity he consoles his fellow-prisoners, and exposes himself to the risk of every torment and of death itself with composure of spirit. He is insensible to all the power and threats of the emperor, and he defends himself from the accusation of being a god.

8. Lastly, the death ascribed to him, if death it can be called, is miraculous, is in correspondence with his birth and worthy of his life. Without pain and suffering which other men undergo, as he is welcomed into life by the song of birds consecrated to the god of light, whose religion he practises, so he disappears from the earth and is invited to ascend to heaven by a choir of virgins, hymning from the recesses of a temple.

Now it is much to be noted that the whole pre-

ceding picture of doctrine is conveyed to us in the
form of a biography. The career of Apollonius is
followed out from before his birth to after his death,
and the narrative of his actions is the exhibition of
his religion. But as the whole Greek and Roman
history does not furnish us with a single instance
of a man who spent his life in going about teaching
and doing good, so the whole Greek and Roman
literature before Philostratus does not furnish us
with a single example of an attempt to convey a
system of religious teaching in the form of biography.
There are indeed two instances, one before and one
after Christ, of men whose life furnishes a point of
resemblance with the life here assigned to Apollonius.
The one is Socrates, inquiring and discussing with all
men at Athens; the other is Epictetus, who devotes
himself to philosophic teaching with a select circle
of disciples. And in both these instances their
friends and pupils have put together books which
contain some of their conversations. But neither
the conversations of Socrates as recorded by Xenophon,
nor those of Epictetus by Arrian, come up to the design of Philostratus. That design, as it reveals itself
by internal evidence, seems to have been to supply to
the Hellenic religion and civilisation a person as its
bearer and representative in the same manner as the
Christians had such a bearer and representative in
Christ. Thus Philostratus, carefully abstaining from
any mention of Christ or the Christian Church, tacitly
imitates what he ignores. But likewise his imitation is
twofold. The first and very remarkable imitation is that
his book purports to set forth the life of a religious
teacher, whose doctrine is unfolded by his acts. In this
it has for its only adequate prototype the life of Christ

contained in the four Gospels. The second imitation is not less noteworthy. The character which he ascribes to Apollonius is not a simple copy of the character of Christ, but a heathen reflection of it. It is so drawn as to be to the Greek and Roman heathens what Christ is to Christians. We have an adequate reason for this double imitation in the fact that the Christian society was, at the moment he wrote, in the highest degree aggressive, advancing, and influential. He wished to show that his own heathenism could do as well or better. If Christ went about doing good for three years in one small country, Apollonius should do the same for sixty years through the whole region from Syria to Spain, from Rome to India and Ethiopia. If Christ worked miracles and cast out evil spirits, Apollonius should do as much. If Christ could despise external goods, practise continence, face betrayal, danger, and death, the heathen champion should match Him in this. Christ's birth even and disappearance from the earth should have their parallel, nay, be outdone, as his biographer might think, by those of Apollonius. And Apollonius should remain throughout true to his Hellenic race, should stand throughout on his own ground. For, as we have said, it is not a simple copy which he sought to make.

We have just been specifying the very striking points of similarity which this pretended life of Apollonius offers to the life of Christ. Let us now glance at the points of contrast, which no less illustrate the design of Philostratus, and the state of the mental conflict then carried on.

1. The doctrine which runs through the whole book is the relationship of the human soul with the divinity. The ethereal light-substance, which is the supreme

God, is shared also by every human soul. Apollonius thought it the highest wisdom of the Indian Brahmans when they told him that they were gods because they were good men. So in parting with him they told him that he would be considered a god not only after his death but during his life.[1] So, in the long defence which he is said to have composed but did not deliver before Domitian, in answering the accusation that he made himself a god, he explained in what sense the title could be used of him by the oracle of Apollo so calling Lycurgus. For the oracle, first doubting whether it should address him as god or man, finally decreed to him the style and title of god, as being a good man. It is in this sense, as kindling into full flame that spark of the divine nature which is in him, that Apollonius is represented throughout his life to be wise, divine, and even a god. This is the source of his knowledge, his power, and his goodness. In virtue of this he works miracles, and passes instantaneously from one place to another.

2. In the same passage Apollonius describes the true doctrine, as he conceives, of the nature of God, which is, he says, the doctrine both of the Indians and Egyptians. This doctrine recognises God as the Constructor, by whom all things have their generation[2] and being, and his goodness is the cause of his devising them. Since, then, there is kindred in these things, he asserts that good men have something of God in them. Now, by that ordered universe which rests upon God its Constructor, we understand all things in heaven and earth and sea, of which all men

---

[1] Book iii. 50.
[2] This word γένεσις has in this philosophy a special meaning, which I think Tzschirner, p. 433, very well renders, "Dieser Zusammenhang der enstehenden und vergehenden Dinge."

equally partake, save as to differences of fortune. But there is a world of order in every good man's power not surpassing the limits of his wisdom, and to attain this, as Domitian himself will admit, requires a man like unto God. What, then, is the appearance which this world wears? Souls in a state of disorder madly assume every sort of shape. Laws seem to them obsolete, moderation is lost, the worship of the gods neglected, idle talking is in fashion, and dissipation, from which flows indolence, the counsellor of every evil deed. Souls thus besotted by intemperance plunge into every excess, and nothing can restrain this wild irregularity, not if they were to swallow all those potions which like mandragora are medicined to sleep. But to regulate such a world of souls as these needs a man who shall come to them as a god in wisdom. Such a man is able to recall them from loves to which they are devoted, and from avarice which is never sated by riches until choked. Perhaps such a man may restrain them beforehand from disorder, but when once committed, he adds, "neither I, nor God, who is the Constructor of all things, can wash them from its stain."[1]

Now in these words we have a picture of the whole action attributed to Apollonius throughout his life. This and no more he aspired to do in virtue of the innate power of the soul, as being a part of the divine ethereal nature. Such he conceived to be the true task of philosophy; so much, as it thought, required to be done, and so much it attempted to do. And as the soul, being a portion of the divine intelligence, is the source of all good to man, so the body, which is regarded as the prison of its higher nature, must be

[1] Book viii. 7, 7, pp. 311, 312. Edit. Kayser.

the source of the disordered affections which gain mastery over the soul. All the ascetic life of Apollonius is therefore directed to subdue this tyranny of the body. His notion of evil is physical; the notion of the body overmastering the high and pure nature of the soul. His notion of good is, the subduing the body to the control of the soul. Thus the work of the wise man in the world corresponds to the work of the Demiurge in chaos, to reduce everything to the order of reason. This he must do, first in himself, then in those around him, and finally in the commonwealth. It is this idea consistently carried out which makes the Pythagorean philosophy.

From all this we see how far Philostratus and his hero are removed from approaching the Christian notion of sin. They would not even understand the conception of a purely immaterial spirit who was in rebellion against God. The soul, according to them, became liable to evil by its contact with matter, became evil so far as it was ruled by the matter which concerned it, that is, its own body; but in itself it was identical in quality, not in quantity, with the one supreme nature. And when the soul exerted this, its original power, the man became wise, divine, or even god. The doctrine of the pre-existence, post-existence, and transmigration of souls is evidently an essential part of such philosophy, which is as evidently at the bottom pure pantheism.

Thus the similarity between the picture of Apollonius, as drawn by Philostratus, and that of Christ in the Gospels, to which we have alluded, is merely external. Beneath it lies the most absolute antagonism, which may be further illustrated by pointing out that the opposition to the tyranny of Nero and Domitian occupies in the life of Apollonius the place which opposition to the tyranny of sin takes in the life of Christ.

3. The biographer plainly conceives that he is exalting his hero to the utmost when he makes him teach philosophy at Rome in spite of Nero's tyranny, to which, however, he gives way by retiring upon the definitive banishment of philosophers: and that he does this still more when he makes Apollonius go to Rome to meet the accusations brought against him before Domitian, and take this occasion to rebuke his despotism. In fact, in the Pythagorean philosophy the tyranny of despotism would be that malady in the commonwealth which corresponds to the malady in the individual whereby the unseemly passions of the body invade and subject the soul, both again being images of that chaos in the universe which existed in shapeless conflict before the divine reason reduced it to order. The function of wisdom, which is the soul acting by the energy of its divine nature, is to restore harmony in the inner world of man and the outer world of human society. But Philostratus is far from going any deeper than this into the malady of human nature; nay, he expressly declares that God Himself, the Constructor of the universe, cannot wash the soul from the guilt of blood once shed.

4. We see, then, that Philostratus had caught and imitated that portion of our Lord's character which consisted in His being a public teacher, going about doing good: but he had not the least entered into His character as a Redeemer from sin, and a Victim. And the next contrast we shall note very curiously illustrates this defect in the heathen apprehension. Thus he gives his hero a miraculous birth and a miraculous departure from the earth, and it is difficult to

read them without at once thinking of our Lord's Nativity and Ascension. They are plainly heathen counterparts of these, intended to be more brilliant and more triumphant. But the circumstances of pain, which belong to the real events, are carefully detached from their imitation. There is nothing in the birth upon the flowery meadow, heralded by the song of swans, and foretold by the god Proteus, to correspond to the Cave of Bethlehem and the Flight into Egypt. There is similarity in the disappearance from a temple amid the songs of virgins calling upon Apollonius to mount to heaven, and the Ascent from the Mount of Olives, but there is no Gethsemane and no Golgotha preceding it in the heathen life, for there was nothing in the heathen mind to call for these. There is, however, the recognition that real greatness is not accomplished without suffering. Philostratus strives to make his hero confront the loss of goods, torment, imprisonment, and death. But it is only seeming. The reality of suffering is away. Thus Apollonius on his way to Rome says to his friends: "Neither fire nor sword would terrify a wise man: none of these things prevail on him to make him flinch or utter falsehood." But he adds: "I know more than all men, since I know all things: but that I am not come here on a fool's errand you may see by this. I run no risk as to my own body, nor can I meet with my death from the tyrant's power even if I would."[1] So a little later he dismisses Damis, being perfectly sure as to his own escape. And all through the trial he is in no disquietude, knowing well that at the critical moment he will vanish from the tribunal and elude Domitian's grasp. Thus, in the heathen's copy

[1] Book vii. 14.

of Christ, while the ideal of suffering is admitted the reality is expunged. The glory of endurance is admired; but its actual cross abominated. The only outrage which Apollonius is described as having really endured is the cutting off his hair and beard in derision by order of Domitian, which is the feeblest possible imitation of the mocking and scourging of the Divine Original, while it is accompanied by the unfailing assurance of ultimate and painless delivery. The sense of the reality of an actual human life fails us throughout in the supposed biography, but most of all in the attempt to make the hero suffer, which is transparently counterfeit. Philostratus admitted that perfect virtue must be suffering virtue, but Plato's anticipation of the torments which the perfectly good man would undergo in such an actual world as ours is far more vivid and life-like than the feeble imitation of the real event on which Philostratus ventured. He never succeeds in making us think that his hero is not imaginary: but most of all in the attempt to give him the glory without the reality of suffering the imposture is evident. But the heathen had nothing in his mind to make the cross acceptable. It inflicted upon him the horror which St. Peter before his conversion felt when his Master declared that He would undergo it. It had not for him that meaning and that power which led St. Peter afterwards to embrace it for himself.

5. This whole state of mind will become most clear when we consider that doctrine of the soul's immortality which Philostratus makes Apollonius teach after his death. For he represents him as appearing in vision to a young man who had disputed the soul's post-existence, and this is the doctrine which the form of Apollonius returns to the earth to reveal to the

doubting disciple: "The soul is deathless, not thy property, but that of Providence, and when the body is dissolved in corruption, like a mettlesome courser freed from all restraint, it mingles with thin air, casting off at length its long-endured and hateful servitude."[1] The individual man then ceases to be: why should the body, which drops away and is never to be glorified, suffer crucifixion? Unless man needs redemption, there is no reason for the cross. Unless body and soul live together for ever, there is no reward for it. Philostratus neither accepted the reason nor aspired after the reward.

The sum then of the contrast we have been noting is this. Apollonius is the man-god, by virtue of the spark of divine intelligence, of which his soul is enkindled, and his ideal task is to restore the order of the universe first in the individual man and then in the commonwealth. In doing this the appearance of suffering and shame may rest upon him, but not its reality, and the soul which seems in its divine action like a god upon earth reaches its full power when delivered from the trammels of the body. If the manifold resemblances before noted assure us that Apollonius was intended to be a heathen Christ, the contrast here shown goes to the very bottom of the fundamental antagonism between philosophic heathenism in what we may certainly call its highest form, and the Christian faith.

We now come to the question, what was the attitude of Philostratus in this work towards the Christian religion? We have found him completely ignoring it, yet delineating a character which had no original in heathen history, for the Pythagoras referred to is so

[1] Book viii. 31.

dressed up in the school to which Philostratus belonged as to be a mere fiction, but which is a tacit imitation of Christ so far as His example of a public teacher extends. Further, the peculiarity of the imitation lies in this, that while the supposed Apollonius is to be made at least equal to Christ in wisdom, wonder-working power, piety, and good-will to all men, he is to be all this on a heathen basis, by the kindred, that is, which his soul possesses to the divinity. He is to call forth in a high degree the power which belongs to every human soul: he is wise, wonder-working, pious, benevolent towards other men, but all men may be such as he is, for he is but the representative of humanity. He is a man-god, but in no exclusive sense. Thus the outward similarity of the man-god reveals an intense inward antagonism to the God-man. Philostratus then is far removed from the position of Trajan a hundred years before condemning Christianity as a State offence. He is no less removed from the scoffing derision of Christ by Celsus, and the mocking spirit of Lucian, to which his piety is in the strongest contrast. In his whole conception of Apollonius we see the strongest proof of the force with which the Christian Church was acting on the world. It was a conquest of that Church that one outside of it should seek to give to a heathen personage a character and detailed life which should be to heathenism what the character and life of Christ are to Christians. The degree of the resemblance measures the force with which the character of Christ was influencing men who were not Christians; and a heathen ideal is produced which but for the life and actions of Christ would never have been thought of. But heathenism does not therefore abdicate its own right of existence.

It is said of the Emperor Alexander Severus, who reigned just at the time that this book was published, that he set up in his private chapel images of Abraham, the father of the Jewish people, and of Christ, the founder of the Christian Faith, as well as of Orpheus, the institutor of the Hellenic mysteries, and of Apollonius, as the teacher of Indian, Egyptian, and Grecian wisdom. The same emperor, we are told, in his public government, "permitted the Christians to exist," and Christian churches were in his days publicly frequented at Rome for the first time. It is this sort of liberal fusion of creeds which the book of Philostratus represents. A favourite of the Empress Julia Domna, writing under her commission, very naturally reproduces the policy which was followed by her son Caracalla, as well as by her sister's grandsons, Elagabalus and Alexander Severus. These emperors would have been content if all the worships of the Roman empire could have been comprehended in a solar religion, which is exactly that of Apollonius: and they were willing to admit Christ as a god into it, if the god so admitted would acknowledge his brotherhood with the deities embraced by the like comprehension. This period lasted from the death of Septimius Severus in 211 to the accession of Decius in 250. But from the time of Decius the Roman emperors became aware of two things, the one that Christ would accept no such brotherhood, and the other that His religion was contesting with them the possession of the Roman world. And a new period ensued, which contains the great and what may be termed scientific persecutions of the Church.

We can now, then, sum up the results which we gain from the work of Philostratus.

THE GOSPEL OF PHILOSOPHIC HEATHENISM 259

Nothing is more afflicting to the student of history in the first three centuries than the want of anything like a continuous record of events, and especially of the action which the Roman State exerted upon the Christian Church. Thus the brief reference of Pliny, as the governor of a province, to the Emperor Trajan, respecting the Christians with whom he had to deal, illuminates, as it were, a whole period which is dark from the absence of authentic information. But for this, modern scepticism would probably have denied that Trajan persecuted at all. In like manner the Romance of Philostratus, utterly worthless as history, is of the utmost value as revealing to us the state of mind among learned and reflecting heathens in the first half of the third century, and how great was the change which had passed over society since the time of Seneca. All the preceding tendencies which we have been following since the rise of the Neopythagorean school are fully developed in the Apollonius of Philostratus. With regard to the bearing of philosophy upon religion, we may take as three stages, the several positions of Seneca, of Plutarch, and of Philostratus. Seneca's god, if we can say that he has any, is nature or reason. He utterly scorns the existing worship; he considers prayer useless, he has no notion of reconciling philosophy with the worship of the gods. His Stoic doctrine would be the complete subversion of that worship, for not only does he reduce the multiplicity of its objects to unity, but his notion of the god within him is incompatible with piety or religion at all. A man cannot be pious to himself. Not such is the mind, and still less such the heart of Plutarch. He, too, holds a unity of the godhead, but one by which all the ancestral and traditional deities have sunk into subordinate parts of the chief God, while they retain their own rites and worship. Prayer to him is of the utmost moment. Sacrifice and worship are god-pleasing acts, and they are not only the bond of human society, but the pleasure and support of the individual soul. The whole existing worship, in all its multiplicity, is taken under the protection of the philosophic mind, and the restoration of piety in connection with it makes up the character of Plutarch. But how far does Philostratus go beyond Plutarch, Maximus, Apuleius, Celsus, and the like? In his conception of God perhaps not at all. So far as this, his Apollonius is only a visible embodiment of such a belief and worship as these writers had. But besides this he constructs an ideal of the philosophic life which is a heathen copy of Christ in birth, life, scope, knowledge, miracles, and not death but ascension. And as in doing this Philostratus carefully ignores Christ and Christians, so if in all the works of Plutarch there is no hint that such a religion was existing, it cannot be taken as a conclusive proof either that Plutarch knew nothing about it, or that knowing it he did not think it worthy of notice. But how vast is the difference between the heathendom which Seneca represents, and that which Philostratus portrays, is shown most of all in that spirit of piety with which his Apollonius fosters religious worship wherever he goes. An active principle of belief has been substituted for the principle of negation which prevailed in the century closed by Seneca. Further, the value of the work of Philostratus to us consists in its being a full-length picture of the Neopythagorean system of thought. It contains the best that cultured heathenism had to say for itself in the first half of the third century. It also indicates unmistakably the position which it took up in the face of the advancing Church. The one is its absolute, the other its relative meaning. Hardly a learned man has studied this work without coming to the conclusion that its author was well acquainted with the letter at least of the Gospels; and the inference has likewise been general that it was his intention to give a concrete example of human life which should be to the religion and philosophy of the Greek mind—the object throughout which he seeks to exalt—what the example of Christ was to the Christian. However convinced the reader becomes that the pretended life is a pure fiction, this purpose retains its value. The work is anything but historical in its facts, but its appearance at that time and its intention contain history. It is in this view that the points of similarity and the points of contrast between Christ in the Gospels and Apollonius as imagined by Philostratus are equally striking; for if the man who devoted his life to the communication of religious truth, in whom knowledge and power were perfect and equal, and who used both only in going about and doing good, while they had up to that time no sort of counterpart in actual heathen history, point unmistakably to the Original thus copied, so on the other hand the power in virtue of which all this is said to be done, that is, the divine particle in virtue of which the human soul is one with the supreme God, indicates as decisively the heathen standing-ground on which Philostratus rested. It is a counter-system which Philostratus thus set up; and while his imitation shows his knowledge of the great inimitable life which he presumed to attempt to transfer to another, it also shows that the counter-system which he tried to set up had a special reference to the Christian original. Thus his work is the answer of philosophic heathenism to the Christian Church and its doctrine. It gathers up the elements of the preceding progress which had taken place in this direction, and hardly anticipates in time the full development of the Neoplatonic philosophy which we have next to consider.

LECTURE XX

THE NEOPLATONIC PHILOSOPHY AND EPOCH

I.

In the character of Apollonius, as delineated by Philostratus in his pretended biography, we find a complete union of philosophy and religion. It is not the abstract pursuit of knowledge, but the governing his own life and the directing the lives of others by the principles of divine wisdom which is represented to be the philosopher's motive. So, again, he is represented as living in the temples, as consulting the oracles, and especially that of Trophonius, from which he receives a sort of authentication of his doctrine in the book of Pythagoras. Thus he acknowledges the need of a revelation for the acquisition of truth. Philostratus likewise has invested his creature with the power to work miracles, and this power is assigned to him as a result of his piety, and in order to accredit his teaching. It is, moreover, an inherent power, belonging to the soul as identical in its nature with the one divine ethereal essence which Apollonius worships underneath all the various manifestations of Hellenic or Indian or Egyptian deities. For the author is careful to express by the practice of his hero the notion that the unity of this god is unimpaired by the variety of rites with which these several deities are worshipped. And, further, union with this godhead is the end after which Apollonius strives, and he is supposed to return after death for the purpose of convincing a doubting youth that it has been accomplished in the soul as soon as set free from the bondage of its imprisonment in matter, that is to say, the body borne about by it on earth. Thus in Apollonius the union of philosophy with religion is associated with another union, in which the multitudinous deities of Hellenic, Indian, and Egyptian worship are taken up and absorbed. They become in a manner which is nowhere defined manifestations of one power, in which, as the producer of all things, the source of that generation whose evolutions are countless, the whole universe is lying.

This is one side of the biography by Philostratus. It is its aspect viewed absolutely. If we look at it relatively, the latest historian[1] of Greek philosophy is only summing up what is the concurrent judgment of almost all who have studied the work, where he says: "The delineation of Apollonius as a whole and in many particular traits is so remarkable a counterpart to the representation of Christ in the Gospels, that we have every ground for assuming the purpose of its author to have really been to set an equally distinguished representative of the old religion over against the wonder-working Prophet of the new one." Thus both the knowledge of the Gospels and the imitation of Christ by Philostratus are indisputable, although both Christ and Christians are completely ignored by him, and although his system has its own positive and entirely heathen standing-ground. For the thorough contrast of his doctrine with the Christian is as remarkable as the covert imitation of Christ. Nor is this, as has been already observed, a simple and direct imitation, but a heathen rendering

[1] Zeller, v. 135.

THE NEOPLATONIC PHILOSOPHY AND EPOCH 265

of his features. Apollonius is to be to the heathen what Christ is to the Christian, with a view to show that the religion which produced Apollonius was at least equal to the religion set up by Christ. The fact of a tacit reference to Christ throughout the supposed character of Apollonius would not be overthrown, nay, would not be impaired in force, by showing that the principles from which the two characters spring, as well as the results in which they terminate, are quite different. Rather the imitation and the contrast illustrate each other.

In all the points above mentioned, that is, in the complete union of philosophy and religion, in acknowledging the need of revelation in order to attain that truth which is the object of both, in claiming the power to work miracles as a result of piety and in order to accredit teaching, in maintaining the absolute unity of the Godhead, and the relationship of the human soul to it, and consequently in proposing union with that Godhead as the end of man's life, and further in the close alliance of this religious philosophy, notwithstanding its tenet of the divine unity, with the existing polytheistic worship, the doctrine which Philostratus was exhibiting under the form of a biography was about the same time put forth in the schools of Alexandria in a system of philosophic teaching. Ammonius Sakkas, the reputed founder of the Neoplatonic school, was indeed the exact contemporary of Philostratus, as the lives of both ran from about A.D. 180 to 250. Porphyrius declares that Ammonius[1] was of Christian parents, and brought up a Christian; but asserts that when he began to think and philosophise, he changed to the established religion. This is denied by Euse-

[1] Quoted by Eusebius, *Hist.* vi. 19.

bius, who says that he remained a Christian to the
last. The pupils of Ammonius considered his doctrine
as the revelation of a higher wisdom, which should
not be communicated to the uninitiated. Porphyrius
asserts Plotinus to have derived his system from the
oral teaching of Ammonius. But as no writing by
Ammonius is extant, it is from the treatises of the
disciple that we learn the Neoplatonic system. This
very eminent philosopher [1] was born A.D. 205, at
Lykopolis in Egypt. In his twenty-eighth year, A.D.
232, he gave himself up to the study of philosophy.
After frequenting the schools of various teachers he
came to that of Ammonius, and the doctrine and
demeanour of this teacher so attracted him, that he
exclaimed, "That is the man for me," and he remained
in faithful and devoted attendance on him for eleven
years. He then attempted to visit the East in order
to learn the wisdom of the Persians and Indians, and
for this purpose accompanied the army of the Emperor
Gordian. But this expedition did not succeed, and
thereupon Plotinus betook himself to Rome in the year
244. In this place he gave philosophical lectures
which were much frequented by the higher classes.
He won great applause, not merely by the originality
of his thoughts and by the skilful and attractive
manner of his instruction, but likewise by the dignity
of his person, his intense earnestness, and the purity
of his moral character. He practised the Pythagorean
life in all the severity of its abstinence. His whole
heart was in the work of teaching. So highly was he
esteemed, that a great many friends chose him for
guardian of their children of both sexes. Those who
were in closest intercourse with him looked up to him

[1] See Zeller, v. 413.

THE NEOPLATONIC PHILOSOPHY AND EPOCH 267

with veneration. His disciple Porphyrius, in his Life, attributes to him a gift of working miracles and of prophecy, such as that assigned to Apollonius by Philostratus. The great ladies of Rome hung upon his lips. His extant treatises were composed at Rome from his fiftieth to his sixty-fifth year, A.D. 254–269. The next year he died of a sickness in Campania.

Philostratus had given in the form of a pretended biography the principles of the Neopythagorean philosophy as they had been more or less prevalent from the time of Plutarch. The system of Plotinus proceeds from the same principles, but is drawn out with greater philosophic accuracy, with a more defined purpose, with clearer knowledge of the ultimate issues. If the character of Apollonius was fictitious, the real Plotinus appears to have been as devoted to his work of teaching as the philosopher imagined by Philostratus. His whole life, from the time that he gave himself up to study in the school of Ammonius to his death in Campania, was noble and blameless upon the heathen model. He is described as searching for truth through all the systems of philosophy; and after his attendance of eleven years upon Ammonius, he endeavours to visit the Persian and the Indian wise men, exactly after the manner and with the motive which Philostratus attributes to Apollonius. It cannot be pretended that a man so devoted to inquiry in religious systems was ignorant of Christianity. Not only was his master Ammonius originally a Christian, whether or not he afterwards became a heathen, as Porphyrius, the traducer of Christians, maintains, and Eusebius, the Church historian, denies, but in the twenty-five years which Plotinus spent at Rome, he witnessed the great persecutions of Decius, of Gallus,

and of Valerian, the martyrdoms of at least two
Pontiffs, St. Stephen and St. Sixtus, with that of St.
Laurence. The time of his greatest mental activity
was exactly that of which St. Cyprian said that the
emperor would rather endure a competitor for his
throne than a successor to the Chair of Peter. Thus
during the fifteen years in which Plotinus was com-
mitting to paper the philosophy which in the previous
decade of years he had delivered orally to the most
distinguished circles of Rome, the Christian Church,
teaching and suffering, was visibly contesting with
heathenism the possession of society, and was recognised by the emperors as the foe they had to dread
and were resolved to exterminate. The truce under
which Origen had spent so large a part of his life had
been rudely broken, and if in his answer to Celsus he
had remarked that the number of martyrs up to that
time had been comparatively few, he lived long enough
to enter upon a period in which it would be largely
increased. It is a fact that the appearance of the
Neoplatonic philosophy, as set forth by Plotinus, syn-
chronised with the great persecutions which assaulted
the Church, when in all the domain of thought the
Christian doctrine was the burning question of the
day, and in the daily life of men Christian conduct
was the spectacle of all beholders. If the systems of
Philostratus and Plotinus are in their positive tenets
identical, it will not be surprising to find that they
take up a similar position towards the Christian
Church. It will hereafter be shown that the same
reference which the person and character of the
invented Apollonius as a teacher bear to the person
and character of Christ is found in the religious
system of Plotinus when considered over against

Christian doctrine. As in the one a complete heathen standing-ground did not exclude a tacit imitation of Christ, so in the other the summing up, classifying, and rearranging heathen elements derived from Plato, Aristotle, and the Stoics, will not exclude that force of Christian thought permeating the lettered world, which caused heathenism to collect its whole strength against an advancing enemy.

The system of Plotinus is nothing [1] but a methodical description of the gradations by which the procession of the world from the divinity and the return of man to the divinity is brought about. Its motive [2] may be said to be a yearning after perfect union with the divinity. It may be divided objectively into three main parts: his view of the world above the senses, that is, the intellectual and invisible world; and, springing out of this, his view of the world which meets the senses, and specially of man its chief denizen; and thirdly, the raising of the mind to the invisible world and its return thither, which it is the proper function of philosophy to direct and effectuate.

1. As to the first point, Plato had [3] distinguished the world of ideas from the world of appearance, and placed the soul in the mean between them. Though he had set the Idea of the Good above all the rest, yet it was only the first of them. And he had attempted to explain the world of appearance by the existence of Matter, which he made independent of Ideas. In these respects Plotinus differed from him. While Plato had two original principles, one positive, the Ideas, and one negative, Matter, Plotinus, distinguishing as Plato had done, between the world beyond the

[1] Zeller, v. 370.   [2] Ibid. v. 420.   [3] Ibid. v. 422.

senses and the world of which they are cognisant, the general foundation of which is Matter, did away with that original duality of principles, and deduced in the last resort everything from one supreme cause. But his invisible world was triply graduated. First there was the Primal Being, exalted above all existence and thought: secondly, there was Mind, comprehending the pure thoughts into which it parts itself: thirdly, there was Soul, the supersensuous being which has a propensity to Matter. In these three principles he included all the powers of the invisible world.

As to the conception of the Primal Being by Plotinus it may be [1] summed up in the triple description of the Infinite, the One and Good, and the Absolute Cause of all things. And in this he seems to have employed in fact the three philosophical methods for reaching the knowledge of God, though he never names them, the way of negation, the way of eminence, and the way of causality, which afterwards came through the so-called Dionysius Areopagites into usage in the Christian schools. The conception of the Infinite belongs to the first way, that of the One and the Good to the second way, that of Absolute Causality to the third way. It [2] is especially in the last that his conception becomes intelligible: as when he says, that only the conclusion from effect to cause leads us to the Primal Being. As the Good is not seldom described as the cause of all things, so it is called infinite power, the power from which everything is derived. It is this [3] point of view which especially rules in Plotinus the relation of the finite to the infinite. As [4] the Primal Being is conceived to be efficient power, it necessarily produces another down

[1] Zeller, v. 429. [2] *Ibid.* v. 439. [3] *Ibid.* v. 440. [4] *Ibid.* v. 441.

to the furthest limit of the possible: and this production is not one of reflection and free-will, which have no place in the First One, but simple necessity of nature. As every complete being strives to produce another, the most perfect and the most powerful must above all work producingly, the best communicate itself ungrudgingly. The First One overflows, and in overflowing produces another. But in this he would not only exclude all thought of generation in time; he would likewise expressly guard against the thought of emanation by remarking that the inferior must not be conceived as an efflux of the superior. The First One remains in itself unmoved and unlessened, while the stream of being goes forth from it; the Derived is in It, but not It in the Derived. He uses other images expressly to show the immanence of this relation. The First One is the Root; the Derived, the Plant: that the Sun, and this its Light—atmosphere. The Derived stands to the First One not as a part to the whole, but as the effect to its cause. It is not taken from the substance of the First One, but without lessening or change of this substance is established and supported by its power. In fact these images serve to conceal want of precision in the conception. There is a contradiction to be covered by them, and it consists in this, that the First One is the cause of the Derived, but yet is required to be enclosed in itself, and to need no completion. Now, cause as such cannot be conceived without effect, nor power without its result. Here, on the contrary, a cause is maintained which is essentially outside its effect, and does not need it for the completion of its being.

That which is produced [1] is entirely dependent upon

[1] Zeller, v. 444.

that from which it is originated, that is, not merely receives its condition in its origin, but only subsists in dependence on it, is borne and supported by it. The power which goes forth from the First One diffuses itself into every being, without, however, dividing itself from its origin. The First One is therefore present to each being with its whole undivided infinite power: it is one life which issuing from it pervades all and confers on each its proper being. Plotinus expresses this by a metaphor. The whole is enlightened by the beams of the Primal Being. This is the Sun, which pours forth the universe, as a circle of light, around: the Centre, which rules by its power the whole circumference of existence. Thus everything is essentially related to the First One in its being and activity: has in it the end of its operation: the centre about which it turns.

Now [1] so far as the First One reveals itself in the Derived, the Derived stands to it in a relation of identity, partakes of it: but so far as this revelation is only appearance in another, the representation of the supreme cause in its effects, the two stand negatively to each other. The Original can only communicate itself imperfectly to the Derived. In proportion as the chain of beings is removed from its origin its completeness diminishes. Plotinus dwells on both these sides of his doctrine. The One is present to everything which is, as penetrating it with its power. All is an imitation, or more accurately, a shadowed or mirrored image of the First: that is, is not merely similar, but produced as a copy by the continuous effect of the Primal Being. To Be comes to a being only so far as it is one, and the completeness of its

[1] Zeller, v. 447.

THE NEOPLATONIC PHILOSOPHY AND EPOCH 273

being is in proportion to its unity. But everything is one only so far as it imitates the original unity. So likewise everything has the end of its effort and the measure of its activity in the Primal Being as the absolute Good: or, as Plotinus represents this, everything seeks to contemplate the Good, and what it does or produces is only an attempt to reach this contemplation. But, however near the relationship of that which is After to that which is Before may be, it is far removed from actual sameness. That which has become can never be of the same being as that out of which it has become. The Cause is of necessity more complete and powerful than the Effect: the origin more one than the Derived. Thus the further that we descend the chain of causes and effects, the more intermediate causes separate a thing from the first cause, the more imperfect it is. The sum of being forms a graduated scale, or a series of concentric circles, in which perfectness of being decreases in proportion to distance from the First One, Unity passes into Multiplicity, and the light radiated from the Primal Being pales until it is at length extinguished in the darkness of non-being. On[1] the other hand, the Primal Being is complete and content in itself, and by no means goes out of itself in producing the finite. It receives thereby no increase in perfection, not even any object for its activity. The Derived only is inwardly drawn to the First, not the First to the Derived. The Second is derived only from the overflowing of the First, but is something superfluous to it.

But here we must note two things. The first is,[2] that this procession from the First One to the Finite

[1] Zeller, v. 450.   [2] *Ibid.* v. 451.

takes place neither by an act of Thought or Will, nor by a logical necessity, but by a purely physical effect, being moreover a procession which ever diminishes in completeness, though this weakening is not the substance but only the effect of the Original Being. And we must note secondly, that in the relation thus maintained between the Divine and the Finite, the Finite has no being of its own, is mere accident, mere appearance of the Divine. Everything which is Derived is upborne by the powers which stream forth from the Primal Being, which are not separated from their origin, so that one operation embraces, penetrates, determines all things.

This presence[1] of the Divine is always brought into act for the lower degrees of being by the higher. The part works first upon the part, then the whole through the part. The corporeal world is in the Soul; the Soul in the Mind; the Mind in the One. Or, again, of the unfolding spheres, the Innermost, or Mind, is enlightened by the Centre; the Second, or Soul, by the Mind; the Third, or Corporeal, by the Soul. Hence the Corporeal moves itself first towards the Soul; the Soul towards the Mind; and both only in this gradation towards the First One.

The Primal Being,[2] the Original Unity, the One which is likewise Good, being above reason and the knowledge of reason, out of the superabundance of its power causes an image of itself to go forth, as the sun sends forth its beams. The likeness of necessity turns itself to its original, in order to contemplate it, and thereby becomes Mind. The Ideas are immanent in the Mind, but not as mere thoughts, rather as portions of itself substantially existing in it. They make in

[1] Zeller, v. 453.   [2] Ueberweg, i. 244.

their unity the Mind, as theorems in their unity make a science. Plato's Ideas [1] become to Plotinus, as to Philo, intelligences which are embraced by the Mind as universal intelligence, which the Mind works out in itself, and of which it consists: spiritual powers, thinking spirits, which are contained in it and under it, as species in genus, or as particular sciences in science as a whole. Thus the conception of Mind, inasmuch as it contains in itself a multiplicity of forms and powers, broadens into that of the intelligible world. It is the very Living Being which contains the archetypes of all living beings in itself. In it the multifold intelligible powers are one power, the many gods one god.

As the Second proceeds from the First,[2] so by the same necessity a Third proceeds from the Second, which stands in the same relation to it as it to the First, and its generation is no more in the one case than in the other a work of intention or purpose, or connected with change in the Producer. This production of the Mind is the Soul.

The conception of the Soul is determined in general by its being the next to the Mind, and the mean between it and the world of appearance, being on the one side filled, moved, and illumined by the Mind, on the other side touching the corporeal which is produced by it. It stands, however, nearer to the Intelligible, and with it is reckoned to belong to "the Divine." In its essence it is Number and Form, like the Idea, Life, and Activity, like the Mind: the outermost of the light-circles which surround the Primal Light, beyond which darkness begins. In its nature it is eternal and outside of time, though it produces

---

[1] Zeller, v. 471, 473. αὐτοζῶον, 475.   [2] Zeller, v. 476.

time. Proceeding[1] forth from the Mind it stretches itself out into bodies, as a point extends itself to a line. Thus it has an ideal indivisible element, and likewise a divisible element which enters into the corporeal world. The indivisible element[2] belongs to it as totality, or world-soul. That which proceeds immediately from the Second Principle is only the universal Soul. Particular souls spring from this. They are only operations of the universal Soul, different manifestations of the one life which streams through all. Therefore, though individually different, they are yet one and the same, as science in its different parts is one, as there is one light which illumines the most various places. The Soul of the universe remains undivided, but each several being takes from it what it can hold.

At this point we reach the boundary of the intelligible world, and if the universal Soul does not pass out of it, yet in its division among particular souls we enter upon the world of appearance.

2. As the invisible divine world proceeds forth by necessity from the Primal Being, first in the Mind and then in the Soul, so the whole visible world which meets the senses proceeds forth from the Soul by the same necessity. The Soul,[3] standing at the limit of these two worlds, illuminates, in accordance with the system of nature, that which is beneath it, namely, Matter, enters into Matter with a portion of its powers, becomes in its operation bound up with it, and advances out of the eternal and intelligible into the life of time. It is only through this connection of the Soul's powers with Matter that the visible world comes into existence. Without it, Matter, as being devoid of

[1] Ueberweg, i. 253.   [2] Zeller, v. 480, 484.   [3] Ibid. v. 491.

THE NEOPLATONIC PHILOSOPHY AND EPOCH 277

quality, and of body, would be no object of perception. So far Plotinus,[1] following Plato and Aristotle, considers Matter as the basis of everything which meets the senses, and distinguishes it from the Intelligible. It is a universal Substratum of that which has body, distinct from every particular body. It is the mere possibility of being. Only by the accession of Form to it, it becomes definite.

By this coming down of the Soul upon Matter, the whole visible world starts into being,[2] not by an act of thought and will, but by simple natural necessity, for the Soul could do no otherwise than give shape to the Matter which needed shaping, no otherwise than enlighten that which lay beneath it. And since this necessity ever equally existed and will ever equally exist, Plotinus absolutely contradicts any temporal beginning and any temporal end of the world. But though this operation of the Soul in forming the world is necessary, yet its connection with Matter is a sinking down into an unfitting state, a fall of the Soul. For Plotinus,[3] passing herein beyond Plato, places the cause of evil in the connection of the Soul with Matter. The Soul, in virtue of its higher nature, is of itself free from evil. Evil can only arise to it from the polluting connection with something in itself evil. For, if evil is the absence of good, Matter is the original and absolute privation, pure want. If evil consists in motion without rest, in absence of limit, in want of form, proportion, and definiteness, of Matter alone these properties are not only predicated, but make up its essence. Hence Matter is the Primal Evil; corporeality is a secondary evil; and only in the third degree can the Soul, in so far as it

[1] Zeller, v. 486.   [2] Ibid. v. 493.   [3] Ibid. v. 489.

gives itself up to an evil which is foreign to it, be termed evil.

This doctrine,[1] that the nature of evil consists in the connection of the soul with matter, is the special characteristic of Neoplatonism, and, it must be added, a special contradiction in itself, and one which leads to a disarrangement and confusion in the whole view of human nature. The contradiction consists in this, that Plotinus makes everything, without exception, including Matter itself, proceed forth in orderly sequence from the Primal Being, the absolute One and Good. But Matter is evil, as being privation and pure want. Thus, that which in quality is the absolute contradiction of the One, the Good, and the Spiritual, is made to arise out of it by the quantitative way of a progressive weakening or deterioration. The whole visible universe, which Plotinus otherwise marks as a work of transcendent wisdom and power, is produced by the connection of the Soul with Matter, which very connection is at the same time stigmatised as evil. Yet to this predicament Plotinus was reduced, since from his point of view he could neither derive Matter from the Divinity as a positive condition of the Divine being carried into act, nor place it as a second original principle beside the Divinity.

But this conception of Matter as evil is neither that of the natural philosopher nor that of the metaphysician; it arises clearly from the moralist's view of the effect of a bodily nature on the human subject. Let us proceed then from it to the doctrine of man, as set forth by Plotinus.

This divides itself into three parts: the first will concern the condition of the human soul in its state

[1] Zeller, v. 490, 422.

THE NEOPLATONIC PHILOSOPHY AND EPOCH 279

before this life; the second, its condition during this life; the third, its condition after this life.

As to the pre-existence of the soul, Plotinus says,[1] "Before this generation had taken place (that is, before our entrance into this life), we were there as other men, and some as gods, pure souls, mind bound up with the universal substance, being portions of the intelligible not parted off nor detached from it, but being of the Whole." As long as souls[2] continue in this state they are free from all sufferings, and as portions of the World-soul rule with it the world, without being in it. They are outside the world, since in that which is beyond the senses there is neither time nor change. There is in them neither the faculty of discursive thought, nor self-consciousness, nor remembrance, for they do not need to seek knowledge, which they either do not yet or no longer possess, but as they are perfectly transparent to each other, they see immediately in themselves the Mind, and all Essence, and the superessential Good. But yet souls cannot continue in this their original state. As the original unity produces multiplicity, so by the same necessity the Soul must produce something else, and communicate itself to that which is beneath it. And thus individual souls by a necessity, which is at the same time called a fall and a fault, pass by an eternal law into a body suited to their quality and will. This descent[3] is at once by an internal impulse, by the power of the absolute cause, and for the adornment of the corporeal world. Souls pass into a body because the Soul of the universe, according to the

---

[1] *Ennead*, vi. 4, 14. Quoted by Zeller, v. 512. [2] *Ibid.* v. 513.
[3] *Ennead*, iv. 8, 5. ῥοπῇ αὐτεξουσίῳ καὶ αἰτίᾳ δυνάμεως, καὶ τοῦ μετ' αὐτὴν κοσμήσει ὡδὶ ἔρχεται. Quoted by Zeller, v. 515.

conception of it in the system, is the point of union between the intelligible and the sensible world.

We must bear in mind this previous state of the soul in considering man as he is in this life. By its connection with the body something strange and foreign has been attached to the soul, which is in its nature incorporeal, and likewise was once without a body. Another being of opposite qualities has now hung on to the pure being of man. The soul has been transferred from its natural element into a new one, and has been subjected to the necessity of a double life. "We [1] are twofold, as we take into account the wild beast, or that which is above it. The body is a wild beast animated, but the true man is another who is pure of these things, and possesses the intellectual virtues, which have their seat in the soul as it is apart." But the genuine substance of the man, the real man, is our higher nature only. Through it our soul is related to the Soul of the All, and of like quality. It is the pure form which is not touched by that which is of the senses. It has the divine reason not merely above it, but also to its whole extent within it. "In what relation,"[2] he asks, "does the soul stand to the Mind? or have we this above us? We have it either as common to all, or as peculiar to ourselves, or, and this last is plainly the meaning of Plotinus, both as common to all and peculiar to ourselves. It is common, because indivisible and one and everywhere the same: it is our own, because every one has it entire in the First Soul." But this want of clearness affects the whole Plotinic system, in that the Mind is made at once our reason and a being

---

[1] *Ennead*, i. 1, 10. Quoted by Zeller, v. 516.
[2] Quoted by Zeller, v. 517.

superior to us, and that the Soul is made equivalent to the human I, at one time as distinguished from the Mind, at another as identified with it.

The result is that in the Plotinic theory, soul and body do not make up one nature of man.[1] But if there is no real unity in the parts which compose him during his life on earth, with the end of this life these parts separate again, and the return of the soul from the world of sense to the world which is above the senses follows. This is a simple consequence of what precedes. If the soul before this life was bodiless, it can be so likewise after it. If the present life is merely a disturbing of its original state, we shall consider the leaving it only a return to a higher and more natural being. Further, Plotinus points to the soul's relationship with "the Divine." If any soul, for instance, the World-soul, be immortal, our soul must be so likewise, since it is of the like essence. But as it is of the soul's essence to be immortal, so a restoration of the body is not to be thought of, since it would be a perpetuation of the prison in which the soul now finds itself. "The true waking up," says Plotinus,[2] "is a resurrection not together with the body, but away from it: to wake up with the body would be but a change as it were of bed from one sleep to another. To wake up absolutely without bodies is the real waking." Plotinus, like the whole Greek philosophy, abhors the doctrine of the resurrection of the body. But he embraces the old Pythagorean and Platonic doctrine of the transmigration of souls. As souls were originally

---

[1] The difficulties and inconsistencies of the theory in this respect are dwelt upon by Zeller, v. 519–527.
[2] *Ennead*, iii. 6, 6. Quoted by Zeller, v. 528.

drawn down into bodies by the attraction of the senses, so at their issue from the body the souls which have not freed themselves from this attraction will pass into new bodies, whether of beasts or of men, which shall correspond to their quality, and thus each shall receive a retribution for what it has here deserved. The purest souls rise above the world of sense altogether, and return to their original country.

It may be remarked, that according to this doctrine the conception of personality, as belonging to the soul, is wanting in the period before its earthly existence and in the period after it. In its original state its condition is clearly impersonal altogether. The words above quoted express this. In such a state souls are "pure," that is, disencumbered from matter, "mind bound up with the universal substance." To this state the completely-purified souls return. They behold the universe. As [1] in the intelligible world there is no change and no time, upon entering into it life in time, and with it remembrance, is extinguished in an absolutely uniform thought of the supersensuous world. Thus the soul proceeds into the body, as into a prison, out of an impersonal state; and when it is best and purest it returns out of that prison into an impersonal state. But what is it in the interval? What in this life constitutes the human being? The soul alone is said to be the real man. It is of its own nature free from error and free from fault. It is only by connection with a body that it can become involved in either. Sensuality, which is the source of all evil, belongs to the body only, yet the soul alone is punished for it in the retribution which follows after death. According

[1] Zeller, v. 532.

to the doctrine of transmigration, to which imperfectly purified souls are subject, the body in which they did well or ill is neither rewarded nor punished, but the soul is punished by passing into another body, of man or beast, corresponding to the quality which it has acquired by its transitory union with the former body. It is plainly regarded as the only principle of identity in the man, but its reward consists in becoming again impersonal, as its punishment lies in being again connected with a body. But this is not all. Even during its imprisonment in the body it has no substantial existence of its own, but is a portion cut off from the World-soul. It follows that in Neoplatonic doctrine there is no such union between soul and body as to constitute a personality made up of the two. If we regard the soul's own nature, it is divine; if we regard its connection with the body, it is an imprisonment of the divine in matter; if we regard the body, it is a portion of matter, which by its connection with the soul becomes to it the intrinsic seat of evil. The man, in whom these two antagonistic elements co-exist, indeed, but do not coalesce, is literally "half dust, half deity," but he is not a whole at all. According to this system of thought, the unity of body and soul, which constitutes a proper human personality, does not exist.

3. If the soul [1] has come into its present condition only by a darkening of its original being, and during its connection with the body can never cease to look upon it as something foreign and disturbing, and can only hope for a return to its original state by absolute freedom from the dominion of sense, its proper task is to work for this deliverance and so to reach the end of

[1] Zeller, v. 533.

its nature. Accordingly this elevation of the mind above the world of sense forms the third portion of the Plotinic system.

As to the end at which man should aim, his doctrine is Stoic. Perfect life must be life in accordance with nature, nature however so understood as that which is highest in man, and most proper to him, and this is thought, the activity of the thinking mind. All the rest is but accessory. External circumstances are merely the shell, the mind the kernel. Happiness consists in the bearing of the man towards this real inward self.

The doctrine respecting moral good and evil which follows upon this is of the highest moment in the system.

As [1] it is not an inward perversion of the spiritual being, but only the connection of the soul with the body from which the imperfection of its present life springs, no more than the dissolution of this connection is required to get rid of this imperfection; or, so far as it is affected by the soul's own inclination to sensuousness, the mere cessation of this external bias, not a change of its inward character, will be required to take back the soul to its purity and perfectness. The soul has no more to do than to turn itself away from what is foreign to it, and to confine itself to its own original activity. A change in this activity, as such, is neither possible nor necessary, since the proper being of the soul, its real self, has remained without fault and without error. The decision in man's moral condition consists in the turning away from sensuousness; the turning towards that which is above the senses follows immediately, as a natural consequence,

[1] Zeller, v. 537.

THE NEOPLATONIC PHILOSOPHY AND EPOCH 285

and requires no special working of the will upon itself, no further inward process, to bring it about. So soon as the impediment which the sensuous inclination puts in the way of the soul's natural activity is removed, this is resumed, and the soul pursues its course to that which is above the senses with the same certainty and necessity with which a balloon mounts into the air when the ropes which bind it down are cut. Thus the notion of purification understood as a deliverance from the body forms the basis of this moral system. That, at least, is the negative side; the positive is, that conversion to the invisible world, that becoming like to God, which follows immediately from it. As the soul's badness consists in its mixture with the body, and its dependence on the body, its goodness can only consist in its detaching itself from the body, and working for itself alone. All virtues are nothing more than a purifying, but this purifying does not touch the soul as such, which in itself has no stain, but only its relation to the body. Accordingly, the becoming like to God is contained in the purifying. As soon as the impure elements are removed, the soul appears again in its original being. As the sculptor only needs to cut away a portion of the marble to bring out the divine image, so the man working upon himself only needs to remove the superfluity in order to stand revealed in his pure beauty. Nor only this, but at the same time he will see the Divine above him, for kith only can discern kin. On which Plotinus[1] remarks, "For never did eye gaze on the sun without being of sun-like nature, nor the soul behold beauty, without already being beautiful."

[1] *Ennead*, i. 6, 9. Quoted by Zeller.

All moral activity, then, in its last resort, leads back to the delivery of the soul from the body.

But[1] highly as Plotinus prizes the activity of discursive thought, it is not to him the highest thing of all. It presupposes an immediate knowledge of that which is above the senses. The soul of itself is limited to mere reflection; it can only borrow from the Mind the principles of a higher knowledge. Spirit only can reveal itself to spirit; kin only can know kin; mind only can understand the Mind. This higher knowing is an immediate possession of what is known. In the contemplation which thus takes place the distinction between the divine and the human Mind ceases. The human thought, retiring into the purity of its being, thereby unites itself with the divine thought of which it is a part. In the words of Plotinus:[2] "If he who has mind is himself such as to be all things, when he conceives self he conceives all things with it; so that such an one with energetic inworking, beholding himself, holds all things as contained in himself, and himself as containing all things." The highest degree of this state is that doctrine of Ecstasy which is in contradiction to the whole original direction of Græco-Roman thought. Plotinus makes the ultimate end of philosophy to consist in a beholding of the divinity, in which all definiteness of thought and all self-consciousness disappear in mystic trance. When[3] God appears suddenly in the soul, there is nothing more between him and it; they are no longer two, but an indistinguishable unity. The soul becomes in this contemplation of the divinity not

---

[1] Zeller, v. 547.
[2] *Ennead*, iv. 4, 2. Quoted by Zeller, v. 548.
[3] Zeller, v. 551.

THE NEOPLATONIC PHILOSOPHY AND EPOCH 287

only one with itself, in that the opposition between mind[1] and soul disappears, but one with the divinity. The Primal Being unites itself with its being; the Soul has no part which it does not touch, but falls into one point with it. It can then no longer be called a contemplation of God, but a being God. The soul becomes pure light, free from all gravity; becomes God, or, yet more rightly, knows that it is God. In this unconditional unity with the highest, how could self-consciousness or conscious thought remain? Self-consciousness is only where the subject can distinguish itself from the object; thought only where these are determinate conceptions; but here we have gone beyond everything determinate and conceivable. If[2] we ask how the soul can reach this state, the reply is, through absolute abstraction from external things, through complete sinking into itself. If the soul removes every inclination and every image of what is outside it, if it draws back into itself from everything which is not itself, then it is at once immediately in the divinity, being entirely in itself. This higher light may not be pursued, but must be waited for till it appear. It dawns on the soul without means or preparation, by a sudden enlightening. The soul cannot say whence it comes, from within or from without. Indeed, strictly speaking, it does not come, but is there, and fills us with delight and blessing.

We may suppose that with a character so inward and concentrated as that of Plotinus, and with a system the culminating point of which is the identification of the soul with the Divinity, his philosophy would be also his religion: the two would be to him convertible terms. We have seen this to have been a marked

---

[1] *I.e.*, νοῦς and ψυχή.   [2] Zeller, v. 553.

feature in the character of Apollonius as imagined by Philostratus. No doubt it became a reality in the living Plotinus. But the imagined Apollonius was likewise devoted to the worship of the gods: and the apparently absolute monotheism of Plotinus found room in his system for an unlimited number of deities, in which he could comprehend the ancestral gods of the popular worship, and the visible gods, the stars and heavenly bodies. The Mind, the Second God, the most immediate revelation of the Inconceivable, produces all the Ideas, all the invisible gods. They are portions of his substance, and so make up collectively the supersensuous world. The divine Mind comprehends these several minds: they are personified into gods, and gifted with the contemplative knowledge of the intellectual world; but then again their separate personality vanishes away into identity with the divine Mind. They are indescribably beautiful and venerable, but only through the Mind which works in them. "They are not,"[1] he says, "at one time intelligent, at another time unintelligent, but are always wise in the impassible, stable, pure Mind, and know all things, and are acquainted not with human affairs, but their own, and all things which the mind beholds." Here, then, he can find room for all the deities of the Greek or any other mythology, and by using the interpretation of the myth which had become common in philosophy, his Primal[2] Being can become Uranos, the father of the gods, and Kronos, who swallows his own children, is the Mind, in that he encloses in himself his offspring which is the intelligible world, and if Zeus is said to escape from that destiny, the real meaning here indicated is the production of the

[1] *Ennead*, v. 8, 3. Quoted by Zeller, v. 558.   [2] Zeller, v. 560.

World-soul, the Third Deity, out of the Mind. This World-soul is Jupiter. Apollo is the One, as the negation of the multiple. Hermes is intelligible Form, the Logos. The most degrading symbol of Greek worship represents the productive power of the Logos, and the mother of the gods is the abstract conception of Matter, as the general substratum of Forms. In fact, just as the Stoic Monotheism with its one all-embracing god did not scruple to recognise innumerable particular gods under various apparent shapes, so Plotinus,[1] laying down one great King of whom all things are the production, did not hesitate to assert that his greatness was shown by the multitude of the gods who were ranged beneath him and dependent on him, and that those who knew his power would not contract God into one, but declare him to be many.

Nor was it[2] only the whole range of mythology which Plotinus defended by philosophical argument. He extended this defence to the concrete worship carried on in thousands of temples and paid to the statues of the gods who represented the qualities which he interpreted after the manner we have just indicated. For inasmuch as the whole universe is bound together by sympathy, the higher powers communicate themselves in preference to that which is like them. Now as the statue is formed after the idea of a particular definite god, it is through this idea connected with that god, in the same manner as the world of sense is connected with the intelligible world by the medium of the Soul. Thus, though he did not admit that the godhead descended into the statue, yet the power imparted from the godhead to the visible world has in

[1] Plotinus, ii. 9, 9. Quoted by Zeller, v. 557.   [2] Zeller, v. 562.

a special manner its seat in it. The statue is, as it were, a mirror reflecting a portion of the divine radiance, which the worshipper thus catches up.

Now in all this system of religious philosophy, which was committed to writing at Rome between the years 254–270, and which has been arranged for us by Porphyrius, the chief disciple of Plotinus, there is no mention of the Christian religion. We have seen that there was none in the life of Apollonius by Philostratus. Plotinus presents his system as the result of ancient Greek thought: the harmony of Pythagoras, Plato, and Aristotle. But the master of Plotinus, that Ammonius Sakkas on whom he had sedulously and reverently attended for eleven years, and from whose oral teaching Porphyrius, who worships his own master, declares that he drew his inspiration, was a Christian. Moreover, the character of the mind of Plotinus, as well as the time and circumstances of his life, leave scarcely a possibility that he was not informed in Christian doctrine. Nor must we fail to remember that the actual arranger of his writings, his chief disciple Porphyrius, was a man very well acquainted with Christianity, and wrote an elaborate attack upon it, an attack which the chief defenders of the Church thought worthy of refutation. Into the bearing of the Plotinic philosophy upon Christian doctrine we shall enter presently. Here it is sufficient to say that it cannot with any show of probability be doubted that the author of it was acquainted with the Christian belief, as he was beyond question a witness of a time of unparalleled suffering undergone by the Church while he was resident at Rome. The man who philosophised in the very city and at the very time when the martyrdom of St. Laurence thrilled through every breast, knew what Christianity was, both in belief and in action.

But here a word must be said about Porphyrius, and it need not be more than a word, because he did not himself[1] add to the Plotinic philosophy, which he expounded and popularised, and which he laboured to make clear and intelligible. That philosophy already stood under its founder in the closest relation to religion, having a practical scope; but in Porphyrius it is the main object to work a reform of religion by philosophy, to cultivate piety in connection with the heathen gods. Some Christian writers state that he was originally a Christian, but on account of some ill-treatment which he experienced fell off to heathenism. This, however, seems contrary to the language of St. Augustine,[2] who laments over him that pride, and especially his disgust at the doctrine that God assumed a body, prevented him from becoming a Christian. But it is beyond question that the man who laboured above all others to arrange and make clear the Plotinic system of philosophy was himself imbued with many Christian sentiments. Moreover he was at once well acquainted with the Christian religion and its bitterest enemy. But he did not add anything material to that philosophy. Such as Plotinus made it it continued to be during the whole period in which heathenism carried on the struggle with the Christian Church. From Plotinus to Julian, who carried out with the power of the Roman Empire the principles of that philosophy, the great opponents and persecutors of the Christian Faith were heathens of this fashion. From Julian to Proclus, during which the power of persecu-

[1] Zeller, v. 580. [2] *De Civitate Dei*, x. 29.

tion was taken from them, they maintained exactly the same principles respecting the supreme God, His relation to the world, and respecting man and his place in the world, as Plotinus. They maintained likewise the same intense abhorrence of the Christian Faith. They united devotion to the heathen worship and defence of its gods, its fables, and its practices with such an exoteric belief as that of Plotinus. To meet the Christian objection against plurality in the godhead, they were monotheists in the sense of Plotinus; while on the part of all those who maintained the deity of Jupiter, Juno, and Venus, and the rest, they defended the worship and all the manifold practices which belonged to that worship with such an interpretation as we have seen above.

What has been said of Porphyrius,[1] that he took up philosophy mainly on its religious and practical side, is yet more applicable to Iamblichus. If the former had found the help of religion and the assistance of the gods necessary to enable philosophy to discharge its work, much stronger was this feeling in the latter, since he still more distrusted the strength of human nature, and was still more convinced of his own helplessness. How the gods produce what is finite we cannot tell; enough for us the conviction that all is done by them. The first condition of a true knowledge of God is the belief that nothing is impossible to the gods. He who has this belief will betake himself to a theology which allows him to assume everything which is taught about the gods. To a philosopher who proceeded from these principles no popular belief could appear absurd, no blending of tenets in a system of mixed philosophy and religion

[1] Zeller, v. 619.

be extravagant. The wider the grasp with which he embraced in his speculation the religions of all peoples, the more perfectly he must have thought himself to have reached the end at which his philosophy aimed.

It is needless to enter into more detail as to the particular views of Porphyrius and Iamblichus, or of Proclus, the last exponent of this philosophy. Such as it appears in Plotinus, it continues in its main principles and conclusions to the end.

There can be no doubt that this Philosophy, as it is the last production of the Greek mind, so it is the issue and the outcome of a long preceding train of thought. We are told that Plotinus, like his great predecessors who were the objects of his professed veneration, Pythagoras, Plato, and Aristotle, was a man of the most curious mind. He had, in fact, followed up with a sort of devotion the lives of the philosophers who preceded him, and examined their several tenets; and he composed a system which was the working out and arrangement of certain fundamental ideas inherited from Pythagoras, Plato, and the Stoics on the one hand, from Philo and the Alexandrine school of thought on the other. The work so accomplished was the logical issue of the whole Neopythagorean movement, a movement which in the days of Cicero and Seneca, as we have seen them declare, did not exist, but which we have found so strong in the time of Plutarch. Plotinus, indeed, may be said to be his interpreter, to give a logical and connected expression to that which was at the bottom of Plutarch's mind. But what was the cause of all this movement? What resuscitated, with a force which it had never before possessed, a train of thought which had apparently come to an end in

Seneca's time? Plotinus, like Philostratus, was fully aware of the new power which was stirring the world, and he searched the whole arsenal of Greek thought for a counter force. His philosophy is the ultimate ground taken up by Hellenism, on which to fight its last and desperate battle with the advancing Christian Church.

Nor is it only the last chosen ground of conflict, but likewise the development of a complete antagonism in which heathendom gathers itself up to produce on its own domain and from its own principles all those effects which it saw the Christian Church in the train of accomplishing. It aimed at satisfying the mind and heart of man with regard to the same objects which the Christian Church had made of primary interest in the world. At the moment [1] when Ammonius Sakkas and Plotinus founded their school, the search after the Absolute was the capital problem which agitated and troubled minds. What the Philosopher calls the Absolute, the Christian calls God. But to produce such a state of things had been the work of the Christian Church. In Seneca's time such a question would have been otiose, a complaint which he makes in fact, when he says that so few regard philosophy. Plotinus felt that the unity of the Godhead had assaulted the polytheistic worship with a prodigious force, and he set up a counter unity to it with which he wished to satisfy the reason on one side, and spread an ægis over the whole pantheon of Greek and Oriental gods on the other.

For, further, his system is a heathen analogon of Christianity, to which it stands just as the pretended Apollonius stands to Christ. Apollonius was the

---

[1] Jules Simon, *Alexandrine Philosophy*, Preface, p. l.

man-god, in that, possessing in his soul a portion of the divine reason, in virtue of it he possessed all knowledge and the power of working miracles. As such, he was set over against the God-man. As a specimen of human nature in its highest condition, he was to bear a comparison with human nature as assumed by a Divine Person, in which fact the whole Christian revelation is summed up. The force of the simultaneous connection and contrast lies precisely in this, that Apollonius not only stood entirely on heathen ground, but represented unassisted human nature. Such as he was, Pythagoras had been and others might be. On this ground he was to rival, encounter, and, as Philostratus thought, to prevail over Christ. Just so the system of Plotinus was intended on a heathen basis to meet and encounter the Christian Church at all points, wage war with it for the possession of human hearts, satisfy the yearnings which it had called forth, and all this in virtue of a force belonging to human nature itself.

This triple thesis, that the Philosophy which we have above contemplated in its chief features was the last production and outcome of Hellenic thought, that it was the development of a complete antagonism with the Christian mind, and at the same time a heathen analogon of it, I shall now proceed to illustrate.

II.

This will be done sufficiently, I think, if we consider under three heads the opposition between the Neoplatonic system and the Christian Creed. The first opposition will be between the Primal Being as conceived in the system, and God as He is in Himself according to the Creed, between the Impersonal and the Personal God. The problem of God and the World, as stated by the one and the other, makes the second opposition. The relation between God and man, issuing out of these two several conceptions of this problem, forms the third.

The Primal Being of Plotinus appears to be formed by logical abstraction after this wise. All which meets the senses he generalises under the conception of Matter; all which thinks he generalises under the conception of Mind, as Spinoza did after him.[1] But beyond both Mind and Matter lies the conception of Being. Not content, however, with this, he tries to invent something beyond not only Mind but Being, which he terms the Absolute Unity. He personifies[2] the result of his abstraction, holds it for the principle of that from which it is abstracted, and identifies it accordingly with what he calls the Godhead. Then, following the inverse process, and descending from the abstraction to which he had mounted, he makes the first production of the Absolute Unity to be Mind, that is, the conception of Intellect as distinct from Matter, the second to be Soul, which he considers already to touch upon the corporeal world, or Matter: and then through the connection of the Soul with Matter he supposes the whole visible world to roll itself out into existence.

The procession of all things from this so conceived Unity is necessary and eternal: not of thought or purpose. And all that which so proceeds has no real substance of its own. It is mere accident, an appearance of the Divine: for it is one operation which

---

[1] See note at the end of the chapter.
[2] Ueberweg, p. 251.

embraces, penetrates through, and determines all things.[1]

If we attempt to reach the meaning of all this, it would seem to be that the Unity which is called the Deity has no real existence. It is merely the substitution of the highest logical abstraction for the really Absolute. It puts the emptiness of all being, which may become anything, which exists only in our thought, and nowhere in reality, instead of the fulness of Being, Mind, and Life.

Such a conception of the Primal Being is logical Pantheism; and its relation with the universe that of dynamical Pantheism.

But it was from a physical view of the world and a desire to reduce it to a physical unity, that Greek philosophy took its start; and the confusion of God with the world, as it was involved in its beginning, so remains its great error during the course of nine hundred years from Thales to Plotinus. In the seventh century before Christ, the wise men of Greece all proceeded from the expressed or the tacit assumption of one world-forming force, whether they considered this as bound up with matter, or as severed from it, whether they called it Nature, or the Divine, or by any other name.[2] This conception forms the common basis of the mechanical doctrine of nature on the one hand, and of the dynamical doctrine of nature on the other. All the various schools of materialistic Pantheism, of which the Ionic is the first, spring from the former; all the various schools of idealistic Pantheism, of which the Eleatic is the

[1] The appearance of this thought almost at the beginning of Greek philosophy is noted by Kleutgen, *Philosophie der Vorzeit*, ii. 204, sec. 649. See note at the end of the chapter.
[2] Zeller's *Vorträge*, p. 9.

first, spring from the latter. In the former the confusion of God with the world consists in making him its material cause; in the latter it consists in making him its formal cause: in both the relation of all existing things to him is that of the Appearance to the Essence, that of the Part to the Whole.

In the first stirrings of Greek philosophic thought Matter and Mind were not distinguished, but Anaxagoras clearly brought out the conception of Mind as distinct from Matter, of one universal Mind as the disposer and controller of all things. This conception appeared to Aristotle so important, that he called Anaxagoras, in comparison with those who preceded him, a sober man among drunkards. And in truth this conception was the highest reached, whether by Plato or by himself. Brought up in the belief of a multitude of gods, and with the material figures which represented the functions of those gods continually before their eyes from childhood, their merit was that they conceived one supreme God distinct from Matter, pure Mind: but when they considered the relation of this God, who was pure Mind, to Matter, of which the endless manifestations in the universe may be summed up in the word Nature, Plato did not reach beyond the conclusion that this Matter had always existed, and was in some undefined way over against the supreme Mind, who worked upon it indeed, and reduced it to order, but who found it there, a something to be counted with, and not wholly to be subdued. Aristotle, while he carried out the conception of Anaxagoras to the point that this Mind, distinct from all contact with Matter, was eternal, the first mover, and the cause of motion, but himself incapable of change, incapable of becoming, pure Act, yet in dealing with the problem of Matter, and its relation to this Mind, held that the universe was eternal. Thus the two princes of Greek thought, while not Pantheists, so far as they conceived one Supreme Mind, entirely detached from Matter, yet failed to solve the problem of the relation of this Mind to the universe in such a manner as would escape the error of Pantheism. For not only was Matter conceived by them as ever existing over against Mind, but their conception of Mind itself appears to have been only an abstraction from the human mind; a generalising of Intellect parallel to the conception of *Materia prima* as the substratum of all body. At least the result in those who followed them was that the one Supreme Mind and the human mind fell under the same genus with only a quantitative difference. And so they made this mind not indeed the material but yet the formal cause of the world: the formal cause inasmuch as the world subsisted as it does because Mind was in it arranging and ordering it, as the soul is in the body. And if the notion of creation out of nothing is excluded, then this arranging and ordering must be by the substance of the arranging and ordering power being likewise the substance of things. This in philosophic language is to make God the formal cause of the world.

Now, excepting the Epicurean school, which was materialistic, that is, placed in Matter itself the force which made the world, it seems to have been the universal doctrine of Greek philosophy after Plato and Aristotle that the Logos in man is part of the one divine Logos. We have seen this run through Stoicism as its generating and characteristic doctrine, the basis of such moral teaching as it possessed. Cicero represented this not only as his own conclusion, the result of reasoning and discussion, but likewise accepted it on the authority of the highest philosophers. Pythagoras and his school had never doubted that our minds are drops of the universal divine Mind. The human spirit having been severed off from the divine Mind can be compared with nothing else, if this may be reverentially spoken, but with God Himself. Elsewhere he affirms that "there is one infinite nature and power of mind, separate from these natures usual and known to us. And so whatever that is which feels, which understands, which wills, which energises, it is heavenly and divine, and therefore must be eternal. Nor, indeed, can God himself, who is conceived by us, be otherwise conceived than as Mind, pure and free, distinct and apart from all mortal composition, feeling and moving all things, and itself endowed with eternal motion. Of this kind and of the same nature is the human mind." The view is completed by the parallel between the soul in the body and God in the world, which he puts in the mouth of the elder Scipio, addressing the younger with a sort of revelation from the supernal region in which his soul as a part of the universal soul was dwelling. "Know then thyself to be God, if, indeed, he is God who energises, feels, remembers, provides: who as much rules and directs and moves that body over which he presides as the supreme God does with regard to this universe. And as God, who is himself eternal, moves the universe which is in one part of it subject to death, so the everlasting mind moves a corruptible body."

Cicero[1] may be said to be here expressing the out-

---

[1] Cicero, *De Senectute*, 21; *Tusc. Disp.* v. 13, i. 27. Somnium Scipionis from *De Republica*.

come of the Pythagorean, Platonic, and Peripatetic philosophy as to the important point of the relation of God to the universe.

Thus the highest reach of pre-Christian philosophic thought in the Græco-Roman world may amount to this, the admission of one Supreme God who is a purely immaterial intelligence without beginning and without end; the belief that the soul of man is an immaterial intelligence of the same nature, and related to it as a part to the whole, the images most in use being that it is in regard to the universal Mind as a drop of the ocean, as a spiration of the breath, as a spark of the fire. And the God so conceived is to the universe as the human soul is to its body.

In the three centuries which elapse between Cicero and Plotinus, Greek philosophy does not shift its standing-ground as to the relation between the substance of that which it terms by a neuter and abstract noun "the Divine," and the intellectual part in man. We have seen how this kinship, or rather, identity, of nature between the divine and human mind runs through the doctrine of Epictetus and Marcus Aurelius; how it no less rules the opposite school of Plutarch, Dio, and Maximus Tyrius; how it makes up as it were the whole philosophy of the pretended Apollonius, as drawn by Philostratus.

But if the confusion of the substance of God with the substance of the world, in the one or the other shape, of making something which is denominated God either the material or formal cause of the visible and intelligible universe, runs in various degrees through all the philosophic thought of the nine hundred years before Plotinus, the doctrine of Plotinus may be considered one in which Pantheism obtains a complete sway. The universe is the evolution of the One; the Absolute Unity is immanent in the world, which is its eternal and necessary development, not merely the human soul but matter itself being part of this procession, in which there is but one life, one being, one substance. And as to the important point on which we have been treating, the assertion of a merely quantitative difference between the human and the universal soul, no more conclusive proof of the belief of Plotinus can be given than the words of the dying philosopher as recorded by his friend, admirer, and disciple, Porphyrius: "I am going to lead back the God that is in me to the God of the universe." That movement of thought which is apparent at the starting of Greek philosophy, to reduce all things to a physical unity, receives its completion in the system of Plotinus. But in two hundred years which elapse from Seneca to that philosopher there had been a further effort which shows itself equally in the Neostoic and the Neopythagorean school, an effort to reconcile the gods of Polytheism and the worship of them with this one power or cause. In Plotinus we find this reconciliation carried out with the greatest completeness. His Absolute Unity admits into its capacious bosom all gods, for the gods so admitted are simply parts of one universal power, which is the substance of all things. Pantheism and Polytheism share the same error [1] of giving the incommunicable Name to stocks and stones; for if the being of God is the being of all things, it is as true to say a stone is God, as to say a stone is a being. If God be at once the matter and the soul of the world, and in both, in spite of his

---

[1] See St. Thomas, *Contra Gentiles*, i. 26, and Kleutgen, *Philosophie der Vorzeit*, ii. 418.

THE NEOPLATONIC PHILOSOPHY AND EPOCH 303

eternity and unchangeableness, be subject to every change in time, the idolaters were not to be blamed for honouring with divine worship the air, or the fire, or irrational animals; rather the only blame they deserved was that they did not worship everything.

Plotinus was only faithful to the whole course of Greek philosophy from its rise in rejecting the doctrine of creation. Even Plato and Aristotle had never risen above the conception of a Mind who arranged and ordered matter, an architect of the universe, who built from pre-existent materials. The creation of matter and mind equally out of nothing was not reached by them; or we may rather say it was opposed to certain principles which were the basis of all their thought. That out of nothing nothing comes, was an axiom with all Greek thinkers. It was the Stoic conception of utmost impossibility that anything should come out of nothing. And that anything should happen without a cause they said was similar. Their view of the order of the world was this: "The universe is a unity governed by a living, reasonable, and intelligent nature, in which all things proceed by an eternal series linked and strung together; so that in this process of becoming, every antecedent has its result necessarily suspended from it as a cause. Nothing therefore in the universe is, or becomes, without a cause, inasmuch as there is nothing in it unattached or severed from all the constituents preceding it. For the universe would be distracted, divided, and no longer retain its unity, nor the one order and series of its distribution, if a single uncaused movement could be introduced." Again, the conception is brought out by Cicero with all the lucidity of the master of Roman diction. "Fate I call the order and series of causes, in which cause linked to cause generates from itself the real. That[1] is everlasting truth flowing out of the abyss of eternity. According to this nothing has taken place which would not have taken place; and in like manner nothing will take place of which nature does not contain within her the exactly efficient causes. By which we may understand that fate is not a superstitious but a physical expression, the eternal cause of things, why all that is past has taken effect, all which is instant is taking effect, all which follows shall take effect."[2]

No words could more exactly express the procession of all things from the Absolute Unity as conceived by Plotinus. And as herein he exactly followed his Stoic predecessors, so has he anticipated his modern successors; for this is the very kernel of Pantheism. This procession was the deity of Plotinus, and is the only deity which his modern successors admit. "God, through the activity of thought determining His originally undetermined being, produces things. The meaning of which is, that He generates things according to their proper and real being out of His own essence, and that accordingly this, His essence, is in things under manifold forms; a metamorphosis of the Absolute which Hegel could not characterise more sharply than by naming God the eternal procession."[3] And in this respect Plotinus and Hegel are exactly at one.

We have, then, now before us the Neoplatonic conception of God and of his relation to the world, in which it is clear that he has neither unity nor per-

[1] "Ea est ex omni æternitate fluens veritas sempiterna."
[2] Alexander, *De Fato*, p. 70, and Cicero, *De Divinatione*, i. 55. Referred to by Zeller, iv. 149.
[3] Kleutgen, *Philosophie der Vorzeit*, i. 48.

sonality, nor even any being of his own apart from the world and independent of it. He is, in fact, merely a logical conception, drawn from abstraction and assumed to be real. And the world is his eternal and necessary procession, under an infinite variety of appearance.

The antagonism in the teaching of the Christian Church respecting the being of God and His relation to the world with the Neoplatonic system may be summed up under four heads. The first will be the unity and unicity of God; the second, the Trinity of Personal Relations in God; the third, the doctrine of Creation; and the fourth, the infinite gulf between the being of God and the being of creatures which that doctrine establishes.

1. The Church proclaimed belief in one God, who was not the abstract conception of unity or being formed by the mind, the highest generality which arises in the thought when it considers the universe, which is a thing of logic, not real nor actual, but who is the Being apart from all other being, subsisting in Himself, conscious and free. His Being is not abstract, but concrete; not general, but peculiar; not the possible basis of all being, which is nothing and may be anything, but the fulness of being, infinite on all sides, incapable of mixture, incapable of addition, incapable of becoming, that is, of change; determined in Himself, and divided from all other beings because no addition can be made to Him.[1] Such is the One God viewed as over against the Absolute Unity.

2. In this One God the Christian Church proclaimed a Trinity of Personal Relations, eternal as God Himself, the Father eternally generating, the Son eternally generated, the Holy Ghost eternally proceeding, but

[1] See Kleutgen, *Theologie der Vorzeit*, i. 364; i. 208.

having one eternity, immensity, infinity, immutability; one omnipresence, one omniscience, one goodness, one sanctity. But in the Plotinic Trinity the first procession of the Absolute Unity was the Universal Mind, and the second procession from the Universal Mind was the Universal Soul, both being successive weakenings of the First One, and the latter touching already on the world of matter. There was, therefore, no real resemblance between the two. The Plotinic Trinity is as remote from the Christian as the Plotinic Unity is from the One God. It stands, however, to that Unity as the Christian Trinity stands to the Christian Unity. For the Plotinic Trinity is an attempt to explain the origin of things, and is produced in furtherance of that attempt; but the Christian Trinity is a revelation of the ever-blessed Being of God, His inner Life and Blessedness in Himself, independent of creatures.

3. But the force of the Plotinic conception lay in the relation which it established between the world and God; and here the antagonism with the Christian Faith comes into yet fuller light. The procession of all things from the Absolute Unity through the Mind and the Soul, down to the last particle of Matter, was as eternal and necessary as the procession of "the Divine" itself; a procession devoid of will, in which there was one only substance, and one only operation, under every variety of appearance. But the Triune Christian God creates all things out of nothing, and this in a threefold sense. Out of nothing, because there is no pre-existent matter; again, out of nothing, because non-being precedes in nature; and, once more, out of nothing, because non-being precedes in time.[1] And hence is seen the truth

[1] See Stöckl, *Philosophie des Mittelalters*, ii. 542, from St. Thomas.

THE NEOPLATONIC PHILOSOPHY AND EPOCH 307

and reality of that being which God confers; for what thus arises out of nothing is not an appearance of something else, but a being consisting in itself; and again, it is not drawn out of any other substance, but made out of nothing. Equally, whether Matter or Mind, it is a simple creation out of nothing. And lastly, which is not the least important point of the contrast, what thus arises springs from the free-will and choice of the Creator. Being perfect in Himself, He chooses to create, as He might have chosen to remain without creatures. There is no necessity in His Being for this choice, for which there is no other cause conceivable than the divine Will.

4. We have seen how the Absolute Unity of Plotinus took into itself the Polytheism with which its author was surrounded. This was part of its use. The multitude of the manifestations of the one force, as conceived by Plotinus, might be endless: it only needed to personify each manifestation with the name of a god, as the Stoics had done before him. Also, if there is only one substance, this abstract god of Plotinus may be a stone as well as Jupiter. But the One God who creates Mind and Matter alike out of nothing, excludes all other beings from approaching Him by an infinite chasm. Their being and His do not fall under one genus. And so the gods of heathendom dropped away before Him. In His presence they were simply nowhere: vanity, non-entity. This was the meaning of the reproach of "godless" addressed to the ancient Christians; and this too was at the bottom of the profound hatred with which Neoplatonists, when in power, persecuted the Christians. They saw and felt the full force of the antagonism between their pantheistic unity and the One God of

the Christians: between a necessary force proceeding through all nature to its utmost limit, and the Lord of Hosts, surrounded by hierarchies of spirits, who are called into existence, and maintained in it, by His omnipotent Fiat: between a universe in which man is the product of a nature eternally unfolding itself without will, and man the creature of God.

This brings us to the third point of contrast which we had to consider, the being, position, duties, and hopes of man in Neoplatonism and in Christianity.

The God of Plotinus does not create, but evolves itself in an eternal becoming; and the human spirit is a portion of the divine Universal Mind. This latter pantheistic doctrine seems to date from Pythagoras, and coming down through Plato and the Stoics, to form the basis of the conception of human nature in all the course of Greek philosophy, and in its last effort shows itself as part of a complete pantheistic system. If such be the nature of the human spirit, its conjunction with matter would seem of itself to be the cause of evil, and so, as we have seen, it is reckoned by Plotinus to be. Yet that the will is free,[1] that virtue is without a master, that every one bears the fault of his own actions, all this, he says, is a fact which is grounded so immediately in the being of man, that without free-will we should be no men, but mere portions of the universe, moved from without. But he totally fails, or rather does not endeavour, to reconcile these statements with that necessary chain of cause and effect according to which the universe goes forth without any will or choice of a contriver, and in which man's actions are bound as part of the machine. Human nature in fact has no unity under

[1] Zeller, v. 525.

his hand. The soul, as such, in virtue of its divine origin and nature, is incapable of error, while matter, as such, is incapable of good; and so far as concerns the whole question of moral evil and the freedom of human actions, its two parts, mind and matter, start asunder, and we are left in an insuperable contradiction.

This contradiction indeed had beset Greek philosophy even in the hands of Aristotle. Strongly as he maintained that man is the master of his own actions,[1] and has it in his own power to be good or bad, yet he could find no place for true freedom of the will between the movement which proceeds from sensuous desire, and the other which proceeds from the divine mind dwelling in the soul. Necessity broke in on both sides, from the action of things on the sensuous soul, and from the divine intelligence.

But so much as this is plain, that in the system of Plotinus man is not bound to God as a creature to the Creator. He has not that dependence which one whose whole being is made by another owes to that other. Thus in this, as in the Stoic system, the spring of virtue lay in the pride engendered by the belief that the soul is of the same nature as God. This God is not self-conscious, not free, but a blind force of nature, Power without Will. Somehow or another the soul, a portion of this God, has been joined with a portion of matter, and human life is the result.

But in the practical scope at which it aims is seen the closest point of connection and at the same time the fundamental opposition between this system and the Christian Faith. The divine intelligence dwell-

[1] Döllinger, *Heidenthum und Judenthum*, p. 311.

ing in man must according to its nature seek for a restoration of order, first in the little universe of the individual, secondly in the larger one of the commonwealth. This is put forth in the person of an ideal Pythagoras, which Iamblichus dressed up in a pretended life of that sage, at the beginning of the fourth century. In it he attributed to his hero three things.[1]

First he communicated to men a higher religious and speculative knowledge. Secondly, he sought to bring them by the religious and moral principles which he set up for their everyday life into a relation with the deity which should correspond to their kinship with it. Thirdly, the idea of order was the central point and main substance of the religious and philosophical knowledge which he communicated. To realise this in human society was his purpose, and the union of disciples which Pythagoras set up was the means thereto. As the Christian Church was to present a visible appearance of the kingdom of heaven, so the Pythagorean union was to have an organisation which should incorporate its founder's idea of order. Its members had certain reciprocal engagements to each other, and all were in subjection to the founder, whose person was so sacred that no one uttered his name, but during his life termed him "the Divine," and after his death spoke only of "him," or "that man." Thus the influence exercised by Pythagoras was not only religious and moral, but political, by which he sought to banish the two greatest evils, anarchy and tyranny, and to give a constitution to civil society in which law alone, as the expression of

---

[1] I take these remarks on the *Pythagoras* of Iamblichus from Baur's review of the *Life of Apollonius* by Philostratus.

order, should bear sway, and Pythagoras is praised by Iamblichus as the discoverer of all political education.

In this work the Neopythagorean conception of *friendship* appears as the exact counterpart of the Christian charity, but the one is based upon the natural cognation of the soul with the deity, as the other is founded on supernatural union with Christ by His Spirit. An instance where both the language is similar and the thought is parallel may be seen in the words of Iamblichus. "All that is commanded to be done or left undone aims at intercourse with the deity; and this is the principle: and the whole life is ordered so as to be an imitation of God: this is the function of philosophy." Here philosophy corresponds to religion, and friendship to charity.

As the Neopythagorean good was the carrying out order, that is, the Kosmos, through the whole body of the universe including man, so to its thought the first germ of sin lay in the connection of the soul with the material body. By this connection alone man was in his birth impure, besides the guilt of a previous life which lay upon him.

Thus, in this system, the conception of good was the acting of the soul according to its divine nature; the conception of evil was physical, as resulting from the imprisonment of mind in matter. The conception of the revolt of the soul itself from God was entirely wanting. A disorder was indeed recognised, and it was sometimes called "sin," or "a fall of the soul," or "guilt," but the root of it was placed in the union of the soul with a body, not in the destruction of the union of the soul with God. The notion of moral perversity in the soul itself, as the intellectual principle of man, was an absolute contradiction to its belief that the soul was a particle of the divine intelligence.

These notions run through the whole movement of Greek thought from Seneca to Plotinus, and akin to them, one may say their corollary, is a theory of immortality. While the restoration of the Kosmos in man and human society is the good aimed at for this life, as to anything beyond it is the union with "the Divine" by the return of the spirit freed from matter to that of which it was a portion, and from which it was severed at its entrance into bodily life. The Pythagorean and Platonic pre-existence and post-existence of the soul, with the doctrine of transmigration which attends upon it, and the obscure and confused view of retribution hovering over that doctrine, is part and parcel of the Pantheistic conception that the soul is a particle of the divine reason. Such post-existence is not a living on of the human being, a perpetuation of the human identity. Cicero, when platonising, makes the mind of Scipio speak to his descendant as one living indeed an immortal life, but identified with the universal Mind, and without an existence of his own. The Stoic raptures of Seneca as to the future condition of the mind when purified from contact with matter, amount to a philosophic Nirvana. The same thought inspires the proud exclamation of the dying Plotinus above mentioned, that he was leading back the god that was in him to the god of the universe. Such a notion of the post-existence of the soul offers exactly the same contrast to the Christian doctrine of eternal life as the Primal Being offers to the one living God. It is, indeed, but reasonable that, if the universe is the eternal procession of one impersonal substance, mind also, though for a few years intercepted by the bars of its fleshly prison, should presently rejoin the universal Mind. It is but just and logical that a god who has no being of his own should be incapable of creating.

The culminating point in such a system is, as we have seen, such a conception as the imaginary Apollonius or the ideal Pythagoras. Every good man is god: specially such men as these in whom the soul asserts its original and inherent power, lives according to its nature, restores harmony in the being over which it presides, and works for the restoration of the same harmony in the commonwealth of man, and in the whole universe. We have seen in the romance of Apollonius how far a tacit imitation of the life and conduct of Christ could be carried upon this entirely natural basis, upon which likewise Iamblichus attributed to his Pythagoras the formation of a society which was the exact counterpart of the Christian Church. In both these instances we may trace the workings of minds which saw the Christian Church in operation before them, profoundly admired the work, but wished to transfer it to their own hereditary standing-ground.

Both these authors can speak, as Stoics had spoken before them, of the unity of the human race, of the brotherhood of man with man, even how man, as Epictetus had said, is a "son of God," how all gradations of human rank vanish before that divine equality, how an emperor is less than a wise man. All this unity of the human race rested upon the common possession of the divine intelligence within it.

But if in a few choice minds such as Seneca, Epictetus, Marcus Aurelius, or Plotinus, such a conception served for the basis of many kindly thoughts concerning universal brotherhood and benevolence, how very far was it from taking root in society! The brotherhood they extolled remained for the mass an unknown thing. It did not pass the limit of their school; it touched only refined and contemplative minds. But the whole heathen society was affected by the absence of belief in the relation between God and man as Creator and creature, and by that which was an inevitable sequence, the absence equally of belief in the relation between man and man as fellow-creatures of one God. The inner life of each human being, his domestic life, his social life, his political life, all were touched in all their springs by that opposing doctrine of philosophy according to which the Absolute Unity, the Primal Being, the Divine, was either the material or the formal cause working in and through all things. This is best seen by concisely stating the antagonistic truths which the Christian Church set forth not to the select votaries of a school, not to the learned, the rich, and the refined alone, but to the poor, to the slave, to the enthralled female sex; which it poured forth as the light of the sun to gladden every human eye, and ennoble every human affection.

1. Instead of the notion that the human mind, being a portion of the divine intelligence, had become in some unexplained manner connected for a time with a body, and that the man was this mind, the Church taught that it was an entirely free act of God which called every man into existence. This act of the divine volition created the soul out of nothing, and infused it into a body derived immediately from the parents but ultimately made likewise out of nothing, and thus constituted the one man, the human being, by a union most unsearchable in its inner

nature, most clear in its results, in which the soul is the form of the body. The tie between the creature thus made and the Creator is so stringent, the dependence of the one on the other so absolute, that nature through its whole realm offers no parallel. For in every operation of nature that which is produced is produced out of something pre-existing. So far and no farther experience carries us, and an observation proceeding only from experience and limited to physical appearances had left the Greek philosophic mind short of the idea itself of creation. The parental relation led up the nearest to that between the Creator and the creature. But the parent communicates only a part of his nature to the child, and that part the less noble. The distance which remains between the function of the natural parent and the act of creation transcends altogether the conception of such fathership; and the exercise of illimitable power on one side finds adequate correspondence only in absolute dependence on the other. Such a dependence was the foundation of all that the Church taught respecting the duties and the hopes of man.

2. The philosophy, proceeding from its false notion as to the nature of the human soul, gave a physical notion of evil as inherent in the junction of mind and matter. The notion of evil which the Church asserted was one purely spiritual, that is, rebellion against the eternal law in thought, word, or deed. The eternal law is the sanctity of God exhibited in His commands. These commands were summed up in the first and second tables of the law. The rebellion of man against his Creator was therefore the radical notion of sin, and this rebellion would extend through the whole of his nature, beginning from the spirit,

and stretching out to the body as informed by the spirit. And though the conjunction of body with spirit afforded a large matter and occasion for sin by the body being subject to one class of desires, while the spirit was moved by another, yet the seat of the rebellion would be in the spirit alone, and from it alone infringement of the command of the Creator in thought, word, or deed could proceed.

3. In the Neoplatonic system, as in the Stoic, we find a perpetual assertion of man's free-will counter-worked and contradicted by the whole theory of the production of the world. For as they made that production to be not the result of will but the necessary going forth of an absolute power, in which a physical concatenation of cause and effect could not suffer the slightest break, they could not but consider that the actions of man, as part of this machine, were bound by this necessity. Most pointed is the opposition of the Church's doctrine here, and on both sides. The greatness and majesty of the Creator are specially seen in that freedom by which, being ineffably blessed in His own inner life, in that Fathership, Sonship, and Procession of the Spirit, which is the Triune God, He chose to create. And the freedom of the reasonable creature so made is the image of the Creator's freedom in making. "The reasonable creature indeed cannot create, that is, call out of nothing into existence, but it can produce changes in itself, and in something outside itself, which by God's will is there. And so as the freedom of the Creator consists in that His will is the last ground of the being of creatures, the freedom of the creature consists in that the last ground of such changes lies in its will. This is to say that in the sphere which God has assigned to our freedom

the operations which we can produce are but possible through the nature of things, through the will of God, and our own constitution: to make them actual depends on our will. We determine whether they shall be, which of them shall be, how long and in what circumstances they shall be."[1]

As a world evolved by necessity cannot admit a freedom of will in a subordinate part of itself, so a God free to create makes a creature free in the choice of his actions. This created dignity in man answers to that uncreated dignity of will in God, which is the source of all beings outside of Himself.

4. The evil which the philosophy saw was that the mind should not act according to its nature as an effluence of the divine mind, being drawn down by the contact with matter. The good was such a restoration of order that everything in man and in society should be done according to this nature. But the Church taught that the malady of human nature consisted in an inward rebellion of the spirit itself against its Maker. Its good was the removal of that rebellion by the sanctification of man. Thus the word "sin" was used in the philosophy in a sense entirely opposed to that which belonged to it in the Christian teaching. In the philosophy it was the soul missing its aim, falling short of its intrinsic dignity as a portion of "the Divine," and the body with which it was encumbered was the perpetual cause of such a fall. In the Christian sense Sin was the disobedience of the creature to the will of the Creator; and if in the actual state of man the body perpetually solicited the will to such a disobedience, yet the mind likewise was liable to classes of sins more dangerous and more difficult to overcome

[1] Kleutgen, *Theologie der Vorzeit*, i. 514.

than those of which the body was the occasion; and in the will itself, that is, in an erring use of the liberty which made its dignity, lay the seat of all sin. Of Redemption it is clear that the philosophy knew and could know nothing, and in like manner of Sanctification. Both were repugnant to its conception of the human mind. But these two ideas were the spring of Christian ethics and of Christian politics. From them started the whole moral order to the individual and to the body politic.

5. The difference in the *end* after life corresponded to the difference in the view of the nature of *good* during life. In the philosophy the mind freed from matter returned to that from which it had been severed. Individual identity was lost. The body, prison of the mind, was for ever dissolved. The mind, after a longer or shorter sojourn in some new prison, was absorbed again in the universal mind. Instead of this shadowy dream of immortality the Church taught the everlasting union of the human person with the Triune God, the Giver of that personality which is the highest completion of the creature's being. But in this union the personal being was for ever maintained by the preservation of identity in the whole man, body and soul. As truly as in this world each man had been "the individual substance of a rational nature," so in that world in which man would find his true end the full man and the same man should exult in the glory of body and soul under the divine light of a vision unfolding to him the divine essence. If to be a person, enjoying free-will, is the natural dignity bestowed upon man by God in creating him, so, when he attained his true end, he was not to lose that dignity, but retain it ineffably

exalted. If the use of free-will on earth constituted his trial, and made up the quality of his virtue, the reward of both would not consist in the suppression of the gift, but in such a union of the will with God as left it free and made it blessed. The sight of God is the accomplishment of this.

6. It is in the doctrine on which the Christian belief is founded that the most thorough antagonism between the Neoplatonic system and the Church was rooted. To the Neoplatonist the union of mind with matter was the fall of the soul: the encumbrance, the imposition, so to say, of the body upon the mind, in which lay the ever-present cause of evil. Nothing therefore could be more abhorrent from his principles than the assumption of a human body by the Divine Word. Thus what to the Christian was the greatest, the most magnificent, the tenderest work of God, was to the Neoplatonist a scandal, a degradation, a blasphemy. That God should take to Him a material body, and work through that body the sanctification of matter, that His body should become the tree of life to every generation of His people, was to overthrow from its very foundation the philosophy we have been considering, for it was a denial equally of its two parts, its doctrine as to mind and its doctrine as to matter. The human mind was not a particle of the divine mind, for God assumed a human soul in order to destroy the rebellion of every human soul against its Maker. The union of the body with the mind was not the cause of evil in man, for God assumed a body in order to give eternal life to every human body. Thus the Incarnation carried in itself the cure for all those erroneous notions respecting both mind and body which had travelled down to Plotinus, if

not from the teaching of Pythagoras, at any rate from his time, through the stream of Greek philosophy. St. Augustine, who was almost the contemporary of Porphyrius, reproached him with having been deterred from becoming a Christian by this very doctrine,[1] for he could not give up his cardinal tenet that all contact with the body was to be shunned, in order that the soul may dwell blessed with God.

7. This error no doubt was radical in the philosophy. The unity of the whole human race, as possessing reason, which was the ground of Stoic and Neoplatonic doctrine as to fraternity and equality, was falsely exalted by it into a divine unity by the assertion that reason was part of the divine mind. It was only by this fiction that it could be set against the Christian unity founded on the gift of the Holy Ghost, which was bestowed upon the members of Christ as the fruit of the Incarnation. This deification of reason is the completion of the contrast which we have been noting between the philosophy and the faith. It sets up nature against grace, as by asserting a natural affinity and identity of essence between the human mind and the divine it attempts to give to man in his natural condition all that union with God which in the supernatural order is conferred upon him as a gratuitous gift, the effect of an unspeakable love on the part of God in becoming man.

8. The summing up of the whole is this. In the philosophy the Primal Being is the cause of things by their being produced out of him, though not voluntarily,

---

[1] *De Civitate Dei*, x. 28. "Contemnis enim eum propter corpus ex foemina acceptum." 29. "Ideo viluit superbis Deus ille magister, quia Verbum caro factum est et habitavit in nobis: ut parum sit miseris quod ægrotant, nisi se in ipsa etiam ægritudine extollant, et pe medicina qua sanari poterant, erubescant."

but by a natural necessity. In the faith, God is the cause of all things by creating them out of nothing, by creating them according to an idea which is in Himself, by creating them for Himself. He is the Power which works, the Exemplar which guides, the End to which all things tend. Being in these three relations the cause of the world, He is its sole author, yet absolutely independent of it, for it is not His Being and Substance which are the being and substance of the world. He is as little the form of the world as He is its matter, for He created both out of nothing, and with them called into existence the universe in its all but infinite variety.[1]

It is in His character of Creator that God is the Revealer of His will, the Giver of law, the Governor of mankind, the Rewarder and the Punisher of man. It is part of natural religion to believe in Him as all these. In the poets and historians of Greece, grievously as Polytheism had lowered the conception of divine things, yet a divine power was recognised to which these attributes belonged. And a like recognition lay at the basis of the religious rites. In the popular mind and feeling such a power was still appealed to, often with a singular and personal appellation, as God, or Father, especially in times of emotion, amid the troubles and sorrows of public and private life. It is in the philosophical teaching from Thales to Plotinus that we find this conception of God most obscured and least recognised. And the reason seems to be that such a conception springs out of that Creatorship which this philosophy from beginning to end denied, and in the most emphatic denial of it, the Neoplatonic system, expired.

[1] See Kleutgen, *Philosophie der Vorzeit*, ii. 865, 866.

The above remarks have all pointed to the conclusion that that pantheistic origin of things, from which Greek thought in its highest representatives was not free, but which formed the very core of its latest system, is incompatible with a God who is independent of the world, with any free ruling of the world by the power directing it, with moral freedom on the part of man, which cannot exist without the freedom of the will, with all moral dignity, which depends on free-will, with any real immortality of reasonable natures, with retribution after death to man as a personal being. On the other hand, a God who gives their whole being to things, of whom mind no less than matter is the mere creature, who places forms in matter at His pleasure, whose most finished work in the creature is the endowing it with personality—a self-conscious moral being, which is its own, and not another's, and as such an image of the divine immortality and self-subsistence—such a God can never desert the universe so made. And the signs of His presence are that He communicates His will, and in so doing establishes law, that He governs, rewards, and punishes. And if His government here is manifestly not complete, because reward and punishment by no means always follow according to His own law, yet His own being, the inviolable Sanctity which is His nature, forbids that they should not follow hereafter. Among men the evil often triumph in this life, and the good suffer, of which the crucifixion of our Lord is the great example. But in this, the world's utter condemnation, is contained also its imperishable hope, the well-head of Christian life, since the failure of justice here makes certain that hereafter in which it will be fully attained. All these conceptions, that is, the revelation of God's will as a rule to His creatures, the law thus established, the government of them which thence ensues, their permanent reward for the good exercise of their will, or their permanent punishment for the bad exercise of it, are in fact component parts of the idea of Creator, of that Lord who is at once the Power which makes all things, the Rule which guides them, the End for which they are made.

CONNECTION OF ANCIENT WITH MODERN PANTHEISM.

Note to p. 296.

That the whole contest lies between a Personal and an Impersonal God, between a God who because He has created and maintains all things and all beings is their Lord, and a force which by an innate necessity develops itself in the universe, seems to be proved by the history of philosophy from its earliest time to the present day. Of the seventh century A.C. Kleutgen, *Theologie der Vorzeit*, vol ii. pp. 204, 205, sect. 649, 650, observes:

" Over against these systems of the Ionian school a pantheistic view of the world was formed in the Eleatic school, in which the pantheism of our own days itself recognises its commencement. Whilst the Ionians searched for the substantial foundation of all beings in the endless multiplicity of atoms, the Eleatics, Xenophanes, Parmenides, and Zeno, declared the Many to be mere appearance, since there can be only One that is real. That which is, they inferred, is Being, and that which is not Being, is not. Things therefore can only be, in so far as they are the Being. This Being, which is the All, can neither be originated, nor pass away: therefore as the Many and the distinctions of things, so likewise all Origination and Passing away, which the senses perceive, belong to the world of appearance. Thus we find already here that interchange of the Logical and the Real, of the General and the Absolute, which lies at the bottom of all idealistic and logical Pantheism. What the highest conception contains, that is, Being in general, is put as something actual; and since everything which is certainly falls under that conception, it is made to coincide with this Being. Further, since Being, as embraced in the conception, is without distinction because of the conception's indeterminateness, so the distinctions of things are made to disappear by means of the unity which they have in this Being. But the root of logical Pantheism comes out yet more definitely, inasmuch as the Eleatics also explained this One, which they made to be the All, as the Reason, or the Thought, which permeates and holds together the Universal Whole of things as their proper and true essence. This conception, which is the All, is their God.

"The two opposing schools of the Ionians and Eleatics were yet accordant in two errors. Neither the one nor the other considered God as a Being distinct from the world, nor did they recognise substantial distinctions in the things of nature. According to the Eleatics there is only one Substance, and all multiplicity of things, which appears to the senses, disappears before the thinking reason. According to the Ionians there are indeed as many Substances as there are elements or atoms, but things are only distinct through the multifold composition of this material which is common to all. Thus likewise in nature nothing substantial is produced or destroyed."

Spinoza's doctrine is thus summed up by Zeller, *Geschichte der Deutschen Philosophie*, p. 62—

"The unity of all Being, to which the whole development of Cartesianism tended, was the spring of Spinoza's system, and the point on which it all turned. There can only be one Being, which is of itself, the all-embracing infinite Being, since each particular Being is limited, and therefore also conditioned, is not of itself. God is the one only Substance which is thinkable. In this infinite Substance all finite things must be contained as to their being and essence, and must spring out of it by virtue of the unalterable necessity of their nature : for we cannot ascribe a proper being to them, nor ought we to represent it to us in its producing after the analogy of imperfect causes, which do not operate with unconditional regularity. Accordingly all things are only modifications, all which takes place only operations of the one Substance. God and the World, the producing and the produced nature, are one and the same, only considered under distinct points of view. What as unity we call God, as the Many, as the Totality of all its particular manifestations, we call the World. What presents itself to our imagination under the form of time, our thought recognises under the form of eternity, as one undivided, unchangeable, infinite Being : which for that very reason we must not change into a single Being, nor endow with qualities which can only belong to finite beings, such as understanding and will. In virtue of the infiniteness of this Being there are in it infinitely many realities; it exists under innumerable attributes, of which however we can only know two, Extension and Thought, because these only are given us in our own nature. But the real in both is only the divine Substance. The corporeal world is Substance as it presents itself under the form, or attribute, of Extension; the totality of souls or spirits is Substance as it presents itself under the attribute of Thought. But as it is one and the same Substance which is discerned under both these forms, both have in the whole and in the particular the like contents. . . . Man, as much as every other being, is a portion of nature, and nothing can happen in his life which does not proceed with strict necessity from natural reasons. Hence the human will, as our philosopher expressly declares, is not a free but a compelled cause. The actions of men are to be regarded just as any other appearance of nature, and their passions likewise are just as much in agreement with nature as their virtues. For the philosopher they are not an object of blame and abhorrence, but of scientific explanation."

In all this Spinoza seems to have simply reproduced and carried out to its furthest consequences a thought which lay at the root of the eldest Greek philosophy, and was probably transmitted to it from the Indian; which formed the core of Stoicism, and which Plotinus also made the centre of his system. Moreover, all modern systems of the infidel philosophy appear to be merely variations played upon the same thought. Professor Tyndall's lecture at Belfast is the last exhibition of it.

LECTURE XXI

THE RESPECTIVE POWER OF THE GREEK PHILOSOPHY AND THE CHRISTIAN CHURCH TO CONSTRUCT A SOCIETY

"Who then and what is this Christ, who has filled the whole world with His teaching? . . . When and in whom of men that have been born has the teaching prevailed everywhere from end to end of the earth one and the same, so that His worship found itself wings to traverse the world?"

St. Athanasius on the assumption of human nature by the Word, and on His appearance to us in a body. Written about A.D. 318, sect. 48, 49.

IN a former lecture, tracing from the time of Thales to the accession of the Emperor Claudius the effect of philosophy in the way of forming a society which should be ruled by its doctrine, I had occasion to remark its utter impotence to unite together belief, morality, and worship, and by such union to satisfy the needs of the human heart and conscience in the individual, or to construct a commonwealth. Having now in the last five lectures dwelt upon the teaching of philosophy as it concerned the most important problems of human life, and deduced the logical issue of that teaching as set forth in the Neoplatonic system, it remains briefly to consider the power which philosophy showed to organise society during this same period, from Claudius to Constantine. As to doctrine, I have spoken successively of Seneca, Musonius, Epictetus, and Marcus Aurelius, who give us the spirit of the Neostoic school for the first one hundred and forty years of this period. Then, again, I have described another movement which was affected by Philo, and represented by Plutarch, Dio Chrysostomus, Maximus Tyrius, Apuleius, and Celsus, in the course of which it occurred to touch upon the functions which philosophy attempted to execute in the private life of the Romans and by the teaching of its professorial chairs in the great centres of Athens, Alexandria, and Rome itself. Before the end of the second century this latter school of thought had obtained a complete predominance. In the romance of Philostratus we have seen it exhibited at full length in an ideal portrait of Apollonius, with which another life of an imaginary Pythagoras by Iamblichus, which seems to have been published in the reign of Constantine,[1] is identical in spirit. But the movement is already complete and final, and the last standing-ground of defence taken up when, two hundred years after Seneca, Plotinus, in a series of lectures at Rome, unfolds to the cultured classes of the great metropolis of heathendom the system by which he hopes to stem the progress of the Christian religion; the system which gathers up for a final effort the whole force of pagan philosophy, and fights for the multitude of gods with the arms of the pantheistic unity. I have just considered the three oppositions presented by that system to the Christian Faith, the first and second in its conception of God, and of His connection with the world, and the third as shown in that whole relation between God and man which may be termed the collective result of the former two principles. Having then dealt with the development of heathen doctrine over against the

---

[1] Zeller, v. 613, n. 2, remarks that the death of Iamblichus may be set about 330.

doctrine of the Church, it is full time to consider the respective power to form society exercised by the one and by the other.

I.

But first, in order to obtain the right point of view from which to look at this society, let us trace back to its source not merely the Græco-Roman civilisation, but this great stream of nations of which it formed the most cultivated part. We may leap over the intervening period since its origin stands out to us in clear light. Its starting-point is definitely fixed for all Christian believers, and the direction given which it was intended to take. "God spake unto Noah, saying, Go forth from the ark, thou, and thy wife, thy sons, and thy sons' wives with thee. Walk abroad upon the earth, increase and multiply upon it. Noah therefore went forth, and his sons, and his wife, and his sons' wives with him. But Noah built an altar to the Lord, and took of all clean cattle and birds, and offered holocausts upon the altar. . . . And the Lord blessed Noah and his sons, and said to them, Increase and multiply, and replenish the earth. . . . Whosoever hath shed man's blood, his blood shall be shed; for man is made after the image of God. . . . Thus also said God to Noah and to his sons with him, Behold I will establish My covenant with you, and with your seed after you. . . . And the sons of Noah who came out of the ark were Shem, Cham, and Japhet. These three are the sons of Noah, and from these was all mankind spread over the whole earth."

Thus human society was planted on the soil of the earth wet with the Flood, and belief, conduct, and worship had one root at the cradle of the race. For this sacrifice to the One God was the witness of belief in Him, and the actions of men rested on their belief, which was mirrored in their worship. So strong, so perfect, so self-supporting was the triple cord by which God bound in one the new society of rescued man. And let us well note that He joined together the civil and the divine society. The new father of the race was its priest. The covenant for perpetual generations was made with sacrifice, and so rested upon a positive right of the deepest signification. The family from which nations should spring was thus consecrated, and the State sanctified in its birth by its homage to God its Founder. And this connection was the *ideal* relation between the commonwealth and religion for the whole race.

Again, it is to be noted that at the head of the civil and religious society of man thus founded there stood one who had seen all the glory and civilisation of the old world before the Flood, and had moreover been a "preacher of justice" to that "world of the impious" in its corruption. It is not from man making the tentative efforts of an inexperienced childhood, and far less from man as he grovelled on the penal descent of savagery, that the second society of the human race took its rise; but it was set up in the fathership and headship of a Patriarch renowned for long-tried wisdom and eminent sanctity.[1] Thus his first step upon the recovered earth is to offer sacrifice; in which is contained potentially the whole of man's religion to God; and the importance of the act is signified by the words following it: "And God

---

[1] Ezech. xiv. 14. "And if these three men, Noah, Daniel, and Job, shall be in it, they shall deliver their own souls by their justice, saith the Lord of Hosts."

smelt an odour of sweet smell, and said, I will no longer curse the earth on account of men." Moreover, beside Noah stood his sons, likewise of full manhood, and likewise witnesses of what the old world had been and how it had perished. Thus human society was based at its second rise upon belief in the unity of God and upon a perpetual covenant made with Him in the rite of sacrifice, which was a confession of that belief; and so it was at the same time based upon the conjunction of belief in Him and worship of Him with the first springs of human action as a corporate body. At that moment, big with the destiny of a world, the race was in the family, and the word of the father became the constituent law of his descendants. A whole mass of belief as to the future of man was contained in this rite of sacrifice, which was a prophecy and promise of redemption and restoration, made perpetually visible to the eyes and minds of men by recurring acts of daily life.

A part of sacrifice was the public institution of prayer, so that with the offering of it the daily wants of man were presented before God, the daily praise and thanksgiving of man to God as the Author of his being was made, and the daily confession of man's guilt and request for pardon associated with the blood of the victim. Thus the essential parts of man's inner life with God were connected with the outward religious rite, and the whole conduct of man inseparably bound up with his belief and worship.

The sacrifice carries with it the priest, and the rite of sacrifice everywhere established among the children of Noah brought with it likewise altars and temples, festivals, and processions. Let us consider these things for the moment as they existed without corruption and before that process had set in; as they existed in all the portions of the human family, which had now run out into tribes and nations. All these things are legitimately contained at least in germ in that account which we have cited of Noah, as he emerged from the ark and set foot upon the earth. If we reflect upon them, we shall find that the union of the religious worship with the civil society was a common good bestowed by God on all the descendants of Noah. It was not a development of human civilisation; not a work of human craft; but the signet of divine care and providence stamped upon the forehead of the race, and guarded by every device with which reverence for a primeval institution and the natural feelings of family affection could surround it.

The depth of the fall and the multiplicity of the corruption which we are afterwards to witness ought not to blind us to the tenderness of the divine providence in bestowing this original good on the race; nor to the provision with which every care compatible with the existence of free-will in man had been taken to assure its continuance, and the purity of that worship of God in His unapproachable unity on the maintenance of which its beneficent action depended.

If we look upon the nations of the world as presented to us when history first opens on them, we find that all of them were communities in which the civil power and the religious worship are in close alliance. Nay, this alliance is one of the "unwritten laws," more powerful and influential than any positive enactment of which the date can be given; for these laws are the life of the community, the blood which runs in its veins. Assyria and Egypt, Medea and Persia, Hellenic tribes, first monarchies and then republics, Etruria and Rome, and no less the great realm of India, and China stretching through all times in her vast peopled isolation, bear alike witness to this alliance. Not only the house has its household god, but the city and its worship are blended together, and sacrilege is likewise treason. That in itself is the legitimate carrying out of Noah's first sacrifice: the normal state of human life according to the divine ideal given in the fathership of Noah, wherein belief, action, and worship are harmoniously joined together for the man, the family, and the commonwealth.

It is hard to calculate the enormous disturbance of this triple union produced by the denial of God's unity. By such denial man's conception of God was essentially corrupted. As soon as God was multiplied, He ceased to be immense and infinite, all-powerful and all-wise: He ceased likewise to be the God of the whole earth, and of the whole race of man. The conception of the One God corrupted by the division of His Being ran speedily out into all the abominations of false worship, as seen in its three main lines, worship of dead men exalted into heroes, worship of inferior spirits, worship of the powers of nature. The various false gods thus set up became national gods, and were made after the imagination of those whom they were supposed to protect. We are led to conclude from the passage of Scripture recording the confusion of languages that it was a punishment for some great act of pride and rebellion on man's part. It may be conjectured that the earth ceased to be of one tongue at the same time that it ceased to worship one God, and it is certain that the variety of languages ensuing upon the dispersion of men over the earth was rivalled by the variety of gods whom the dispersed peoples began to worship. In fact, when the corruption had gone on for some centuries, it would have seemed as difficult to reduce to that original worship of one God the worship offered by men to their various deities, in which they had even sunk to the conception of male and female gods, as to reduce all the speeches which man in his dispersion had produced to his original language. There is indeed a singular and mysterious parallel as well as synchronism between the two, between the deflection of the human speech from the original language, and the deflection of polytheistic worship from the worship offered to God by Noah.

But the union of worship with the civil authority, which had been the foundation-stone of human society as laid by God its architect, and would have ensured a solid and beautiful structure, fitted for all the needs of man, was deeply and fatally affected by the rise of Polytheism. The fissure thus introduced struck down to the very foundations of the house. The union indeed did not cease to exist, but its blessing was impaired: in cases where the corruption was extreme it might seem to be almost changed into a curse. For every act of human life, both domestic and civil, being connected with religious rites and worship, that worship, when falsified in its objects, might lend itself to the desecration of most sacred things, and turn religion into a weapon against morality, as in the case not only of Babylonian and other Asiatic deities, but of Greek and Roman. And the Grecian gods generally had come to be immortal men of human passions and superhuman power. Yet they were in the thought of the people the guardians of the Acropolis, the defenders of the land, the givers of the harvest, and to them the original rite of sacrifice was still offered, and to them the mental sacrifice of prayer still ascended. Now prayer and sacrifice were the primary goods of human nature, the heirloom of Noah's fathership, which his children in the depth of their moral descent had retained, but so strangely degraded. And for prayer and sacrifice the moral nature of man, still possessing from age to age sound reason and upright natural sense, and so persisting to be the witness of the one true God in His fallen world, continued to yearn amid all the corruptions with which they had been tainted.

When philosophy first raised its head in Greece the corruption of the public worship had proceeded very far: but the union between the city and its worship was still unbroken. Moreover the great lineaments of an original revelation from God to man were preserved in the popular mind. The monarchy of Jupiter, a witness imperfect indeed and faltering, but still a witness to the original doctrine of the divine unity, was impaired by a multitude of deities his assessors. Then again the support which the conception of creation gives to the relation of the Godhead to the world was wanting to the Greek, who only recognised a world generating itself out of Primal Matter or Chaos, not a world which the Godhead made by an act of free-will. Moses set at the head of all being a God who created because He willed to create, whilst in the whole Greek mythology there is not to be met the conception of a Creator, that is, a Being before all things, who in absolute freedom produces the universe as it pleases Him.[1]

[1] Nägelsbach, *Nachhomerische Theologie*, p. 71, who refers also to Braun, *Griechische Götterlehre*, p. 7.

Yet in spite of this defect it would appear that in Greek belief the gods collectively maintained the whole world in its existing order. It was believed also that the individual man in all his circumstances, in his whole spiritual and moral nature, was ruled and determined by the deity. Nor was it supposed that the gods only worked upon the individual, but likewise that they guided and ruled the lot of peoples and states, and sent punishments upon them. And this divine rule was believed to be not only one of power but a moral government. Men conceived the gods not only to determine the course of events, but to maintain the right which they had established among men, and on the maintenance of which the moral order of the world rested. They had made and they supported what we call the law of nature. Thus in a well-known passage Sophocles speaks of "that holy purity of word and deed, whose laws are inscribed on high, born in the celestial sky, whose sire is heaven alone, nor hath the mortal nature of men produced them, nor will oblivion ever lull them to sleep. In these God is great, and grows not old."[1] So further, as the foundations of the State are laid upon marriage and the family, marriage itself was deemed to be the creation of the gods, together with the variety of character and occupation given to the man and the woman, which make the tie possible and desirable. It is also to be noted that penal justice formed a part of the divine idea in the Greek mind, and that so strongly as to lead them to believe that the deity exercised his office of punishing with a law so stringent that he would rather destroy the innocent with the wicked, if they were bound up indivisibly together, than pardon

[1] Œdipus Rex, 863-872.

the sinner for the sake of the good. It is a summary of the general belief in this respect to say that penal justice was represented as an original and everlasting principle of the world's government, maintained by Zeus himself.[1] Thus the individual thought of inquiring minds found itself in the presence of a society which offered to the observer two very different aspects; on the one hand a civil and religious order, closely united, coming down from remote antiquity, with the tokens of an original divine sanction upon it, with large portions of a divine tradition preserved in it, with great and venerable institutions, that of sacrifice bearing traces of a primeval covenant between God and man, under which lay a revelation and a promise, that of prayer, which formed part of the ordinance of sacrifice, expressing the perpetual relation between God and man, a divine government of the world. Together with these were oracles, in which man professed to seek divine guidance in the trials and obscurities of his private lot, as well as in public dangers; and further mysteries, in which he also sought for deliverance from guilt. This on the one hand. On the other the whole of this religious order had suffered an incredible corruption. First the unity of God had been divided, and by that division the conception of His eternal and infinite Being unspeakably degraded: next His sanctity

---

[1] The above propositions are proved by a great array of quotations from Greek authors by Nägelsbach, pp. 71–84 and 30–36. I take one truly Æschylean passage, *Choeph,* 309.

ἀντὶ μὲν ἐχθρᾶς γλώσσης ἐχθρὰ
γλῶσσα τελείσθω· τοὐφειλόμενον
πράσσουσα Δίκη. μέγ' ἀυτεῖ·
ἀντὶ δὲ πληγῆς φονίας φονίαν
πληγὴν τινέτω · δράσαντι παθεῖν
τριγέρων μῦθος τάδε φωνεῖ.

had been tainted by the character of the false gods which mythology had invented. Thus a priesthood, which had everywhere been established to discharge the functions of His worship and declare a daily belief in His government of the world, became the instrument of corruption in offering this worship both to those to whom it was not due, to false gods, and to those who were besides unworthy of any honour, as impure and unholy beings. And so the four great heads which contain the whole religious life of man, whether individual or aggregated, Prayer, Sacrifice, the instruction of man in the divine will, and his deliverance from sin incurred, had suffered as it were an usurpation by an evil possessor, were held down in injustice. The original good of the great primary revelation had passed under the power of an enemy.

Now, as I began by stating, I have elsewhere [1] dwelt upon the conduct of philosophy in the presence of this complex aspect of human society during the period from its first rise in the seventh century before Christ to the reign of Claudius, and have drawn out the results which it produced on the belief and actions of men. When the Christian Church appeared in the world it may be said that the corruption of the good which I have been noting had reached its ultimate point of intensity. Let us then, bearing in mind what had been the original constitution of society, and what was the nature and extent of the corruption under which it had fallen, consider the respective action of philosophy and of the Christian Church from the time they began to co-exist during ten generations, in the face of this perplexed and difficult problem, and with a view to restore what had been corrupted.

[1] Lectures xiii. and xiv. vol. ii.

II.

1. In all the various peoples composing the Roman empire, except the Jews, belief as influencing action had been detached from worship. The great act of worship, sacrifice, subsisted in its material integrity, and was performed daily on countless altars, and was still connected with various priesthoods belonging to the several deities. And certain stated prayers were offered still in conjunction with the sacrifice. But these priesthoods were not connected with each other by any hierarchical rule and institution. The religious traditions to which their very existence bore witness were not drawn out by any religious writings into any specific form. Throughout this whole realm of heathendom, in all its regions, no religious instruction was habitually given. The priests discharged their several liturgic offices, but the cure of souls, the forming the religious character of their people, did not enter into their practice, and made in the opinion of the people no part of their function.

Thus sacrifice itself had long ceased to point to that great religious doctrine with a view to which it had been instituted, and so had ceased both to prophesy and to promise. It was performed mechanically, and the good of the nation or individual for whom it was offered, and the favour of the gods, was supposed to depend upon its performance, but the reason of this dependence was lost to the mind both of people and priest. There was then absence not only of church but of religious dogma: there was only remaining a traditional belief, which still acted as a ground of conduct for such as followed the leading of conscience, and there was a customary worship from which latter conduct had been detached. And the most striking sign and proof of this detachment is the fact that the priest was nowhere approached as the adviser, exhorter, and trainer in the religious life. This fact, the gravity of which it is difficult to realise, is beyond question; but if we seek its reason it will be found that it was the division of the divine unity which had broken down and laid waste the union of belief and conduct with worship. Mythology, which is the mirror of popular belief, is itself the result of false, that is, polytheistic worship. As long as men believe in one only God, no mythology is possible, as there is none among Jews, or Christians, or Mahometans. But the division of the divine unity introduced gods of three sorts, deified men, deified spirits, deified powers of nature, and mythology is the endless play of human fancy, differing according to the mental quality of various peoples in describing the various attributes and actions of these various deities. Such wild fictions, mixed up indeed with religion, and containing some disguised and disfigured religious truth, could not be reduced to the severe and orderly arrangement of religious instruction, could not form a consistent code of human duty, any more than a theory of correct belief. So the priest of the false god ceased to teach his people religious truth and a rule of life. He became a mere sacrificant; he was no longer an instructor; and specially he ceased to teach what the sacrifice which he outwardly performed carried in its inward meaning. And in his own life there had equally ceased to be a connection between upright conduct and the priestly office.

Thus in all this period the strange result is seen that in the various trials of life, in bereavement, anxieties, and perplexity recourse was not had to any priest. Again, in whatever attempt there was to form and maintain a moral conduct of life, it was the philosopher whose advice and exhortation were sought. And once more, it was to the philosopher that the education of youth was entrusted. Everywhere and at all times human nature has three abiding needs, and the higher its civilisation the more it feels them. These needs are to be consoled in its trials, to be directed in its difficulties, to be instructed in its belief, and in the duties which spring out of that belief. As to all these at this period men turned away from the priest, for he had forfeited his charter by serving false gods, but some men betook themselves to the philosopher. Let us see how he sped in the work thus put on him.

2. Cicero and Seneca, as we have seen, both proclaimed philosophy, not religion, to be the guide of life: that is, they turned entirely away from the worship offered to the "immortal gods" upon innumerable altars by all the various nations who did homage to the rule of Rome, and sought for peace, tranquillity of mind, and all the dignity of moral nature from the effort of human thought, the search for wisdom. Their countrymen generally accepted this view and ratified it by their practice. In the retinue of a Roman noble was usually to be found one who was termed "his" philosopher, as another might be called his steward. From casual mention of philosophers at the Courts of Augustus, Nero, Trajan, Hadrian, Julia Domna, and Elagabalus, we learn that these professors of wisdom were, if not as a rule, yet frequently to be found living in the closest intercourse with the emperors. One remark-

able instance given us by Seneca in the case of the most sagacious of princes, Augustus, will serve to indicate the part which they played. In his Consolation to Marcia, Seneca bids her to follow the example of her friend, the Empress Julia. In the first outburst of her grief for the loss of her son Drusus, she sought consolation from Areus, "her husband's philosopher." And she found him of great service; more than the Roman people, whose sorrow she would not increase by her own; more than Augustus, who was already overthrown by losing one of his supports; more than the affection of her son Tiberius, who by redoubling his devotion to her sought to compensate for his brother's loss. And the influence of Areus upon a woman so chary of her confidence was grounded on this, that up to that day he had been the constant companion of her husband, to whom not only their public acts were made known, but, both as to husband and to wife, their "deep heart-courses and its motive seeds."[1] This instance standing at the head of Cæsarean history will show the wonderful vantage-ground occupied during this period by philosophers in the eclipse of the influence which reasonably and properly belongs to religion. If we add to this confidential position in the bosom of the great Roman families the means of propagating their doctrine given by the possession of the great professorial chairs in large cities, accompanied with ample revenues and high consideration, we can estimate what opportunities were afforded to the pro-

[1] Seneca, *Ad Marciam*, 4. Areus says of his intercourse with Augustus, "Assiduus viri tui *comes*, cui non tantum quæ in publicum emittuntur nota, sed omnes sunt secretiores animorum vestrorum motus." I venture to translate the last words by a beautiful line from Father Newman's poems.

fessors of wisdom for acting upon the public opinion and the private practice of men.

This being so, it becomes the more interesting to know what they taught. Into this confidential situation all the philosophical sects entered. It is stated indeed even of the second century that the greater part of those who as Readers, Educators, and Companions lived in the houses of distinguished Romans, followed the Epicurean principles:[1] but there were likewise Stoics, Peripatetics, Cynics, Platonists, Eclectics, as afterwards Neoplatonists. Now these sects waged a continual war with each other, a war carried on with the most jealous bitterness, and offering to outsiders the spectacle of irreconcilable contradictions even in the first and most important questions. Of them Cicero had said in his own time concerning the first question of all, the Being of God, "We are compelled by the disagreement of the wise to be ignorant of our own Lord and Ruler. We know not whether we are subjects of the Sun or the Ether."[2]

The same remark might have been made of them all for three centuries onward down to Plotinus and Porphyrius. But if they had no common doctrine, still less had they any union of a society between themselves. Not only was the Stoic not a Platonist or an Epicurean, but the Stoics and the Platonists had no society of their own. They were all mere units, each working by himself. But to complete the view of their situation we must bear in mind the split between the inward conviction of the philosopher, whatever he might be, and his outward practice

---

[1] Tzschirner, *Fall des Heidenthums*, p. 150.
[2] Lucullus, v. 41.

of the vulgar worship. Philosophy, in fact, was attempting its cure of souls not only upon the basis of human nature's intrinsic strength, the force of free inquiry, but likewise in complete severance from that foundation of tradition, custom, and public law on which the worship rested, which yet the philosopher himself frequented. He was trying to do the work of religion, but he was not a priest in any sense of the word, nor did the priest attempt the work of the philosopher. But it was not only that they remained apart, and that troubled consciences went to the philosopher and not to the priest. There was likewise this, that the philosopher consoled and instructed not by the hopes, the fears, the ordinances of religion, but by an esoteric teaching of his own quite at variance with the religion. Let us observe the two characters in Marcus Aurelius. He is the most profuse employer of the established rites and offerer of endless sacrifices so that the white oxen threatened to fail, not to say that he is official Pontifex Maximus of all the religions sanctioned by the empire; but his philosophy, and that is the whole inward man, stands quite apart from these. It is a hard Pantheism, an iron order of physical sequence, in which prayer and sacrifice are utterly unavailing and out of place. There is no harmony whatever between the philosophic communer with his soul and the worshipper of the gods.

The same contradiction belongs to Epictetus, to Plotinus, and to Porphyrius. No one of these philosophers stood aloof from the public worship: no one of them frequented it with the belief of the unphilosophic vulgar mind. Their patronage of it, in fact, was setting a new meaning on it which was nothing better than a falsehood. Their frequentation of the public worship gave the lie to their inward teaching. This indicates the temper of the second and third centuries as to the relation between philosophy and religion. It is, in the minds of the cultured class, the juxtaposition of an esoteric belief, like that of Epictetus, or Plutarch, or Plotinus, with an outward and likewise real honouring of the gods, at least as to the visible ceremonies of worship, but with no harmony between the two; nay, with an utter contradiction.

Never before had philosophy been so honourable and so lucrative a profession. We have hitherto spoken of those who practised it seriously, but of course there was a multitude of pretenders, philosophers of the beard, cloak, and stick only, who are described by their rivals and enemies, the Rhetors, as the pests of society. The Cynics especially, under whose name Epictetus has given a portrait of his ideal teacher, bore a bad character. They were credited with every vice contrary to their assumed profession. Lucian has given us a vivid picture of the trickery, vanity, grasping avarice, and immorality of the pretenders to philosophy. And he is surpassed by Aristides, who says their grasping is insatiable; to take from others their property they call community of goods; their envy is termed philosophy, their persistence in begging contempt of money. Insolent to all other men, they crouch before the rich, and even before the cooks and bakers of the rich. Their strength lies in shameless cupidity, insulting, and slandering.[1]

But without dwelling on the abuse, we may remark concerning the work which the best of the class were

---

[1] Quoted by Döllinger, *Heidenthum*, p. 605.

attempting, the men such as Areus among Court chaplains, such as Cornutus, Musonius, and Taurus among eminent Romans, such as Epictetus among the Greeks. These men took human conduct for their field of labour, but they detached it from belief on the one side, and from worship on the other. As to belief, the philosopher was, in spite of himself, member of a society which had inherited large portions of an ancient order of things based upon the government of the world by the godhead. From this, however, he had emancipated himself as far as he could. His philosophy, as a work of simple human reason, was in opposition to religion, tradition, and usage, and to all the rites which belonged to this triple source. But as to worship, he had none of his own. Not once, in any instance from Socrates to Plotinus, did the philosopher proclaim and openly practise the worship of one God, and of one alone. That same effort of reason which had alienated him from the corruption of the popular religion, should have led him to such a proclamation and to the corresponding practice. But he built his system of human conduct on the dignity of that reason as a particle of the divine essence, and as the essential part of man, not on submission to that Lord and Ruler, whom, as Cicero said, the dissensions of the philosophers compelled men not to know. As to the homage of the heart to God, all these philosophers were an unworshipping race. But their accommodation to the worship of the gods from Jupiter to Æsculapius was equally universal with their omission to proclaim and adore "the Lord" of human nature and of human beings.

3. Another characteristic of philosophy is of great importance, both to show its nature and temper and

to calculate its influence. Viewed as a movement, it touched from beginning to end the cultured class only It may almost be termed a pastime for the rich. It sprang from a few men who bore in after times the name of "the Wise," and who were certainly of conspicuous mental power. By those who had reached the highest point, first Pythagoras, then Plato and Aristotle, it was admitted that the study of philosophy was fitted only for the few. Throughout all its existence it was confined to the narrow precincts of "the schools," and expressed contempt for "the unphilosophic mob." It took no account of the poor, the ignorant, the female sex in general, of the vast population engaged in manual labour, which at that time lay almost, without exception, under the ban of slavery. All this means that while it assumed the religious office of being "a cure for the sick," it left the generality of the human race outside of its cure. Being destitute of charity, it despised their ignorance. Let us take a double instance of this. That conception of God into which the last and at length the sole prevailing school of philosophy settled down, the conception, that is, of an abstract power or force running through all things, was a nonentity to ordinary men and women. This philosophic god of Pantheism never was a god of the people, and never can be. It would be a liberal computation to suppose that this notion of "the Divine" could have any existence for one in a thousand of the human race. But while Plotinus discoursed with profound earnestness and false mysticism upon such a god to the great lords and ladies of Rome, in the days when the minister of Valerian was torturing St. Laurence, he left the unphilosophic multitude to frequent the rites of heathen worship. They cared nothing for his "Primal Being," but they burned incense before the statue of Jupiter, and were given up to a most unspiritual devotion of Cybele and Aphrodite. Thus both in what it taught itself, and in what it suffered the vast majority to practise, philosophy was exclusive and eclectic. It was in all its course the exact contradiction of that divine word, "To the poor the Gospel is preached." It may be added, that in its conduct it entirely disregarded that citizenship of the whole human race which it was the boast of Stoicism to set forth. The principle which we are told was inherent in Zeno's doctrine did not develop itself for many generations after him; but it remained always a theory, never carried into effect by philosophers. If Stoics taught universal brotherhood, Christians alone practised it.

4. Taking then the period from Claudius to Constantine, what had philosophy done to reunite the triple strand of human belief, conduct, and worship? It found belief and worship separated from each other, and conduct left to the insufficient support which the remains of an ancestral tradition gave; and it showed itself absolutely impotent to create a society which should live and flourish by the union of the three. This creation of society is the test of power. It was in the beginning a divine work. Human corruption had done its worst upon it, had divided the great parts and made them struggling adversaries in a huge dislocated mass, rather than members yielding their co-operation according to the measure of each part in one body. Philosophy could not repair the corruption. It produced, indeed, individual writers, used in the closet, and affecting cognate minds, such as were

Seneca, Epictetus, Plutarch, Numenius, Plotinus, Porphyrius, and the rest. The utmost that one could say of these, supposing, which is far from the fact, that each had taught truth and accordant truth with the others, would be that they were like irrigated patches in a desert, lying apart, and insufficient even to form an oasis. But where was the philosophic land full of pasture for the human flock, and watered with fountains for human thirst? Philosophy could make no such a country. They who strove to set up an ideal Pythagoras in envy of the work of Christ, never attempted even that society which Pythagoras, fraught with the elder wisdom of Egypt and the East, conceived. All this work of teaching in private families, of philosophers acting as quasi-chaplains to noblemen or emperors, of great professorial chairs, of supposed Cynic missionaries discoursing upon human rights and duties to mixed audiences from city to city, ended in this, that one day the most famous of philosophers asked an emperor, conspicuous for his persecution of Christians, to bestow on him a city wherein to draw together the devotees of philosophic teaching. The emperor refused. Platonopolis never existed in Campania, and philosophy in all the Roman world could make no city of its own. It had, indeed, wielded the arm of demolition against things once sacred, and then worn out or perverted, but it did not possess materials of its own to build with, and still less the art of construction.

The positive result appears to be this. An attempt was made to prop up the falsehood of the polytheistic worship by substituting a pantheistic unity. A handful of philosophers announced this unity, and a sprinkling of the educated classes accepted it. But the people went on worshipping still its ancestral and debased but yet personal deities. And in the meantime the State, led on by the philosophers, furiously persecuted the Christian society which had gathered itself everywhere together under the real unity of the one living God.

But of this we are now to speak.

III.

When Constantine in the possession of the imperial authority cast his eyes over the vast Roman world of which his sword had given him the sovereignty, what did the mind of the statesman discern? He saw that the work inaugurated by Peter in the capital of his empire had had an enduring success; that in the interval of two hundred and seventy years the vigorous tree of the Apostle's planting had been shaken by many a persecution, but had come forth from all with roots more deeply driven below, and branches more widely spread above. Nor was it merely that the spiritual society had divided into regions the whole city of Rome, erected basilicas, portioned them among priests, and filled them with worshippers, so that the emperor's own gift of the Lateran palace for the residence of a Pontiff who had just come forth from the catacombs seemed but in keeping with the importance of the place which he occupied in the mother-city of the Roman dominion. The spiritual mother had been as fruitful in the spiritual order as the creatrix of colonies and municipalities on the banks of the Rhone and the Rhine, the Ebro and the Thames. Constantine held in his hand the network of the Roman administration, and the emperor both saw and felt that in five hundred cities of his empire the work of Peter at Rome had been imitated and repeated. The same structure which I have described in a preceding chapter had grown up, modified in some measure according to the differences of place and circumstance, but identical in character throughout province after province. To use the metaphor of Tertullian, the Apostolic See, like a fruitful vine, had sent out suckers in all directions, and the plant had everywhere preserved the likeness of that from which it was drawn. Nor could he fail to see that the organisation was as complete in the East as in the West; that there also suffragan sees had radiated from two Apostolic centres, on both of which rested the name and power of Peter. The second rank in the Roman empire among cities was held by that wonderful creation of Alexander's genius, the city of Alexandria. Thither Peter had sent his disciple Mark, who had founded a Church in his blood, and in strictest dependence on it each Egyptian city had received its bishop; so that in Constantine's time the whole mass of the bishops of Egypt moved as by one impulse under the hand of Mark's successor and Peter's representative, the Primate of Alexandria. The third city of the empire, Antioch the Great, metropolis of the East, gloried no less in Peter as its first bishop; and stood at the head of a large number of metropolitans and bishops, whose sees had been propagated from its bosom, and covered vast provinces as far as the Tigris and the Euphrates. Here was a principle of spiritual growth which Constantine saw by the experience of nearly three centuries to be as strong, as stable, and as fruitful as any temporal power of the Roman polity which he held in his hands. Here was an authority which he perceived likewise with the evidence of sight not to be of the earth earthy, for it had grown in spite of all worldly influence, in spite of that imperial power whose force none knew better than himself The acts of his predecessors were before him, and of their last and most desperate attack on the Church he had been an eyewitness: and he knew that during all that time it had been at the best and always discouraged by them, at the worst and often persecuted. The sameness of the structure and the multiplicity of its extent in this spiritual creation could not fail to strike the mind of such an observer as Constantine. It was a sight worthy of a Roman emperor, for it was wrought with more than Roman order, wisdom, and pertinacity.

By the side of such a fact, uniform and universal, as it met the eye of Constantine, the existence of which cannot be disputed nor its force parried, all discussion of certain points of detail, as, for instance, how the Apostolic power became restricted in the bishop, yet that of the bishop everywhere superior to the priests, must be termed otiose and fruitless. I take the unquestionable result of the Church's development by her own intrinsic power, since she was not favoured by the State but throughout opposed, as the one fact which I need, and as the only one which I think it worth while to state. Before it all speculations of infidel criticism fall to the ground: the fact is a thousand times more powerful than them all, speaks for itself, and is sufficient. It is enough to look upon the finished structure of the divine building as it rose before the gaze of the first Christian emperor.

When Constantine examined the nature of the authority thus everywhere set up, which so moved his admiration that it won his acceptance, he would find it the same in all places, and its sameness to consist in a triple force distinct yet bound together in its operation. This force corresponds to the intellect and the will in the human soul, which is at once both intellect and will, and, thirdly, to that homage of both these powers, which the soul offers to its Maker. This force is the office of teaching, and so informing the intellect; the office of ruling, and so directing the will in action; the office of sacrificing, which is the presentation of both intellect and will to their author. These are the three rays of the divine sovereignty as partitioned to the Prophet, the King, and the Priest in the great type of the Jewish people, which together form a perfect government and commonwealth, which satisfy the needs of human nature, and produce its good. These are the powers which we have seen dislocated in heathenism, bestowed indeed upon the race in its first ancestor Noah, but disturbed by the treason of man in giving the incommunicable Name to the offspring of his own lusts, and finally, in the lowest descent of corruption, set against each other. These are the powers which the Incarnate God took up into His own Person, giving them by that assumption a divine consecration, and from that Person recommunicated them to men exalted and enhanced. The triple force, as it remains everywhere identical in character, so it is everywhere bound together and no more separable. The teaching cannot be exercised fully without ruling, nor both without the sacrifice, which betokens their completeness. The Teacher, the Shepherd, and the Priest is one in origin, being none other than a divine Person, as He appears in that adorable act of power, wisdom, and love which made and carries on the Christian Church. The work continues one likewise in operation by the Church in all times and places. The teacher who does not hold spiritual rule is an impotent teacher; the teacher who does not offer sacrifice is a false teacher. How poor was the mere sacrificant who did not teach, though he administered a rite in itself full of teaching, we have seen in the fully-ripened heathen corruption. How miserable was the separation of action from belief and worship we have seen in that same corruption. In fact, the efficacy of each several function lies in their union.

The office of the Teacher, the Pastor, and the Priest is carried on undivided in the whole Church, but in its bearers it is seen in three degrees. In its fulness it dwells in the Sovereign Pontificate; in its diocesan derivation it is stored up in each bishop; it is diffused through the whole Church in the priesthood. When Constantine examined it he found the Christian Episcopate in all lands. No Christian community existed which did not form part of a diocese under the rule of a bishop. Between diocese and diocese there was the utmost variety as to extent and population, but in all the same organisation, and the rank of the bishop in each the same with regard to all who were under his care. If this had been all, the Church would not have formed a kingdom, but at the utmost a confederation of provinces far more numerous than the provinces of any temporal kingdom, and in proportion liable to disruption. The power which was to last for ever and to defy the gates of hell, would have been the weakest and most dissoluble of all powers. It was not so that the Church had grown. It was not so that the great commission, "Feed My lambs," "Be shepherd over My sheep," had been understood and carried into practice. The One Flock was to remain One. It was propagated from the Primacy of Peter, and in the Primacy of Peter it remained for ever one and indissoluble. The more the brethren of Peter multiplied, the more they required to be confirmed. This was the bond of the faggot, without which the arm of the opponent could break every separate stick. This the keystone of the arch by which alone it coheres, and bears the weight set upon it. This the form which impressed unity of teaching and government on the whole body. And the Christian priesthood, one and the same throughout the whole, and making up the multitude of teachers in each diocese, might be termed the blood of this body. The great variety of functions which it discharges answers to this similitude. The Church which Constantine beheld acted throughout and in all its work as one body. To contemplate priest or bishop or primate as acting separately and by himself would be to separate and so extinguish the life which makes the body.

That the unity just described is not a sort of superinduced perfection adding a lustre to its subject, but is indeed that without which the subject cannot exist, will be seen by considering what are those great works which in her teaching, her spiritual rule, and her priesthood the Church is bound to exercise, which she exercised in the time of Constantine, which she exercises now, and will exercise for all time.

1. The first of these is the manifestation to the world of the fact that God had become Incarnate, and of the consequences springing from that fact, which begin with the individual man, but permeate the whole human society and transform it. This is the

religious truth which the Church is charged to communicate. It is a word spoken by authority, the concurrent witness of the whole Church, not the speculation of an individual, not a literature, but the deduction of a whole intellectual creation from its first source, a process in which all gifts of the human intellect are to be used. It is a perpetual work from generation to generation, lodged in the whole priesthood, to discharge which a line of men consecrates its mind, but at the same time a work executed under strict laws of order, wherein the priest is subordinate to the bishop, and every bishop to the Apostolic See of Peter in its occupant. Thus there is unity in the truth to be so communicated, which extends through all times and places, and with unity there is all the force derived from impact. The philosophic school scatters itself into endless divergencies; the Christian priesthood remains one and indivisible in its propagation of the truth with which it is charged. But within these lines of unity and order there is room for the play of every human faculty, and the free exercise of every intellectual gift. The truth which is thus endless in its application, which offers so rich and inexhaustible a subject for the labour of every mind, springs indeed from a mystery which is received only by faith. That God the Son has condescended so to touch His creation as to enter Himself into the line of human nature, to have a Mother, and to call men His brethren, as well as God His Father, this is a fact to which the order of men above mentioned bears witness for ever, but its reception rests upon a gift of God, an illumination of the mind to which we give the name of faith. When once so received, the development of the truth offers scope to the most rigorous philosophic thought; nor has the human mind ever reached a higher degree of excellence than in some of those who have exercised its powers in this development, as, for instance, St. Augustine among the Fathers, and St. Thomas among scientific theologians.

The main work of propagating this truth is done by word of mouth. The word thus originally poured forth is often indeed gathered up and stereotyped afterwards, but in its propagating power it is essentially fluent and oral. It is the work of persons upon persons, and therefore of speakers upon hearers; for the whole life of the speaker, his bodily presence, his moral character, impregnate the truth which he delivers for the reception of the hearer.

The oral delivery of the truth divides itself into two main branches, orderly exposition by discourse, and instruction by question and answer. To conceive aright and adequately the force and grandeur of the institution which produced an order of men dedicated to this work we must recall the sight as it met the eyes of Constantine, and regard it from his point of view. In every city of his empire he saw this work of preaching and catechising carried on simultaneously by a body which had arisen in spite of many active persecutions by the imperial government, of invariable and long-continued discouragement, calumny, and ill-will on the part of the influential classes in society, of frequent violence by the people. He saw the heathen priests in attendance upon countless temples rich in statues and works of art, and endowed with costly revenues; he saw them, perfunctory ministers, as they performed a solemn service of sacrifice daily at the altars of their various deities, declaring no religious truth, unvisited by any anxious conscience. Again, his empire was scoured by philosophers who contended with each other in a chaos of ever-varying opinions, all without authority, unpersuasive and fruitless to the mass of mankind, and to the cultured few who listened to their disputations unable to give any definite notion of that cloudy god of fire, or ether, or the universal mind, whom they obscurely hinted at. At the same time, and in every city, he saw an orderly society of bishop, priests, and people taught by them, of the young instructed by laborious interchange of question and answer, of the faithful collected together, cheered, exhorted, and directed by the unfailing proclamation of a religious truth, one, definite, precise in all places. We have preserved for us an instance of this preaching, the more precious because it stands at the beginning of this institution, is addressed to the professors of that philosophy which we have been so long considering, and represents the bearing and attitude of the institution towards the philosophy. It shows at the same time how it set forth those very truths concerning which it was vain to seek for any definite information from philosophy, the One God, the relation of man to Him, and of the various members of the human family to each other.

When St. Paul in his apostolic travel first came to Athens, his spirit was stirred within him at the sight of a city given up to idolatry. His discussions with Stoics and Epicureans in the market-place led to their demanding an account of his doctrine, and of the "strange things which he brought to their ears." He was led to the Areopagus, and at their demand gave them what may be termed a manifesto of the Christian Church to the Greek philosophy. His words are a summary of three hundred years of action, for that which he has set forth in a few pregnant statements of great truths the Church was occupied during all that time in working by suffering as well as by preaching into the hearts of men.

"Paul, standing in the midst of the Areopagus, said: Ye men of Athens, I perceive that in all things you are too superstitious. For passing by and seeing your idols I found also an altar on which was written, 'To the Unknown God.' Him therefore whom you worship without knowing I announce to you. God, who made the world and all things therein, inasmuch as He is Lord of heaven and earth, dwelleth not in temples made with hands, neither is He served with men's hands as though He needed anything, seeing that it is He who giveth to all life and breath and all things, and has made of one blood every nation of men, to dwell upon the whole face of the earth, having determined their appointed times and the limits of their habitation, that they should seek the Lord, if haply they may feel after Him and find Him, although He be not far from every one of us, for in Him we live and move and are, as some also of your own poets have said, 'For we are also His offspring.' Being then the offspring of God, we must not suppose 'the Divine'[1] to be like unto gold or silver or stone, the graving of the art or thought of man. And God indeed, having winked at the times of this ignorance, now declares to all men everywhere to do penance, because He has determined a day wherein He will judge the world in equity, by the Man whom He has

---

[1] It is much to be noted that St. Paul, having just used the personal expression "God," then proceeds to refer to it the favourite expression of Greek philosophy for the deity, τὸ θεῖον. It is here and only here used in the New Testament, which thus as it were cites the pantheistic falsehood before the true God.

POWER OF THE GREEK PHILOSOPHY 359

appointed, giving assurance of this to all by raising Him up from the dead."

The fitness of this doctrine for the circumstances in which it was given will appear if we reflect that it was uttered in the high place of philosophy, at the request of its two most powerful sects, and that it contains a summary of the relation between God and man which will vainly be sought in Plato or Aristotle, or in the whole line of Greek philosophers from Thales to Plotinus. For with the utmost simplicity and precision St. Paul declares there to be One God, who is a living God, inasmuch as He is the Creator of all things, and by the fact of creating the Absolute Lord of all beings. He gives life and breath to all, and wants nothing of them. He has made every nation of men of one blood, and predetermined the times and boundaries of their habitation over the whole earth, leaving them to search and feel after Him, yet remaining so close to every one of His creatures, that they live, move, and have their being in Him, and are His offspring. The fact that they are His offspring ought to prevent their conceiving the Deity to be like any work of man's hand or thought graven in gold or silver or stone, for how much nobler is the mind of man himself than any such works, and this mind is but a faint reflex of the Creator. However, God passing over, as it were, the times of this ignorance, now calls on all men in the whole world to repent, because He will judge not this or that people but the whole earth in justice, by the Man whom He has appointed, giving proof of this appointment to all by raising Him from the dead.

If we compare this proclamation of St. Paul with the evolution of Greek thought from Seneca to Plotinus which we have been tracing, we shall see that the great preacher pointed out to his hearers exactly what was wanting in their conception of God and man. He knitted the unity of God with His Creatorship, and deduced from the latter the entire dependence of man on God, and the absolute sovereignty of God, which is the counterpart of this dependence. Then followed the unity of the human race, and the unfailing providence of God, which encompassed every creature who lived, moved, and had in him the being derived from Him, and every nation, which, wherever it might dwell over the face of the whole earth, only occupied the boundaries predetermined for it by the Creator. This statement of man's creatorship at once struck at that great defect which degraded the conception of God entertained by Greek philosophy from its beginning to its end, while it also contained in itself the censure of that gross idolatry to which both Stoics and Epicureans in their practice showed themselves basely subservient, and which Plotinus and his followers afterwards took under their protection. For the God who creates is a jealous God, who will not give His glory to another; but the pantheistic god of force admits all forces as parts of itself into its universal bosom. St. Paul likewise by the simple statement of God's absolute lordship over all, who were all equally His creatures, cut the root of that arrogation of superiority for one race over another which was fostered alike by the Greek pride of mind, and the Roman pride of dominion, and established thereby quite another bond between men than that devised by the Stoic fiction of the divine reason dwelling in man. Then he drew the practical conclusion from this, that God who had given the nations knowledge of Himself from which they had fallen away, and had maintained a daily witness of Himself in their hearts by the absolute dependence of their life upon His power and goodness, had suffered them indeed to incur an ignorance which was caused by their own will, but now called on all men everywhere to prepare for the judgment of their actions by the Man whom He had appointed Judge of all. And the proof of this appointment lay in that resurrection from the dead, which is the seal of man's undying personality: a doctrine which philosophy had as entirely failed to teach, as it had shrunk from giving to God the glory of creating.

Let us multiply this preaching of St. Paul by the daily voice of the Christian priesthood in five hundred cities, and we reach some conception of that power which was so persuasive in its unity and simplicity, so vast in its range and influence. What was philosophy's lecture-room and the daily contradictions of those who spoke there, in comparison with it? This, however, was but one half of that oral delivery of the truth on which we have been speaking. Its other division consisted in the catechistic instruction. Such doctrine as that of St. Paul's above was distributed into a series of short statements and imparted carefully to those who were under teaching. The catechism not only led to systematic and perspicuous arrangement of doctrine, which is a most powerful security against error, but carried with it a continual nourishment of the mind by the food presented to it in small portions, and by the necessity of reflecting caused in receiving knowledge in the form of question and answer. Thus it came to pass that a child in the Christian community had a distinct conception of that Maker and Father of the universe whom Plato found it both hard to discover, and when discovered impossible to declare to all.

We must endeavour to realise this order of oral teaching by discourse and by catechising as established through the whole Church and in perpetual operation. It was quite new to the actual heathen world. The freedom, the richness, the accuracy thus imparted to religious teaching had nothing similar to it in all the nations forming part of the empire, outside of the Jews. Its connection with the Jewish foreshadowing of it I have treated elsewhere.[1] From it we proceed to consider the second great work of the Church. The first has been addressed to the intellect, the next will be addressed to the will; but the two are not divided in their application. Simultaneously with her instruction of the intellect, the Church unfolded the manifold treasure of her sacramental life.

2. When the philosopher had addressed the reason of his hearers, he had exhausted all his strength. But the whole action of the Church exercised upon the intellect by the imparting of truth in its two divisions, as described above, was accompanied by a parallel action on the will. Revelation and grace went hand in hand. In the case of those who were without the fold, the oral instruction of the proselyte was terminated by the baptismal rite, one name for which was Illumination. But it was likewise a new birth of the soul, investing it with divine virtues of faith, hope, and charity. In the case of those who were within the fold, the oral instruction of the young was accompanied by the grace which belonged to them as baptized, and their appropriation of the

[1] See above, Lecture xv.

truth thus imparted grew with their growth and
strengthened with their strength. It was strong
enough to carry St. Agnes at the age of thirteen to
contempt of the world and to martyrdom. At the
time when human passions ordinarily assault the
heart, the grace of confirmation came to make the
Christian complete. Through the whole time of his
warfare the Bread of Life was offered to him as
the perpetual nourishment of the regenerated soul.
Through the whole time of his warfare another sacrament likewise opened to him the gate of penance,
and enabled him to wipe away the spots of sin contracted through negligence or deeper guilt. Further,
the whole triple order of the teaching, the pastoral,
and the sacerdotal function was conveyed by a divine
gift, and was the subject of a sacrament belonging
to itself. Though every act of this triple function
belonged to the intellectual nature of man, it received
a divine consecration of the will, an imparting of
the power of the One Prophet, King, and Priest, and
by this consecration the intellect was fertilised. The
same divine power likewise touched that bond of the
sexes by which human society is held together, and
human love burned more brightly and lasted more
steadfastly when fed with the oil of charity. Even
sickness and the danger of death were not left without a special force to be exercised upon them by the
priests of the Church. The power of the sacraments,
that is, the unction of the Prophet, Priest, and King,
covered the whole ground of daily life. The human
soul is at once intellect and will, and the acts of each
run into each other and are indivisible; and so in the
great work created by the Author of the soul the
one and the other were equally provided for, and the

illumination of the mind was accompanied by the forming of the will. The whole domain of human conduct was thus touched and encompassed by the sacramental life, which constituted the ordinary state of the Christian.

3. But this union between belief and action, between doctrine and conduct, was powerfully upheld by the offering of the One great Sacrifice to the One God in all lands. This Sacrifice contained the supreme act of worship, the homage to God of both intellect and will; but it likewise contained in itself indivisibly the expression of great truths, those truths on which the human race lives its real life, those very truths which popular heathenism had obscured and degraded, and which scientific heathenism in its philosophy had denied. In the central shrine of Christian belief the point to which all eyes were turned, for which all hearts yearned, was that commemoration of the Offering of Christ which brought in visible form before the Christian daily the supreme act of divine love. He who attended that Sacrifice testified thereby that God was one alone, and that He was the Creator; testified moreover that He had become Incarnate, and had wrought Redemption; testified, thirdly, that He maintained perpetually the work which He had wrought. The offering of this Sacrifice was the perpetual guardian of truth in the Church; it was no less the perpetual guardian of charity. It confirmed daily the charter of that covenant which had been made with Noah, and then broken by his posterity; which was made afresh with Abraham, and established for ever in the Son of Abraham and David. The offering of this Sacrifice was the third work of the Church, indissolubly blended

with her whole task of instructing man's intellect and persuading his will. And Constantine beheld that in five hundred cities of his dominion, and wherever the Christian community existed, this Sacrifice was offered incessantly, and gathered about it the most fervent prayers of all worshippers for the various orders of the great Christian Church, for princes and governments, for relations and friends, for enemies likewise and persecutors, for those who prospered and those who suffered, for those who had departed from this life in a state of grace but yet with the temporal punishment due to sin not fully discharged— in fact, with absolute unanimity of the Christian heart for the living and for the dead.

In the triple function which we have now described, and which made up the perpetual work of the Church, teaching was inseparably bound up with action, the informing of the intellect with the moulding of the will; but equally close was the union of the Christian Sacrifice with both. It taught daily before the eyes what the sacraments communicated. It set forth Jesus Christ crucified; and He was the beginning and end of the teaching; He was the source and giver of the sacraments. The several powers which a corruption, whose seat was in the will much more than in the intellect, had disunited in the society originally set up by God for the whole race, and which philosophy, assuming as it did the office of religion, had utterly failed to reunite, were here once more joined together. The teaching, the sacraments, and the Sacrifice embraced the whole inner life of the individual from childhood to age, from birth to death. The heathen priest had worship without teaching; the philosopher taught without a worship; but to both the wide field of human action and suffering lay apart from the teaching or the worship. On the contrary, that triple work of instruction, spiritual rule, and worship, which occupied the priesthood of the Christian Church, touched every condition of life with its inexhaustible charity. An incident of modern life will serve to show what was as true in the fourth century as it is in the nineteenth. "One day," says M. Cochin, "scarcely a few months ago, I was walking in the court of the Institute with M. Cousin, and a learned professor of philosophy. A young curate had just passed, and as he went from us towards the bridge, M. Cousin, looking at him from a distance, stopped and said to his colleague: 'My friend, we have been teaching philosophy all our life; we call young men of education together, and endeavour to prove to them by laborious arguments that there is a soul. In the meantime what has this young priest been doing, and where has he been going? He goes to reconcile the souls of husband and wife, to strengthen the soul of an old man at the point of death, to struggle with vice in the soul of a bad man, with temptation in the soul of a young girl, with despair in the soul of the unhappy, to enlighten the soul of a child. And we wish to throw such people as that into the river! It would be better for us to be thrown in ourselves with a stone about our necks. Let us be honest enough to admit what they are doing for souls while we are trying to recognise the soul's existence.'"[1]

But the priesthood thus engaged was one in its nature and character through every diocese. So the authority of the bishop was one and the same in all;

[1] Lacordaire's *Correspondence with Madame Swetchine*, p. 570.

and the guardian of both in teaching and spiritual rule was the Primacy of St. Peter. Thus the organisation of the great Christian commonwealth was as perfect as the direction of the individual's life and conduct. There is every reason to believe that this organisation powerfully affected the mind of Constantine, and that he looked upon it as a result beyond human wisdom to contrive or human ability to execute. Let us think of it for a moment from the point of view from which it appeared to him.

For indeed it is in the joint action upon the three great forces which together constitute human life, that is to say, the belief, the conduct, and the worship of man, that the definite formation and establishment of the Christian Kingdom consists. To make such a kingdom is a work by itself, single, and without parallel in all time. It had no predecessor; it has no rival; it will have no successor. It is a distinct work of Christ over and above His teaching, over and above His suffering, built upon both, but a further exercise of power. We shall be helped to see how great this power is by reflecting on the utter impotence of human genius in those who had preceded Him to do anything of the kind. The force of it lies not in the number of bishops or believers, but in the character of a perfect and at the same time an universal society. And it is not a nation which is selected as the recipient of such a society, so that any support for it might be drawn from natural qualities or locality. The embryo of such a society had been set up by God as a type in the Jewish people, but it ceased to be national before it could become universal. The wonder here is that such a society was impressed on the most heterogeneous elements, in the great swarming hive of confederated peoples called the Roman empire. The material elements, the men of various races of whom it was composed, the different classes, rich and poor, learned and ignorant, a multitude of slaves, and a mass of the female sex which had lain for centuries enthralled and degraded by the stronger sex, all these in themselves, and still more in the attempt to weld them together, portended dissolution. The society was maintained not by force of them but in spite of them. Again, it was maintained without break or failure amid a multitude of sects which used the same liberty of internal belief that itself possessed to break away from it: which successively rose like bubbles and dissolved. Again, this society had been formed and attained full effect in the ten generations during which it had never been legally tolerated, and was often actually persecuted. What that persecution could be none could tell so well as an emperor, and Constantine had indeed witnessed the full force in the East of the last and worst himself. And it had been formed right in the teeth of the cultured classes, which turned from it with aversion, and gave themselves in preference to philosophy, that is, to the unaided efforts of human reason. These were the antecedents when Constantine saw it, and no human ingenuity could have suggested any adequate reason for its subsistence except a divine power; and this he recognised, and therefore he set the Cross upon his diadem.

He saw the whole society as based upon the Person of the Son of God Incarnate. This alone was its reason for existence; this alone the adequate support of its existence. The whole teaching, pastoral, and sacerdotal office in all its parts was simply a derivation from Christ. It was He who created the teaching, named the pastors, and invested them with His own priesthood after the order of Melchisedech. They were drawn from His Person. They dated from the Cœnaculum and the Day of Pentecost. Again, every priest throughout the Church by the possession of these three functions and in the union of them represented Christ. The bishop in every diocese by the same possession and union represented Christ likewise; but in him the teaching and the pastoral functions had a larger derivation of the virtue of the Head. So lastly the Primate of the whole Church, inasmuch as he possessed with one and the same priesthood the teaching and pastoral functions in the highest degree and immediately from Christ, was in a pre-eminent sense His Vicar. This was the Rock which Christ had laid so that "though there be in the people of God many priests and many pastors, Peter should rule all with ordinary whom Christ also rules with sovereign power."[1]

In this sense it is that the Church is the realisation of Christ in the world as King and Legislator. No other kingdom is wrapped up in the person of the sovereign, and developed from him. This is the unique glory of the God-man. But that union of belief, conduct, and worship which was perfectly carried out only by Him, was pointed at in the preceding dispensations. As we have seen, the society established by Noah, which itself was a repetition of the original

[1] St. Leo, Epist. iv. 2. It may be noted that the first four sermons of St. Leo, preached the first upon the day of his consecration, and the three following on the subsequent anniversaries, that is, in the years A.D. 440, 441, 442, 443, contain a statement of doctrine respecting the Primacy of St. Peter, as continued in his heir, the Bishop of Rome, which is identical and coextensive with that set forth in the First Dogmatic Constitution concerning the Church of Christ decreed by the Vatican Council.

society as constituted in Adam, and which carried on the same rite of sacrifice, began in this union, and gradually declined from it. The nations as they come before us in a state of moral degradation show traces of it. But in the dispensation given to Moses the triple mediation of Prophet, Priest, and King made a complete society for the Jewish people, and was in this a typical picture of the great world-wide Church which should spring out of its bosom. Nevertheless, to carry that into effect, and to maintain its effect in the world from age to age, the personal action of the Divine Legislator was needed, and Constantine, and in him the Roman empire, acknowledged that action, and did homage to the King in His Kingdom.

LECTURE XXII

THE CHURCH RECONSTRUCTING THE NATURAL ORDER BY THE SUPERNATURAL

In that intellectual battle of three hundred years which we have been narrating in so many preceding lectures, all the power of civilisation from Claudius to Constantine stood on the side of the heathen philosophy. It started in possession of the cultured mind, it was favoured both by the prepossessions of the higher classes and by the wishes and policy of the government. It was not merely free from all interference, but munificently endowed. In all the worthier members of the philosophic profession it brought honour as well as means of living to be a philosopher. It flattered in the highest degree the national feeling of the Grecian part of the empire, which comprehended generally the men of letters, inasmuch as it was the most glorious heirloom of the Greek mind. The very names of Pythagoras, Plato, and Aristotle touched their remotest descendant with a halo of renown. It was favoured no less by the political feeling and instincts of the Romans, who viewing philosophy in its alliance with the established religion considered it to be supporting their empire, which from Romulus and Numa downwards had been associated with their worship. On the other hand its opponent started from the deep opprobrium of Golgotha, to the Jews a stumbling-block and to the Greeks folly; its standard-bearers were fishermen relieved by a publican and a tent-maker, all of them from a despised and odious province. It laid hold of the ignorant, of women, and of slaves, and its adherents among the cultured classes were for a long time few and far between. Under these conditions the contest began and was carried on, and at the end of ten generations Philosophy had proved a rope of sand, utterly powerless to form a society out of its adherents, and the Church, stretching her organisation throughout the empire and discharging her triple but simultaneous work of the teaching, the pastoral, and the sacerdotal function with a unity which no persecution could mar, and no sect rival, presented to the emperor's searching eye a divine society, to which he certainly looked for the revivifying of his empire, when he took the banner of the Cross for his Oriflamme, and inscribed upon it the words of the heavenly vision, "In this sign shalt thou conquer."

It was on such a victory that St. Jerome looked back a hundred years later when he wrote to the noble Roman ladies Paula and Eustochium,[1] "If any one seeks for eloquence and takes pleasure in declamations, he has in the one language Demosthenes and Polemo, in the other Tullius and Quintilian. The Church of Christ was drawn together not from the Academia or the Lyceum, but from the meanest of the multitude. Whence too the Apostle said, 'Consider your vocation, brethren, that you are not many wise according to the flesh, not many powerful, not many noble, but God chose the foolish things of this world to confound the wise, and the weak things of the world to confound the strong, and the base things of the world and the things that are contemptible has God chosen, and

[1] *In Epist. ad Galatas.* tom. vii. 486

RECONSTRUCTING THE NATURAL ORDER 373

things that are not, that He might bring to nought things that are. For because the world had not learnt God by wisdom from the order, the variety, and the settled continuance of creatures, it pleased God by the folly of preaching to save those that believed, not by wisdom of language, lest the Cross of Christ should be made of no effect.' But lest he might be thought in thus speaking to be a preacher of unwisdom, he overthrew with prophetic mind a possible objection, saying, 'We speak the wisdom of God in a mystery which has been concealed, which no one of the princes of this world knew.' Who is there now that reads Aristotle? How many know Plato's books or even his name? Scarcely here and there a few old men in their retirement turn them over. But our countrymen and fishermen the whole world speaks of: they are voiced by the universe."

Perhaps it is well for us in the nineteenth century to refer to this simple mention of a fact in the fifth. For it is a victory never to be forgotten, being indeed that miracle which seemed to the greatest thinker of that same fifth century the greatest of all miracles—for so the Catholic Church viewed in her course up to his own time appeared to St. Augustine.

But it was not only that Philosophy failed to form a society; it likewise failed and utterly failed up to the time of Constantine to implant the belief of one God in the hearts of men. St. Paul addressed the Stoics and Epicureans in the Areopagus of Athens with the words, " I proclaim to you that God whom you unknowing worship." For two centuries and a half from the time these words were spoken the Church pursued her work on the one hand, and Philosophy its discussion on the other. At the end of that time what was the result? The pantheistic god of Philosophy never got beyond the lecture-room, where his audience comprised a sprinkling of cultured men and women, who employed their learned ease in listening to a Plotinus or a Porphyrius, and worshipped at the same time the gods of Greece, or Egypt, or the East. Up to the reign of Constantine it may safely be said that Philosophy had never caused a single idolater to desert his idols, or a single servant of the temple to give up her unholy worship. But had the belief in the philosophic god been far more real than it was, there is yet a vast difference between the existence of a doctrine on paper, and the impressing that doctrine upon the lives and habits of men. The test of spiritual power lies in producing action, in transmuting belief into conduct. Heathen life was action; Christian life was action; Philosophy was talk, or writing; the talk evaporated in the lecture-room; the writing never passed further than the paper. For the recitation in the restricted lecture-room was but a page out of a book which the hearer might receive as he pleased and do what he pleased with. But the statues in myriads of temples to a multitude of gods, the sacrifices upon myriads of altars, the priests who offered them, the national and hereditary traditions which hung about them, the customs of life and the affections of the heart with which they were united, these were a reality, a great and abiding force, which Philosophy did not attempt to overthrow, of which indeed it had made itself the ally. Plotinus and Porphyrius and Iamblichus were perfectly good friends with Jupiter and his wife, and all his children legitimate and illegitimate.

1. The doctrine that there is One God, distinct

from all other beings, subsisting in Himself, intelligent, free, and the Creator of all things out of nothing, is the foundation of human society and of morality. To re-establish this doctrine in the minds and hearts of men, corrupted by a false worship which for ages had obscured it, and was itself tainted with unspeakable profanations, was a task of the greatest difficulty. At the time of Constantine it had been accomplished by the Church through the joint and simultaneous action of her teaching, pastoral, and sacerdotal office. Not only did the whole of this action turn upon the Person of Christ, but the fact that it did so turn led to the result that every doctrine was brought out in the form of a concrete fact. Let us observe this with regard to that master doctrine the Being of God as above set forth.

St. Paul ended his address to the philosophers, in which he so clearly and precisely challenged them to accept the God who was the Author and Preserver of their being, with the words, " Because God has appointed a day wherein He will judge the world in equity by the Man whom He has appointed, giving assurance of it to all by raising Him up from the dead." The resurrection of Christ was a fact which all could comprehend. It formed the basis of the Apostolic teaching. But it led on to the further doctrine that He was the Messiah and the Son of God. Now in what sense was He the Son of God? And what was His work as Messiah? Here again the doctrine when unfolded led up to the mysteries of the Redemption and Incarnation, and to the primal mystery of all, that God was one in Nature yet three in Person, and that the Fathership, the Sonship, and the Procession of the Spirit made a triple personality in the one divine Essence. The preaching of Jesus

Christ crucified—a simple fact, concrete if ever fact was—carried in its bosom all these consequences. And one of the first acts of the Church was to embody them all in a short document which was taught by heart, and so given to each disciple as the symbol of his faith. It was in the main a simple statement of a number of facts concerning a Person, His birth, His life, His death, and His resurrection. The power of a document like the Creed, summing up the chief heads of a perfectly concordant and harmonious doctrine, was very great. It was also new, and nothing like it had been known in the heathen world. It sounded in the disciples' ears like a trumpet to battle in the ears of the soldier. Indelibly impressed on the memory, repeated morning and night, it reminded the disciple with every day's coming and departure whose he was and in what power he stood. Thus it was that the Creed formed Christ in the Christian, and in so forming fixed in him the belief in the Living God the Creator of man, who was at the same time the God and Father of the Lord Jesus Christ.

But this teaching was only one touch of a triple instrument. By the whole hierarchy of the Church, that is, the perpetual daily action of the priest, or the bishop, or the Primate, in continual exercises of authority, all of which had their source and their reason of existence in the Person of Christ alone, and without Him were senseless and profitless, these same doctrines of the Redemption, the Incarnation, and the Godhead were applied to the disciple. All the sacraments uttered them vocally and expressed them in a concrete form. Baptism itself made the Christian in the name of the Triune God; the Eucharist supported him with the flesh of Christ crucified; Penance remitted his guilt with the voice of Christ, and by applying the merits of Christ; Marriage set the blessing of Christ upon the chief relation of civil life, and raised it at the same time to be a type of His union with His Church and of the soul's union with God.

But, thirdly, in the great act of Christian worship, the culminating point of the Christian's life, these same doctrines, the Redemption, the Incarnation, and the Trinity in Unity, were daily set forth in action. There above all the Bishop or the Priest stood in the Person of Christ, spoke the words of Christ, and by the virtue of those words—an act of no less than creative power—accomplished the Sacrifice. In the liturgy above all was enshrined the belief that one of the Divine Persons became incarnate and was crucified, and thereby redeemed the world. The belief thus embodied became a concrete fact, and all who had attained the age of reason could make it their own.

Thus by the joint action of personal teaching, of the hierarchy with its attendant sacraments, and of the Sacrifice, the Church exhibited the mysteries of her faith, the great supernatural doctrines of the Trinity in Unity, the Incarnation, and the Redemption; but in doing so, as it were by a surplusage she brought out, illuminated, and made concrete to every mind and heart the conception of God as distinct from the world, free to create or not to create, and caring for His creatures with intensest love.

But I must note further two points in this mode of establishing belief in the One God.

The first is, the great help which the Person of our Lord made visible to human eyes in His form and fashion as a man, and brought within the grasp of human perception, gave to the conceiving the doctrine of Personality in God. The whole of the above teaching of Christ in the triple office of the Church, as at once God and Man, was thereby of the greatest service to the Christian. The cords of a man enabled him to comprehend God in that respect in which Philosophy had most erred, and wherein the reason of Pythagoras, Plato, and Aristotle had fallen short. And secondly, the distinction of Persons in the One Essence of God afforded help in the same direction, since it is the strongest example of Personality which can be given to the creature, and the most emphatic denial of Pantheism, on which that ancient paganism rested as its ultimate basis, and on which every fresh paganism which has arisen or will arise must equally rest. For the Divine Essence is absolutely One, yet in it the Fathership, the Sonship, and the Procession of the Spirit constitute eternal relations, which are the Divine Persons. There is no other distinction in God but these. And they are inseparably connected with the work of human salvation, in which they co-operate, each in regard to that by which they are Divine Persons, the Father as giving His Son, the Son as conferring His Sonship upon men His brethren, the Holy Spirit as conveying the gift of the divine Love, which He is Himself.

The whole loveliness of the Christian Faith was thus expended in setting forth God as He is in Himself, in His personal relations. Redemption threw back a light upon Creation, and the Unity and Personality of God were conceived in one light of faith.

The restoration of the belief and the worship of the One living God may be said to be among the greatest works of the Church, and in accomplishing it she laid afresh the foundation of human society.

2. The credibility of the Christian Faith was rested

by its heralds and proclaimers upon a fact, the resurrection of their Master in the body in which He had died upon the Cross. This was their guarantee to the world of the truth which they sought to promulgate, When St. Paul said, "If Christ be not risen again, then is our preaching vain, and your faith is also vain ; yes, and we are found false witnesses of God," he expressed the vast importance of this doctrine, and its special position as basis of the Christian fabric of belief. Nor was there any doctrine which more kindled the animosity or sharpened the scorn of the heathen than this of the resurrection of the body. When the Stoics and Epicureans heard it, "some mocked, while others said, We will hear thee again about this matter," a time which probably never came. Yet there was a doctrine about the immortality of the soul, that is, the intellectual principle in man, current at least among philosophers, and that something of man survived after death was generally believed by the multitude of men, and was borne witness to upon their tombs. What then was the reason for this animosity and scorn?

All arguments as to the immortality of the soul were in the force which they exercised to persuade as nothing in comparison with the one fact of Christ's resurrection. For this fact, the foundation of Christian hope, without which Christians were, as they are still, of all men the most miserable, established in the mind the conception of the eternal personal subsistence of the human compound, soul and body, distinct from God, but sustained by Him. It was the corollary to the doctrine of the Personal God : it did for the manhood what the preceding doctrine did for the godhead. But such a conception of the eternal and personal subsistence of the human compound had dropt away from the Gentile mind together with the belief of a God creating and therefore absolutely detached from the world. Thus it was that when the Apostles urged upon their hearers the resurrection of Christ in the body in which He suffered, and with it the resurrection of all men in their several bodies after His example, they set forth a belief which touched the whole life and conduct of the heathen man in its every detail. It was the greatest moral revolution which could be imagined, for it altered the value of everything in the world. If this were true, that also became true, "What shall it profit a man to gain the whole world and lose his own soul?" Not only had Julius Cæsar, and Tiberius, and Nero to look to it, but Zeno and Cato of Utica no less, for what had Philosophy hitherto done with the soul?

Plato, after Pythagoras, and carrying on his doctrine, argued for the post-existence of the soul after the death of the body, on the ground of its pre-existence before it entered into the body. And this again was connected with the doctrine that all intellect is one and divine, and so not subject to death. Thus they held that when man's life on earth in the body began, it was not a creation but a union of the intellectual principle already existing with so much matter, a union which was to terminate at death, when the matter would be resolved into other changes, but the mind would recur to its former state. If therefore any distinct being was thus supposed to be carried on, there was a want of continuity in its condition, unrelieved by any further hope. The body which had been the partner and instrument of all its work on earth ceased to be connected with it. But in point of fact the heathen belief as to the lot of the soul itself was quite vague and undetermined. The philosophic opinion just cited was that the mind in its pre-existent state had, at least originally, not been severed from the universal mind, and apparently in its post-existent state it was, at any rate in the end, to return to its first condition. Thus the conception of man even during his earthly life as a personal being was imperfect, but with the union of the soul and body at any rate the personality disappeared. This was the philosophic belief at the highest point which it reached. But what was the popular belief? It was a struggle of human desire and affection, a whispering too of conscience, and the lingering echo of old tradition against the fear that death was the last determining line of each human life. For the Greek the touching words of Moschus express an universal plaint:

> "O muse of Sicily, begin the dirge,
> Woe—woe—the mallows dying in the garden,
> Or the green parsley and the florid anise
> Revive again, spring up another year.
> But we, the great, the mighty, and the wise,
> Once laid in death, lie voiceless in earth's bosom,
> A long, a boundless, unawakened sleep."

And Catullus mourns for the whole Latin race:

> "Suns set, and suns can rise again,
> But our brief light of day once gone
> Yields to one endless night of sleep."

And the plaint too often turned into the carouse: let us eat and drink, let us crown ourselves with roses, let us love, for to-morrow we die. That we may be sure will be the practical result with the vast majority, if they can bring themselves to believe that after all the joys and sorrows of life, after all its struggles and cares, after its shortcomings and its crimes, with death "like streaks of morning cloud they melt into the infinite azure of the past."[1]

Nothing therefore could be more distinct either from the philosophic doctrine of a qualified post-existence of man's spirit, grounded on the pantheistic notion of an universal mind, or the popular mixture of incertitude, sorrow, desire, and despair as to a life of man after death, than the peremptory doctrine, Christ is risen from the dead to be the Judge of all men, who likewise shall rise in their bodies from death to die no more. As the same Christ who had been crucified, who had been laid in the tomb, rose in the very body in which He had suffered shame and torment, so each man should rise to receive good or evil in the body for the deeds done in the body. It was the setting forth of a complete human responsibility as the counterpart of an enduring human personality. Hence the outcry of the philosopher; hence the mockery of the people. The tremendous seriousness of that belief, conveyed in visible form, and no longer an abstraction, penetrated right through the heathen armour, and touched the man to the quick.

The force then of the fact that Christ was risen from the dead lay in bringing out sharply, practically, and vividly, the doctrine of man's everlasting personality in his compound nature of soul and body. The continuity which was wanting to the vague and indeterminate heathen notion of a surviving intellect was given by the rising of the body. The bodiless shade eluding the grasp like the viewless air, which hovered about the heathen tomb, became the man, with all his

---

[1] The last words of Professor Tyndall's Address at Belfast, as reported in the *Times*.

affections, all his aspirations, and, it must be added, with all his deeds upon him.

Let us note further two corrections which this wonderfully pregnant fact brought with it.

First there was the correction of a long and manifold scientific error which showed itself in the greatest force in the last or Neoplatonic phase of Grecian philosophy. There had been a disposition throughout to make Matter the seat of evil, as if there were something essentially unruly, which was so inherent in it that it baffled even the power of the Demiurge to overcome and reduce it to order. Again, the Platonists made the body a mere instrument of the soul, not an essential part of man's nature; or, again, the prison of the spirit, not its partner and yoke-fellow in the noble work of life. Or further, they considered that the contact of Matter with Mind corrupted the mind and polluted its divine nature. Now all these errors were overthrown together by the resurrection of Christ in His body. This fact restored the body to honour, as being not the seat of evil, not the mere instrument of the soul, far less its prison, and yet less again the cause of its corruption. That resurrection showed the body of man to be the creature of God, and revindicated to it the original part which it had held, when the Creator took earth, moulded it into an organism, and breathed into it the breath of life. When He thus made the soul the form of the body He made the body likewise the partner of the soul, constructing an alliance in which there was nothing debasing, nothing unholy, but which was to be for ever a miracle of divine power and wisdom, and the subject of divine goodness in its highest exhibition. The resurrection of Christ was the full accomplishment of that design, for in it the body of man, which had been raised to inexpressible honour by its assumption on the part of the Divine Word, entered into the visible and everlasting possession of its rank in creation.

But, secondly, from this fact was to spring the correction of an intense moral corruption.

The resurrection of Christ in His Body was not merely proclaimed by word of mouth; it ran structurally through the whole fabric of the Church. It was the seminal principle of the sacraments. And the great Sacrifice of the new covenant—the daily act of Christian worship—presupposed it and rested on it. A comparison will best illustrate this whole view. Some of the worst impurities of heathen life were connected with the worship of Ceres and Bacchus. These false gods were considered to preside over the principle of increase and multiplication in the fruits of the earth; the one over corn and every sort of dry seed, the other over wine and every sort of liquid. Their festivals, celebrated with an extraordinary concourse of people, became infamous for the open exhibition of debauchery, a sort of glorying in deeds of shame. It was the very consummation of turpitude in the devil's kingdom to abuse in this manner for evil that very bounty of the Creator in which He opened His hand to fill all living things with plenteousness. But now it was precisely of corn and wine that the divine Restorer took hold to convey in His sacrament the grace of purity. He caused the corn of wheat which had died in His Body to become the food of His people, and of the natural fruit of the vine He made His Blood to become the wine which produces virgins. Thus the true King, in overthrowing the usurper, took those very elements of natural increase which heathenism had put under two false deities, and perverted in their worship to incitements for evil, and in taking them caused them to become His Body and Blood for the creation of a sacred race. But He took them likewise and constituted them to be the perpetual commemoration of the Sacrifice which He had offered of His Body. He had associated matter with Himself in a wonderful way in taking a body; and now He made that Body itself the means whereby the Creator and Redeemer of man becomes his Sacrifice. This is the part which matter plays when touched by God. In the Neoplatonic philosophy it was deemed the cause of evil. In the Christian Faith it becomes the special instrument which brings about the triumph of good. But the consecration thus given to matter ran all through the doctrine of the sacraments. Water conferred regeneration, and oil was the channel of grace; and the Church took possession of the whole material world for the glory of its Maker. All this was involved in the fact of Christ's resurrection in the body.

The second great fact, therefore, by which the Church in setting forth supernatural mysteries replaced civil society on its true basis, was in establishing by the resurrection of Christ in His Body the eternal personality of man. This doctrine, and this alone, is an adequate foundation for the whole conduct of man in the trial to which he is exposed. Without it morality becomes what it became in the Græco-Roman heathenism, and what it is now in every country where the moral order is not based upon Christian belief.

3. That God is One, that He is intelligent, that by an act of freedom, which had He chosen He need not

have exercised, He created all men and all things; that man so created has an abiding personal subsistence, which in its unity, its intelligence, and its freedom is an image, however faint, of these attributes in God: these are the two great truths on which I have hitherto dwelt, as being re-implanted in the minds of the Gentile nations by the action of the Church. From them follows another truth, the absolute dominion of God on the one hand over the man so formed and sustained, and the duty of absolute obedience to God by man on the other. That, in other words, is the conception of creatureship. Now it is not too much to say that this was the precise want of the Gentile world. The debasement of God's nature by the breaking His unity, the diminution of God's sovereignty by supposing Matter to stand over against Mind, as co-eternal or at least co-original, and at the same time by conceiving the divine and the human intelligence to fall under one genus, and the loss of the sense of man's future everlasting personal subsistence, these untruths prevailing together had greatly impaired the sense of dependence on the divine power, and destroyed the complete loyalty of heart which man owes to that power. The people indeed were better than the philosophers in this respect. There was more reverence, more sense of a divine government, in the popular and untutored mind than in the Neoplatonic fabulist of a Primal Being. But in a universe in which men and women were supposed, by virtue of some force which was everything and nothing, to grow like animals and plants without knowing whence they came or whither they were going, in such a world, the world of the last Greek philosophy, the obedience of man to his

Lord—*Dominus suus*, as Cicero phrased it, using just that Roman word which expressed absolute property—was extinct. And in a world given up to a multitude of deities, who were indeed supposed to be personal, but were full of crimes and inconsistent with each other, and who were not supposed to have made man, though they presided in some sense over human society, and were its guardians, the dependence allowed to exist between man and these beings was not that of creatureship, wanting both its stringency and its tenderness.

Moreover it should be noted that the philosophic school which most exalted the notion of duty rested it on quite a different ground from that of obedience to a person. The Stoic conception of life according to reason or nature was based on the principle that man should submit himself to the control of what was divine in his own nature, the spark of mind which was in him for a time. The ground of this was the reasonableness of the subjection of the part to the whole, of the particular reason to the general, of so much mind and matter put together to the unvarying series of physical cause and effect termed necessity. The particular reason in man which was called upon to submit was no more a creature than the universal reason to which that submission was urged as a duty was a creator. And the submission of the individual to the commonwealth, the basis of heathen patriotism, was closely akin to the Stoic notion of duty. Like that it had no limit; it had no moral reserve. The individual had no fortress in himself inexpugnable to human power, the fortress of the creature's will, supported by the sense of obedience due to the Creator. In all this state there was nothing of personal devotion obedience, and love. These are virtues of the creature towards the Creator, but that relationship had been ignored.

Whatever there was of grand and forcible in the later Roman life was the joint result of the Stoic officium and Roman patriotism. Such men as Trajan, Hadrian, Antoninus Pius, and Marcus Aurelius amongst emperors, such men as Agricola among soldiers and officials, are instances of a considerable class. A certain unbending vigour and even rectitude in their official duties, a certain sacrifice of time and risk of life, gave somewhat of nobility to this temperament, and undoubtedly prolonged the tenure of Roman power. But the private life of these men, as for instance of Trajan and Hadrian, was often an abyss of turpitude. The first of these, the model of constitutional rulers, as Tacitus and Pliny viewed him, deserved to be banished from human society as the worst of criminals; the second, a man of the most restless energy, and the model of imperial generals as he marched bareheaded with his troops, went, if it was possible, even beyond his predecessor by consecrating the foulest of human perversities into a worship.

It has passed into a commonplace among Christian truths that the whole Christian life is built upon the imitation of Christ. This imitation is the symbol which comprehends the root, the motive, and the strength of the whole race, the standard and model of its virtue, the ground of its reward. But we limit here our notice of this imitation to a single point, the character of the perfect creature, the Just Servant of God, which consists in absolute obedience. In this obedience, as the expression of Christ's life from the moment when, coming [1] into the world, He uttered, "A body Thou hast fitted to Me; behold I come; in the head of the book it is written of Me, to do Thy will, O Lord," to the last words upon the Cross, "Father, into Thy hands I commend My spirit," is summed up all His thought and all His action. That conception of creatureship the Church took, and out of it formed the whole of her ritual. Her teaching through the whole order of the year revolves round the life of Christ, and sets forth His example as the perfect creature in His obedience. But no less her hierarchy, from its highest point in the Primate to the humblest doorkeeper, was a carrying out of the *ministry* of Christ. As He *ministered* to His Father in the whole work which He came to do upon earth, so in carrying on that work to the end of time, the hierarchy which He instituted *ministered* to Him. The highest of all in the highest of his functions expresses this ministry when he terms himself Servant of the servants of God, but most of all in the divine Sacrifice, in virtue of which Christ is for ever in the midst of His Church, His obedience unto death is embodied. This perhaps is the most striking of the many great lessons which with every day it perpetually enjoins. From the teaching, the hierarchy, and the Sacrifice, one accordant voice sounds everywhere in the ears of the great Christian people that obedience, unreserved and absolute, is the part of the creature towards the Creator. Thus by the publication of the Christian mysteries, which is the Church's work in the supernatural order, she re-established the shaken basis of the natural order in the world, man's creatureship, and obedience as the mark of it. When the great

[1] Heb. x. 5, from Psalm xxxix. 6.

antichristian revolution burst in the full force of its hurricane upon European society, the blast which it blew was of man's rights, but the order which it attacked rested upon man's duties, the spring of which is the obedience which he owes as a creature. But in the first three centuries of her course—the period of persecution—the Church had immutably based her society upon the principle of obedience. She could not do otherwise, because she is the Kingdom of Christ, the Just Servant; and she made this principle the foundation of all her works, carrying it out consistently, and applying it first in the Roman State, and then in every State which she formed.

It was then by the example of Christ in His absolute obedience that she healed the great wound under which heathen society suffered; that she changed the Stoic pride of an imagined divine dignity in human nature into a confession of absolute dependence upon the Maker of the nature, and so changed also the whole quality of virtue and morality, making it the creature's homage to God. This was simply a victory of the Cross of Christ, the Jewish stumbling-block and the heathen folly, proving itself stronger than human fortitude, and wiser than human philosophy.

4. A most learned observer [1] of the morals and manners of the Roman empire makes the following statement: "Man in the ancient world did not feel himself to be separated by an immeasurable distance from the deity, because he did not stand before it as a creature before the Creator; and the different relation to the divinity carried with it likewise a different relation to humanity. That first principle of Christianity

---

[1] Friedlaender, *Darstellungen aus der Sittengeschichte Roms*, iii. 547.

that all men are made by one Creator, children of one Father, in consequence drawn together by the bond of brotherhood, equally entitled and equally bound to mutual love, this view developed itself in non-Christian antiquity for the first time during the period of the Roman world-empire; nor did it ever become general. Greek and Roman antiquity, in opposition to that undistinguishable equality before God of all created, recognised as subsisting in right those numerous gradations of human existence which political, national, and social developments had produced, and neither a divine command nor a moral law hindered him who had the best of it from making his superior right felt in its whole range over any one less favoured. The existence of man was not in the eyes of men holy and inviolable to that degree in which it must be in presence of a deity from whom all life proceeds, and who not only has not allowed but has expressly forbidden to them the right to destroy His creatures, which belongs to Himself alone. From the position which the ancient view of the order of the world assigned to man, there resulted to him, together with his greater freedom and independence, a far more extended authority to determine upon the existence of those who were given over to his protection or his power. Not only had the master the right over the life of his slaves, the father had it likewise over the life of his children, and Plato and Aristotle expressly recommended the withdrawal of life from those who would be a burden upon society."

Let us note here as of great importance the avowal by so competent a witness, who refers likewise to one as learned and as competent as himself, the last historian of Greek philosophy, that the principle of men being made by one Creator, children of one Father, and so bound together by the bond of brotherhood, and entitled and no less bound to mutual love, was unknown to Greek and Roman antiquity, and first developed itself in the time of the Roman empire. But let us add for greater precision that it did not develop itself until after our Lord had died upon the Cross. When we consider the facts which the author just cited sums up with so much clearness, we cannot doubt that the doctrine of man's brotherhood under a common Father was simply of Christian origin. But I wish to remark further that the view of human fraternity, so far as it does appear in non-Christian Greek and Roman authors after the Sacrifice of Christ, not merely never became general, but was not identical with the Christian doctrine either in its ground or in its character. It was the special boast of the Stoics to claim to be citizens of one commonwealth, the great world commonwealth of gods and men. Plutarch ascribes this renowned doctrine to the founder of Stoicism, and Cicero records it as belonging to the Stoics. It rested upon that supposed joint and exclusive possession of reason by gods and men which made them both "the reasonable race." In its first conception, then, it was an implicit denial of creatureship on the part of man. This denial was fully held and maintained by the chief extollers of the Stoic commonwealth of gods and men who flourished after our Lord's coming, Seneca, Epictetus, and Marcus Aurelius. The brotherhood which these magnified was therefore not fellow-creatureship, and had none of the tenderness which fellow-creatureship inspires towards those whom it embraces, none of its veneration for God the Creator as its origin. And moreover it was severed from any thought of the continuance of man's personal being after death, so that it carried with it none of the preciousness of human life, as the trial-ground and condition of an eternal state, which is part of the Christian brotherhood. It led to contempt of life in general, not to love of brethren. It is also to be observed that this view, belonging, as it does, to the principles of Stoicism, remained otiose from Zeno to Seneca. It was never carried out before our Lord's Passion. It was a mere intellectual conception which the proudest and most selfish of men could entertain without allowing it to influence their conduct; which Cato and Seneca did so entertain, and remained the one a pitiless slave-master and the other a grinding moneylender. But what the observer of history, if he will take care not to disregard chronology, will find, is that from the time that another doctrine, that of Christian fraternity, which we shall presently mark, had been published through the Roman empire, and carried into imperial palaces and the pædagogea of slaves, the Stoic doctrine of human equality and brotherhood seemed to assume new dimensions, as in the pages of Seneca, Epictetus, and Marcus Aurelius, as no less in the whole Platonic and Neoplatonic school of Plutarch, Dio Chrysostomus, and Plotinus afterwards. But we must not forget that here too it remained an intellectual conception alone. The Stoic slave-master neither emancipated his slaves nor treated them as brethren. Epictetus, by far the most consistent, as by far the most real of those who put forward this view of men's confraternity, as possessing reason in common, was unable to transfuse his doctrine into any living society of scholars. From Seneca to Iamblichus the doctrine remained, though stimulated by Christian activity, not only on its entirely heathen basis, but inoperative; a vision of the intellect, not an action of the will; a theory never effectuated.

There is, however, a fact in history, the extension of the right of Roman citizenship by the Emperor Caracalla to all inhabitants, which has sometimes been mentioned as the result of Stoic principles carried into Roman legislation by great jurists, such as Ulpian. However, it is not clear but that fiscal considerations may have had much influence in bringing about this measure, for all who were citizens became liable to very heavy duties. But what is certain is that when this citizenship was conferred, the Church for six generations had been leavening the Roman world with the doctrine of the divine fraternity of men in Christ, which involved in it much more than the equality of Roman citizenship.

For indeed far other both in its character and its efficacy than any Stoic teaching was the brotherhood of men in Christ conveyed, in the first words of our Lord after His resurrection, to the Church in the person of St. Mary Magdalene: "Go to My brethren, and say to them, I ascend to My Father and your Father, and My God and your God:" words of unspeakable tenderness, of immortal consolation, words which carried with them a new creation of never-ending power, which established a family of undying heirs. In them spoke the charity of Christ the God-man, fresh from the Sacrifice of Himself for man; and they form in the brotherhood and the sacrifice united together, because the brotherhood reaches its accomplishment and fulfilment in the sacrifice, the whole conception of the relation of man to his fellow-man which was to form and rule the Christian Kingdom.

From these brethren to whom Christ sent this first Easter greeting of God's Fathership and His own Brotherhood with them, the Church went forth into all lands, being itself a brotherhood in Christ from the beginning. This brotherhood is altogether supernatural, springing from a double source, which we can but trace up to the very Being of God, and leave there to be unfolded in the light of eternity. The one source is the infinite condescension which moved the Eternal Father to send His coequal and coeternal Son in the likeness of man, creating thereby a race of brethren by the tie of the nature which the Son assumed; the other source is the infinite charity in which He gave the Son, when made Man, to be a sacrifice for His brethren. The love of the Creator therefore ran out into the love of the Redeemer, and when both had been combined, they formed that brotherhood of men with Christ, and therefore with each other, of which we are speaking. The Church then in setting forth these transcendent mysteries, upon which she is built, included in them the whole doctrine of the Creator and His creatures and their co-creatureship together, but made it tenfold more amiable by pouring upon it the light of an infinite condescension and an infinite charity. It was in this guise that brotherhood was taught to that vast multitude of separated nations and races which made up the Roman empire; and in this guise it was accepted by a large proportion of them. And thus in the very soil desecrated by centuries of division and enmity, polluted by idolatries without number and expression, the result of gods not to be named for their foulness, was introduced again the conception of the true relation of man to his fellow-men as creatures of one God.

This doctrine of brotherhood ran equally through the whole teaching of the Church, through her living structure in the hierarchy, through her channels of grace in the sacraments, and through her great act of worship, the Sacrifice. For were not all her members children together of one Father? Was not this their baptismal name? Was it not her very distinguishing mark that neither difference of rank nor difference of race affected at all the Christian adoption, from which he who received it arose "renewed unto knowledge according to the image of the Creator, where there is neither Gentile nor Jew, circumcision nor uncircumcision, barbarian nor Scythian, bond nor free, but Christ is all and in all?" Nor did this remain a fine theory, like the Stoic fraternity or the Epicurean and afterwards the Neoplatonic friendship. From the beginning master and slave partook together of the sacraments which conferred the brotherhood, and sustained it when conferred; and God the Creator was never celebrated with such chants of praise as those which arose from the eucharistic altar on which God the Redeemer lay sacrificed, to be the food of His brethren.

Philosophy had been for ages trying to find an adequate basis for the relative duties of man to man. The Stoic conceived that he had found it in the common possession of reason, which he attempted to exalt into a share of the divine nature. This same notion formed the core of the Neoplatonic theory. Hence both deduced a sort of duty of man to himself, and by consequence to other men of like nature. But the theory was tainted at its source with falsehood. Man's spirit was as much made as his body. To represent, therefore, human duty as springing from the possession of reason on the ground that this was a spark of the divine fire, a portion of the universal mind, was to found it upon a fiction. On the contrary, the true foundation of it was that both man's spirit and his body were the work of an infinitely superior power, and the teaching of the Church in revealing that power, and recognising the bond which the creation both of spirit and of matter formed for the being so united, laid afresh the missing basis of morality. Whatever theory may re-attempt, the scheme of forming a morality independent of a moral governor will fail as the Stoic failed; for the first spring of duty lies in the obligation which the act of creation imposes on the being created. The Church, in preaching her great doctrines of Redemption and Adoption, re-established the basis of morality by unveiling the Creator of man. But she availed herself of an infinite attraction in disclosing Him at the same time as Father and Redeemer.

The sum of what I have said is this: that the divine brotherhood of men in Christ, together with the charity of Christ the God-man sacrificing Himself for His brethren, unitedly make up the Christian conception of the relation of man to his fellow-man. And all the relative duties of life are affected by this double fact. This conclusion was drawn by St. Paul from these grounds in the following words: "Be kind to one another, merciful, forgiving one another, even as God has forgiven you in Christ. Be therefore imitators of God, as most dear children, and walk in love, as Christ also has loved us, and delivered Himself for us an oblation and a sacrifice to God for an odour of sweetness."[1]

---

[1] Ephes. iv. 32. It is to be noted that the expression, "odour of sweetness," here ascribed to the Sacrifice of Christ, is the same as that

5. A point of the greatest importance in considering the Græco-Roman civilisation is the attitude of the State towards the individual. It is remarked by Zeller[1] that "an essential difference distinguishes all modern ideal commonwealths from the Platonic republic. Plato's leading idea is the effecting morality by the State. It is the State which must form its citizens to virtue. The State is a vast educational institute which embraces the whole life and being of its members. All other ends must be subordinate to this one; all private interests be unreservedly sacrificed to it. The State can only aim at the happiness and perfection of the Whole. The individual can claim no more than is compatible with the beauty of the Whole." "Plato wishes to do away with private interest; his modern imitators wish to content it. Plato strives after the perfectness of the Whole; these after the happiness of individuals. Plato treats the State as the end, the Person as means; these treat Persons as the end, the State and society as means." The contrast here drawn will serve to bring out the thorough distinction between what we may call the Christian conception of the State's functions and the Hellenic conception. "That consists," says the same observer, "much less in forms of constitution than in the position which is assigned to the State as a whole in regard to individuals, their rights and their conduct. In our view the State is built up from below; individuals are the first. The State arises from the fact that they meet together for the protection of their rights and the general furtherance of

used of God in accepting the first sacrifice of Noah as he came from the ark. See above, p. 329.

[1] Zeller's *Vorträge*. "Der platonische Staat in seiner Bedentung für die Folge-zeit." Pp. 78–80.

their good. For this reason individuals remain the ultimate object of the State's life. We ask of it to provide for the collective mass of those belonging to it as individuals the utmost possible freedom, prosperity, and culture; and we can never be persuaded that it can conduce to the perfection of the State as a whole, or that it is allowable, to sacrifice the essential rights and interests of individuals to its ends. To the Greek, on the contrary, the State appears as the first and most essential; the individual only as a portion of the commonweal. The feeling of political community is so strong in him, the idea of personality recedes so entirely into the background, that it is only in the State that he can picture to himself an existence worthy of man. He knows of no higher function than the political; no more original right than that of the whole mass. The State, says Aristotle, is in its nature earlier than individuals. In all this, accordingly, only so much right is allowed to the Person as his position in the State carries with it. Strictly speaking, there are no general rights of man, but only rights of citizens; and however deeply the interests of individuals may be violated by the State, if the interest of the State require it they cannot complain. The State is the sole original proprietor of all rights, and is not bound to secure to its subjects a greater portion of them than its own interests allow. Plato also shares this point of view, and has even pushed it to an extreme in his republic."

Now why does all modern thought build up the State from below, and consider the individual before the mass? Why does it acknowledge private rights as inviolable. Why does it treat men as men before they are citizens? The ground of this most thorough, this essential difference between not only Greek but Roman and generally heathen thought, and Christian thought, on the position of man as an individual in regard of the State, is the conception of human personality—that counterpart and reflex of the Personal God—which has been wrought into the hearts of men by the Christian Church. It is the force of the divine word, "What shall it profit a man to gain the whole world and lose his own soul?" which has been incorporated by her preaching into human society. The Christian Church taught heathenism the fact that the human soul is greater than the world. With this pebble from her sling the Church struck on the forehead the giant of heathen tyranny, who had exercised autocracy in the State over the actions and the consciences of men. The Church as the City of God, the Body of Christ, established a whole code of treatment in dealing with the individual. This code has only to be applied to the human commonwealth in order to illuminate all the relations of the individual to the State.

How did the Church deal with the individual in respect to the whole body?

Before we answer this question let us note that if we consider heathenism in the ripeness of that corruption which it had reached by the time of the Emperor Claudius, the whole heathen conception of the commonwealth, as it bears upon the individual, was the result of the disregard of any future life, and of the ignoring the true nature of the human personality. If man was not to live after this life, the value of his life here was essentially altered. He was become the property of the State. The general interest would rule every particular interest. In this, therefore, Plato and Aristotle reasoned with the utmost correctness, and Greece and Rome were no less wise than logical in carrying out their conclusion to practical results. But the Church started from this very truth of a human personality continued on after death. She built the whole structure of her society upon the sacredness of that personality. It was, therefore, impossible that she should sacrifice the individual to the corporate body. But likewise she had no motive so to sacrifice him. It was quite otherwise with the heathen State, which considered itself and its subjects as belonging to this life only. The interests of this life ruled it therefore absolutely. But the Christian society—the Body of Christ—went on into eternity together with each Christian man. To it, therefore, the highest good of the Body and the highest good of the Individual were one and the same. Again, the Church had one rule which admitted of no single exception. Sin, that is a deliberate breaking of the eternal law, was not allowable for any conceivable purpose. And this rule protected the individual in every circumstance of his life. Plato and Aristotle could recommend, and the heathen State could carry out the suggestion, that feeble and infirm children, who were little likely to benefit their country, should be exposed and left to perish. The Church insisted that every human life was sacred, and took them from unnatural parents to nurture and educate.[1] Plato had no scruple to impose upon his " Watchers " the prohibition of founding a family, in order that they might belong entirely and exclu-

---

[1] Chinese heathenism repeats at this day the cruelty of the old heathenism—and Christian charity, it must be added, is true in the nineteenth century to the part which it played in the first.

sively to the State. But when the rule of celibacy grew up as a qualification for all spiritual government in the Church, it was a free choice of those who embraced the highest function which can fall to man. It was an imitation of their Lord, in which the voluntary sacrifice of a natural good was accepted by those who made it for the attainment of a supernatural good. Plato trampled down the instincts of nature for the sake of a temporal good; the Christian clergy were content to bear that likeness of Christ in virtue of which they would become not founders of an earthly home, but co-builders in an eternal house, and to make themselves without father, without mother, without genealogy, in the earthly order, if so be that in the spiritual they might be likened to the Son of God. But this great institution of Christian celibacy affords perhaps as good an instance as can be found to show the coincidence in the Christian society of the highest good of the Individual with the highest good of the Body. Plato, in enjoining celibacy on his "Watchers," had a real and excellent object in view, their complete devotion to their work, without the interruption of family cares. For this end he simply sacrificed them to the commonwealth. But all the great works of Christian charity in their heroic degree depend for their fulfilment on freedom from the bonds of domestic life. How did the Church reach this end? By her counsels of perfection she set the virginal or the celibate life before her children as a reward in itself, as carrying higher privileges and a more perfect imitation of the Master for those to whom it was given. She proposed it to them as a choice leading to an infinite recompense, beginning in this life, completed in the life to come, and she reached her end without sacrificing the individual to the commonweal. For the choice exalted the chooser, and gave him a better thing for that which he resigned. Moreover, Plato's ideal remained a dream, but the Christian religious life is a reality. There have been no Platonic "Watchers" in a human republic, but there have been myriads of priests and religious, who have followed to the end the Virgin Son of the Virgin Mother.

The Church then, as a society making individual man her unit of construction, in no case sacrificed the part to the whole. In this she was in contradiction to the heathen State. And whereas that was instinct with a despotic spirit, she breathed freedom to her children by this scrupulous regard to every individual, however weak, friendless, and forlorn. This was within her own society. But now what was the effect of her operation upon the heathen State into which she was cast?

The State, as we have seen, admitted no reserve on the part of the individual to its sovereignty. He was bound to obey the command of emperor, or senate, or demos, in all things. It was Christ who set a limit to this authority in those words which have created a new political as well as a new moral world, "Render to Cæsar the things which are Cæsar's, and to God the things which are God's." It was the Church which during three hundred years of persecution carried those words into effect, and established the domain of the human conscience, not to be infringed by emperor, by parliament, or by democracy.

For let it be considered that liberty does not consist in the form of government but in the nature of the power which the government exercises. The rule of parliament or democracy may be as absolute as that

of an autocrat emperor, and in that case those who
are ruled will not be free because the power is exercised by a joint resolution of many instead of a decree
of one. Freedom consists in such a limit being set
to the power of the government itself, whatever form
it may bear, as will secure to the individual his lawful
rights. The Athenian demos became a byword for its
tyranny; the Roman senate, in the days when Rome
was said to be free, acted with the most arbitrary
licence towards subject nations. The Roman empire
was not more tyrannical than either of these, and probably was much more temperate in the actual exercise
of its power. But all these admitted no limit to that
power. And they had this ground at least for their
claim to illimitable authority, that the power of the
State, so long as it is considered with reference to this
life only, does admit of no limit, and is an absolute
sovereignty. Now these governments were fallen into
such a state as to act only with reference to this life.
The limit to the power of civil government is given by
the fact that the whole of this life is subordinate to
another life; it is given when we introduce "the
things of God" over against "the things of Cæsar."
This truth was conveyed in that sentence of our Lord;
and the Church during ten generations of persecution
carried it into effect, which is quite a different thing
and manifests quite a different power from an intellectual perception of it. The divine power of our
Lord therefore was shown in His Church when He
made her His instrument for separating off "the
things of God" from "the things of Cæsar." The
nature of the Christian religion brought it into constant conflict with the Roman State. It was no doubt
an intellectual and a moral revolution at once which

took its source from the cave of Bethlehem and the cross of Calvary. As often as the Apostles and their successors had to say, "It is better to obey God than man," and to suffer for so saying, they were introducing a new principle into human government; they were limiting the State's supremacy by the force of the human conscience. And thus in fact civil liberty was contained in the bosom of religious liberty, and this was the cause which was being contended for from Claudius to Constantine. Thus a vast store of lessons for all future time is contained in this period. One of these is that in it the battle of human liberty, as against the arbitrary and unlimited power of the civil government, was then won. Every Christian teacher who was occupied in the promulgation of doctrine, who was a member of the Christian hierarchy, who administered the sacraments, who offered the Sacrifice, all of them "things of God," to which our Lord referred, every confessor who suffered for these things, every martyr who died for them, was a witness for the freedom of the human conscience in the face of the civil authority; but by the same act he was establishing civil liberty; he was setting a moral bound to the State's authority, which left room for the exercise of every lawful right by the individual.

This vast result had been definitely gained not for the Roman empire only but for all time, and under all governments, when Constantine accepted the Christian Faith, and as emperor, the possessor of all the rights of the State, the Senatus Populusque Romanus, acknowledged the independent authority of the Church's hierarchy.

Let us then observe a mighty contrast in Roman history. When Peter in the second year of Claudius came to Rome, an unacknowledged stranger of a most unpopular race, he found Claudius exercising the whole power of the Roman empire without any limitation to the obedience which it might demand of its subjects. As the Pontifex Maximus Claudius stood at the head of religious power, as the Princeps he wielded civil authority, and as the Imperator the armed force. When the Emperor Constantine arranged with St. Silvester the summoning of the Nicene Council, the Christian Episcopate met from all the East under the presidency of the West in acknowledged freedom as the Kingdom of Christ to determine a point of Christian doctrine. The State had receded from its own omnipotence. In the whole domain of conscience it allowed man to be free. Cæsar acknowledged "things of God" over which he had no control, and which were given not to his determination, but to the determination of those who bore rule in the Kingdom of God. Therein lay the principle of civil liberty also for the Europe and the World of the future.

6. But yet more than this was then achieved. The Church at the Nicene Council stood forth in the sight of all men as the one Kingdom of God throughout all the world. Those who sat there sat not as subjects of the Roman empire, but as bishops of the Church of God. The great armies of the North and West were already mustering in such force that the Roman unity had scarcely been preserved in the preceding century: they were shortly to prevail, to take captive the mother of nations, and to found distinct kingdoms out of the spoils of her world-empire. Then the successors of these bishops who sat in the Nicene Council would be no

longer members of one civil empire, but they would be equally princes of one divine kingdom. They would equally represent the people of dioceses spread throughout the world. They would be equally bound in the bonds of Christian charity to each other. Could they and their people be in their civil capacity enemies, when in their spiritual they were friends and brethren? The Church then as the one Kingdom of God throughout all the world contained in herself a law of nations, which take their place as harmoniously within her bosom as individuals hold definite rights within their own State over against that State.

Thus the duties of States to States were carried potentially in the establishment of an universal Church. But a law of nations consists precisely in conceiving adequately the proper relation which one nation or State bears to another nation or State. That which divides States, which operates as a perpetual nourishment of jealousies, rivalries, and wars, are temporal interests; the struggle for increase of territory, dominion, and wealth, and the sense that what is gained by one nation in these things must be taken away from another. But what unites nations are eternal interests, and these are the same for all, and one nation does not gain by another's loss of these. They were not indeed the same until a common faith arose to bind nations together; but this was precisely the crowning good brought by the Christian Faith to the various nations, so far as concerns its bearing upon natural society. So far as that Faith was received by them, it became to them an everlasting bond. It destroyed the enmity between Europe and Asia which was coeval with history; it joined the men of the North and South

with the men of the East and West. In the faith
of Christ they had a common home and a central
hearth. The fact was not only new, but when it
began to arise was treated by Celsus in his objections
to Christianity as a pretension so unattainable that
it was deserving of ridicule. But this universal
religion became a fact. The gods of the nations,
the standard-bearers of their petty jealousies, their
national exclusiveness, their moral corruptions, went
down before the Cross. But the Faith of Christ as
an universal religion, raised by its very nature above
the pettiness of nationalities, likewise established
equality between all nations in the exercise of their
rights. It did away with all predominance arising
from superior force or size. This equality, again,
is a necessary condition for a law of nations. The
small must feel that they are respected by the great:
that the fact of great or small in the parties concerned
has nothing to do with the justice of the case. But
one justice flows out of one religion; and more par-
ticularly one justice flows out of men's brotherhood
in Christ. For it is much to be noted that the
equality of *fallen* human nature had never been able
to construct a law of nations. The Stoic doctrine of
reason has never been so persuasive over the hearts
and minds of men as to lead them to admit an universal justice. It was only the equality of *regenerate*
human nature which had that power. But the spring
of duty which touches man and man, and which by
the same movement directs the relation of the individual to the State, reaches also, and by the same
force, to the relation between one State and another.
Morals, politics, international rights, have one and
the same foundation, one and the same measure.

What is wrong in morals can never be right in politics: and crime is not less crime because it is willed by a nation. The nation is as responsible as the man. A parliament which enacts an immoral law is as guilty as a man who commits murder. The establishment of an universal Church made this principle visible to men, and it is one of the greatest boons which that Church has conferred on human society. But it was symbolised and expressed most powerfully in the position which the First Bishop and Primate of the Church possesses as the Common Father of all, equally near to all, equally interested for all. The successor of St. Peter in his office was at the Council of Nice, as he is now, as near to the men of Antioch and Egypt as to the men of Gaul, Spain, Britain, and Germany. And when the time to which I have above alluded had come, when the imperial unity of Rome had been broken, the spiritual unity of Rome shone out clearly to the eyes of men: and the sovereigns of great nations, indifferent whether they were of Teutonic or Latin blood, acknowledged in the Common Father the voice of a living law of nations, the voice of a common Christian duty, the voice of a glorious Christian confederacy; the rule not of blood and iron but of Christian charity, upon which alone a law of nations can be based.

I have now gone through the six principles in which the whole Græco-Roman world, which was by far the most advanced and intelligent portion of the human race, was defective when the Christian Church in the person of its chief Apostle began its work at Rome. They are the conception of the One, the Personal, the Creating God, and subordinate to it the conception of man's everlasting personality, as uniting soul and body in one enduring human being. Next, the conception of the relation thence arising between God and man. And from this the triple range of human duties, what man owes to his fellow-man; inasmuch as they are creatures of one God, what the individual man owes to the commonwealth, and the commonwealth reciprocally to the individual man, and finally what each nation of these men owes to each other nation.

It was my purpose to show that the Christian Church in the exercise of purely supernatural functions, that is, in promulgating a belief in the most Blessed Trinity, in the Incarnation, and in the Redemption, by means of her teaching, her ritual, her hierarchy, her sacraments, and her Sacrifice, effected likewise a wonderful change in the natural order by establishing both the belief and the practice of these six principles in the minds of men. It was further my purpose to show that Philosophy, which means the utmost effort of the unassisted human intelligence, the flower and fruit of Hellenic civilisation, had utterly failed to establish these principles in the minds and practice of men: had gone astray as to the first after a god of forces, a god without morality and sanctity: as to the second, had never accepted a continuous and abiding human personality after death, responsible for its actions in life, and subject to an exact retribution: and as these two conceptions are the conditions of the rest, had equally failed to carry these others into effect.

Further, from what I have said it will be apparent that the effective promulgation of these principles sprung from the declaring and preaching the Person of our Lord as the God-man. They did not at all spring from any effect [of race, or development of natural circumstances, or previous preparation of men by their civil condition. They did not spring from the union of Oriental with Western civilisation. Such a union Philosophy could have brought about, if aided by the powerful bond of a common civil government. Philosophy indeed tried what it could do, but failed ignominiously either to establish belief in one God, or to destroy the worship of a thousand idols. Again, I have shown that the introduction and establishment of these principles were completed as a fact of history before the accession of the Teutonic nations to the Church. Thus the belief in an abiding human personality with all its immense consequences was fully felt and acknowledged and carried out into practice by teachers in their doctrine, by confessors in their life, by martyrs in the tortures which they braved before a single German tribe had been taught the dignity of human nature by its introduction into the great Christian society. The sense of the personal dignity of man, the sense of the rights of the individual, was not the result of the fusion of the natural qualities of the Teuton with the Christian spirit. In Basil, and Gregory, and Athanasius, and Jerome, and Augustine, and in whole generations of Christian men and women who preceded them, we see this sense complete and perfect. It was the gift of our Lord to His people by His doctrine, when He said, " What shall it profit a man to gain the whole world and to lose his own soul ? " by His act when He gave up His body to the extreme of torment and humiliation, and when He raised it to life again from the Cross.

INDEX

ABERLE, his rule as to the writings of the New Testament, 15, *note.*
Æschylus, asserts the penal justice of God, 336.
Alexander, *de Fato,* 304.
Ammonius Sakkas, his time and place, 265.
Apollonius of Tyana, his pretended Life by Philostratus, 207-62; for particulars see table of contents, Lecture xix.
Apuleius of Madaura, his philosophical opinions, 202.
Augustine, St., 75, 291; his reproach of Porphyrius, 320.

BAUR, *Apollonius und Christus,* 222, 223, 246, 310.

CELSUS, his time, work, and positive standing-ground, 203.
Cicero, quoted, 25, 32, 104, 114. Identity of divine and human mind, 300, 303, 342.
Clemens Alexandrinus, states that the Apostles for twelve years preached only to the Jews, 12.
Clement, Pope, St., the First, testimony to foundation of the Roman Church, 14.

DE ROSSI, *Roma Sotteranea,* burial of the Popes in the Crypta Vaticana, 20.
Dio Chrysostomus, 168; his conception of the universe, and the power ruling it, 168; man's intuition of God, 169; his supreme God a Demiurge, 171; man's kinship with God, and the humanitarian doctrine as its result, 172; his Demiurge and Plato's, 172.
Dionysius, Bishop of Corinth in the second century, testifies to the foundation of the Roman Church, 14.
Döllinger, *Heidenthum und Judenthum,* 51, 123, 128, 147, 309, 344. *Christenthum und Kirche,* 39, 41.
Dubois-Cuchan, quoted, 10, *note.*

EPICTETUS, what function he assigns to philosophy, 79; belief as to God and Providence, 80, 183; the human mind and its kindred with God, 80; denies personal subsistence after death, 82, 191; advocates suicide, 84, 166; bearing of his philosophy on polytheism, 82, 192; his religion compared with that of Plutarch, 164; his knowledge of Christians, 165; sole open reference to them, 188; his ideal teacher, 184; a messenger of God, 186; whose office is a bishopric, 186; must be without wife and children, 187; fearless of men, 187; his ideal only realised in the Christian teachers whom he had seen, 188; a heathen in his grounds of action, 191; but who had seen Christians, 192; parent of modern Deism, 165; his treatment of slavery compared with that of St. Paul, 106.

Euripides, gives the Anaxagorean view of immortality, 83.

Eusebius, *History of the Church*, quoted, 13, 14, 20, 265.

"FOLLOW ME," vast meaning of the passages in which it occurs, 35.

Friedlaender, *Darstellungen aus der Sittengeschichte Roms*, his statement that Stoics rose by their own force to conceptions of moral duty like the Christian, 102, *note*; answered, 192; power of the heathen worship, 122; education of heathen youth, 194, 196, 198, 200; gives a reason for the contrast between Græco-Roman and Christian morality, 390.

Future life of man as a personal being, denied by Epictetus, 82; by Marcus Aurelius, 87; by Seneca and the Neostoics in general, 89, 109; by the Neopythagorean school, as set forth by Philostratus in his Apollonius, 255; by Plotinus, 281-3; by the whole line of Greek thinkers from Seneca to Plotinus, 312; how the belief in it was re-established by the Church preaching the Resurrection of Christ, 378-83; overthrow thereby of the whole philosophic error, 383, 384; and correction of a vast moral corruption, 384, 385.

GREEK and Roman mind, contrast in Tacitus, Pliny, Suetonius, Juvenal, and Trajan, to Epictetus, Dio Chrysostomus, and Plutarch, 175-83.

Grote's Plato, 173.

HAGEMANN, *die Römische Kirche*, 13, *note*.

IAMBLICHUS, 292.

Irenæus, St., testifies to the foundation of the Roman Church by St. Peter and St. Paul, 13.

INDEX 415

JEROME, St., states as a fact of his day the result of the conflict between heathen philosophy and the Church, 372.
Judaism and Christianity, their relation, 37-43.
Juvenal, his religious and philosophic standing-ground, 177.

KELLNER, *Hellenismus und Christenthum*, 207.
Kleutgen, *Theologie der Vorzeit*, statement of the Being of God, 304; freedom of the creature an image of the Creator's freedom, 317; early pantheism of Greek philosophy, 323, 324; *Philosophie der Vorzeit*, 45, 297, 302; the doctrine of Pantheism, 304; God, the efficient, exemplary, and final cause of things, not their formal or material cause, 321.

LACORDAIRE, anecdote recorded by, 366.
Lasaulx, 115, 116, 123.
Leo the Great, Pope, St., mentions the presence of St. Peter at Rome, both under Claudius and Nero, 13, *note;* his statement of the Primacy of St. Peter, as continued in the Roman See, identical and coextensive with its definition in the Vatican Council, 369, *note*, 42, 43.

MARCUS AURELIUS, outline of his philosophy, 84; passages referring to man's state after death, 88; his cosmopolitanism, 96.
Maximus Tyrius, his philosophical standing-point, 201.
Merivale, *History of Rome*, quoted, 7, *note*.
Möhler, *Kirchengeschichte*, 123.
Musonius, general sketch of his teaching, 77.

NÄGELSBACH, *die Nachhomerische Theologie*, 83, 184. Greek mythology knows no Creator, 334. Lineaments of an original revelation in the Greek traditional religion, 334-36.
Northcote and Brownlow, quoted, 37.

ORIGEN, 63, 204, 205.
Orosius, cited, 13.
Ott, Dr., in *Tübinger Quartalschrift*, quoted, 67-9.

PANTHEISM, *i.e.*, the confusion of the substance of God with the substance of the world, by making God either the *formal* or the *material* cause of the world, runs in various degrees through all philosophic thought from Thales to Plotinus, 301; carries with it a denial of creation, 302, 308; and of free-will, 308, 309. The contradictory Christian truth that God is the *efficient, exemplary*, and *final* cause of all things, 320-23. The whole contest between ancient and modern infidel Philosophy on the one side, and the Christian Church on the other, summed up in this antagonism, *note*, 323-25. The doctrine of one God, distinct from all other beings, subsisting in Himself, intelligent, free, and the Creator of all things, the foundation of human society and morality, 374 ; how re-established by the preaching of the Church, 375-78. An eternal human personality, the corollary of a personal God, 379. Its denial running through Greek and Latin thought, 380-82. Denial of creatureship a result of pantheism, 385-88; the great wound of heathen society, and how healed by the Church, 388-90. Denial of creatureship made the Greek and Roman morality essentially different from the Christian, 390-94; the Church found a basis for morality, which the whole pantheistic philosophy sought in vain, 394-97 ; and by the same power wrought out the civil liberty of the individual over against the State, 397-405; and cast the outline of a law of nations, 406-9.

Persius, his strong testimony to Cornutus, 197.

Philo, his time and position, 123-26. His attempt to unite Greek science with Hebrew revelation, 127-31 ; his conception of God, 131-33. Man's need of grace, 134; subordination of human science to theology, 135. His possible effect on subsequent Greek philosophy, 137-40; his partiality for the imperial government, 3. Contradiction of his view to that of Tacitus, 4, *note*.

Philosophy. Its work as conceived by Pythagoras, 25 ; by Plato, 26 ; by Aristotle, 27 ; by Zeno, 28; the common effect produced by them, 29-43. Its radical defect the disjunction of the three forces, belief, morality, and worship, 43-6, 338-45. The contrast in these respects presented to it by the Church, 349-70. Its disregard of the ignorant, the poor, and the labouring classes, 22, 345. Its result as to forming a society from Claudius to Constantine, 347. The ideal life which the Neopythagorean philosophy sought to substitute for the Christian life, 249-56, 309-11. The Neoplatonic system a heathen analogon of Christianity, 294 ; as shown in three oppositions, between the Primal Being and God, 296, 320-23; between the confusion of God with the World and the doctrine of creation, 296-308 ; and between the being, position, duties, and hopes of man in Neoplatonism and in Christianity, 308-21. Philosophic and Christian immortality, 312, 318. Philosophic substitute for creation, ancient and modern, 304, and *note*, 323-25. Three positions of Greek philosophy in reference to the Greek religion, 114. The society in which it arose possessed prayer, sacrifice, oracles, and mysteries, 115. The proper ancient philosophy ends not in purifying the primary truths recognised by the polytheistic worship, but in denying them, 120-22. Rise of a believing movement in philosophy, 123. Admits the principle of revelation and the principle of holiness, in opposition to all its previous course, 130, 137. Patronises polytheism and is patronised by the emperors from Nerva's time, 160-63. Accepted by the higher Romans as the guide of life, 340; want of agreement in the teaching of it, 342. Its function as described by Plutarch, 195. Supervision of the whole life exercised by philosophers, 196; house and court philosophers and public teachers, 198.

Philostratus, Life of Apollonius, quoted, *passim*, Lecture xix., 207-62.

Plato, quoted, 27, 119, 131, 174.

Plotinus, his time and place, 265; his character, 267; produces his system at Rome in the midst of the persecution of the Christians, 268. His doctrine as to the Primal Being, 269-75; as to the procession of the world from it, 276-78; as to the human soul before, during, and after this life, 278-83; as to happiness, moral good and evil, 283-85; as to ecstasy, 286. His pantheistic unity amalgamates itself with the polytheistic worship, 287; ignores Christianity, 289; opposition of the whole system to the Christian Faith, 295-323; Plotinus wishes to found a city of philosophers, but is not allowed, 32.

Plutarch: time and circumstances of his life, 141; first representative of Neopythagorean school, 142; his theodicea, the Supreme God, 142; constructor, not creator of the world, 143; the visible gods and demons, 145; Triple Providence, 145; his piety, 146; he sets up a divine monarchy, 148; but supports polytheistic worship, 148. Relation between Plutarch and Philo, 150-54. Review of the change which took place in the interval which passed between them, 154-59. Assigns the work of moral education to philosophy, 194; defends the position of a court philosopher, 200.

Porphyrius, 291.

REUMONT, VON (*Geschichte der Stadt Rom*, i. 347), states the Roman rule of Augustus and Tiberius in the East to have been incomparably milder and juster than that of the native kings, 7.

Roman Church, founded by St. Peter (A.D. 42), 12; recorded by St. Irenæus, Eusebius, Orosius, St. Leo the Great, 13; by St. Clement of Rome, and St. Dionysius of Corinth, 14; probable allusion by Suetonius, 15; testimony of St. Paul to its growth and eminence before he came to Rome, 16; of Tacitus, to its spread among the nobility (A.D. 58), 17; and to its strength at the first persecution, (A.D. 64), 18; nature and strangeness of the work thus accom-

plished, 18-22; its intrinsic contrast with philosophy in the union
of dogma, morality, and worship, 23-5; its success as compared
with the previous efforts of human genius in Pythagoras, Plato,
Aristotle, and Zeno, 25-32; St. Peter's work a personal following
of Christ, 32-35; represented in catacombs and sarcophagi at
Rome, 35-7; carries on into the Christian people the triple
mediation of Prophet, Priest, and King, which made the Jewish
nation, 37-43; this work of St. Peter at Rome seen by Constantine to have been repeated in each city of his empire, 349-53;
in it consists the establishment of a Christian Kingdom, 366-68;
which is based upon the Person of Christ, 368-70.

SANGUINETI, *de Sede Romana B. Petri*, 13, 15, 17.
Seneca, his life and circumstances, 57; his view of the task of philosophy, 58; his conception of God, the World, Cause and Matter,
60; of the human soul, 64; his teaching on beneficence, anger,
revenge, a great advance on his predecessors, 66; but modified
by his view of man's duty to himself, 68; doctrine on slavery, 69;
inconsistency between his life and writings, 72; his superiority to
those before him a singular case, 73; his principles pagan, his
expressions almost Christian, 74; how this problem may be
solved, 75; points common to him with Musonius, Epictetus, and
Marcus Aurelius, 88; his relation to Attalus, 196; Seneca,
Plutarch, and Philostratus, three stages in the bearing of philosophy upon religion, 259; Seneca contrasted with Philo, 138;
passages in his writings which seem to refer to Christian martyrs,
74; assigns to *reason* in his system a parallel place to that which
is given to *charity* in the Christian religion, 92; the analogy of
his language with that of St. Paul as to human wickedness, 101,
102; his teacher, Sotion of Alexandria, a Pythagorean, 139;
anecdote of the trust of Augustus and the Empress Julia in the
philosopher Areus, 341.
Simon, Jules, Alexandrine philosophy, 294.
Sophocles, recognises a moral law, sustained by God, 335.
Stiefelhagen, *Theologie des Heidenthums*, 116, 117.
Stöckl, *Philosophie des Mittelalters*, true doctrine of creation, 306.
Stoicism, alone in force in the reigns of Claudius and Nero, 54; its
kosmology, theology, and ethics, 55; its four chief teachers'
representative men, 57; its doctrine of reason, as a portion of
the divine spirit, 90, 299, 313, 81, 249; virtue, the only good, 92;
science subordinate to virtue, 93; the philosophical life preferred
to the political, 94; cosmopolitanism, 95; its view as to design
and final causes in the world, 98; as to the subordination of all

things to the good of man, 99; considers the mass of men sinners against the law of nature, i.e., reason, 100; its view as to humanity, philanthropy, and beneficence, 102; as to submission to the will of God, 106; Stoic end of man compared with Christian, 109; its effect from Claudius to Marcus Aurelius, 110; ends in negation of primary truth, 120.

Suetonius, 18, *note*; his religion, 177.

TACITUS, admits that the condition of the provinces was improved by the empire, 7, *note*; trial of Pomponia Græcina, the Christian Lucina, 17; on the first persecution of the Christians, 18, 19; his philosophical and religious standing-point, 176; his death of Thrasea, 199.

Thomas Aquinas, St., *Contra Gentiles*, 302, 306.

τὸ Θεῖον, "the Divine," a pantheistic term, 91. Once used by St. Paul in contradistinction to the personal name of God, *note*, 358.

Tocqueville, 95.

Tyndall, Professor, his lecture at Belfast, a restatement of the early Greek materialistic pantheism, 325, 382.

Tzschirner, *Fall des Heidenthums*, 207, 250, 342.

UEBERWEG, *Grundriss der Geschichte der Philosophie des Alterthums*, 55-7, 93, 274, 276, 296.

WERNER, *Geschichte der christlichen Theologie*, 204.

ZELLER, *Philosophie der Griechen*, supposes Christianity and Neoplatonism to have drawn their joint origin from the needs of their time, 9; quoted, 58, 62, 66, 77, 80, 81, 84, 85, 90, 91, 94, 101, 103, 105, 106-8, 124, 128-30, 134, 137, 139, 140, 144-7, 151, 152, 200-2, 211, 264. Doctrine of Plotinus, 269-290, *passim*. Porphyrius, 291. Iamblichus, 292-304, 377, 399. *Vorträge*, physical unity of nature from which Greek philosophy started, 297; the Platonic State, 398. *Geschichte der Deutschen Philosophie*, statement of Spinoza's pantheism, 324.

END OF VOL. III.

No. 1.   1898.

Selection
FROM
Burns & Oates'
Catalogue of Publications.

Latest Publications.

Characteristics from the Writings of Cardinal Wiseman. Edited and with a Preface by the Rev. T. E. BRIDGETT, C.SS.R. Crown 8vo, cloth. 6/-.

Cardinal Wiseman's Meditations on the Sacred Passion of our Lord. With a Preface by H. E. CARDINAL VAUGHAN. Crown 8vo, cloth. 4/-.

THE FOURTH VOLUME OF THE POPULAR EDITION OF
The Formation of Christendom as seen in Church and State. By T. W. ALLIES, K.C.S.G. Crown 8vo, cloth. 5/-.

Genesis and Science. Inspiration of the Mosaic Ideas of Creative Work. By JOHN SMYTH. Crown 8vo, cloth, with Illustrations. 3/6.

Jewels of Prayer and Meditation from Unfamiliar Sources. By PERCY FITZGERALD, M.A., F.S.A. Fancy cloth, gilt. 2/6.

St. Francis de Sales as a Preacher. By the Very Rev. H. B. CANON MACKEY, O.S.B. Wrapper. 1/-.

India: A Sketch of the Madura Mission. By the Rev. H. WHITEHEAD, S.J. Crown 8vo, cloth, with Map and Illustrations. 3/6.

NEW AND POPULAR EDITION.
Life of Don Bosco, Founder of the Salesian Society. Translated from the French of J. M. VILLEFRANCHE by Lady MARTIN. Crown 8vo, 302 pp. Wrapper, 1/- net (postage 3d.).

BURNS & OATES, LIMITED,
Granville Mansions, 28, Orchard Street, London, W.

ALEXIS-LOUIS, PÈRE (O.C.D.).

Five Thrones of Divine Love upon the Earth, The. The Womb of Mary, the Crib, the Cross, the Eucharist, and the Faithful Soul. From the French. Crown 8vo, cloth. 3/6.

"A book of devotion, consisting of a series of short readings or meditations, chiefly on the Incarnation, the Blessed Eucharist, the Crucifixion and the principles which underlie and govern the spiritual life, whether among the Priesthood, the cloistered Religious, or the laity. The sum of the experimental knowledge of a Carmelite priest, it breathes the very inner spirit of St. John of the Cross, and contains the essence of affective theology."—*Monitor.*

ALLIES, T. W. (K.C.S.G.).

A Life's Decision. Second and Cheaper Edition. Crown 8vo, cloth. 5/-.

"Interesting, not only in the way in which all genuine personal narratives are interesting, but also for the many letters from well-known persons that it contains. It is a valuable contribution to the history of the Anglican Church in the eventful years which followed Newman's secession."—*Guardian.*

THE FORMATION OF CHRISTENDOM SERIES.

Vol. I. The Christian Faith and the Individual. Popular Edition. Crown 8vo, cloth. 5/-.

Vol. II. The Christian Faith and Society. Popular Edition. Crown 8vo, cloth. 5/-.

Vol. III. The Christian Faith and Philosophy. Popular Edition. Crown 8vo, cloth. 5/-.

Vol. IV. Church and State. Popular Edition. Crown 8vo, cloth. 5/-.

H. E. CARDINAL VAUGHAN says:—"It is one of the noblest historical works I have ever read. Now that its price has placed it within the reach of all, I earnestly pray that it may become widely known and appreciatively studied. We have nothing like it in the English language."

The Throne of the Fisherman, built by the Carpenter's Son. The Root, the Bond, and the Crown of Christendom. Demy 8vo, cloth. 10/6.

"The most important contribution to ecclesiastical history which has been given to the world for many a long day."—*Tablet.*

The Holy See and the Wandering of the Nations. Demy 8vo, cloth. 10/6.

Peter's Rock in Mohammed's Flood. Being the Seventh Volume of Mr. Allies' great work on the "Formation of Christendom." Demy 8vo, cloth. 10/6.

ALLIES, MARY.

Pius the Seventh, 1800-1823. Crown 8vo, cloth gilt. 5/-.

"Miss Allies has narrated the history of the long and memorable Pontificate of the first Pope of this century with a thoroughness of research and a dignity of style worthy of her illustrious father."—*Irish Monthly.*

Leaves from St. John Chrysostom. With Introduction by T. W. Allies, K.C.S.G. Crown 8vo, cloth. 6/-.

"The selections are well chosen, and Miss Allies' rendering is smooth, idiomatic, and faithful to the original. There is no existing book which is better adapted to make the English reader acquainted with the most eloquent of the Fathers of the Church."—*Dublin Review.*

CATALOGUE OF PUBLICATIONS. 3

ALLIES, MARY—(continued).

History of the Church in England, from the Beginning of the Christian Era to the Death of Queen Elizabeth. In Two Vols. Crown 8vo, cloth. Vol. I. From the Beginning of the Christian Era to the Accession of Henry VIII. 6/-. Vol. II. From the Accession of Henry VIII. to the Death of Queen Elizabeth. 3/6.

"Miss Allies has admirably compressed the substance, or such as was necessary to her purpose, of a number of authorities, judiciously selected. . . . . As a narrative the volume is capitally written, as a summary it is skilful, and not its least excellence is its value as an index of the best available sources which deal with the period it covers."—*Birmingham Daily Gazette.*

ARNOLD, THOMAS (M.A., Fellow of the Royal University of Ireland).

Notes on the Sacrifice of the Altar. Crown 12mo, cloth gilt. 1/6.

"A very useful treatise on the Mass. The end of the Holy Sacrifice is first explained. Then the author takes occasion to point out the essential difference between the Anglican service and the Mass. Lastly, Mr. Arnold, following the course of the ritual, brings out clearly the meaning and object of each part of the sacred function. In his illustrative remarks he imparts a good deal of interesting information."—*Catholic Times.*

BAKER, VEN. FATHER AUGUSTIN (O.S.B.).

Holy Wisdom (*Sancta Sophia*). Directions for the Prayer of Contemplation, &c. Edited by Abbot Sweeney, D.D. New and Cheaper Edition. Crown 8vo. Handsomely bound in half leather, xx.-667 pp. 6/-.

"The thanks of the Catholic public are due to Dr. Sweeney for re-editing this famous work. It does not belong to the catalogue of ephemeral publications. It is of a totally different standard. . . . To lovers of prayer and meditation it will be a most acceptable guide and friend."—*Tablet.*

BIBLES, &c.

N.B.—For full particulars of Bindings, &c., see Illustrated Prayer Book Catalogue, sent post free on application.

Holy Bible. POCKET EDITION (size, 5¼ by 3¼ inches). Embossed cloth, red edges, 2/6; and in leather bindings, from 4/6 to 7/6. MEDIUM EDITION (size, 7¼ by 4¾ inches). Cloth, 3/6; and in leather bindings, from 6/- net to 10/6 net (postage 6d.). OCTAVO EDITION (size, 9 by 6 inches). Cloth, 6/-; and in a great variety of leather bindings, from 8/- to 35/- net. Family Editions in quarto and folio. Prices upon application.

New Testament, The. POCKET EDITION. Limp cloth, 6d. (postage 2d.). Cloth, red edges, 1/-. Roan, 1/6. Paste grain, round corners, 3/-. Best calf or morocco, 4/6 each. ROYAL 8vo EDITION (size, 9 by 6 inches). Cloth, 1/- net (postage 3d.). NEW MEDIUM EDITION. LARGE TYPE. Crown 8vo (size, 7½ by 5 inches). 500 pp. Cloth, boards, gilt lettered, 2/-. Paste grain, limp, round corners, red or gold edges, 4/6. German calf, limp, round corners, red under gold edges, 8/6. Morocco, limp, round corners, red under gold edges, 8/6. Also in better bindings for presentation.

BLESSED SACRAMENT, OUR GOD; or, Practical Thoughts on the Mystery of Love, The. By a Child of St. Teresa. Cloth gilt. 1/-.

"It is written in the spirit of reverence and earnestness in simple and forcible language. This little work is calculated to do much good, and we heartily commend it."—*Dublin Review.*

BOWDEN, REV. H. S. (of the Oratory), Edited by.

Dante's Divina Commedia: Its scope and value. From the German of Francis Hettinger, D.D. With an engraving of Dante. Second Edition. 10/6.

Natural Religion. Being Vol. I. of Dr. Hettinger's "Evidences of Christianity." With an Introduction on "Certainty." Third Edition. Crown 8vo, cloth. 7/6.

Revealed Religion. Vol. II. of Dr. Hettinger's "Evidences of Christianity." With an Introduction on the "Assent of Faith." Crown 8vo, cloth. 5/-.

"The two together ('Natural Religion' and 'Revealed Religion') supply a real want in our Catholic literature. Nothing is more common nowadays than for a priest to be asked to recommend a book, written from a Catholic point of view, on the evidence for the Christian religion. And in future he will be able to recommend Father Bowden's 'Hettinger'. . . . It may be confidently affirmed that all who have taken interest in the war against religion raised by its modern adversaries will find in Father Bowden's pages many of their chief difficulties helpfully dealt with."—*Month.*

BRIDGETT, REV. T. E. (C.SS.R.).

Lyra Hieratica: Poems on the Priesthood. Collected from many sources by the Rev. T. E. Bridgett, C.SS.R. Fcap. 8vo, cloth. 2/6 net (postage 3d.).

"The idea of gathering an anthology of Poems on the Priesthood was a happy one, and has been happily carried out. Priests and laity alike owe a debt of gratitude to Father Bridgett for the many beautiful things he has brought together."—*Tablet.*

The True Story of the Catholic Hierarchy deposed by Queen Elizabeth, with fuller Memoirs of its last Two Survivors. By the Rev. T. E. Bridgett, C.SS.R., and the late Rev. T. F. Knox, D.D., of the London Oratory. Crown 8vo, cloth. 7/6.

Wisdom and Wit of Sir Thomas More, The. Crown 8vo, cloth. 6/-.

"Every page in this delightful volume bespeaks the master hand, the clear head, the deep and tender heart. It is lively, eloquent, impressive, genial; without stiffness of parade of learning, but as full as good things as it can hold."—*Catholic Times.*

BROWNLOW, BISHOP.

Memoir of Mother Rose Columba Adams, O.P., first Prioress of St. Dominic's Convent, and Foundress of the Perpetual Adoration at North Adelaide. With Portrait and Plates. Crown 8vo, cloth, 384 pp. 6/6.

"It is a work of the deepest interest and edification. In a handsomely printed and beautifully illustrated volume, Bishop Brownlow tells us the story of a remarkable woman's life and work, drawing on his own recollections of her career, and with the help of her own letters and reminiscences of many friends, giving us a life-like picture of a singularly earnest, devoted, and saintly soul."—*Tablet.*

BUTLER, REV. ALBAN.
People's Edition of the Lives of the Saints. Twelve Pocket Volumes, each Volume containing the Saints of the Month. Superfine paper, neat cloth binding, gilt lettered. 1/6 each; or the complete set (comprising over 6,000 pages), in handsome cloth case to match, 18/-.

DALE, REV. J. D. HILARIUS.
Ceremonial according to the Roman Rite. Translated from the Italian of Joseph Baldeschi. New and Revised Edition. Crown 8vo, cloth. 6/6.

"This work is our standard English directory on the subject. Few functions of any importance are carried on without a glance at it. It is a familiar guide and friend—in short, a classic."—*Catholic Times.*

The Sacristan's Manual; or, Handbook of Church Furniture, Ornament, &c. Fourth and Enlarged Edition. Crown 8vo, cloth. 2/6.

DIGNAM, FATHER (S.J.).
Conferences given by Father Dignam, S.J., with Retreats, Sermons, and Notes of Spiritual Direction. With a Preface by His Eminence Cardinal Mazzella, S.J. Crown 8vo, cloth gilt. 6/- net (postage 4d.).

FABER, FATHER.
All for Jesus; or, The Easy Ways of Divine Love. New Edition. Crown 8vo, cloth, 407 pp. 5/-.

Bethlehem. New Edition. Crown 8vo, cloth, 500 pp. 7/-.

Ethel's Book; or, Tales of the Angels. A New and Cheaper Edition. Beautifully bound in cloth, extra gilt, gilt edges. 2/6.

Growth in Holiness; or, The Progress of the Spiritual Life. New Edition. Crown 8vo, cloth, 464 pp. 6/-.

Hymns. Complete Edition. Crown 8vo, cloth, 427 pp. 6/-.

Notes on Doctrinal and Spiritual Subjects. Fourth Edition. Two Vols. Crown 8vo, cloth, 759 pp. 10/-.

Poems. Complete Edition. Crown 8vo, cloth, 582 pp. 5/-.

Sir Lancelot. A Legend of the Middle Ages. Crown 8vo, cloth, 347 pp. 5/-.

Spiritual Conferences. Eighth Edition. Crown 8vo, cloth, 403 pp. 6/-.

The Blessed Sacrament; or, The Works and Ways of God. New Edition. Crown 8vo, cloth, 548 pp. 7/6.

The Creator and the Creature; or, The Wonders of Divine Love. New Edition. Crown 8vo, cloth, 416 pp. 6/-.

The Easiness of Salvation. Cloth gilt. 1/-.

The Foot of the Cross; or, The Sorrows of Mary. Crown 8vo, cloth, 432 pp. 6/-.

The Precious Blood; or, The Price of our Salvation. Fifth Edition. Crown 8vo, cloth, 308 pp. 5/-.

FABER, FATHER—(*continued*).
  The Life and Letters of Frederick William Faber, D.D.
  By Rev. John E. Bowden, of the Oratory. Third Edition. Crown 8vo, cloth, 447 pp. 6/-.

  Father Faber's May Book. Compiled by an Oblate of Mary Immaculate. A New Month of May, arranged for Daily Reading, from the writings of Father Faber. 18mo, cloth, gilt edges, with Steel Frontispiece. 2/-.

  A Brief Sketch of the Early Life of Frederick William Faber, D.D. By his Brother. Limp cloth. 1/-.

FITZGERALD, PERCY.
  Jewels of Prayer and Meditation from Unfamiliar Sources. Fancy cloth, gilt. 2/6.

  Jewels of the Imitation. A Selection of Passages with a Little Commentary. Cloth, extra gilt. 2/-.
  "It is an excellent book for spiritual reading in itself, and it will help its readers to read that holiest of books with more relish and fruit. Mr. Fitzgerald's pithy, up-to-date comments throw a new light on many a wise saying of Thomas à Kempis."
  —*Irish Monthly.*

  Eucharistic Jewels. Second Edition. Fancy cloth, gilt. 2/6.
  "Every page is bright with some exquisite passage, and Mr. Fitzgerald's little commentaries, as he carries us along, are not unworthy of the glorious companionship in which he has placed them."—*Freeman's Journal.*

  Jewels of the Mass. A Short Account of the Rites and Prayers used in the Holy Sacrifice. Sixth Edition. Fancy cloth gilt. 2/-.
  "A treatise on the Mass, in which the author proves himself a sound theologian, an accomplished master of ecclesiastical history bearing on the question, a cultured scholar, and the possessor of a very charming style."—*Nation.*

  The Layman's Day ; or, Jewels of Practical Piety. Second Edition. Cloth, extra gilt. 2/-.
  "An effort to induce people to consider their every-day life from the point of view of practical common-sense. . . . Admirably done."—*Catholic News.*

FULLERTON, LADY GEORGIANA.
  Grantley Manor. An Interesting Story of Catholic Life and Society. New Edition. Cloth gilt, gilt edges, 349 pp. 3/6.

  Life of St. Frances of Rome. New Edition. Cloth gilt. 2/-.

  Life of Mère Marie de la Providence, Foundress of the Helpers of the Holy Souls. Third Edition. With Preface and Appendix by the Rev. Sydney F. Smith, S.J. Cloth. 1/6 net (postage 3d.).

GIBSON, REV. HENRY.
  Catechism made Easy: being a Familiar Explanation of the Catechism of Christian Doctrine. Tenth Edition. Two Vols. Fcap. 8vo, cloth, 800 pp. 7/6.
  "Contains a course of fifty-eight instructions on Catholic doctrines, each accompanied by from one to eleven stories, legends, anecdotes, &c., expressly designed to illustrate their meanings and to fix them in the minds of children.
  "This work must be of priceless worth to any who are engaged in any form of catechetical instruction. The best book of the kind that we have seen in English."
  —*Irish Monthly.*

GILLOW, JOSEPH.
Biographical History, and Bibliographical Dictionary of the English Catholics. From the Breach with Rome in 1534 to the Present Time. Vol. I., A-C, 612 pp. Vol. II., D-Grad, 557 pp. Vol. III., Grah-Kem, 688 pp. Vol. IV., Kem-Met, 572 pp. Demy 8vo, cloth. 15/- each.

"The patient research of Mr. Gillow, his conscientious record of minute particulars, and especially his exhaustive bibliographical information in connection with each name are beyond praise."—*British Quarterly Review.*

HAMMERSTEIN, REV. L. VON (S.J.).
Foundations of Faith: The Existence of God Demonstrated. From the German of Fr. Ludwig von Hammerstein, S.J. With an Introduction by the Rev. W. L. Gildea, D.D. Crown 8vo, cloth. 6/-.

"Popular, interesting, forcible, and sound. It is well to have a book like Father von Hammerstein's to put into the hands of serious inquirers; it forms a valuable addition to our apologetic literature."—*Tablet.*

HEDLEY, BISHOP.
The Christian Inheritance. Second Edition. Crown 8vo, cloth gilt, 430 pp. 6/-.

"We do not know any book we could more confidently recommend to intelligent inquirers after truth, perplexed by the prevailing unbelief, than this new volume, in which the Bishop of Newport prints some twenty discourses preached by him on various occasions."—*Tablet.*

Our Divine Saviour, and other Discourses. Second Edition. Crown 8vo, cloth gilt. 6/-.

A Retreat: Consisting of Thirty-three Discourses, with Meditations: for the use of the Clergy, Religious, and Others. Fourth Edition. In handsome half-leather binding. Crown 8vo, 428 pp. 6/-.

"The book is one which, beyond the purpose for which it is directly intended, may be strongly recommended for spiritual reading."—*Month.*

LIGUORI, ST. ALPHONSUS.
A Translation of the Works of St. Alphonsus, edited by the late Bishop Coffin:—

Christian Virtues, and the Means for obtaining them, The. Cloth gilt. 3/-. Or separately, cloth flush—1. The Love of Our Lord Jesus Christ. 1/-. 2. Treatise on Prayer (in many Editions a great part of this work is omitted). 1/-. 3. A Christian's Rule of Life. 1/-.

Eternal Truths. Preparation for Death. 2/6.

The Redemption. Meditations on the Passion. 2/6.

Glories of Mary. New Edition. 3/6.

Reflections on Spiritual Subjects and on the Passion of Jesus Christ. 2/6.

LIVIUS, REV. T. (M.A., C.SS.R.).
St. Peter, Bishop of Rome; or, the Roman Episcopate of the Prince of the Apostles. Demy 8vo, cloth. 12/-.

LIVIUS, REV. T. (M.A., C.SS.R.)—*(continued)*.
   Explanation of the Psalms and Canticles in the Divine Office. By St. Alphonsus Liguori. Translated from the Italian by Thomas Livius, C.SS.R. With a Preface by his Eminence Cardinal Manning. Crown 8vo, cloth, xxx.-512 pp. 7/6.
   Mary in the Epistles; or, The Implicit Teaching of the Apostles concerning the Blessed Virgin. Crown 8vo, cloth. 5/-.
   The Blessed Virgin in the Fathers of the First Six Centuries. Demy 8vo, cloth. 12/-.

McDONALD, REV. WALTER (D.D.).
   Motion: Its Origin and Conservation. An Essay by the Rev. Walter McDonald, D.D., Prefect of the Dunboyne Establishment, St. Patrick's College, Maynooth. Demy 8vo, xii.-458 pp. 7/6 net (postage 4d.).

MADDEN, REV. W. J.
   Disunion and Reunion. Crown 8vo, cloth. 3/-.
   "The volume contains a good deal of practical information in a plain and popular style."—*Catholic Times.*

MANNING, CARDINAL.
   Confidence in God. 32mo, neat cloth gilt. 1/-.
   Lost Sheep Found. A Sermon. Wrapper. 6d. Being an Appeal for the Convents of the Good Shepherd.
   Miscellanies. First Series. Crown 8vo, cloth, 387 pp. 6/-.
   Miscellanies. Second Series. Crown 8vo, cloth, 391 pp. 6/-.
   Religio Viatoris. Crown 8vo, cloth. 1/6.
   Sermons on Ecclesiastical Subjects. Crown 8vo, cloth, 456 pp. 6/-.
   Sin and its Consequences. Crown 8vo, cloth. 4/-.
   The Blessed Sacrament the Centre of Immutable Truth. 32mo, neat cloth gilt. 1/-.
   The Eternal Priesthood. Crown 8vo, cloth. 2/6.
   The Four Great Evils of the Day. Crown 8vo, cloth. 2/6.
   The Fourfold Sovereignty of God. Crown 8vo, cloth. 2/6.
   The Glories of the Sacred Heart. Crown 8vo, cloth. 4/-.
   The Grounds of Faith. Crown 8vo, cloth. 1/6.
   The Holy Ghost the Sanctifier. 32mo, neat cloth gilt. 2/-.
   The Independence of the Holy See. Crown 8vo, cloth. 2/6.
   The Internal Mission of the Holy Ghost. Crown 8vo, cloth, 494 pp. 5/-.
   The Love of Jesus to Penitents. 32mo, neat cloth gilt. 1/-.
   The Office of the Church in Higher Catholic Education. 6d.

MANNING, CARDINAL—*(continued)*.

The Temporal Mission of the Holy Ghost; or, Reason and Revelation. Crown 8vo, cloth. 5/-.

The True Story of the Vatican Council. Crown 8vo, cloth. 2/6.

The Workings of the Holy Spirit in the Church of England. New Edition. Crown 8vo, cloth. 1/6.

MARTIN, LADY.

Life of Don Bosco, Founder of the Salesian Society. Translated from the French of J. M. Villefranche. New Popular Edition. Crown 8vo, 302 pp. Wrapper. 1/- net (postage 3d.).

"We possess in this volume a popular life of a saintly man whose good works are bearing abundant fruit, and the glory of whose life will continue to stimulate zeal in many lands. Lady Martin's translation is admirable, and the book is extremely cheap at a shilling."—*Catholic Times*.

Life of Princess Borghese (*née* Gwendalin Talbot). Translated from the French. Crown 8vo, tastefully bound in cloth gilt. 4/-.

"The life of the charming and saint-like young Englishwoman will come as a welcome surprise to the readers of a later generation, who will find how completely the spirit of Catholic faith and charity was combined in the person of Lady Gwendalin Talbot with the rarest beauty and the most accomplished talents."—*Tablet*.

MEMORIES OF THE CRIMEA. By Sister Mary Aloysius. With Preface by the Very Rev. J. Fahey, D.D., V.G. Crown 8vo, cloth gilt. 2/6.

"The venerable Sister, upon whom Her Majesty the Queen bestowed the decoration of the Royal Red Cross a few months ago, tells her touching story of heroic self-abnegation with a modest simplicity that is far more impressive than the most elaborate and picturesque style of descriptive writing."—*Daily Telegraph*.

NEWMAN, CARDINAL.

The Church of the Fathers. Fcap. 8vo, cloth, 361 pp. 4/-.

An attempt to illustrate the tone and modes of thought, the habits and manners, of the early times of the Church.

Detailed List of Cardinal Newman's Works on application.

NORTHCOTE, VERY REV. PROVOST (D.D.).

Mary in the Gospels; or, Lectures on the History of our Blessed Lady as recorded by the Evangelists. Second Edition. Cloth gilt, 344 pp. 3/6.

PERRY, REV. JOHN.

Practical Sermons, for all the Sundays of the Year. First and Second Series. Sixth Edition. Fcap. 8vo, cloth. 3/6 each.

POPE, REV. T. A. (of the Oratory).

Life of St. Philip Neri. Translated from the Italian of Cardinal Capecelatro. Second and Revised Edition. Two Volumes. Crown 8vo, cloth. 12/6.

"Altogether this is a most fascinating work, full of spiritual lore and historic erudition, and with all the intense interest of a remarkable biography. Take it up where you will, it is hard to lay it down. We think it one of the most completely satisfactory lives of a Saint that has been written in modern times."—*Tablet*.

PORTER, ARCHBISHOP (S.J.).
 The Banquet of the Angels: Preparation and Thanksgiving for Holy Communion. New Edition. 18mo, blue cloth, gilt. 2/-. Also bound in a variety of handsome leather bindings suitable for First Communion memorial gifts. From 6/6 to 12/6 net.

PRACTICAL MEDITATIONS FOR EVERY DAY IN THE Year, on the Life of our Lord Jesus Christ. Chiefly for the use of Religious. By a Father of the Society of Jesus. With Imprimatur of Cardinal Manning. New Edition, Revised. In two Volumes. Cloth, red edges. 9/-.

These volumes give three different daily points for consideration and application. "A work of great practical utility, and we give it our earnest recommendation."— *Weekly Register.*

PRAYER BOOKS, &c.

N.B.—For full particulars of Prayer Books, see *Illustrated Prayer Book Catalogue*, sent post free on application.

Catholic's Daily Companion. With Epistles and Gospels. Roan, 1/-; and in various leather bindings, 1/6 to 5/-.

Catholic Piety. Containing a Selection of Prayers, Reflections, Meditations, and Instructions adapted to every state in life. By the late Rev. Wm. Gahan, O.S.A. 32mo Edition, with Ordinary of the Mass. Cloth, 6d.; post free, 8d.; roan, 1/-. With Epistles and Gospels, 1/6, 2/-, 2/6, 4/6, &c. Messrs. BURNS & OATES also publish two other Editions of this book.

Catholic's Vade Mecum. A Select Manual of Prayers for Daily Use. Compiled from approved sources. 34th Thousand. With Epistles and Gospels. Calf, 5/6, and also in better bindings.

Children's Pictorial Mass Book. (Abridged.) New Edition. Forty-three Illustrations. 2d.; cloth, 6d.

Daily Exercise. Cloth limp. 6d.

Flowers of Devotion. Being a Collection of Favourite Devotions, for Public and Private use. Compiled from approved sources, and with the Imprimatur of His Eminence Cardinal Vaughan. New Edition. Leather bindings. 1/6 to 5/-.

Spirit of the Sacred Heart, The. A new large-type Prayer Book. Cloth, 3/6; leather, 5/6; German calf or morocco, 8/6.

Garden of the Soul. 700th Thousand. Approved by the Cardinal Archbishop of Westminster, and revised by a Priest of the Archdiocese. New Edition. In which many devotions will be found which now form a necessary part of every Catholic Prayer Book. Cloth, 6d.; post free, 8d.; roan, 1/-. With Epistles and Gospels, cloth, 1/-; and in leather bindings, at 1/6, 2/-, 2/6, 3/-, 3/6, 4/-, 5/-, and upwards.

Messrs. BURNS & OATES have just issued a new Pocket Edition of the "Garden of the Soul," size $3\frac{3}{4}$ by $2\frac{1}{2}$ inches, with red line borders, and Devotions for Mass in large type. This Edition can now be had in various bindings, from 1/- to 5/-. They also publish three other Editions.

CATALOGUE OF PUBLICATIONS. 11

PRAYER BOOKS, &c.—(*continued*).

Golden Manual. A Guide to Catholic Devotion, Public and Private, Compiled from approved sources. Fine Paper. Leather, 6/-. With Epistles and Gospels, 7/- and upwards.

Imitation of Christ, Of the. By Thomas à Kempis. NEW POPULAR EDITION FOR DISTRIBUTION. Cloth, red edges, 6d. (postage, 2d.). Leather, red edges, 1/-. SUPERFINE POCKET EDITION. Fancy cloth extra, with red borders, 1/6. And in leather bindings, from 2/6 to 10/-. PRESENTATION EDITION (size, 6¼ by 4¼ inches). With red border on each page. Cloth extra, 3/6. And in leather bindings, from 7/- to 15/-.

Key of Heaven. A Manual of Devout Prayers. 32mo Edition. Cloth, 6d.; post free, 8d.; roan, 1/-. With Epistles and Gospels, 1/6, 2/-, 2/6, 3/-, 4/6, &c. They also publish two Smaller Editions.

Manual of Prayers for Congregational Use. As authorized by the Bishops of England and Wales. With an Appendix containing Prayers for Mass, Confession, and Communion. Cloth, 1/-; leather, 2/6, 5/-, and upwards.

Manual of the Sacred Heart. Compiled and Translated from approved sources. New Edition. Cloth. 2/- upwards.

Missal. New and Complete Pocket Missal, with the Imprimatur of H. E. Cardinal Vaughan, in Latin and English, with all the New Offices, and the propers for Ireland, Scotland, and the Jesuits. (Size, 5¼ by 3¾ inches). Roan or French morocco, 5/-; Rutland roan, limp, 7/-; best calf or morocco, four styles, 8/6 each. Also in better bindings, from 11/- to 30/- net.

Missal for the Laity. Cheap Edition. 6d.; post free, 8d.; and in leather bindings, at 1/6, 2/6, 4/6, and 5/-.

Path to Heaven. Containing Epistles, Gospels, and Hymns, &c. Cloth, 2/- and 2/6; leather, 3/-, 4/-, 4/6, 6/-, and upwards.

Prayers for the People. By the Rev. F. D. Byrne. Imperial 32mo, cloth, extra gilt. 2/-.

QUARTERLY SERIES. Edited by the Jesuit Fathers. 98 Volumes published to date.

SELECTION.

The Life and Letters of St. Francis Xavier. By the Rev. H. J. Coleridge, S.J. Second Edition. Two Volumes. 10/6.

The Life and Letters of St. Teresa. By the Rev. H. J. Coleridge, S.J. Three Volumes. 7/6 each.

Pious Affections towards God and the Saints. Meditations for every Day in the Year, and for the principal Festivals, From the Latin of the Ven. Nicholas Lancicius, S.J. 7/6.

The Life and Teaching of Jesus Christ in Meditations for every Day in the Year. By Fr. Nicholas Avancino, S.J. Two Volumes. 10/6.

QUARTERLY SERIES—(continued).

The Life of St. Alonso Rodriguez. By Francis Goldie, of the Society of Jesus. 7/6.

Letters of St. Augustine. Selected and Arranged by Mary H. Allies. 6/6.

Acts of the English Martyrs, hitherto unpublished. By the Rev. John H. Pollen, S.J. 7/6.

The Life of St. Francis di Geronimo, S.J. By A. M. Clarke. 7/6.

Aquinas Ethicus; or, The Moral Teaching of St. Thomas. By the Rev. Joseph Rickaby, S.J. Second Edition. Two Volumes. 12/-.

The Spirit of St. Ignatius. From the French of the Rev. Fr. Xavier de Franciosi, S.J. 6/-.

Jesus, the All-Beautiful. A Devotional Treatise on the Character and Actions of our Lord. Edited by the Rev. J. G. Macleod, S.J. Second Edition. 6/6.

The Manna of the Soul. By Fr. Paul Segneri. New Edition. In Two Volumes. 12/-.

Life of Ven. Joseph Benedict Cottolengo. From the Italian of Don P. Gastaldi. 4/6.

Life of St. Francis Borgia. By A. M. Clarke. 6/6.

Life of Blessed Antony Baldinucci. By the Rev. F. Goldie, S.J. 6/-.

Distinguished Irishmen of the Sixteenth Century. By Rev. E. Hogan, S.J. 6/-.

Journals kept during Times of Retreat. By the late Fr. John Morris, S.J. Edited by Rev. J. Pollen, S.J. 6/-.

Life of the Rev. Mother Mary of St. Euphrasia Pelletier. By A. M. Clarke. 6/-.

Jesus: His Life, in the very Words of the Four Gospels. A Diatessaron by Henry Beauclerk, S.J. Cloth. 5/-.

First Communion. A Book of Preparation for First Communion. Edited by Fr. Thurston, S.J. Third and Cheaper Edition. With nineteen Illustrations. 3/6.

The Life and Letters of Fr. John Morris, S.J. By Fr. J. H. Pollen, S.J. Cloth. 6/-.

The Story of Mary Aikenhead, Foundress of the Irish Sisters of Charity. By Maria Nethercott. Crown 8vo, cloth. 3/-.

Life of the Blessed Master John of Avila. Secular Priest, called the Apostle of Andalusia. By Father Longaro Degli Oddi, S.J. Edited by J. G. Macleod, S.J. Cloth. 4/-.

Notes on St. Paul; Corinthians, Galatians, Romans. By Joseph Rickaby, S.J. 7/6.

RENDU, A. (LL.D.).
The Jewish Race in Ancient and Roman History. Translated from the Eleventh Corrected Edition by S. T. Crook. Crown 8vo, 440 pp. 6/-.

"This should prove a very useful book."—*Dublin Review.*
"The story is well and lucidly told."—*Schoolmaster.*

RICKABY, REV. JOSEPH (S.J.).
Oxford Conferences. Lent and Summer Terms, 1897. Crown 8vo. Wrapper, 1/- net (postage 2d.).

RIVINGTON, REV. LUKE (D.D.).
Rome and England; or, Ecclesiastical Continuity. Crown 8vo, cloth. 3/6.

"Fr. Rivington's method of exposition is admirable—brief and lucid without meagreness, pointed and telling without harshness. . . . . A book to be grateful for; useful alike to the controversialist, the historical student, and the general reader."—*Tablet.*

RUSHE, VERY REV. JAMES P. (O.D.C.) (Father Patrick of St. Joseph).
Carmel in Ireland. A Narrative of the Irish Province of Teresian or Discalced Carmelites. A.D. 1625-1896. Crown 8vo, cloth. 3/6 net (postage 4d.).

". . . . Written in an easy, historical style. The history of the Carmelite Abbeys in Ireland is here told with much graphic power in a series of interesting chapters, which will be valued by very many readers. . . . . The author is most painstaking, and has consulted all available books of reference to make his record complete."—*Irish Times.*

ST. BENEDICT'S SERIES.
The Life and the Rule of our Holy Father, St. Benedict. Being the Second Book of the Dialogues of St. Gregory the Great, with the Rule of the same Holy Patriarch. In Latin and English. Cloth gilt. 5/-.

St. Benedict and Grottaferrata. Limp cloth, gilt. 1/-.

A Visit to Sublaco, the Cradle of the Benedictine Order. 47 pp., 8vo, wrapper. 6d.

Life of Helen Lucretia Cornaro Piscopia, Benedictine Oblate, and Doctor of the University of Padua. Cloth gilt. 4/6.

Life of the Blessed Joanna Mary Bonomo. With Portrait. Cloth gilt. 3/6.

ST. FRANCIS DE SALES, The Works of.
Translated into the English Language by the Very Rev. Canon Mackey, O.S.B., under the Direction of the Right Rev. Bishop Hedley, O.S.B.

Vol. I. Letters to Persons in the World. Third Edition. Crown 8vo, cloth. 6/-.

Vol. II. The Treatise on the Love of God. Fr. Carr's Translation of 1630 has been taken as a basis, but it has been Modernised and thoroughly Revised and Corrected. Second Edition. 6/-.

ST. FRANCIS DE SALES —(continued).

Vol. III. The Catholic Controversy. Crown 8vo, cloth. 6/-.

Vol. IV. Letters to Persons in Religion, with Introduction by Bishop Hedley on "St. Francis de Sales and the Religious State." Second Edition. Crown 8vo, cloth. 6/-.

"We earnestly commend these volumes to all readers, and we desire their widest diffusion, as we desire also that the doctrine and spirit of St. Francis may reign in all our hearts, both of pastors and of people."—Cardinal Manning in the *Dublin Review*.

St. Francis de Sales as a Preacher. Wrapper. 1/-.

SALVATORI'S PRACTICAL INSTRUCTIONS FOR NEW Confessors. Edited by Fr. Anthony Ballerini, S.J., and Translated by Very Rev. William Hutch, D.D. Third Edition. 18mo, cloth gilt, 314 pp. 4/-.

SCHOUPPE, REV. F. X. (S.J.).

Purgatory: Illustrated by the Lives and Legends of the Saints. Second Edition. Crown 8vo, cloth. 6/-.

"Solid, instructive, practical, and interesting as a romance, this book will go far to dispel the vague and erroneous ideas entertained among the faithful on the subject of Purgatory. Its careful perusal will repay the thoughtless Christian, the devout Catholic, and the zealous priest."—*Irish Ecclesiastical Record*.

SMYTH, JOHN.

Genesis and Science. Inspiration of the Mosaic Ideas of Creative Work. Crown 8vo, cloth, with Illustrations. 3/6.

"In the following pages abundant proof is given that the several phenomena recorded in the first chapter of Genesis are scientifically certain. And as the Mosaic days can be shown to embrace, and include, the æons of the geologist, all apparent contradictions vanish. With the Mosaic ideas of creative work thus unfolded in their true light, the inspiration of the first chapter of Genesis becomes manifest."—PREFACE.

SWEENEY, RIGHT REV. ABBOT (O.S.B.).

Sermons for all Sundays and Festivals of the Year. Fourth Edition. Crown 8vo, handsomely bound in half-leather. 10/6.

"For such priests as are in search of matter to aid them in their round of Sunday discourses, and have not read this volume, we can assure them that they will find in these 600 pages a mine of solid and simple Catholic teaching."—*Tablet*.

THOMPSON, EDWARD HEALY (M.A.).

Letters and Writings of Marie Lataste, with Critical and Expository Notes. By two Fathers of the Society of Jesus. Translated from the French. Three Volumes. 8vo, cloth. 5/- each.

Life of Jean-Jacques Olier, Founder of the Seminary of St. Sulpice. New and Enlarged Edition. Post 8vo, xxxvi.-628 pp. 15/-.

The Hidden Life of Jesus. A Lesson and Model to Christians. By Henri-Marie Boudon. Translated from the French by E. Healy Thompson, M.A. Third Edition. Cloth gilt. 3/-.

The Life and Glories of St. Joseph. Grounded on the Dissertations of Canon Vitali, Fr. José Moreno, and other Writers. Second Edition. Crown 8vo, cloth. 6/-.

The Unity of the Episcopate. Crown 8vo, cloth. 4/6.

CATALOGUE OF PUBLICATIONS. 15

THOMPSON, EDWARD HEALY (M.A.), Edited by.
LIBRARY OF RELIGIOUS BIOGRAPHY.

Life of St. Aloysius Gonzaga (S.J.). Eleventh Edition.
Globe 8vo, cloth, xxiv.-373 pp. 5/-.

Life of Marie Eustelle Harpain; or, The Angel of the Eucharist. Fifth Edition. Cloth, xxi.-388 pp. 5/-.

Life of St. Stanislaus Kostka. Fifth Edition. Cloth. 5/-.

Life of Marie Lataste, Lay Sister of the Congregation of the Sacred Heart. With a Brief Notice of her Sister Quitterie. Second Edition. Cloth. 5/-.

Life of Leon Papin-Dupont, The Holy Man of Tours. Fourth Edition. Cloth. 5/-.

Life of Jean Baptiste Muard, Founder of the Congregation of St. Edme and of the Monastery of La Pierre-qui-Vire. 8vo, cloth, xix.-540 pp. 6/-.

Life of St. Charles Borromeo, Cardinal Archbishop of Milan. Second Edition. Cloth gilt. 3/-.

ULLATHORNE, ARCHBISHOP.

Christian Patience: The Strength and Discipline of the Soul. Sixth and Cheaper Edition. Demy 8vo, cloth, 256 pp. 7/-.

The Endowments of Man considered in their Relations with his Final End. Fifth and Cheaper Edition. Demy 8vo, cloth, 404 pp. 7/-.

The Groundwork of the Christian Virtues. Fifth and Cheaper Edition. Demy 8vo, cloth, 411 pp. 7/-.

Memoir of Bishop Willson, first Bishop of Hobart, Tasmania. With Portrait. Crown 8vo, cloth. 2/6.

The Autobiography of Archbishop Ullathorne. Edited by Augusta Theodosia Drane. Second Edition. Demy 8vo, cloth. 7/6.

"As a plucky Yorkshireman, as a sailor, as a missionary, as a great traveller, as a ravenous reader, and as a great prelate, Dr. Ullathorne was able to write down most fascinating accounts of his experiences. The book is full of shrewd glimpses from a Roman point of view of the man himself, of the position of Roman Catholics in this country, of the condition of the country, of the Colonies, and of the Anglican Church in various parts of the world, in the earlier half of this century."—*Guardian*.

The Letters of Archbishop Ullathorne. Arranged by A. T. Drane. (Sequel to the "Autobiography.") Demy 8vo, cloth, 550 pp. 9/-.

"Compiled with admirable judgment for the purpose of displaying in a thousand various ways the real man who was Archbishop Ullathorne. . . . . This book is very cordially recommended, not only for the intrinsic interest, but also for the sage and prudent counsel which characterizes the intimate correspondence of Archbishop Ullathorne."—*Tablet*.

ULLATHORNE, ARCHBISHOP—(continued).

Characteristics from the Writings of Archbishop Ullathorne, together with a Bibliographical Account of the Archbishop's Works. By the Rev. M. F. Glancey, Crown 8vo, cloth. 6/-.

WALPOLE, F. GOULBURN.

A Short History of the Catholic Church. Crown 8vo, cloth. 3/-.

This work may be described as a Skeleton History of the Church. It is been compiled from notes made by the author for his own instruction, and he hopes that it may prove useful to those who may not have leisure or inclination to study the voluminous standard works upon which it is based.

WHITEHEAD, REV. H. (S.J.).

India: A Sketch of the Madura Mission. Crown 8vo, cloth, with Map and Illustrations. 3/6.

"There are few books of missionary experiences which equal this in interest. This sketch will be deeply appreciated by all who read it."—*Catholic Times.*

WISEMAN, CARDINAL.

Meditations on the Sacred Passion of our Lord. Crown 8vo, cloth. 4/-.

In the Preface H. E. CARDINAL VAUGHAN says:—"The characteristic of these Meditations, as indeed of most of Cardinal Wiseman's writings, is that you will nearly always find in them a 'Hidden Gem.' The beauty and richness of his mind seemed to illustrate and justify every topic he treated by suddenly striking some vein of thought or some point of feeling which, if not new, is at least presented in a new light or reference."

Fabiola. A Tale of the Catacombs. New Cheap Edition. Crown 8vo, cloth, xii.-304 pp. 2/-. Also an Edition on better paper, bound in cloth, richly gilt, gilt edges. 3/6. And an *Edition de luxe* printed on large 4to paper, embellished with thirty-one Full-page Illustrations and a Coloured Portrait of St. Agnes. Handsomely bound. £1 1/-.

A Few Flowers from the Roman Campagna. Small 4to, cloth gilt, printed in red and black. 1/- net (postage 2d.).

New Visits to the Blessed Sacrament. Edited by Cardinal Wiseman. Containing Devotions to the Quarant' Ore and other Occasions of Exposition and Benediction. Cloth, red edges. 2/-.

Characteristics from the Writings of Cardinal Wiseman. Edited, and with a Preface by the Rev. T. E. Bridgett, C.SS.R. Crown 8vo, cloth. 6/-.

New Classified Catalogue of Standard Books (84 pages), comprising every class of book in demand among Catholic Readers, post free on application.

BURNS & OATES, LIMITED,
Granville Mansions, 28, Orchard Street, London, W.

www.ingramcontent.com/pod-product-compliance
Lightning Source LLC
Chambersburg PA
CBHW022140300426
44115CB00006B/276